Web Design & Development Using XHTML

Jeff Griffin
Purdue University

Carlos Morales
Purdue University

John Finnegan
Purdue University

Franklin, Beedle & Associates, Incorporated
8536 SW St. Helens Drive, Suite D
Wilsonville, OR 97070
(503) 682-7668
www.fbeedle.com

President and Publisher	Jim Leisy (jimleisy@fbeedle.com)
Manuscript Editor	Jeni Lee
Production	Tom Sumner
	Bill DeRouchey
	Stephanie Welch
Cover	Ian Shadburne
Proofreader	Stephanie Welch
Developmental Editor	Sue Page
Marketing	Chris Collier
Order Processing	Krista Brown

Printed in the U.S.A.

Rights and Permissions
Franklin, Beedle & Associates, Incorporated
8536 SW St. Helens Drive, Suite D
Wilsonville, Oregon 97070

Library of Congress Cataloging-in-Publication Data is available from the publisher.

dedication

*To my parents, Jerry and Evelyn Griffin, for providing a
loving and secure environment to grow up in; it has made
me into the person I am today.*

—J.G.

To my family.

—C.M.

*To my parents, Alice, Bill and Carol Finnegan, for
everything you taught me on the way to my becoming who
I am. To my students for the things you have taught me.
To Susan, Jonathan, and Jamie for thier never flagging
love and support.*

—J.F.

contents

This book is intended for a first course covering Web design and development topics taken by students majoring in computer science (CS), management information systems (MIS), and information technology (IT). The prerequisites are a familiarity with basic computer operations and the ability to launch, use, and close applications such as a Web browser, word processor, and email program. No prior experience with computer programming or Web development tools is assumed. Our course is entitled "Internet Foundations, Technologies, and Development" and is offered at the 100 level.

We deal with the practical aspects of XHTML, JavaScript, CGI scripts, file sizes, and file formats. We address the ideas of human computer interface (HCI) psychology and how we perceive information. Additionally, the study of current graphic design and how to adapt it for the electronic medium—technically and aesthetically—is explored. This is so the student can learn to design visually for the target audience in the best and most efficient manner. This conscious and deliberate approach makes a solid basis from which students can then push themselves and explore further the world of information design.

For the design aesthetics and HCI portion of the book we integrate ideas from Gestalt psychology, HCI research concerning graphical user interfaces, current graphic design concepts, and design ideas from outside the field of computing. For the IS/CS portions of the text, we primarily use XHTML 1.0 and related applications for the creation of content and support structures associated with Websites and Web design.

Why use XHTML? HTML has been the de facto standard for many years, but it is important to keep in mind that HTML is a simple markup language for formatting data. HTML has a fixed set of tags to define the structure and style of text and provides no provisions for expansion. It is this inflexibility that has allowed browser vendors to add many proprietary tags that may be supported by only their browsers. HTML also does not allow individuals to add custom tags because none of the browsers would know how to parse the custom tags. The

Web is full of poorly written HTML that violates the basic HTML rules. This has led to browsers having to include code to handle this poorly written HTML. We feel XHTML addresses these problems.

As the use of the Web continues to grow, it is increasingly being accessed by a variety of devices such as cell phones, PDAs, and pagers. These devices, with displays that are not visually oriented, are driving the change in how we mark up documents for the Web. The Extensible Markup Language (XML) promises to solve most of our problems. This is because content creators will have to focus on the structure of a document, not just on how it looks. XHTML is a reformulation of HTML 4 into an XML application; it provides a migration path while maintaining backwards compatibility. XHTML 1.0 is the current recommended standard of the World Wide Web Consortium.

WHAT THIS BOOK IS AND IS NOT

This book is a practical approach to Web design and coding. We believe that a person should have a good understanding of the basic concepts of design and a basic understanding of XHTML before using a WYSIWYG application to develop Web pages. By developing an understanding of these concepts, students will be able to use their skill and creativity to control their designs. The best way to learn these basic concepts is by doing. The three most popular visual editing software applications currently do not support XHTML and often have extraneous code problems with HTML. If students want to keep up with current standards, they have to understand the code.

This book is not a complete reference for XHTML or Web design.

WHY WE WROTE THIS BOOK

This book is largely a product of our frustration in being unable to find an academic textbook with which to teach a course on Internet technologies and application development that covers more than just Web page creation.

HOW TO USE THIS BOOK

Conventions Used in This Book

This book uses two conventions in an effort to highlight important points:

tip: This symbol points out important information, tricks, handy hints, and

warning: This symbol warns you of situations and procedures that could lead to undesired results. *Be careful!*

How This Book Is Organized

Chapter 1   The Internet and the World Wide Web
This chapter introduces the history, development, philosophy, and practical aspects of the Internet. The Internet is a technology, culture, and much more, linking together computers and people literally all over the world. This chapter explores the crude beginnings of the Internet, from ARPANET to Tim Burners-Lee to searching the Web for information. It focuses on a subset of the Internet, the World Wide Web. The discussion includes Web page access, software protocols, and networks. The explanations given are purposefully general and simplified.

Chapter 2   XHTML: Making the Transition from HTML
This chapter focuses on the differences between the HTML 4 specification and XHTML 1.0. The environment that HTML was originally designed for has changed into a very demanding high-tech world of e-commerce. The markup languages HTML, XHTML, and XML all are derived from the more complex markup language SGML; it is important to know the relationships between these languages. This chapter discusses the main differences in these areas: attributes, case, document type definitions, document structure, and closure.

Chapter 3   Design Basics for the Information Designer
This chapter focuses on the vocabulary and principles of visual design based on the Gestalt theories of information perception

pioneered by Max Wertheimer. It also explores the interrelationships of forms using Boolean operations (union, difference,
and intersection). This hands-on exploration includes design
exercises and projects that stimulate the imagination and lead
to strengthening the visualization skills of the student. The
techniques and theories discussed in this chapter lead directly to
the students' own Web page designs.

Chapter 4   Site Design
This chapter focuses on the concepts necessary to build effective
Websites. Before getting into the nuts-and-bolts development of
a Website, it's important to think about its overall organization.
In previous chapters, design considerations have been focused
on individual pages, but these pages are just part of a Website.
How will the pages relate to each other? This is one of many
questions that is explored in this chapter, along with concepts of
good site design, site structure, planning, content, and management.

Chapter 5   Page Design
This chapter focuses on what goes into the design of a stand-out
Web page. A Website's presentation is everything: its look and
feel, the organization of pages and information, the flow, and
so on. The bad news is that it's easy to create a bad or boring
presentation; they proliferate on the Web. The good news is
that it's also fairly easy to create an interesting, even inventive
presentation. All that it requires is some good advice and a little
forethought. The topics covered in this chapter include the use
of color, page layout, fonts, use of images, and content. One of
the best ways to learn good W eb page design is observe both
good and bad Web pages.

Chapter 6   Introduction to XHTML
This chapter introduces the basic building blocks that enable
students to write well-formed XHTML documents. We start by
looking at how we present information in a document by using

tags and attributes. The process of writing XHTML starts by using the proper document structure and structure/syntax of elements and tags. This chapter presents elements that deal with how the document is rendered by the browser. In this chapter XHTML block-level elements are used to organize or group text into easily understandable blocks of text. Once block-level elements have been covered, the chapter presents XHTML inline elements, which are use to control specific formatting changes to text within block-level elements.

Chapter 7   Hypertext Links
This chapter introduces how to add hypertext links to Web pages. Hypertext links are what makes accessing other documents or another section of the same document from a Web page possible. Without links, the Web would be just a collection of documents. It is this linking of documents in a non-linear fashion that provides the real power of the Web. Although links provide users easy access to other documents, they can also be a source of frustration as students try to correctly implement them. Only one element is required to add a hypertext link to a Web page and one attribute enables the link to function properly. This chapter discusses the use and difference between absolute and relative linking.

Chapter 8   Tables
This chapter presents tables, which are a very useful method of displaying data. It discusses the difference between a table structure and style (table presentation). The structure topics include elements for table creation, captions, cell widths, and spanning rows and columns. The style topics include borders, frames, and rules. A brief look at style sheets and their impact on table style is also discussed. Cascading style sheets is covered in detail in another chapter, but a look is warranted here.

Portions of Chapter 8 were contributed by
Victor Barlow
Purdue University

Chapter 9   Frames
Frames are an exciting feature in the HTML 4 standard and can be used in XHTML using the frameset DTD. Using frames, students can enhance the navigational possibilities and achieve layout control over Web pages. This feature is controversial among Web designers because it divides the available space, which is already in short supply. It also causes the browser to load more than one XHTML file, which may result in a delay for the user. This chapter covers the following frame topics: creation, elements, nesting, and the use of frames.

Chapter 10   Working with Images and Multimedia

This chapter presents basic and advanced information on preparing graphics for the Web, creating usable interfaces, and using sound and video on the Web. Anyone that has surfed the Web knows that graphics play an important role in any Web page design. This chapter explains the different types of images and how to add them to Web pages. While adding graphics is often very appealing, it can also cause some problems downloading, so optimizing of images is discussed. Additionally, image maps, video, and sounds are discussed.

Chapter 11   Forms
Web pages can do more than just display information to users; it can also gather information using forms. This chapter explores the use of forms as an opportunity for interaction with users. It briefly discusses server-side interaction with forms using CGI (Common Gateway Interface) and Active Server Pages (ASP). This chapter focuses on the browser side of forms and accessing them with JavaScript. Topics included are creating forms, using input elements, and creating user interfaces.

Chapter 12   Cascading Style Sheets
This chapter introduces style sheets and how to apply them. Previous chapters worked with attributes to determine how certain elements were presented. How all elements are presented can

be changed by using the cascading style sheet language. With this language students can control the text size and color, font, background color, and white space around a particular element. Cascading style sheets allow them to take more control over the presentation of a Web page.

Chapter 13   Publishing Your Page
Publishing a Website consists of three main areas: hosting the files, registering a domain name, and promoting the site. In this chapter students explore how to accomplish these tasks.

Chapter 14   Programming with JavaScript: Introduction
The pages created in previous chapters have been static, allowing limited interaction through links. This chapter introduces JavaScript concepts, which allow students to build applications that actively process user inputs. This chapter covers the following topics: capabilities, client-side and server-side scripting, incorporating scripts into XHTML pages, language and syntax, built-in operators, and functions.

Chapter 15   Programming with JavaScript: Intermediate
This chapter is not intended to make students programmers, but students do need to have a basic understanding of some programming principles in order to do some basic JavaScript. The pages created in previous chapters have been static, allowing limited interaction through links. This chapter introduces more JavaScript concepts, which allow students to build applications that actively process user inputs. This chapter covers the following topics: operators, conditional statements, loops, and incorporating dates into XHTML pages. This chapter demonstrates how to validate user input before the data is submitted to the server for processing.

Chapter 16   Active Server Pages
This chapter provides a brief introduction to Active Server Pages (ASP). ASP is a server-based technology from Microsoft,

designed to create interactive Web pages. The topics covered include what is ASP, basic Web servers, creating an Active Server Page, and some common problems working with Active Server Pages.

Chapter 17   Extensible Markup Language (XML)
The Extensible Markup Language (XML) enables students to create highly flexible documents by separating the content of a document from its appearance. Using XML to store information and then using other technologies such as XSL enables students to efficiently disseminate data in multiple forms. This chapter covers how to create XML documents to maintain data, use document type definitions to validate data, and use namespaces for extending XML documents.

Chapter 18   Extensible Stylesheet Language (XSL)
The Extensible Stylesheet Language (XSL) allows us to transform XML data into any number of forms, including HTML, XHTML, and plain text. By using different XSL documents to access the same XML data, it is possible to more efficiently create documents that rely on the same underlying data. This chapter covers the structure of XSL and how to integrate it with XML on both the client and the server. Emphasis is placed on the role of XSLT.

FOR THE INSTRUCTOR

This textbook was designed to be used in a course covering Internet technologies during a typical 15-week semester. It assumes that the students have no prior knowledge of HTML or XHTML.

The first 13 chapters cover a brief history of the Internet, design basics, page/site design, creating pages using XHTML, links, tables, frames, images, forms, style sheets, and publishing a Web page. Chapter 13 is a logical break in the text, with more advanced topics covered in Chapters 14 through 18. These advanced topics include JavaScript, Active Server Pages, and XML. Since these chapters are independent of Chapters 1 through 13, they can be included in an introductory course or used in a second course. We like to cover the material presented in Chapters 1 through 14 in a semester-long introductory course.

It is our intention to provide adopters with support materials that will aid in teaching, not just a textbook. A comprehensive package of supporting materials is available. The supplements for *Web Design and Development Using XHTML* include the following items:

- Answers to all end-of-chapter review questions
- Possible solutions to the end-of-chapter exercises
- Possible solutions to the chapter-by-chapter project as it progresses through each chapter
- Simple PowerPoint slides for each chapter
- A test bank that covers all of the chapters in this book. The test bank contains questions in multiple-choice and true/false formats.

FOR THE STUDENT

CD ROM. A CD-ROM is included with this book. It contains XHTML code examples from each chapter, useful references, and tutorials on software packages used in the process of Website development.

ACKNOWLEDGMENTS

As a long project comes to an end, it's time to reflect on what has brought this project to a successful close. It would not have been possible without a very supportive family. Thanks go to my wife, Mary Ellen, and our daughters, Kelly,

Kadra, and Kelsey, for the love and support they offered during the writing of this book. I think my daughters were beginning to believe that my laptop was attached to my body. Also I would like to acknowledge my parents, whose love and support of whatever I attempted to do over the years has been very much appreciated.

My thanks also go to my co-authors John and Carlos for their work on this project and putting up with my demanding requirements. Thanks to my colleagues in the Computer Technology Department at Purdue University for their support during this project. I appreciate the valuable suggestions from the book's reviewers; thank you for your time:

Gretchen V. Douglas	*State University of New York at Cortland*
Gerald M. Santoro	*The Pennsylvania State University*
Cherie L. Zieleniewski	*University of Cincinnati*

Thanks to the many fine people at Franklin, Beedle & Associates: Sue Page for keeping this project on track, Jim Leisy for his strong support of this project, Tom Sumner, Stephanie Welch, Bill DeRouchey, and Jeni Lee for their editing and production work; and Ian Shadburne, Christine Collier, and Krista Brown for all their hard work.

> —Jeff Griffin
> Assistant Professor of Computer Information
> Systems and Technology
> Purdue University

I'd like to thank my family.

> —Carlos Morales
> Assistant Professor of
> Computer Graphics Technology
> Purdue University

I would like to thank my wife Susan and our children, Jonathan and Bethany (Jamie), for their love, their support, and the sacrifices they made while I pursued the teaching of this discipline and the writing of this book. Thanks go also to Alice, Bill, and Carol Finnegan for instilling in me the love of learning and the pursuit of higher education. Thanks to my colleagues, especially those at Purdue in South Bend and at the West Lafayette and New Albany campus, for their support and feedback on this project. Many thanks go to my teachers over the years. To those at Wellesley High School, especially Jeanne Goddard and Myles Corey, who were inspirational in their care and attention to students and learning. To my professors at the University of Massachusetts Department of Theatre who taught me to question, to explore, and to love the pursuit. To the graduate school faculty at Ohio State University, who taught me the importance of research, writing, and a commitment to principles. Thanks to the graduate teaching assistants in Art Education at OSU for your patience while I discovered computer graphics and the beginning of the path on which I find myself today. Last, but not least, thanks to my co-authors and publisher. To Jeff Griffin for driving this project and to Carlos Morales for joining Jeff and I on this journey, which began with an idea and has grown into this book. To Jim Leisy, Sue Page, Tom Sumner, Stephanie Welch, Ian Shadburne, Christine Collier, and Krista Brown at Franklin, Beedle & Associates. Many thanks to all.

—John Finnegan
Assistant Professor of
Computer Graphics Technology
Purdue University

chapter 1
the internet and the world wide web

CHAPTER OVERVIEW

This chapter introduces the history, development, philosophy, and practical aspects of the Internet. The Internet is a technology, culture, and much more, linking together computers and people all over the world. We will explore the crude beginnings of the Internet, from ARPANET to Tim Berners-Lee. We will learn about searching the Web for information. We will focus on a subset of the Internet, the World Wide Web. Our discussion will include Web page access, software protocols, and networks. The explanations given here are purposefully general and simplified.

CHAPTER OBJECTIVES

- Discuss the history and development of the Internet and the World Wide Web (WWW)
- Describe the differences between the Internet and the World Wide Web
- Explain the importance of Hypertext Markup Language (HTML)
- Discuss the role of Web browsers
- Understand the different services of the Internet

INTRODUCTION

Over the centuries, we have sought ways to communicate with others. From spoken words to hieroglyphics to the printed language, our methods of communicating have evolved from simple to more complicated.

The computer has been an important tool in aiding our ability to communicate, helping us to perform even the most difficult tasks efficiently and effectively. This speed and accuracy have made computers invaluable to the business world. The addition of the Internet now allows us to communicate and share information on a global level.

WHAT IS THE INTERNET?

The Internet is basically a global collection of computer networks. Some might refer to it as a network of networks. The power of the Internet lies in the fact that information can be exchanged between any number of computers; communication is now based on a fixed set of protocols that have been adopted worldwide.

History of the Internet

The Internet began as a simple network of only four computers. The project, named ARPANET (Advanced Research Projects Agency Network), was funded by the Department of Defense. Its purpose was to share resources among Department of Defense–funded research contractors and to encourage more research in the area of computer networking.

Interest in this project grew quickly, and many academic institutions joined ARPANET and became a part of Internet history. ARPANET quickly grew into two distinct networks: one for military traffic and a second for mostly academic use.

ARPANET continued to grow for many years; starting with four nodes in 1969, it went through a transition to the NSFNET (sponsored by the National Science Foundation) in 1990, and grew to an amazing 56,218,000 nodes in 1999! The transformation of this fantastic network continues, as NSFNET is getting phased out and commercial and private companies are taking up the task of maintaining and upgrading this vast array of communications equipment. The graph below is an illustration of this incredible growth in the number of connections to the Internet.

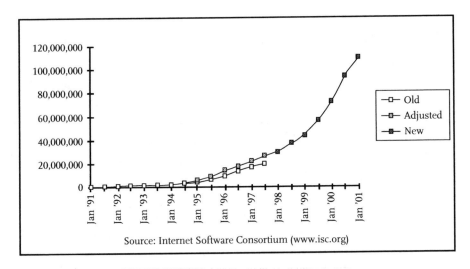

Source: Internet Software Consortium (www.isc.org)

FIGURE 1.1: INTERNET DOMAIN SURVEY HOST COUNT

What will the future bring for the Internet? Congress is actively planning for Internet II, a new and faster network that forms an additional backbone. Internet II has become a necessity due to the overcrowding of the Internet as it exists today. The creation of Internet II will include the addition of Network Access Points (NAPs), probably located at major university–based supercomputing centers. Internet II won't replace the current Internet but will run in conjunction with the current Internet. This will provide much-needed additional routes for universities, research facilities, and governmental agencies to exchange data quickly and easily, avoiding the "traffic jams" that are a part of the current network.

ISPs

An Internet Service Provider (ISP) is a company that allows subscribers to connect to the Internet. This is done traditionally with the use of telephone lines; however, cable television services are beginning to offer this connection as well.

ISPs typically offer some other basic services to subscribers, including email addresses and access to a server to post Web pages.

When selecting an ISP, some important characteristics to consider include:
- Local access to avoid long distance phone charges;
- Adequate capacity to enable access to the Internet at any time;
- Reliability;

- Monthly fees; and
- Modem speed to assure fast connections.

Backbones

To gain a basic understanding of how information travels across the Internet, consider the wide variety of transportation methods that exist today. To move from one location to another, a traveler may use sidewalks, streets, boulevards, highways, and even interstate roadways. The Internet is a similar system, but instead of linking houses or businesses, it links computers. These linked computers may be large systems, called nodes, or smaller systems, such as desktop personal computers.

The Internet equivalent of an interstate consists of lines that form what is called the Internet backbone. The large networks of lines are owned and maintained by companies like MCI: WorldCom, Sprint, and AT&T, to name a few. Together, these networks allow for very fast transfers of vast amounts of data. Of course, these networks also exist overseas, so every country is connected to every other country around the world. If the travel metaphor is continued, a traveler can get to Europe or Asia or Australia by ship or plane. The Internet allows information to travel from one continent to another by way of transoceanic cables.

In the United States, there are five major "ports of call" for data that is traveling over the Internet. These ports, or hubs, are known as Network Access Points (NAPs). The NAPs are located in San Francisco, San Jose, Chicago, New York, and Washington, D.C. The hubs connect the backbone of the Internet to the other regionally maintained networks. It is these regional networks that eventually connect individual computer users to each other. This is done through the use of ISPs.

Internet Services

There's more to the Internet than just "surfing the Web." Although the World Wide Web is certainly one of the most popular Internet services available, it is just one of many services available on the Internet. In the following paragraphs, we'll provide a brief description of various Internet services.

Email

Once an ISP subscriber has selected an email address, communication from one computer to another is possible. Email's popularity has skyrocketed, and email is now commonplace in both business and private settings. The speed and efficiency of email allows people on opposite sides of the world to communicate easily and inexpensively. This is probably the biggest advantage of email.

When a message is sent using email, that message leaves the sender's computer and travels to the ISP's server. From there, the email message is sent out to the Internet, which "delivers" the message to the recipient's mailbox. The message is stored in the recipient's mailbox until it is retrieved. This process is accomplished in only seconds or minutes!

But email users must be aware that these electronic messages are far from private, especially in the business sector, where email that is sent on a company computer is considered company property.

World Wide Web

In 1989, scientist Tim Berners-Lee of the European Particle Physics Laboratory (CERN) came up with the idea and the means to strengthen the ways in which scientists and colleagues could communicate and share information. Codifying the HTML language, which was based on the SGML (Standard Generalized Markup Language) formatting standard that had been around for a while, Berners-Lee created a way to distribute and share information—both text and graphics—that revolutionized the way scientists communicated. The rest of us took a little longer to catch on because of the technical nature of how HTML and HTTP worked. More will be said on that in a moment. The idea of hyperlinking documents was not necessarily new; there were hyperlinking applications prior to 1989, but the way in which Berners-Lee utilized the idea and implemented it with HTML made it accessible in a way that was previously not explored. The metaphor of the Web really acknowledges the connectivity levels of the information available and compares it to the intricacies of a spider's web, where the strands are all interwoven and one can follow the strands for a very long way in many directions.

It wasn't until 1993 and the work of Marc Andreesen at the University of Illinois at the NCSA (National Center for Supercomputing Applications) that the average advanced user could really make use of the Web. The first graphically capable Web browser as we know them today was Mosaic. Andreesen, of course, went on to found Netscape Communications Corporation; Netscape soon surpassed Mosaic in terms of capability and was contributing to the furtherment of the HTML standards.

FTP

Before the advent of graphical Web browsers, computer users could search the Internet for information in a text-only format. Although most users don't need or use most of the capabilities of the Internet, some users need more than an email program to exchange information. These users need the tools that will enable them to "get" and "put" files remotely over the Internet.

FTP, or File Transfer Protocol, is just the tool these users need. FTP allows users to get, or download, files from an FTP server file directory. This protocol also allows users to put, or upload, a file from their local machine to the remote FTP server. Many Websites offer software to Internet users that can be downloaded without charge using "shareware," as it has come to be known, has become very popular; however, the user must be cautious in downloading these files to avoid the viruses that sometimes accompany them.

Telnet allows users to log onto Unix servers mostly at universities and libraries. You can access directories and search for files. You can often search databases of information remotely.

Usenet

A kind of electronic newspaper, Usenet is a means of communicating news over the Internet. Individuals or organizations can write an article and then post the article on a news server. These articles can be read by anyone with access to a newsreader, a piece of software that allows an individual to access a newsgroup.

Newsgroups are interactive in that users can respond to articles by posting their own articles on the news server. As subsequent articles are posted, a discussion thread is formed. Newsgroup participants are expected to abide by the rules of "netiquette," the unofficial guide to communicating on the Internet with good manners.

Internet Protocols (TCP/IP)

Let's return to our metaphor of traveling the highways. Just as a driver follows a map to move from location to location, computers need a "road map" to move information from one computer to another. This road map of Internet communication is called TCP/IP, or Transmission Control Protocol/Internet Protocol.

TCP/IP was developed in order to allow all of the U.S. military computers to communicate with each other easily, regardless of the manufacturer of the system. TCP/IP is the universal translator between all of the different hardware combinations that might exist. It also was designed for auto recovery and rerouting in case a node is damaged or down. It is a very robust protocol with a "seek and find" mentality that goes around traffic jams.

TCP/IP is a check/recheck protocol, with each part doing something a little different and the other part checking to see that the task is done. TCP/IP creates what is called a packet-switched network, which breaks down every large chunk of data into smaller ones called "packets." Then IP moves one packet of data from node to node. IP forwards each packet based on the IP number. IP numbers are like phone numbers or street addresses for each machine. There are machines, called gateways, that are the equivalent of regional post offices. They contain the information for specific machines in their area. That's how information gets to where it is supposed to go.

TCP is the verification part. It puts it all back together at the other end. It also checks to make sure there is no data loss in the exchange. If it detects any, it requests that the data packet be re-sent and then makes sure it is all received at the other end.

IP is the protocol that defines Internet addresses. Internet addresses are made up of numbers divided into four parts by periods (e.g., 123.456.789.0). With IP, when one computer attempts to contact another computer, it will continue trying until it's successful; thus, two communicating computers don't both have to be online at the same time in order to move information from one location to another.

Domain Name System

Remember that every computer on the Internet has a unique IP address. This address is made up of a series of four numbers separated by periods. To humans, this address is not very meaningful, so the Internet supports a text version of the IP address. This text version is referred to as a domain name. Every domain name is associated with a specific IP address.

The domain name system (DNS) is software that translates domain names into IP addresses. Think of the domain name system as the directory assistance of the Internet. Distributed databases containing domain names and their corresponding IP addresses are located all over the Internet on domain name servers.

Hypertext

Hypertext links are what make accessing other documents or other sections of the same document on the Web possible. Without hypertext links, the Web would just be a collection of documents. It is this linking that provides the real power of the Web.

Hypertext Transfer Protocol (HTTP)

Protocols are the rules by which digital devices, such as computers, communicate. Hypertext Transfer Protocol, HTTP, is the protocol used to send information across the World Wide Web. HTTP sends documents and other types of information in hypertext from one computer to another.

When you enter a URL into the browser, the browser sends a message to the specified Web server indicating the name of the file being requested. This is known as the HTTP request. When the server receives this message, it checks to see if it has the file. If the file is located, the contents of the XHTML file are packaged into packets using TCP and addressed to the browser using HTTP. The packets are then sent back to the browser. This is known as the HTTP response.

Once the browser receives the file, it interprets the file and then renders it on the screen.

Extensible Hypertext Markup Language

Extensible Hypertext Markup Language (XHTML) is the language used to create Web pages. XHTML is a set of codes or commands that control how text will appear when it is displayed. For example, if text were to be displayed in italics, the code would look like this:

```
XHTML is a <i> very useful </i> markup language.
```

The code contained in the brackets is a tag. Tags indicate page elements such as a header, page breaks, boldface type, or clickable hyperlinks. Tags can also designate where graphic images go on a page. At the place where the formatting no longer applies, there is a closing tag that is the same as the opening tag with the addition of a forward slash character. Tags are interpreted by the browser and are then displayed on the user's monitor.

Text marked up using the tags in the example above would look like this:

XHTML is a *very useful* markup language.

Web Browsers

A browser is a program that sends a message to a server requesting information. The browser then displays this information in either text or graphical format. Today, Netscape Navigator and Microsoft Internet Explorer are browsers familiar to most Internet users.

- Non-graphical (or text-only) browsers were the first Web browsers developed. These browsers simply display ASCII text on the computer screen. No pictures can be included. The main advantage of this type of a browser is that they are very fast.
- Graphical browsers have the capability of including both text and pictures. Examples include Microsoft Internet Explorer and Netscape Navigator. Graphical browsers have the ability to display pictures, play sounds, and even show video clips. Unfortunately, graphical browsers tend to run much more slowly than text-only browsers.

Browsers also include tools, or features, that make using the Internet simple. Probably the most commonly used feature is "bookmarking." This tool allows the user to mark a favorite Website. The browser will store that Website on the user's "favorites" list, so it can be easily accessed in the future.

Web Addresses

As we continue our travels on the Internet, the URL is the address of the information being sought. URL stands for Uniform Resource Locator. Like the various parts of an address, each part of a URL helps the traveler reach the final destination. Let's take a closer look at the following URL and what each part means:

http://www.tech.purdue.edu/cpt/information/about.html

http

This is the protocol used to transfer data. All Web page URLs begin with the familiar http://. Other Internet services use different protocols, such as File Transfer Protocol (FTP).

www.tech.purdue.edu
This is the domain name that identifies the Web server that stores the requested Web page.
cpt/information/
This is the directory path, which indicates where on the Web server the Web page is stored.
about.html
This is the name of the requested document.

The domain name itself contains several parts:
Top level domain. This is probably the most familiar part of the URL. This indicates what domain the organization belongs to on the Internet. These types include:

.edu	educational
.gov	government
.com	commercial
.mil	military
.net	networking
.org	nonprofit

In November 2000, a proposal was made to add seven new top-level domains to the domain name system. These include:

.aero	air-transport
.biz	businesses
.coop	cooperatives
.info	for all uses
.museum	museums (you probably guessed that one)
.name	individuals
.pro	professions

In 2001, the .biz, .info, and .name domains were the first of the new top-level domains to become operational.

Second level domain. This is the part that is registered and identifies the organization. In the above URL "purdue" is the second-level domain.

Search Engines

The vast amount of information available on the Web sometimes makes finding specific information difficult. It's hard to tell by looking at the surface what information is there. That's where search engines come in. They are the card catalogs of the Internet. Instead of sifting through them with your finger, you can let the Web itself do the work for you. Search engines allow you to look for specific information or types of information.

Search services typically offer subject guides to assist in locating needed information. These subject guides are clickable lists including search topics such as arts and humanities, education, health, travel, and so on. These subject guides don't provide access to every piece of information available on the Web related to a specific topic. Instead, they narrow the focus to a few well-designed and highly informative pages.

If the subject guide doesn't contain enough information, the next step is to try a search engine. Some familiar search engines include Lycos, Alta Vista, or InfoSeek. By typing in just a two-word description, the user gains access to a huge pool of information on a specific subject. Narrowing the list to find just the right information takes some practice.

Not all search engines are the same. Basically, you have three types of search engine: true search engines, Web directories, and metasearch engines. True search engines like Excite use an automated process to search for information on the Web. These "Web crawlers" or "spiders" go from Website to Website gathering information such as URLs, site titles, and some page content. The automation allows the searching of millions of sites, and the search engine remains fairly current. These search engines often have information about the most obscure sites and pages. These search engines use metatags to assist in the searching of the Web. The use of metatags are discussed in Chapter 6.

One of the most popular search engines at one time was Yahoo! But in reality, Yahoo! is not a search engine but a Web directory. What this means is that sites and pages must be registered "manually" with the hosting directory. There is usually an owner-entered description, an owner-entered URL, and some other pertinent information. Yahoo! also has people working to search out information that may be beneficial to catalog and categorize. It gains a limited editorialized snapshot of a Website. Then, like a huge database, Yahoo! logs the entry. When a search is requested, the searching software looks up the entries, gathers them all together, and presents them. The trouble here is that Yahoo! can't present what it doesn't know exists.

Metasearch engines are really just search engines that access more than one Web crawler site at the same time and then return the information to a single page for you to read through. Metasearch sites also make the process of deciding how to structure your search easier.

Search Techniques

The success of a Web search can be greatly enhanced by learning some simple search techniques:

- If AND is placed between two words in a search, the search engine will find only those documents containing both words.
- Using the word OR between two words in a search tells the search engine to retrieve documents with either of the words or both of the words.
- NOT used in a search results in a search that omits the specified words.

Each of these search strategies listed above are examples of Boolean logic.

The plus (+) and minus (-) signs can also be used to narrow a search. For instance, a search defined like this:

+flowers+shade+perennials

will provide a listing of pages that contain all three of the words contained in the search. This type of search is called inclusion.

Exclusion, using the minus sign, assists in narrowing the search even more. For instance, if the inclusion search above isn't specific enough, the search could be enhanced as follows:

+flowers+shade+perennials-bulbs

This search will provide a listing of pages that contain the first three words with the exception of any pages addressing bulbs.

CHAPTER SUMMARY

The Internet is a complex and vast array of information that is exchanged between users over a physical wire using different protocols such as TCP/IP, HTTP, FTP, Telnet, and others. The Internet is not controlled by any one entity but is managed and influenced by various groups of people.

Users who surf the Net use Web browsers to do it. Web browsers speak the various protocols and a language known as HTML. Web browsers need to know the URL of a site or file on the Internet in order to locate it. The URL contains the direct address information of the site or file.

Information can be searched on the Internet using search engines, Web directories, and metasearch engines. The information is returned to the browser in an organized fashion for the user to sift through.

KEY TERMS

ARPANET	IETF
browser	Internet
CERN	IP address
domain name	search engine
FTP	TCP/IP
HTML	Telnet
HTTP	Tim Berners-Lee
IAB	URL

REVIEW QUESTIONS

1. What is a URL?
2. The ARPANET began with how many computers?
3. Which year is said to have been the first year of the ARPANET?
4. Tim Berners-Lee was working at which European lab when he created HTML?
5. What is the purpose of DNS?
6. If the Internet is the physical wire on which data travels, what is the World Wide Web?
7. Before Marc Andreesen founded Netscape Communications Corporation, he worked for what computing research lab?

8. True or false: The Internet is owned by the telephone companies.
9. What does TCP/IP stand for?
10. Are HTML and HTTP the same thing?
11. What is the part of a URL that is between the double slash (//) and the single slash (/) called?

EXERCISES

1. Search the Internet for information on the subject of tessellations. Use Yahoo!, Alta Vista, and Google. Compare and contrast the results of your search. Search on at least one other subject that you discover in your initial research and include this information in your findings. Condense the information you find into a one- to two-page paper with half-inch margins, using a 10-point Times or Times New Roman font. Include a page that indicates the URLs for the sites you used and at least five other URLs for sites you didn't use.
2. Pick a subject from the chapter (such as ARPANET) and do a search of the Internet for additional information not found in the reading. Share this with your professor and classmates in a short oral presentation.
3. Do an online search for the origin of hypertext and hypermedia. Hint: Look for 1945 and an academic paper entitled "As We May Think" by Vanivar Bush. Report your findings to the class either orally or in writing (instructor's choice).

PROJECT

Throughout the book, we will develop a larger project that will require the skill set developed in each chapter. Each chapter will ask you develop an interconnected portion of the project. It is critical that you do each of the chapters.

We'll start with a realistic scenario and build on it.

Scenario

You have been asked to create a Web site for your community. The site needs to provide members of the community with a way to share information about events and community-related information. Your client, the city, has determined that the site should contain at least the following sections:

1. An events area where people can view upcoming events, post events, and search for events.
2. A classifieds section that would allow people to post items for sale and view items.
3. A chat area that would allow people to create private rooms; for example, a chat channel on gardening.

While your client is not a Web designer, they do have some ideas as to what the site should look like and how it should function. He has indicated that he wants the site to be rapidly searchable and that no piece of information should be more than three links away. He has specifically indicated that he likes the look and feel of the major portal sites, such as www.yahoo.com, www.excite.com, and www.xoom.com.

Project Assignment:

- Research what would be an appropriate domain for your site. Should it be placed in the .com or .gov domain?
- Propose a name for the site and do research to determine if the domain name you have suggested has been taken.
- Do a preliminary audience analysis of the computer users in your community. What percentage of the users have computers and Internet access? How fast is the average connection in your community? Is broadband, such as cable modem or DSL, access available?

REFERENCES

All About the Internet, http://www.isoc.org/internet-history/

Life on the Internet, http://www.pbs.org/internet/timeline/index.html

A Brief History of the Internet, http://www.isoc.org/internet/history/brief.html

Press FAQ by Tim Berners-Lee,
http://www.w3.org/People/Berners-Lee/FAQ.html

History of the Internet and WWW, http://www.netvalley.com/intval.html

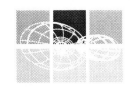

chapter 2

XHTML: making the transition from HTML

CHAPTER OVERVIEW

This chapter will focus on the differences between the HTML 4.01 specification and XHTML 1.0. The environment HTML was originally designed for has changed into a very demanding high-tech world of e-commerce. The markup languages HTML, XHTML, and XML are derived from the more complex markup language SGML; it is important to know the relationships between them. This chapter will discuss the main differences in these areas: attributes, case, document type definitions, document structure, and closure.

CHAPTER OBJECTIVES

- Understand the relationships between markup languages
- Understand the advantages of XHTML
- Understand the differences between HTML and XHTML
- Understand the concept of well-formed documents
- Understand XHTML syntax
- Use Document Type Definitions
- Use XML namespaces
- Understand the criteria for a valid XHTML document
- Create a simple XHTML document

XHTML

We know many of you are wondering why you should use *XHTML (Extensible Hypertext Markup Language)* or what is wrong with HTML. HTML has been the de facto standard for many years, but it is important to keep in mind that HTML is a simple markup language for formatting data. HTML has a fixed set of tags to define the structure and style of text and provides no provisions for expansion. It is this inflexibility that has allowed browser vendors to add many proprietary tags that may be supported only by their browser. It also does not allow individuals to add custom tags because none of the browsers would know how to parse the custom tag. The Web is full of poorly written HTML that violates the basic HTML rules. This has led to browsers having to include code to handle this poorly written HTML.

As the use of the Web continues to grow, it is increasingly being accessed by a variety of devices such as cell phones, personal digital assistants (PDAs), and pagers. These devices, with their displays that are not visually oriented, are driving the change in how we mark up documents for the Web. The *Extensible Markup Language (XML)* should solve many problems because content creators will have to focus on the structure of a document, not just how it looks. XHTML is a reformulation of HTML 4 into an XML application and will provide a migration path while maintaining backwards compatibility. XHTML 1.0 is the current recommended standard of the World Wide Web Consortium (W3C).

RELATIONSHIPS BETWEEN MARKUP LANGUAGES

Before we move on to XHTML, let's take a look at the relationship between the various markup languages.

In the middle 1980s, an international standard called *Standard Generalized Markup Language (SGML)* was published. SGML is written in such a way as to define what a piece of information is. It allows for very clearly defined and marked text, so searching for a specific piece of information was simple. However, because of SGML's complexity, it is a difficult markup language to learn. To become an "expert" in SGML may take years of study. In addition, because of this complexity, SGML was impractical for uncomplicated documents.

Along came HTML, the first "offspring" of SGML developed to respond to the demand for a simpler markup language. HTML was developed to use the grammar of SGML, but it is a much less complex markup language to learn. It uses a limited number of tags that can be written in either upper or lower case or in a combination of both. Rather than defining what a piece of information is, HTML defines how the information should appear.

But it's this simplicity and lack of structured rules that has resulted in "sloppy" markup. The unstructured format requires a lot of processing power to interpret. With the advent of the cellular telephone and the growing popularity of tools such as the handheld computer, HTML has become too cumbersome to process.

Another of SGML's offspring, XML (Extensible Markup Language), had many promising features, including its compatibility with SGML. XML was an easier language to learn and to use than its predecessor, SGML. Like SGML, information written in XML is defined as what type of information it is rather than how it should look. This allows Web users to search for specific information much more quickly. Although XML is a very structured language, it is extensible, meaning new tags could be developed by anyone. But there's one major problem, and that is that many of the older browsers still in use today can't read XML.

What was needed was a language that was easy to use and easy to learn that would also be compatible with old browsers. XHTML was developed to bridge the gap between the current HTML and the exciting possibilities of XML. XHTML is the result of combining the advantages of the "sibling languages," HTML and XML. XHTML uses the exact tags and elements of HTML and syntax of SGML, but has the structure of XML. XHTML is considered to be an application of XML.

A BRIEF LOOK AT HTML

Hypertext Markup Language (HTML) is the popular language used to write Web pages. But why talk about HTML in an XHTML book? A little background on HTML is important since XHTML is a reformulation of HTML 4 into an XML application. So let's take a quick look. The HTML commands used to generate a Web page are called tags and are contained in a plain ASCII text file. The browser interprets the markup tags, and the results are then displayed on your monitor. The following is an example of a simple HTML document:

```
<HTML>
  <HEAD>
    <TITLE>
        Simple HTML Document
    </TITLE>
  </HEAD>
  <BODY>
    <H1>
        Hello HTML World!
    </H1>
    <P>
        This is the first paragraph of text.
    <P>
        This is the second paragraph of text.
  </BODY>
</HTML>
```

The results of the above HTML are in Figure 2.1.

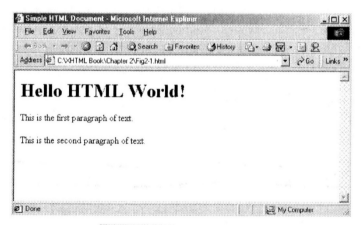

FIGURE 2.1: SIMPLE HTML DOCUMENT

Now that we have seen what a simple HTML document looks like and how the browser interprets the file to render a page on the screen, it's time to discuss some of the terms and syntax associated with HTML. The HTML file contains tags, which can be identified by the fact that they are enclosed in angle brackets, < and >. In the above example, we used the <HTML> tag to indicate that this is an HTML document and will enclose the entire document. The <HEAD> and <BODY> tags are used to create two necessary sections of an HTML document. The information enclosed between the <HEAD> </HEAD> tags will be information about the page that will not be displayed on the page itself.

The <BODY> </BODY> tags will enclose the material to be displayed on the Web page.

Tags can be used to identify structural elements of a document as well as to control the appearance of the Web page. There are two types of tags in HTML, container and stand-alone. A container tag is used to enclose some text, which is called content. Container elements have the following syntax:

```
<opening tag> text content </closing tag>
```

The opening tag indicates where the browser is to begin to mark up the text. The closing tag indicates where the formatting no longer applies. The closing tag will be the same as the opening tag except for the inclusion of a forward slash. The following is an example from the HTML document created above:

```
<H1>
    Hello HTML World!
</H1>
```

The <H1> tag is the opening tag followed by the content, while the </H1> is the closing tag. The opening tag, content, and closing tag are collectively referred to as an HTML element. In HTML, the <H1> tag is used to display a heading, which is large and bold. This tag also needs to have a closing tag </H1>, to indicate where the heading style is to end. Another tag used in our example is the paragraph tag <P>. This tag is used to start a new paragraph of text and to add some space between the previous paragraphs. In HTML, the closing tag for the <P> tag is optional. Our simple HTML contained the following two paragraphs:

```
<P>
   This is the first paragraph of text.
<P>
   This is the second paragraph of text.
```

How does the browser know where to begin the second paragraph without a closing tag on the first paragraph? When the browser encounters the second paragraph tag without encountering a closing paragraph </P> tag for the first paragraph, it assumes that the first paragraph has ended and a new paragraph is to begin.

Using optional or required attributes can change the behavior of tags. Tag attributes are used to specify how the tag is to be processed by the browser. Attributes are added to the opening tag by using keywords that give the browser additional information on how to render the tag on the page. For example, in our simple HTML document, if we wanted to center the heading on the page, we would include the align attribute and give it the value of "center." The opening heading tag would then look like the following:

```
<H1 align = CENTER>
    Hello HTML World!
</H1>
```

The result of adding the attribute to the <H1> tag is shown in Figure 2.2.

FIGURE 2.2: SIMPLE HTML DOCUMENT USING ATTRIBUTE

Tags are not limited to using only a single attribute; they can contain multiple attributes and values.

Over the years, HTML has gone through many versions, with each one adding features and depreciating others. For more information about the evolution of HTML, visit the *World Wide Web Consortium (W3C)* at **http://www.w3c.org**. The W3C organization is responsible for setting and maintaining the standards for HTML.

XHTML ADVANTAGES

Since XHTML follows the rules of XML, it has the advantages of *extensibility* and *portability*.

Extensibility

HTML has a fixed set of elements and has evolved very little over the years. If additional elements were required, the entire *document type definition (DTD)* would need to be changed. Since XHTML is an application of XML, its functionality can be extended beyond its predefined elements. By using XML namespaces, new elements can be added without changing the DTD on which the document is based.

Portability

Currently, most Internet access is through the PC. This is changing rapidly as more devices are becoming Web-enabled. These devices have less power than PCs and have a problem rendering current HTML documents. XHTML makes Web documents accessible across platforms.

DIFFERENCES BETWEEN HTML AND XHTML

XHTML simply redefines HTML using XML rules. Although XHTML is just a redefinition of HTML 4, it provides a stricter implementation of those standards and was developed to bridge the gap between XML and HTML. By adopting the new standards, developers can create documents that work with current browsers as well as be processed by XML applications. There are several ways that XHTML documents differ from HTML documents:

- They must be well-formed
- Element and attribute names must be in lower case
- Non-empty elements require end tags
- Attribute values must always be quoted
- They have no attribute minimization
- They end empty elements
- They use elements with id and name attributes
- They use Document Type Definitions
- They use XML namespaces

WELL-FORMED DOCUMENTS

This concept was introduced in XML, and a document is considered well-formed when it conforms to the rules defined in the XML specification. For an XHTML document, this means all elements:

- Must have an opening and closing tag
- Must be properly nested
- If empty, must be written in a special form

Opening and Closing Tags

In XHTML, all tags are required to be closed, so a closing tag must accompany every open tag. This is a change from HTML, where some closing tags were optional. Some examples of such tags are <p>, <td>, and <li>. For example, in HTML, we could use the <p> tag like:

```
<p>This was a legal use of this tag in HTML
<p>Second paragraph
```

In XHTML, we would close the <p> tag like

```
<p>This is a properly closed XHTML tag</p>
<p>With a second paragraph</p>
```

Properly Nested

Elements must nest properly, which means there can be no overlapping. Overlapping occurs when one element is

> tip: Remember to close every XHTML tag.

not contained within the other. Although overlapping was technically illegal, HTML browsers would tolerate code such as:

```
<p>This is<b> bolded text</p></b>
```

Here is this text in XHTML, without overlapping elements:

```
<p>This is<b> bolded text</b></p>
```

Empty Elements

In HTML, some elements are allowed to omit the closing tag because they do not enclose any content. Two common elements

> tip: Remember to close every XHTML tag in the proper order.

are the <hr> and <br>. For example, the following would be acceptable:

```
<hr>
<br>
```

In XHTML, all empty elements must have a closing tag. This can be accomplished through the use of a shortcut. This is an example of the correct way:

> tip: Leave a space before the / character.

```
<hr />
<br />
```

ELEMENT AND ATTRIBUTE NAMES MUST BE LOWER CASE

XML is case-sensitive, which means that it would treat the tags <P> and <p> differently. In XHTML, all element and attribute names must use lowercase.

In HTML, the following could be used:

```
<A HREF="first.html" TARGET=MAIN>Link to the first page</A>
```

In XHTML, the same line would appear as follows:

```
<a href="first.html" target="main">Link to the first page</a>
```

ATTRIBUTE VALUES MUST ALWAYS BE QUOTED

In XHTML, all values assigned to attributes must be quoted, even numeric values. In HTML, the following could be used:

```
<table align = center width = 85% border = 2 height = 200>
```

In XHTML, the same line would appear as follows:

```
<table align= "center" width= "85%" border= "2" height= "200">
```

NO ATTRIBUTE MINIMIZATION

Attribute minimization (stand-alone attribute) is not supported by XML. HTML has several attributes that do not require a value.

In HTML, the following could be used:

```
<FRAME SRC="frame1.html" NORESIZE>
```

In XHTML, the same line would appear as follows:

```
<frame src="frame1.html" noresize="noresize"/>
```

USING ELEMENTS WITH ID AND NAME ATTRIBUTES

Another change under XHTML is the use of the name attribute, which is defined in HTML 4 for use with the elements <a>, <frame>, <iframe>, <img>, and <map>. The name attribute has been deprecated, but some browsers do not support the id attribute. For compatibility, use both id and name attributes.

> tip: Since future versions of XHTML will drop the name attribute, use both id and name attributes to ensure future compatibility.

In HTML, the following could be used:

```
<FRAME SRC="toc.html" NAME="toc_menu">
```

In XHTML, the same line would appear as follows:

```
<frame src="toc.html" id="toc_menu" name="toc_menu"/>
```

USE OF DOCUMENT TYPE DEFINITIONS

The W3C defines a DTD as "a collection of XML declarations that, as a collection, defines the legal structure, elements, and attributes that are available for use in a document that complies to the DTD." Simply put, it is going to define how the contents of the XHTML document are going to be displayed by the browser.

In an XHTML document, the DTD is referenced in the <!DOCTYPE> element, which is used to declare and define the type of the document. The DTD declaration must be at the top of the document. XHTML documents should reference one of the DTDs, which correspond to the three HTML 4 DTDs. The XHTML DTDs are strict, transitional, and frameset.

Strict DTD

Strict DTD is used for a document that will conform exactly to the XHTML 1.0 standard. This means that the document will not contain any deprecated or frame elements. It is used when presentational markup can be separated from document structure. This is typically used when formatting is being done with cascading style sheets (CSS). Here's an example of the strict DTD:

```
<!DOCTYPE html PUBLIC "-//W3C//DTD/XHTML 1.0 Strict//EN"
"http://www.w3.org/TR/xhtml1/DTD/xhtml1-strict.dtd">
```

Transitional DTD

Transitional DTD is used when presentational markup needs to be embedded in the document. This includes all of the elements, transitional in addition to the frame elements. Here's an example of the *transitional DTD*:

```
<!DOCTYPE html PUBLIC "-//W3C//DTD/XHTML 1.0 Transitional//EN"
"http://www.w3.org/TR/xhtml1/DTD/xhtml1-transitional.dtd">
```

Frameset DTD

This DTD is used when the document needs frames. For compatibility, it includes deprecated elements. Here's an example of the *frameset DTD*:

```
<!DOCTYPE html PUBLIC "-//W3C//DTD/XHTML 1.0 Frameset//EN"
"http://www.w3.org/TR/xhtml1/DTD/xhtml1-frameset.dtd ">
```

XML NAMESPACES

The W3C defines an *XML namespace* as "a collection of names, identified by a URI (uniform resource identifier) reference, which is used in XML documents as element types and attribute names." Earlier in the chapter, we talked about the advantages of extensibility and portability. To make use of these advantages, we must declare an XML namespace that will indicate that it is an XHTML document and how it should be interpreted. The XHTML namespace declaration is an attribute in the <html> element. The XHTML namespace is:

```
<html xmlns="http://www.w3.org/1999/xhtml" xml:lang="en" lang="en">
```

XHTML DOCUMENTS

An XHTML document must meet the following criteria:
1. It must validate against one of the three DTDs.
2. The root element of the document must be <html> and designate the XHTML namespace by using the xmlns attribute.
3. A DOCTYPE declaration must be in the document and placed before the root element.

SIMPLE XHTML DOCUMENT

We start our simple XHTML document with the <?xml> declaration to indicate that the document is based on XML and what version. This is not required, but it is highly recommended. The following is our simple XHTML document:

```
<?xml version="1.0" encoding="UTF-8"?>
<!DOCTYPE html PUBLIC "-//W3C//DTD/XHTML 1.0 Transitional//EN"
"http://www.w3.org/TR/xhtml1/DTD/xhtml1-transitional.dtd">
<html xmlns="http://www.w3.org/1999/xhtml" xml:lang="en" lang="en">
<head>
<title>Simple XHTML Document</title>
</head>
<body>
<h1>Hello XHTML World</h1>
</body>
</html>
```

The results of the above XHTML are in Figure 2.3.

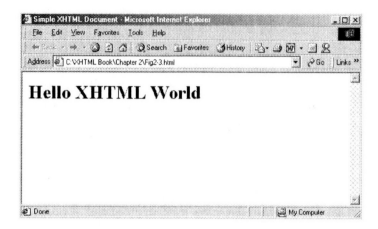

FIGURE 2.3: SIMPLE XHTML DOCUMENT

Before we can start learning about XHTML elements and tags that are used to create Web pages, we must discuss the tools that are available to aid in this development process also known as coding. Currently, there are many HTML development tools but very few XHTML tools.

APPROACHES TO CREATING XHTML DOCUMENTS

There are several ways that can be used to code an XHTML document. HTML tools can be used to create XHTML and then modified to XHTML standards, or we could just code our XHTML in a simple text editor. The following are four types of tools that could be used to create an XHTML file:

- What You See Is What You Get (WYSIWYG) applications
- Tag-based editors
- Conversion applications
- Text editors

You are probably asking yourself, "Why would I use a text editor when I can use an application that generates the code for me?" The answer is simple: If you know XHTML, you can easily learn any development system that comes along, but the converse is not true. In the long run, people who know only how to use a Web development editor are limiting their job marketability. So it is important to learn the basics of XHTML in an ASCII editor and then move on to development systems for their added productivity and functionality when that is appropriate.

Let's look at the four types of tools that could be used to create an XHTML file.

WYSIWYG APPLICATIONS

The WYSIWYG visual development environment makes creating great-looking Web pages so easy, anyone can do it without ever writing any HTML. The Web page is created by selecting items from menus and placing them on the page. This ease of use may sound great, but there are some disadvantages. The first is loss of control; remember that the application will do all your coding. This will allow the application to insert tags that are not necessary or proprietary. Also, as things change, these applications often do not contain the latest standards.

Some popular WYSIWYG applications include Microsoft FrontPage and Macromedia Dreamweaver. FrontPage is discussed in a separate tutorial on the CD included with this book. Figure 2.4 shows the HTML for a simple two-paragraph Web page created using FrontPage 2000. Figure 2.5 shows the code created using a text editor that would render the same Web page. Can you see any differences? Did the WYSIWYG application add any code that is unnecessary?

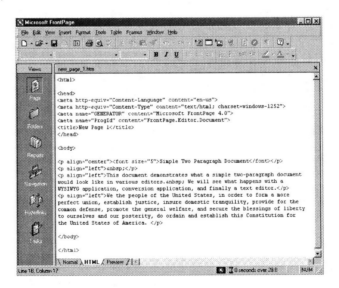

FIGURE 2.4: FRONTPAGE 2000 CODE

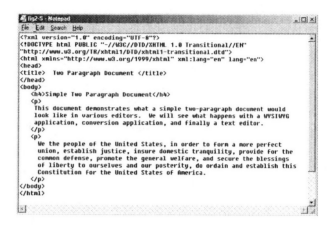

FIGURE 2.5: TEXT EDITOR CODE

TAG-BASED EDITORS

Basically, tag-based editors are text editors with additional features that aid the user during the coding process. These additional features allow the user to enter a tag with a click of a mouse button and have it automatically placed in the document. Some other features include spell checkers and syntax checkers, and some will even highlight tags in a different color to make them easier to identify in the document.

Some popular tag-based editors include Allaire's HomeSite and Sausage Software's HotDog Pro. An editor in this category specific to XHTML is Mozquito Factory. Figure 2.6 shows the HotDog Pro editor. Figure 2.7 shows the XHTML editor Mozquito Factory.

CONVERSION APPLICATIONS

Conversion applications can be stand-alone or integrated into another application such as a word processor. They may seem very useful because you don't need to know any HTML and very little time is required to create the HTML document. There must be a down side to all this ease of use. That's right—there is one; the code generated is full of unnecessary tags. Microsoft Word 2000, for example, allows you to save your work as an HTML file. Allowing you to

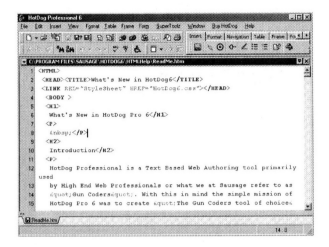

FIGURE 2.6: HOTDOG PRO

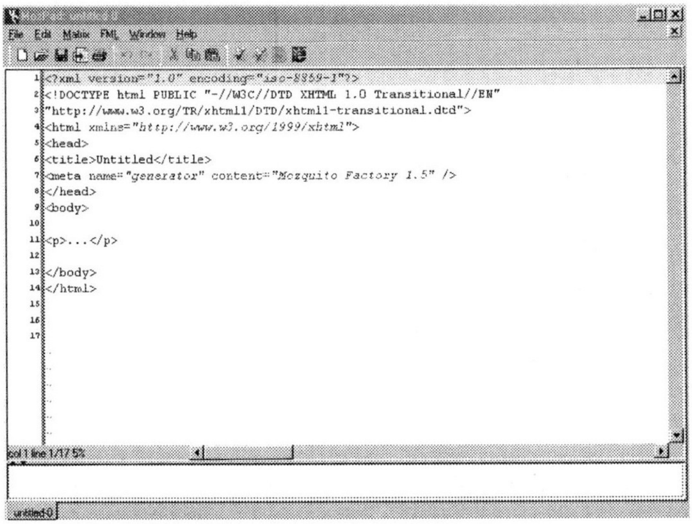

FIGURE 2.7: MOZQUITO FACTORY

use your word processor as a WYSIWYG application, the converter takes out
all of the document formatting information and replaces it with the appropriate
HTML. Figure 2.8 shows the code used in the earlier examples after it has been
saved with Microsoft Word as an HTML file.

```
Fig2-8 - Notepad
File Edit Search Help
<html xmlns:o="urn:schemas-microsoft-com:office:office"
xmlns:w="urn:schemas-microsoft-com:office:word"
xmlns="http://www.w3.org/TR/REC-html40">

<head>
<meta http-equiv=Content-Type content="text/html; charset=windows-1252">
<meta name=ProgId content=Word.Document>
<meta name=Generator content="Microsoft Word 9">
<meta name=Originator content="Microsoft Word 9">
<link rel=File-List href="./fig3-5_files/filelist.xml">
<title>Simple Two Paragraph Document</title>
<!--[if gte mso 9]><xml>
 <o:DocumentProperties>
  <o:Author>Jeff Griffin</o:Author>
  <o:Template>Normal</o:Template>
  <o:LastAuthor>Jeff Griffin</o:LastAuthor>
  <o:Revision>2</o:Revision>
  <o:TotalTime>20</o:TotalTime>
  <o:Created>2001-06-13T14:30:00Z</o:Created>
  <o:LastSaved>2001-06-13T14:30:00Z</o:LastSaved>
  <o:Pages>1</o:Pages>
  <o:Company>Laptop</o:Company>
  <o:Lines>1</o:Lines>
  <o:Paragraphs>1</o:Paragraphs>
  <o:Version>9.2720</o:Version>
 </o:DocumentProperties>
</xml><![endif]-->
<style>
<!--
 /* Style Definitions */
p.MsoNormal, li.MsoNormal, div.MsoNormal
```

```
Fig2-8 - Notepad
File Edit Search Help
@page Section1
        {size:8.5in 11.0in;
        margin:1.0in 1.25in 1.0in 1.25in;
        mso-header-margin:.5in;
        mso-footer-margin:.5in;
        mso-paper-source:0;}
div.Section1
        {page:Section1;}
-->
</style>
</head>

<body lang=EN-US style='tab-interval:.5in'>

<div class=Section1>

<p class=MsoTitle>Simple Two Paragraph Document</p>

<p class=MsoNormal><span style='font-size:16.0pt;mso-bidi-font-size:12.0pt'><![if !supportEmptyParas]> <![

<p class=MsoNormal>This document demonstrates what a simple two-paragraph
document would look like in various editors.<span style="mso-spacerun: yes">
</span>We will see what happens with a WYSIWYG application, conversion
application, and finally a text editor.</p>

<p class=MsoNormal><![if !supportEmptyParas]> <![endif]><o:p></o:p></p>

<p class=MsoNormal>We the people of the United States, in order to form a more
perfect union, establish justice, insure domestic tranquility, provide for the
common defense, promote the general welfare, and secure the blessings of
liberty to ourselves and our posterity, do ordain and establish this
Constitution for the United States of America. </p>

</div>

</body>

</html>
```

FIGURE 2.8: MICROSOFT WORD DOCUMENT CONVERTED TO HTML

TEXT EDITORS

I have saved the best for last, and in case you haven't guessed, this is how we encourage people to learn how to code XHTML. Text editors create ASCII text files (plain text) and are the simplest way to enter and edit text. This is great because XHTML documents are saved as plain-text files. Most computer systems include a text editor; for example, Windows includes Notepad. On Unix and Linux systems, vi and Emacs are the popular text editors. So there is no need to run out and buy a WYSIWYG application to create your Web page.

tip: Often the code generated by converters is less than desirable and will require a great deal of cleanup.

By now you might be wondering why would anyone want to use a text editor to code XHTML, when it could be generated for you? When you write code with a text editor, there is no way around it—you have to know the code. Sooner or later, you will have to get into the code to fix something, convert HTML to XHTML, clean up code that has been generated by a WYSIWYG application, or add a feature that is not supported by the other editors. This type of coding is referred to as "hand-coding." By knowing the coding rules, you will be able to use your skills to be creative and innovative when creating your applications. Figure 2.5 showed XHTML code created using Notepad.

When saving your XHTML files, it is important to remember to save them as plain-text files with the extension of htm or html.

tip: Understanding how and why things are done in XHTML will make you a much better developer and able to solve difficult problems.

Viewing a Document Source

When learning how to write XHTML, it is sometimes beneficial to view the source code of other documents and actually see how some good pages are put together. Remember that the Web pages you are looking at are just text documents that the browser interprets for display. The two leading browsers have menu items that allow you to view the source code for the Web page you are currently viewing. If you are using Microsoft Internet Explorer, choose Source from the View menu. If you are using Netscape Navigator, select Page Source from the View menu.

Although this is relatively easy to do and sometimes it is good to see what goes on behind the scenes, we would add these words of caution:

- The code could be poorly written or contain problems (bugs).
- You think you have learned to write the code, but you may have only learned to cut and paste.
- Since someone else created it, there is the issue of copyright.

Let's look at an example of a Web page and then view its source. This is illustrated in Figures 2.9 and 2.10.

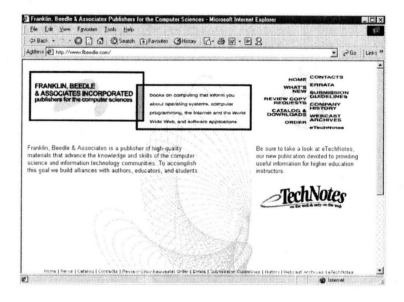

FIGURE 2.9: SAMPLE WEB PAGE

```
www.fbeedle[1] - Notepad                                    _ □ ×
File  Edit  Search  Help
<HTML>
<HEAD>
  <META NAME="GENERATOR" CONTENT="Adobe PageMill 3.0 Win">
  <META HTTP-EQUIV="Content-Type" CONTENT="text/html; charset=iso-8859-1">
  <META NAME="FORMATTER" CONTENT="Microsoft FrontPage 2.0">
  <TITLE>Franklin, Beedle &amp; Associates Publishers for the Computer Sciences</TITLE>
</HEAD>
<BODY BGCOLOR="#FFFFFF" BACKGROUND="art/bakgrond2.gif" LINK="#990000">

<BASEFONT SIZE=2>
<P><TABLE WIDTH="744" BORDER="0" CELLSPACING="2" CELLPADDING="0">
  <TR>
    <TD WIDTH="70%"><BASEFONT SIZE=2>
    <IMG SRC="art/ban-3.gif" WIDTH="501" HEIGHT="133" ALIGN="BOTTOM"
    BORDER="0" NATURALSIZEFLAG="3">
</TD>
    <TD WIDTH="30%"><BASEFONT SIZE=2>
    <MAP NAME="navbar2Map23">
    <AREA SHAPE="rect" COORDS="110,121,190,135" HREF="technote/03-01/03-01.html"
    ALT="View the latest edition of eTechNotes">
    <AREA SHAPE="rect" COORDS="108,96,186,118" HREF="webcast.html"
    ALT="Download files from our webcasts">
    <AREA SHAPE="rect" COORDS="109,71,183,91" HREF="history.html"
    ALT="Read our company history">
    <AREA SHAPE="rect" COORDS="109,46,198,66" HREF="submit.html"
    ALT="Guidelines for prospective authors">
    <AREA SHAPE="rect" COORDS="110,28,169,40" HREF="errata.html"
    ALT="Get the latest updates for our books">
    <AREA SHAPE="rect" COORDS="109,12,188,25" HREF="contacts.html"
    ALT="Contact your representative">
    <AREA SHAPE="rect" COORDS="51,110,105,122" HREF="order.html"
```

FIGURE 2.10 SOURCE CODE FOR SAMPLE WEB PAGE

CHAPTER SUMMARY

To support the next generation of Web-enabled devices, it will be necessary for us to concern ourselves with more than just the presentation of Web pages. We will also have to consider content and how to get that information to all these new devices. That is where XHTML comes in. This chapter briefly looked at HTML 4.01 and the differences with the XHTML 1.0 specification. The differences between HTML and XHTML documents included:

- Documents must be well-formed
- Element and attribute names must be in lower case
- Non-empty elements require tags
- Attribute values must always be quoted
- No attribute minimization
- Use elements with id and name attributes
- Use Document Type Definitions
- End empty elements
- XML namespaces

This chapter also discussed different approaches to creating XHTML documents, such as:

- What You See Is What You Get (WYSIWYG) applications
- Tag-based editors
- Conversion applications
- Text editors

KEY TERMS

attribute minimization
document type definition (DTD)
Extensible Hypertext Markup Language (XHTML)
extensibility
Extensible Markup Language (XML)
frameset DTD
Hypertext Markup Language (HTML)
portability
Standard Generalized Markup Language (SGML)
strict DTD
transitional DTD
World Wide Web Consortium (W3C)
XML namespace

REVIEW QUESTIONS

1. What is the purpose of the Document Type Definition (DTD)?
2. What are the two advantages of XHTML? Explain.
3. What is SGML?
4. What is XML?
5. How are SGML, HTML, and XML related?
6. What is the importance of XHTML?
7. What are the criteria that an XHTML document must conform to?
8. What is attribute minimization?
9. What are the three XHTML DTDs?
10. How are the empty attributes <hr> and <br> closed?

EXERCISES

1. Convert the HTML below to XHTML using the standards discussed in this chapter.

```
<HTML>
<HEAD>
<TITLE>This is an HTML document</TITLE>
<BODY>
    <P>This is an HTML document that you should convert to XHTML. The
    link below will take you to the W3C.
    <BR>
    <A HREF="http://www.w3c.org" TARGET=MAIN>W3C</A>
    <BR>
</BODY>
</HTML>
```

2. Go to the Franklin, Beedle & Associates Website (www.fbeedle.com) and view its source code. Determine what would need to be done to convert the home page to XHTML standards.

3. Using Notepad, create the following XHTML document. Save the document as simple.html.

```
<?xml version="1.0" encoding="UTF-8"?>
<!DOCTYPE html PUBLIC "-//W3C//DTD/XHTML 1.0 Transitional//EN"
"http://www.w3.org/TR/xhtml1/DTD/xhtml1-transitional.dtd">
<html xmlns="http://www.w3.org/1999/xhtml" xml:lang="en" lang="en">
<head>
<title>Simple XHTML Document</title>
</head>
<body>
<h1>Hello XHTML World</h1>
</body>
</html>
```

PROJECT

Your client has hired you to create a portal site in response to a problem. He would like to facilitate communication and collaboration among community members. His decision to have you develop this site is predicated on the assumption that a hyperlinked Website will solve this problem. As a Web designer, you know the strengths and weakness of the Web as a communication medium. Do the following:

* Based on the preliminary audience analysis you created in Chapter 1, write a proposal validating the use of a Website for this purpose. Will a Website

really help members of your community communicate and collaborate better? Make sure to consider attributes specific to your audience. Some questions you should consider:

- Is the percentage of people in your community with computers and Internet access large enough to justify spending money on developing the site?
- Why would an XHTML site solve this problem more effectively than a print-based solution, such as a newspaper?
- What standard will you use to measure success? The number of hits? The number of unique users?

chapter 3
design basics for the information designer

CHAPTER OVERVIEW

This chapter will focus on an introduction to the vocabulary
and principles of visual design based on the Gestalt theories
of information perception pioneered by Max Wertheimer.
Additionally, it will explore the relationships of forms utilizing Boolean operations: union, difference, and intersection.
These hands-on explorations will include design exercises
and projects that stimulate the imagination and will lead to
strengthening your visualization skills. The techniques and
theories discussed in this chapter will lead directly to your
own Web page designs.

CHAPTER OBJECTIVES

- Use and understand the terms in the chapter
- Use the principles to create compositions
- Recognize the use of the principles in other compositions
- Have an understanding and appreciation for visual design
  as it applies to Web pages

INTRODUCTION

At this time, the beginning of a new millennium, thoughts everywhere turn to the rhetorical question, "What does the future hold?" It is a question of great magnitude and one that is not really answerable in full. In part, we can speculate on the state of the economy, the ecological impact current technologies will have on the earth, and what if, what if...? But what does the future hold for the computer industry? What new advances will present themselves in the years to come? In 1949, Arthur C. Clarke wrote a story that came to be known as *2001: A Space Odyssey*. In it he predicted what life might be like in that year. Though we are a lot further from the kind of casual space travel he envisioned, we aren't far from the communications abilities computer networks and wireless networks provide. In spite of its great ability, IBM's Big Blue is no HAL 9000, but we are working hard to close the gap and develop AI (artificial intelligence) to a greater degree. One wonders how Clarke was able to come as close as he did with his ideas. He did it by utilizing as much of his brain as he could, both the left side (logic) and the right side (creativity). This allowed him to have an expansive imagination and vision. It is this imagination, the ability to think, to process non-linear ideas, and to organize and speculate based on new information that is the driving force behind creative individuals. This force results in graphic and product design that is unique and interesting and captures the audience's attention.

The purpose of this chapter, in the middle of a seemingly straightforward text on XHTML, is to expose the student of Web design who comes from the computer/programming side (read left-brained/logical side) to some of the basic vocabulary and techniques that graphic designers utilize to engage in and explore the creation and execution of visual ideas. It doesn't amount to just taste or talent. There are some rules that work; the ability to go outside those rules to make even greater discoveries and connections constitutes conscious, purposeful design.

With the advent and ease of Web technology, more and more of the interaction with computers is being performed via a browser; the traditional operating system becomes a staid backdrop against which dynamic human/computer interface takes place. This is to be expected since even Windows 98 and MacOS 9 are a little long in the tooth, having been birthed and remaining relatively unchanged since the mid-1970s. The current "Office" metaphor was in the original Xerox Palo Alto Research Center's vision for human/computer interface design. Atari and Amiga both used an incarnation of the metaphor for the interface for their systems in the early 1980s. Certainly, Super Bowl 1984 (and Apple's "Big Brother" commercial, with its own literary allusions to predictions of the future from George Orwell) and Apple's release of the Macintosh mark the popular introduction of the desktop/office metaphor, complete with file folder icons and a trash can! Microsoft's idea of Internet Explorer and Web page navigation is just a different way of looking at the same old interface. What's new about that?

The visual front end to the Web was the next revolution in the current wave of interaction with a computer using the point-and-click idea. (Certainly, voice communication will be a wonderful addition to the human/computer interface options, but even the best voice-recognition engines are hard to train and not yet really mass marketable. The days of a computer performing like the system that controls the Starship Enterprise are still in a galaxy far, far away.) Transforming from a primarily science-based, text-based resource to a visually interactive one was an awesome leap. What it also did is reduce our need to rely on Windows or the Mac OS and to experience individualized interfaces created by unique individuals for the multitudes. This is the future of the point-and-click interface.

This freedom is exciting on the one hand but disconcerting on the other. It goes against the strict standards imposed by Microsoft and Apple (and others, but for clarity's sake we will only mention these popular, mass-marketed operating systems). Though HTML imposes other limitations on the interfaces people create, it allows for much more access to interface creation for the layman than either Microsoft or Apple. One cannot easily say, "I think I want to interact with my desktop computer in a different way today," and easily whip up whatever one's visual heart desires. The Web and HTML allow just that idea to come to fruition. Just ask any high-school kid with his or her own Web page.

This hodgepodge of visual information is becoming tedious. The next generation will bring a cleansing and visual clarity to the Web that will make it a wonderful place to spend time and interact with computers. How can we assist you, who will be called upon to design these interfaces and make the leap to this next generation?

The best option would be to require you to take one or two semesters of traditional fine arts fundamentals. There is a trend in this direction, with some computer science curriculums adding a computer graphics track to their majors and partnering with the fine arts departments on their campuses to get

CS/IS/MIS/CPT students into beginning design classes. The artists recognized early that the Web was a place for them and that the computer side ot it (HTML/FTP, and so on) was not so difficult. So they jumped on the Web design bandwagon early. It is time for the technologists and computer people to play catch up.

Since it is not always possible to alter curriculums to accommodate in-depth study into a seemingly unrelated field, our suggestion is to incorporate a traditional fine arts fundamental exploration into the computer-programming curriculum. This is the purpose of this chapter in this text.

The following theories and related exercises or problems are constructed to allow the student to discover the vocabulary of visual design. You are encouraged to explore visual communication concepts and the principles of design. This approach allows personal expression in the solving of complex communication problems of interface and Web design.

This approach to interface and Web design allows intuitive conceptual ways of problem solving to be developed. There are no clearly correct ways of solving the problems, but it is most important to develop thoughtful choices based on some of the rules learned here and in other courses related to human behavior, interface design, and communication.

VOCABULARY AND PRINCIPLES

It is important to understand that design is not just at the whim of the artist or designer. It is not just an amorphous feeling or perception of what is right. So often artists and designers are stereotyped by the idea that the work they do comes from some mysterious place and that the mantle of greatness can only be bestowed on those that "have it." This isn't true. Great artists and visionaries are just very good at applying the rules and making it seem as if there are no rules. They are also very perceptive as to when to break the rules. I am fond of telling my students

"Creativity is in how you break the rules."

Learning the rules, which in this case would be the principles and vocabulary of the visual language, is the first step in achieving better results in your design work. The ability to create good visual design is within every individual. There are no right or wrong choices; however, there are some basic rules. Learn the rules and apply them in your work, and it will stand on its own and serve the purpose you envisioned.

The building blocks of the visual language, like the letters of the alphabet, are described below. Note the similarity to the mathematical definitions of the same entities. This mathematical similarity is also true of some of the other principles discussed later.

- **Point**—A *point* is just that, a single identifiable x,y coordinate in space. It has no breadth or length. It is the beginning and end of a line or the place where lines meet or cross.
- **Line**—A *line* is made up of an infinite number of points. It is also the path a point would make if a point moved through space. It forms the edge of a plane.
- **Plane**—A *plane* is made up of an infinite number of lines. It is also the area a line would scribe if it traveled through space. If a plane traveled through space, it would describe an area of volume that we would represent with a three-dimensional symbol, though the third dimension doesn't truly exist in two-dimensional design.

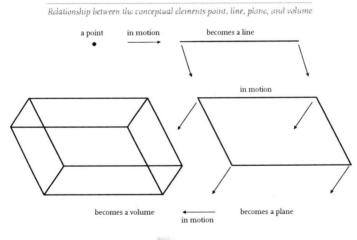

Relationship between the conceptual elements point, line, plane, and volume

FIGURE 3.1

- **Path**—The direction in which a point, line, or plane travels.
- **Shape**—The organization of points and lines to form recognizable, named images in the field of perception. Some shapes are predefined, as in geometric shapes.

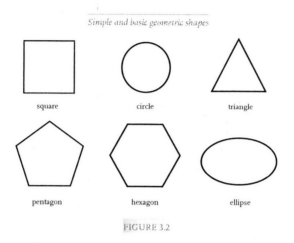

Simple and basic geometric shapes

square   circle   triangle

pentagon   hexagon   ellipse

FIGURE 3.2

Other shapes are free-form and irregular, with either curved lines, straight lines, or a combination of both. Highly complex shapes can be created by the exploitation and use of lines and curves in multiple directions simultaneously.

Shapes can have various attributes assigned to them. Those attributes are:

- **Size**—physically measurable (2 inches) or relative to other shapes described in terms of largeness or smallness.
- **Texture**—referring to the surface attributes of a shape. Plain or ornate, rough or smooth are terms that might be employed when describing the texture of a shape. Texture often appeals to the sense of touch (based on past associations of the observer) as well as to the sense of sight.
- **Color**—the characteristic of a shape that makes it stand out from its surroundings.

Shapes tend to have an inside, an outside, and an outline. We can use the attribute of color to delineate these features of a shape to our advantage in a design, and we will see that advantage when we talk about the *interaction* of shapes with one another.

A shape generally looks as if it either is occupying space or is a hole in occupied space. This is the idea of *positive* (occupying) *space* and *negative* (a hole) *space*. Which part of a composition becomes positive or negative depends on how the observer perceives the form. We tend to perceive darkness as occupying space and lighter values as the hole surrounded by occupied space.

The Stroke and Fill Attributes of a Shape

For the purposes of simplification, we will assume the composition being discussed is limited. We will limit the color palette of this composition to two colors, black and white, and to a single shape (in this case, the geometric shape we call a square).

Remember that earlier we said that shapes tend to have an inside and an outline. Persons familiar with vector illustration software (such as Macromedia FreeHand or Adobe Illustrator) will recognize the following concepts as the *stroke* and the fill of lines and shapes.

If we think about the possible combinations of those two attributes in a framed composition, we can come up with seven possible states the composition can have.

- ▦ It can have a white outline with a white fill on a white background, resulting in the form disappearing (A).
- ▦ It can have a black outline with a white fill on a white background (B).
- ▦ It can have a black outline with a black fill on a white background (C).
- ▦ It can have a black outline with a black fill on a black background, again resulting in the shape disappearing (D).
- ▦ It can have a white outline with a black fill on a black background (E).
- ▦ It can have a black outline with a white fill on a black background (F).
- ▦ It can have a white outline with a white fill on a black background. The visual result of this is the same as F.

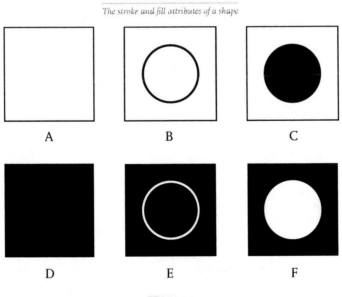

The stroke and fill attributes of a shape

FIGURE 3.3

By understanding and visualizing these basic rules, we can now explore the way two forms might intersect.

THE INTERSECTION OF MULTIPLE FORMS

Some of the terms used to describe the way in which shapes can intersect each other will again be familiar to those who are mathematically inclined. Some of them share names with geometric and algebraic functions. Those who have experience in 3-D modeling will recognize them as Boolean operations.

In a given composition with two shapes, the shapes can be:

- Apart, each occupying space separate from the other (A).
- Touching, where only a single point is shared by both shapes (B).
- Overlapping, which requires one shape to have a stroke of a contrasting color (C).
- Transparent overlapping, in which both shapes have a stroke of a contrasting color and their intersection is filled with a contrasting color (D).
- United, in which the overlapping shapes are filled and have a stroke of the same color. A new form is generally created and perceived in a *union* (E).
- Punched, in which one shape is used like a cookie cutter to carve away part of the other shape. This is sometimes referred to as *subtraction* (F).
- Intersected, in which only the part shared by both remains (G).
- Coincident, in which the two shapes both are the same color and size and appear as one or in which the larger shape totally covers the smaller shape, leaving the perception of only one shape. This choice still involves two shapes to start with but involves the choice to cover one shape with the other by moving them into the same space (H).

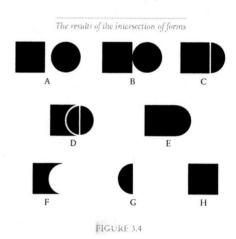

The results of the intersection of forms

FIGURE 3.4

Of course, if we were to repeat the above and use white forms on a black background, we would get eight more compositions for a total of 16 possible combinations. With the use of additional colors, the choices become infinite. It is the making of and manipulation of these choices that add zest to a design. We as designers can choose which of the above behaviors we will use and when we will use them, then follow that path to create a composition. We can also change our minds part way through and follow a different set of rules. With additional information, we can create very complex rule sets, almost like programs or batch files, in which we explore organizing visual information. There is no right or wrong, only choices—make some and go with them.

GESTALT PRINCIPLES

The study of information perception is best summed up by the work of *Gestalt* psychologists, principally Max Wertheimer. The study of how humans perceive and group information by assigning it value relative to other information presented in the same field of view is extremely important to programmers responsible for interface and Web page design. We are familiar with some of the following illustrations, but others will underscore the importance of understanding these building blocks for the presentation of visual information. These, combined with the building blocks we explored in the ideas behind shape and the interaction of shapes, should expand our command of the language significantly. Even if you don't go further into this section of the chapter, you can already create some interesting and purposeful designs.

The Gestalt psychologists broke presentation and perception of two-dimensional information down into what they called grouping principles. The grouping principles help artists and designers understand how humans perceive the visual field of view. Though each principle looks at the parts of an image, the overriding idea is that the whole is greater than the sum of the parts. The patterns that are formed by the parts take precedence over the individual parts. Observe the composition below. It contains multiple filled circles. What is the thing that sticks out about how they are arranged in the field of view? Can you just see the dots, or will they always organize themselves into the recognizable pattern?

Figure and *ground* (sometimes called *field*) are two inseparable ideas in visual design. They refer primarily to the *frame* that exists around everything (often assigned by the brain) in order to provide a context for the perception to focus on. The first

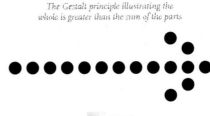

The Gestalt principle illustrating the whole is greater than the sum of the parts

FIGURE 3.5

*An ambiguous figure/ground relationship
and a clear figure/ground relationship*

FIGURE 3.6

figure illustrating this concept is a classic one that demonstrates a figure/ground relationship in equilibrium that creates an ambiguous focus. We cannot see both figures (the faces or the goblet) at the same time, but we switch between them. The other figure/ground illustrates a more useful concept. We are not fighting with our brains as to which part of the composition should receive our focus.

The paper on which the design resides, the computer screen, and the application or browser window inside the screen are all frames that shouldn't be ignored when designing for the screen. They are a part of the perception field and should be used like the proscenium of a stage that seeks to hide and tantalizes to reveal what is beyond the visible edge.

The *grouping principles* of *proximity, similarity, continuation,* and *closure* are key ideas in the organization of visual elements and their relative importance to each other and the user. There is a hierarchy of perception to these grouping principles. Greater importance is perceived in objects that are in close proximity to each other. The converse is also true in that we tend to diminish the importance of the relationship between two objects as they recede from each other. Viewers have a tendency to assign greater importance to objects that are similar. Similarity is given greater weight than proximity. Items that form a continuation or the perception of a continuation tend to take precedence over items that are similar or close to each other.

Proximity—The brain organizes information and visual patterns by grouping. One way that this occurs is by proximity of elements to each other. They appear to be associated just because they are close to one another.

*The same elements distributed with greater or lesser proximity
in the x and y directions yield different results. We have an equally
balanced effect with rows and columns occurring as well.*

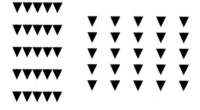

FIGURE 3.7

Similarity—In the visual field, our brains (through the use of our eyes) can pick out things that are similar to one another, even though they share the same proximity as previously illustrated. Items of similar shape, color, texture, or other variable attributes seem to belong together just because they look alike. Figure 3.9 demonstrates this idea.

Similarity also refers to the idea that an object resembles another object, like circles and ellipses, and that we tend to identify those items together if there is not an exact similarity. This idea is helpful in choosing layouts for elements

Though the three items in the field of view are all noticed, we tend to group the two closest to each other and recognize the group as different from the item that is apart.

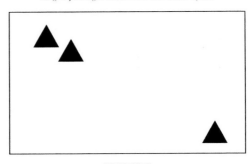

FIGURE 3.8

Similarity overrides proximity, and we see the hexagons as a group though they are apart from each other.

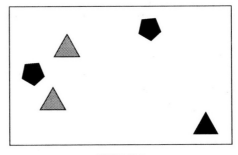

FIGURE 3.9

on a page. If the forms used on a page are circular in their construction, it might be good to lay the elements out along a curved path instead of a linear one. This idea combines the idea of similarity of shape and the idea of continuation as explained next.

Continuation—Continuation is the principle of leading the eye to where you want the viewer to focus. It is an instinctive trait of humans to follow a visual path. The path can be literal or imagined. Literally, objects that point use the idea of continuation. Another way to use continuation is the connect-the-dots approach. Our ability to imagine pictures in the stars (Ursa Major for example) is an example of our use of continuation that leads to closure (as explained next).

The ancients saw pictures in the stars, and it is the principle of continuation that our brains use to organize this information to see the pictures.

FIGURE 3.10

Though the square doesn't exist, our brains do the work so that we see the implied outline of the square.

FIGURE 3.11

Can you read the word? Humans have an easier time with the tops of letters.

FIGURE 3.12

Here is the same word with only the bottom available. Even knowing what it is, it is still very hard to read.

FIGURE 3.13

Closure—Humans possess the innate need to close gaps and complete shapes. This is how we read text and view visual information. We make assumptions regarding the finishing of visual input. Visually, a closed shape leaves nothing for the mind and imagination to do, but an open shape is much more interesting and leaves exploration to the viewer.

Even without all the visual information intact, our brains are able to decipher information because of their ability to use the principles of closure.

Upright and **horizontal**—Viewers are very comfortable with things that are level and plumb. We seem to instinctively know how to deal with the major axis that relate to 90 and 180 degrees and even the major subdivisions of 45 degrees. Humans have a tendency to become uneasy with anything that strays from this expected norm. Deviating from these norms can be disconcerting, but this can also be utilized to create an emphasis and focus. It certainly draws your attention, as illustrated by crooked pictures hanging on the walls of a house always being fussed over by someone. Societal tempering keeps us from doing it in other people's homes, but boy we wish we could.

Grid systems, used extensively by graphic designers and artists for centuries, might also help illustrate this idea. If we use the edges of forms on a page or screen to align other objects in the composition, the whole thing seems to be more cohesive than if we just sort of place things here and there without regard to the horizontal and vertical lines implied in the composition. We will talk more specifically about grids later in this chapter.

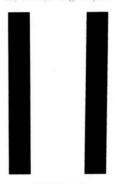

Cover the right figure and just look at the left one. Now cover the left one and see if you can spot the difference. Even though the one on the right is only a few degrees off center, humans are very aware of it. Just think about the pictures on the walls of your house. You can't let them stay askew for long, can you?

FIGURE 3.14

The concept of *direction* addresses the *horizontal* and *vertical* alignment of forms in the frame. This is similar but more deliberate than continuation and has to do with established expectations. Direction, when used effectively, can manipulate the viewer's line of sight in order to create emphasis and focus. Direction is effective when used in a logical approach, such as the arrangement of forms in a left-to-right pattern—the way people in most Western countries read text. However, breaking the logical directional expectation can also be useful in guiding the user to a particular point in the visual field.

OTHER PRINCIPLES

Many design principles don't fall into a particular school of thought, but appear to be common to the various schools. These are described below. Again, though even non-artists/designers may be familiar with the terms below, by suspending judgment and respecting (*re: again + spect: look* = to look again) them enough to really examine and understand them, visual information architects can discover new avenues of design.

Balance, symmetry, and *asymmetry* are key design principles that are almost assumed. A clear understanding of the use of these principles and their effect on the user's perception is essential in successful design. Symmetry, although fairly simple for any user to achieve, can result in a less-than-exciting design in that it places equal value on all forms within the field. This results in

a lesser sense of emphasis and importance for key forms. Asymmetry becomes important then in creating the visual road map that viewers must explore as they interact with the design.

Balance refers to the visual balance of all the items in a composition. Putting too much dense text and accompanying pictures on one side of a page can lead to an overbalance or "tipping" feeling in a composition.

Use of *positive* and *negative space* is another seemingly minor, yet essential, ingredient in visual design. You must understand that form occupies space (positive space) and that there is space around each form (negative space).

Repetition, rhythm, and *pattern* are design principles that complement each other. Repetition is an example of grouping similar forms in an effort to satisfy the user's perceptual need for a sense of order and wholeness. The user recognizes these traits, and the eye is drawn to them. Repetition is the most powerful when the variables of size, shape, texture, and color are equal. Variations of those same attributes can be quite stunning, as when an oversized letter is

Visual balance, unbalance

this text is too light to balance against the black circle

this text is visually heavier and is in balance against the black circle

FIGURE 3.15

An example of symmetrical balance and asymmetrical balance at work

This text and the circle above it are centered visually to the page and each other creating symmetry

This text and the circle above it are balanced in an offset or asymmetrical arrangement

FIGURE 3.16

Forms tend to be perceived as positive and advancing toward the viewer. Negative space appears to recede.

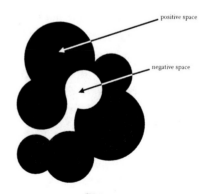

positive space

negative space

FIGURE 3.17

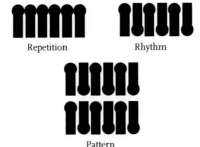

The relationship between repetition, rhythm, and pattern. Pattern is sustained rhythmic repetition.

Repetition   Rhythm

Pattern

FIGURE 3.18

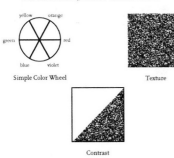

Examples of a simple color wheel, a texture, and a contrast of texture and no texture

Simple Color Wheel   Texture

Contrast

FIGURE 3.19

Here is an example of value used to organize a hierarchy of information. The bold and advancing text is available, the lesser value text is receding and unavailable.

FIGURE 3.20

used both as a background and as a drop capital at the beginning of a paragraph.

The use of rhythm is the designer's ability to use sustained repetition to assist in the provision of a sense of order. Pattern is simply the expression of this rhythm over a continuous area. The design student should be knowledgeable about the impact of *color, texture,* and *contrast.* These tools can be used to create emphasis, focus, hierarchical importance, and pure aesthetic appeal. Instruction in the use of these tools could be a course in and of itself.

Value is the lightness or darkness of a form that supports the perception of the user in developing focus and appeal. This concept must be grasped early in the visual design learning process. Greater or lesser value is assigned to an item dependent on its relative value to other items in a group (or items in close proximity). A common use of this technique in software design is the "graying out" of items that in a particular context are not available or needed. Students of design should be able to reproduce the 10-point value scale accurately with a single pencil weight using shading and hatching techniques.

The 10-point tonal value scale

FIGURE 3.21

Information can be organized over an area or on a screen with the use of *grid systems*. This technique has been employed in graphic design for centuries. The key to using this tool lies in the designer's ability to utilize an underlying and invisible grid to aid in the alignment of visual information. The development of this skill can be exciting and empowering to the student. A related challenge exists in learning how and when to deviate from this grid.

Examples of a three- and a five-column grid layout used in publishing

FIGURE 3.22

USING COLOR/THE AESTHETICS OF COLOR

In Chapter 5, we will learn how to specify color in HTML. The information here is presented from a design and aesthetic point of view. For further study on color, there are many good references on color theory and the use of color on the Web and in design that speak far more eloquently and succinctly on the subject than we could ever hope to. These books are also filled with full-color illustrations, and we highly recommend that you read them. Included on our list would be *Color Harmony* by Hideaki Chijiiwa, *Color Harmony 2: A Guide to Creative Color Combinations* by Bride M. Whelan, and *The Art of Color* by Joannes Itten. At this point our discussion of color uses the traditional artist's color wheel as the reference point for the definitions and examples that follow. Computer-specific color is covered in Chapter 5.

Color Wheel

You can use the color wheel (see the full-color file on the CD) to assist you with color selection. Generally, the three primary colors can go together well. They create a child-like, bright, playful mood. The pure primaries are sometimes overpowering. The primary colors are red, blue, and yellow.

Secondary Colors

Secondary colors are achieved by mixing two primaries together. So the use of those two primaries and their secondary color would create a usable palette. The secondary colors are green, orange, and violet.

Tertiary Colors

Orange red, yellow orange, yellow green, blue green, blue violet, and red violet are considered to be the tertiary colors. This group of colors includes the mixture of a primary with a secondary color.

Complementary Colors

Complementary colors are the colors that are exactly opposite each other on the color wheel. If direct complements are too intense against one another (as in orange text on a blue background), then tint or tone one of the colors in the pair to aid in readability. Starting with the complement brings about a harmony and unity of color.

Split Complements

Another way of using complements without tinting or toning is to use the split complement of a color. This is the color on the wheel that is directly to the left or right of the pure complement.

Analogous Colors

Analogous colors are the four colors on the wheel that are right next to each other. You can start anywhere on the wheel and go one color on one side and two more colors on the other side, and you will have an analogous color group.

Limit Your Palette/Choose It Before You Begin

Try to keep the number of colors down to a reasonable amount. Use the color schemes mentioned previously as a way of limiting your palette. Think about a Web page the same way you might introduce color into a room. You don't want the sofa to clash with the wall or the pillows to clash with the sofa, so why would you want your Web page elements to clash? Using the already defined color logic of HTML that centers around the number 6 (more on this in Chapter 5), it is our suggestion that you pick a set of six colors that contrast and complement each other. Extraneous use of color, like using too many typefaces, is the mark of the amateur.

Contrast

This is one of the biggest rules about color. Make sure your colors are far enough apart in terms of lightness and darkness (color value) that when combined, as in text on a background, the text shows up and stands out from the background. This would be applying high contrast to a design. If all of your colors share the same value, the legibility and readability go way down.

Warm and Cool Colors

You can organize colors based on their warmness or coolness. These terms are relative terms, in that some colors appear warm or cool in relation to each other. The color wheel can be divided into warm and cool colors, with the reds, oranges, and yellows falling on the warm side and the blues, greens and purples falling on the cool side. Then, within each hue, the colors are warmer or cooler in relation to each other.

Use Tints and Tones to Create Unity

The process of adding white or black to a hue or color is known as tinting and toning, respectively. This process is one way to ensure that colors go together. By starting with a single hue, you can create a tint and a tone of that hue, and all three colors will relate to each other because they share a common base color. This is also a way to achieve high contrast in colors. If you used only one color as a base and all other color was achieved using tints and tones, you would be creating a monochromatic color scheme. Some artists create tones of a color by adding the complement of the color.

TYPOGRAPHY

Last, but not least, the student of any kind of design or visual information must concern himself or herself with *typography* and its terminology and issues. Readability being first and foremost on the list of things to achieve with text, all of the above terms, coupled with the following, can and will affect readability. Add the fact that screen resolutions are still only at the level of good, with 72 dpi rendered images, and type on the screen can be a nightmare. Though typography is an in-depth field in and of itself, the student of visual information design should be familiar with the following information and terms surrounding typography. For further information, you should consult Sean Cavanaugh's *Digital Type Design Guide: The Page Designer's Guide to Working with Type.*

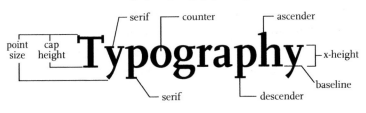

The major parts of the typographic letterforms

FIGURE 3.23

Like color, typography is an area of design that should get a devoted amount of study. Students of design spend lifetimes just looking at and understanding type. There are some simple basic ideas and rules that we present here. But, as with any of the deeper design related areas of Web design, we recommend greater in-depth study either in the academic setting or on your own. The references section at the end of this chapter contains many of the more widely used references on typography.

CAVEAT EMPTOR

If you know your Web page is to be printed, then you need to remember that the HTML-specified background of a Web page does not get sent to the printer. So if you use a dark background and light or white type, what gets sent to the printer is the light or white type, which won't show up on white paper! If you know that people will be printing your pages, make sure by testing it yourself. If your design is such that it doesn't print properly, but you wish people to be able to do just that, provide them with an alternative version of the text either in a downloadable format or in the Portable Document Format (PDF).

Type Terminology

The following terminology is essential to understanding typography, printed and onscreen. Knowing this information will allow you to talk articulately and specifically about type with graphic designers, who spend much of their time studying just type.

- **Font**—all the characters of a typeface, including punctuation, accents, fractions, and so on. We mistakenly use this term when we mean type family or typeface.
- **Type family**—range of typeface designs that are variations of one basic style of design (Helvetica bold, light, light italic, condensed, and so on).

- **Stroke**—the main line of a character.
- **Thick/thin**—the contrast in the thickness of the curved strokes.
- **Condensed type**—typeface with an elongated or narrow appearance.
- **Expanded/extended type**—wider version of a typeface's standard design.
- **Tracking**—adding or decreasing the same amount of space between all the letters.
- **Kerning**—adjusting the space between letters.
- **Baseline**—imaginary line on which the base of a line of type (excluding descenders) rests.
- **x-height**—creates the impression of the font's size.

Measuring Type

Much of the work in publishing and graphic design is based around type, its size and spacing. Understanding the measurement system of type will aid the designer in specifying type for projects on the Web or in print.

- **Point**—standard unit of typographic measurement (72 points = 1 inch).
- **Pica**—typographical measurement equal to 12 points (1 pica = 12 points, 6 picas = 1 inch). *Picas* are actually easier to work with than inches when converting or calculating. For example, 6 points = .083 inches, but 11 inches = 66 picas.

  The points and picas measurement system has its own notation. Most publishing programs and PostScript drawing programs, such as Adobe Illustrator and Macromedia FreeHand, allow you to specify points and picas as the measuring system for a layout or illustration. They will take input in dialogue boxes and such in the pica/point notation. For example, 3 picas, 4 points is written as "3p4."

- **Line spacing** or **leading**—the space between lines of type. It gets its name from the olden days of metal typesetting when slugs of lead were used to separate lines of type. Leading is measured in points, just like type. Most publishing programs allow you to specify leading and also have a setting called auto leading. Generally, leading is equal to your type size plus 2 points. Thus, 12-point type + 2 points of leading = 14 points of total space.

  If the typeface you are using has a large x-height, you need to increase the leading. If your chosen typeface has a small x-height, you should decrease the leading. You can increase or decrease leading dramatically for a special effect. Negative leading will cause type to *overlap*.

Typeface Classification

Type for designers is classified into roughly seven categories. Those categories are *oldstyle, transitional, modern, sans serif, serif, script,* and *decorative* (including the major subcategories of uncial and black letter and the emerging grunge category).

Serifs

Serifs are the "hands" and "feet" of a letter form. They lend stability to a letter and provide continuity and flow to a typeface. Serif typefaces are either oldstyle, transitional, or modern. The way the serif is handled and the way in which the stress of the face is expressed determines which is which. Scientific study has shown that serif faces at smaller sizes (body-text size as in the text you are reading now) are more legible and readable by the human eye. The thought is that the serifs lead the eye from letter to letter. Body copy should always use serif faces. Body-text size is recommended to be in the 10-point to 12-point range. Print body-text size is most often 10 point.

Some examples of serif faces are shown in Figure 3.24.

Sans Serif

Sans serif refers to typefaces that don't have "hands" and "feet." "Sans" is French for "without," so sans serif is without serifs. Examples of sans serif typefaces are shown in Figure 3.25.

Decorative, Script, and Specialty Typefaces

Decorative typefaces are usually reserved for titles, headlines, and other short bits of text. They are designed to be used at a size greater than that of body text, often 18 point and above. Script faces and other specialty faces can fall under the decorative heading. Figure 3.26 shows just some of the thousands of decorative faces available today.

Examples of serif typefaces

Times New Roman
Adobe Garamond
New Baskerville
Bookman Oldstyle
COPPERPLATE GOTHIC
Minion

FIGURE 3.24

Examples of sans serif typefaces

Arial (Helvetica)
Franklin Gothic Book
Gill Sans MT
Weissach
Verdana
Myriad

FIGURE 3.15

Monospace

Though monospace is not really a type category, its use in Web design is fairly popular. Typefaces today, as used with the computer, are generally what is referred to as proportionally spaced. The digital typeface takes care of the kerning (the space between letters) of letterforms automatically. Designers have the ability to kern letters manually if the situation arises where they need to do this. Typewriters, however, had letterforms that were a fixed width and a fixed space apart from each other letter. This is monospacing. There are digital typefaces that mimic this, and there are ways in HTML to request monospacing type to appear on a Web page. Some examples of monospacing are shown in Figure 3.27.

Examples of decorative typefaces

STENCIL
Tekton
Waldorf Script
Westminster
ANNA
Dorchester Script MT

FIGURE 3.26

Examples of monospaced typefaces

OCR-A
Courier
Corporate Mono

FIGURE 3.27

Platform and Browser Differences and Type Handling

In the mix of things to keep track of in the differences between Macintoshes and PCs, you have to add that they display type differently. Macintoshes display type at 72 ppi, and PCs display it at 96 ppi. This is a chief reason that things look different on each platform. The solution is that you shouldn't use small type sizes when you design on the PC because your Macintosh audience will see it as much smaller than you intended. There are reports that browsers also handle a screen inch in differing proportions. Always check your pages on both platforms (and in both major browsers, for that matter).

Type-Use Basics

We are mentioning this information at this point because it is hard to separate the use of type from the other information regarding typography. You should refer back to this information when you begin to create your Websites. This information could very well also go in the chapter on page design, but we choose to offer it here.

Stick to commonly used fonts that are available on both platforms. Those fonts would be Arial, Verdana, Trebuchet, and Times Roman. These choices are good for body text and headings. Times is the most common body-text face available and is a good one to use. Most Macintoshes now utilize the basic Microsoft typefaces, so cross-platform issues aren't such a big deal as long as you stick with the standards.

Decorative type should be used only for headings and such. More often than not, the decorative face you choose is not going to be one that others have access to. In this case, you should make your heading a graphic, with the background matching your chosen background color and the text in the decorative face of your choice.

When choosing colors, stick to six or fewer. When you talk about typeface choices, three or less is a good rule of thumb. Overuse of typefaces is the mark of the amateur. Utilizing too many serif or sans serif faces causes a clashing effect. Be careful when mixing serif or sans serif faces with each other. It is best to stick to a single family of serif or sans serif faces and utilize the different weights for variety.

The way to *tint* and *shade* type is to utilize different weights of the same face. Some typefaces come designed with a bold or ultra bold version and an italic version. Using these other "colors" of the same typeface will expand your type choices while still achieving balance and unity of the type.

Use margins and white space to aid in readability of the text on a page. Cramming large amounts of text into a small space makes the text too dense and hard to read. Give your readers islands of eye-resting space through the use of white space.

When choosing typefaces, start with only a few typefaces and families. Only add additional typefaces if they complement, strengthen, and underscore the concept of your site and only if they enhance the communication value of the information.

Always leave lots of white space to emphasize type.

Readability refers to whether an extended amount of text is easy to read. This is usually referring to body copy/text. Legibility refers to whether a short burst of text is instantly recognizable, such as in a title or headline. Remember not to set text type too large. Smaller sizes with additional leading are generally more readable than larger sizes with tight leading. Be careful using a typeface with delicate thin strokes. Often these features get lost on screen, and the type becomes difficult to read. Be very careful using the built-in outline and shadow functions of your word processor or publishing program. Those kinds of programs do a mildly poor job of creating these effects, and overuse of them looks amateurish. If you want that effect, use it sparingly; create it in an illustration program for a specific text and output it as a graphic.

When mixing typefaces, it is a very common mistake to use typefaces that are so similar in style that a great enough contrast is not achieved. Be sure to make choices that are high contrast such as serif vs. sans serif and light vs. heavy. The kerning of type most often needs to be adjusted in headlines, where too much space between characters shows up more noticeably.

Much of the look of a column of type is dependent on the size of the type. Related to that is the length of the line of type and the overall width of a column of type. For instance, if you specify 10-point type, the minimum column width should be 10 picas and the maximum column width would be 20 picas. Remember that 6 picas = 1 inch.

You should shorten your line length if the typeface has a very large or small x-height, if the typeface is sans serif, or if you are reversing type out of a dark background. This tends to make type look smaller, so you should increase the type size by 1 point so that it appears the same. For example, if you have 12-point black type on a white background, the reverse of that would be 13-point white type on a black background. These two blocks of text would appear to be the same if they appeared in close proximity to each other.

Need we mention not to use clever devices like blinking text? Blinking text is like the lava lamp of the 1960s and 1970s. It was a novel idea for about five seconds and then you wonder "Why?" Blinking text is reported to be a number one reason people leave a site. Animated GIFs that don't stop are another. If you use blinking text, make it stop after its initial use; the same with an animated GIF.

Always use the text alternative with graphics. This isn't really a text tip, but it is a good idea since this is the text that is "read" to the visually impaired Web surfer.

As with colors, you, the Web designer, don't have the kind of control over typeface choice that a print graphic designer has. Web designers are dependent on the typefaces that are installed on the end user's machine. As explained in the tagging portion of this book, you can specify font choices and types of fonts.

There are certain assumptions you can make about what typefaces might be on a user's machine, but if users have set their browser preferences to something obscure for their body-text typeface, it's currently difficult to force your choice upon them. This is changing as the technology progresses.

Cascading style sheets can help accomplish many typographical things that HTML cannot do, such as leading adjustments (the space between lines), tracking (the space between all letters), kerning (the space between individual characters), and baseline shifting (the ability to adjust a single character above or below the baseline).

Another idea in the works for greater typographic control is the idea of font embedding. It is actually possible, but each major browser (Netscape and Internet Explorer) chooses to do it a different way. We don't recommend using it until the specifications have been fully fleshed out (and both major browsers accept and recognize either a single way of employing it or recognize both ways of doing it). You can find out more about Open Type at **www.adobe.com** and TrueDoc technology at **www.bitstream.com**.

The other way around the HTML limitations is to design your text as a graphic. This way, the user won't have to have the font you specify, and you can design the type to look how you want it. Since the text is a graphic, so it can't be copied or searched by Web bots or search engines. But it is the one way to make sure your design displays the way you want it to.

CHAPTER SUMMARY

The history of design of visual information is thousands of years old, and that tradition is still intact today almost in its entirety. The advent of computers and their use in this field in some ways complicate but mostly complement the architecture of visual information. The computer makes things more efficient in terms of revisions and multiple iterations of an idea. They make output less messy (no glue!) and changes on the fly possible. But for the most part, to use computers in the field of visual design requires learning all the non-computer techniques in order to understand the discipline and then applying the computer as an additional tool used to execute the final iteration. Even traditional designers do much work before they pick up a paintbrush or palette knife. So, too, should the architect of information in the electronic era.

KEY TERMS

balance	plane
closure	point
color	positive space
continuation	proximity
contrast	repetition
decorative	rhythm
direction	similarity
field	sans serif
figure	script
frame	separation
Gestalt	serif
grid	shade
ground	shape
grouping principles	stroke
horizontal	subtraction
interaction	symmetry/asymmetry
line	texture
modern	tint
monospace	touching
negative space	transitional
oldstyle	typography
overlap	union
pattern	value
pica	vertical

REVIEW QUESTIONS

1. Gestalt principles were codified primarily by:
2. True or false? "The point size of a typeface extends from the top of the ascenders to the bottom of the descender."
3. Label the type/font parts of Figure 3.28.

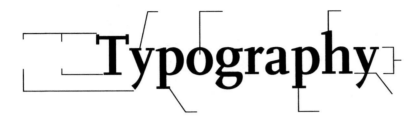

FIGURE 3.28

4. Graphic designers use _____ to help facilitate layout.

5. Fill in the progression: point, _____, plane, _____.

6. List the eight states two forms can have in terms of the interrelationships of these two forms.

7. Pattern, _____, and repetition are all part of the same idea.

8. Around every form or element in a composition, there exists _____.

9. List and define the four grouping principles of Gestalt theory as discussed in this chapter.

10. "The patterns formed by the parts of an image take precedence over the individual parts." True or false?

PROJECTS

Below we have included some projects that are designed to challenge and build your visual literacy. Honest work is needed in order to make these projects useful. There are no right or wrong answers or choices. Some choices will rise to the top, but sometimes there are more effective solutions.

Visual literacy is an important skill to have in this visual world. More and more people are reading less, and the information exchange is becoming a cacophony of imagery. The problems in this book are merely the beginning of what should be a lifelong pursuit of visual literacy, human perception, information exchange, and interface design.

Some of the following problems are based on exercises presented in Judith and Richard Wilde's book entitled *Visual Literacy: A Conceptual Approach to Graphic Problem Solving*. Other exercises are from the authors' own experience as students and teachers of visual design and computer graphics.

Authors' note: These exercises can be done with or without the use of a computer. The CD contains files and tutorials for some graphics programs that will be helpful in completing these assignments. The directions are given for how to achieve them without the computer, and this method is recommended in order to separate the creative process from the computer software, but it is up to your instructor as to how they wish you to accomplish these exercises. In the case of the quilt composition, acetate should be used to protect the glass of the scanner while objects such as nuts and bolts, macaroni, money, and perhaps twigs and leaves are placed on the glass to be scanned and then printed out to be used as textures.

Design Project Work
For any artist, getting over the fear of making marks on a blank sheet of paper can be difficult. This first exercise assists you in getting over this fear as well as in developing your design eye. The exercise is purposely limiting.

1. Nine Square
In this exercise, you will need to copy the following arrangement of nine squares onto an 8.5x11 piece of paper. You can trace, redraw, or use the sheet included on the CD.

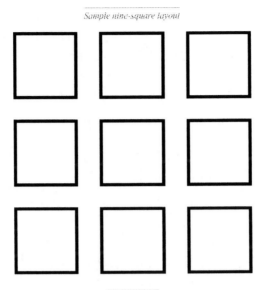

FIGURE 3.29

Using a black Sharpie marker, color in the squares as you wish to create a design. Do not at this time subdivide any of the squares or use the gutter space between the squares. See how many different designs you can come up with.

Once you have exhausted the possbilities with the above, repeat the exercise; this time, you can subdivide the squares horizontally or vertically. Limit yourself to dividing equally in half. Again, stay inside the squares.

What could you come up with if you could divide into thirds? Quarters?

Repeat again. This time you have the ability to divide the squares horizontally, vertically (halves, quarters, and thirds) and from corner to corner. Stay inside the squares.

Try any or all of the above, but just use lines to divide the squares and don't fill in any of the subdivisions.

Now using all you have discovered so far, allow yourself to color outside the squares and include the space between.

After each exploration, you should share what you have discovered with your classmates and take in what they have discovered. Analyze why you made choices and why they made choices.

2. Infinite Subdivide Exercise

The pattern below is a variation on the nine square above. Using the grid pattern provided (included on the CD), color in or connect the various subdivisions, using lines, to create a complex pattern. Attempt to define some rules for yourself, before you begin, about how you might proceed.

Sample of the layout of the grid to be filled in for this exercise. The CD contains a template of this grid.

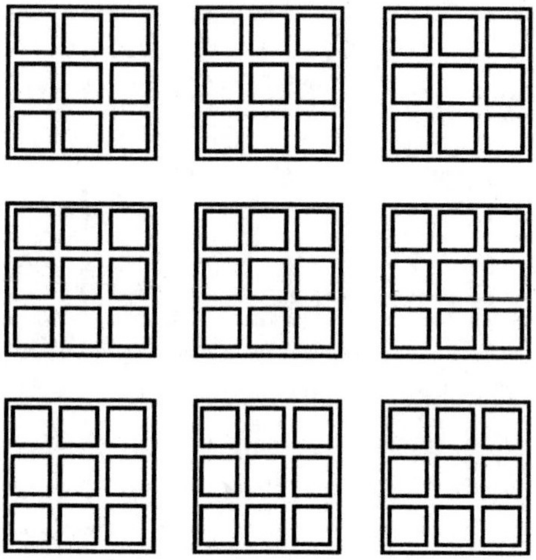

FIGURE 3.30

3. Grids and Color

The purpose of this exercise is to allow you to explore how space is broken up through the use of a grid. It also serves to see more than just straight line grids, which tend to be the easiest and most prevalent choice at first. Once the grid is created, the choice to color or not color the newly created shapes and spaces becomes a conscious act.

Using a straight edge, create a rectilinear grid of your own choosing. Make the composition 10x10 inches. Color in more or fewer of the spaces, using your black marker to create a design. Share your work with your classmates.

Create another rectilinear grid. Overlay a non-rectilinear shape on your grid so that it creates interesting intersections with the lines that are already drawn. Color or leave open the spaces as you see fit to create a composition. Do one that is 10x10. Repeat the exercise in a 5x5 format.

Create a third grid using only straight lines (you should be varying each rectilinear grid as much as possible from the previous one for variety) and overlay the outline of your first initial. Color or leave open the spaces so as to emphasize the letter form. This composition should be 10x10 or 5x5 inches.

4. Type Explorations

The purpose of this exercise is to use the previous exercise in a more delineated way. The interaction of the grid with letterforms allows you to see how your choices to color or not color can reveal or diminish a known form, in this case a letter shape. This technique is often used in design and usually produces a pleasing and interesting design no matter what grid is used or what letter shape. It is important to see how coloring outside the letter shape is as important, if not more so, than coloring inside the letter shape.

For a part of this exercise, you may use the computer since so many typefaces are available on the computer. Other sources for type samples include magazines, books on type, and posters around campus. You can trace, scan, print, and photocopy to scale or shrink the type to suit your purposes.

Pick a letter form (a,b, c...z) that is to your liking. Choose a typeface (Arial, Vivante, Tahoma, and so on) that you like. Create a composition using the outline of the letterform. Duplicate, scale, rotate, and mirror the letter form in order to create your composition. Color the spaces created by the interaction of the letterforms to produce an interesting design.

Student solutions using type and a grid and exploring the interaction of the letter form and the grid. Can you identify the letters used here?

FIGURE 3.31

Create at least three of these compositions using various typefaces of your choosing.

5. The Quilt Project

The purpose of this project is to explore texture and how it can be used as a design element. Using an already-established pattern, the quilt block, and creating "fabric" gives you the experience of actually creating a visual element that they then use in a composition. The more textures you create and the zanier they are, the more invested you become in the process. You don't have to rely on most of the ineffective choices already posted to the Internet to strengthen your compositions.

Create textures for this project by either photocopying or scanning things like screws, coins, leaves, twigs, macaroni, crumpled foil, and other items that you can find around your house or room. Print out the results of your texture creations. This will become the "fabric" with which you create your quilts. You can use colored paper in this exercise and print or photocopy the textures onto different colors. Remember that no texture in contrast to some texture makes a nice statement as well.

Go to the library or some other source (bookstore or sewing store) and find some traditional quilt patterns to which you are drawn. photocopy or sketch them so you have a record of them.

Pick two or three that you want to reproduce using the fabric you created by scanning interesting items. Lightly sketch the pattern on a 10x10 piece of white Bristol board paper. The paper to which you will glue your fabric should be somewhat stiff. Now trace your pattern pieces onto your textured "fabric" and cut them out. Assemble your quilt square.

Student solutions to the quilt project. Can you identify the textures used here?

FIGURE 3.32

6. Black Square Problem

A basic problem with inexperienced designers is the tendency to put too much into a design just because they can. The ability to self-monitor and self-limit is an ability that must be learned, nurtured, and practiced over and over. This exercise addresses this idea in that at first it seems limiting, but once the exploration begins you can see the infinite possibilities that exist in the solutions. The exercise also focuses on composition, use of space, scale, and skewed perspective to create depth. You can explore the idea of the frame hiding and revealing as well as the ideas of the figure/ground relationship.

By using four black squares, initially of the same dimension, create a graphic image to communicate and express the meaning of the following words: *order, increase, bold, congested, tension,* and *playful.* Make eight preliminary sketches for each word. Then select the most effective solution for each word and execute it in a larger area (10x10 inches).

The exploration here is suited to discovering a visual and geometric idiom relating to the ideas of framal reference; *touching;* overlapping and cropping of unit forms; contrast of elements utilizing size, direction, space, and position; and the dynamics of positive and negative spatial relationships.

Using the principles of perspective, the squares can be of differing sizes and shapes as long as perspective dictates the changes. This furthers the range of solutions to explore.

Materials used are black construction paper, a knife, white cover stock, and adhesive.

Student solution to the black square problem

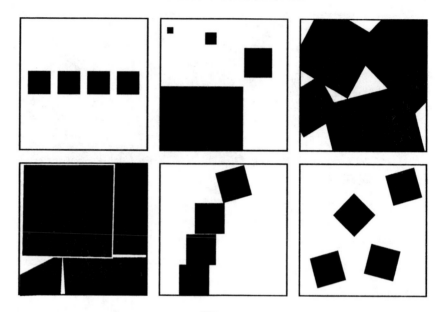

FIGURE 3.24

7. Picture Rearrangement with a Grid

This project emphasizes risk-taking in visual choices, the ability to set and apply some choices without knowing the outcome, and combining techniques (the grid creation with the need to rearrange visual information) to solve a visual problem. Many of us are concrete cognitive thinkers, and we need to know we can think abstractly, too, in order to solve a problem.

This project is a variation on the grid creation described above. It involves using a previously constructed grid or a new one (recommended) and overlaying the grid on a picture from a magazine. Then rearrange the picture based on a written set of rules that you create. The rules will dictate how the pieces, once cut to match the grid, will be rearranged. For example, first the pieces are numbered. Then a list of previously written instructions (a program) determines that piece 1 will move two pieces to the left and that piece 3 will go to piece 5 and so on until all the visual information is in a different place. Emphasis should be placed on pre-creating the instructions once the grid is made and before the picture is chosen. This prevents you from forcing the new composition, and allows it to just happen based your rules. If you're a student of computer science or programming, you should recognize this exercise as the creation of a simple program that you then execute by hand.

Student solutions to picture rearrangement with the grid problem. Can you recreate the grid that is here? Can you determine the rule set created in order to rearrange the picture in this way?

FIGURE 3.25

8. Jack and Jill Problem
Create visual solutions for each line of the nursery rhyme "Jack and Jill" by using the limited symbol vocabulary provided (see examples below). This vocabulary can consist of "dingbats" and "symbols" of your choosing. Only use black and white, unless there is a compelling reason to use color. Even then it should be limited. The space for each solution should be uniform, no larger than 10x10 and no smaller than 5x5.

The intent of this project is to get you developing a visual vocabulary that goes beyond the literal. The student should be moved to understand the infinite possibilities within the limited language offered by the symbology. The expansion of the designer's problem-solving vocabulary is at the heart of this project. It is also closely related to the developing iconography at the core of interface and Web design—allowing freedom to redefine and reshape the language of computer icons on the screen.

The problem touches on the dynamics of composition and scale in relationship to the framal reference (visual literacy book reference). Cropping and overlapping of images are also a factor to be explored. Positive and negative space are strong ideas in this project, as is the idea that one thing can accurately and succinctly symbolize and communicate something that it is not.

The idea of flow from one thing to another is particularly important as the rhyme visually progresses from one frame to the next.

Materials may include the use of a photocopier to reduce or enlarge, a knife for cutting, and adhesive to affix the symbols to white cover stock.

Do this for more than one nursery rhyme.

Jack and Jill
Went up the hill
To fetch a pail of water
Jack fell down
And broke his crown
And Jill came tumbling after.

Three blind mice, three blind mice;
See how they run, see how they run!
They all ran after the farmer's wife,
Who cut off their tails with a carving knife.
Have you ever seen such a sight
In your life as three blind mice?

Rock-a-bye, baby, on the treetop
When the wind blows,
The cradle will rock.
When the bough breaks,
The cradle will fall.
Down will come baby,
Cradle and all.

Humpty Dumpty
Sat on a wall;
Humpty Dumpty had a great fall!
All the king's horses
And all the king's men
Couldn't put Humpty
Together again.

Student solution to Jack and Jill problem using limited symbol vocabulary pictured in Figure 3.36

FIGURE 3.35

Sample limited symbol vocabulary for nursery rhymes

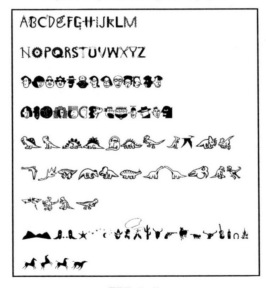

FIGURE 3.36

REFERENCES

Berryman, Gregg. 1990. *Notes on Graphic Design and Visual Communication.* Menlo Park, California: Crisp Learning.

Bever, G. 1997. "Electronic Data Systems Corporation," Private Communication, (January).

Galitz, Wilbert O. 1996. "The Importance of Good Screen Design," *Essential Guide to User Interface Design.* New York: Wiley Computer Publishing.

Larkin, Eugene. 1985. *Design, The Search for Unity.* Iowa: Wm. C. Brown Publishers.

Myers, B.A. & M.B. Rosson. 1992. "Survey on user interface programming," Proceedings: CHI '92, May 3–7, Monterey, CA.

Wilde, Judith & Richard Wilde. 1991. *Visual Literacy: A Conceptual Approach to Graphic Problem Solving.* New York: Watson-Guptill.

Wong, Wucius. 1993. *The Principles of Form and Design.* New York: Van Nostrand Reinhold.

chapter 4
site design

CHAPTER OVERVIEW

Planning and organization are key to the success of any Website. This often requires a team of people, each with a set of tasks, a single individual doing many tasks. It also requires managing many tasks at once. One of the many organizational tasks in creating a Website is the planning of the structure, links, and flow of information. This chapter will discuss creating mission objective statements and brain-storming about a site. This chapter will also focus on the underlying structure of a Website: how pages relate to one another, the organization and flow of information, getting from one page to another, and keeping track of where a user is in a site. Whether your site is linear, hierarchical, or organized in another way, flow-charting is one of the best ways to engage in this activity. This all happens well before deciding which buttons to use and what colors to employ.

CHAPTER OBJECTIVES

- Know who the Web team members are and have an overview of their duties
- Create a mission statement
- List the goals and objectives of a site
- Understand the importance of the audience to the goals of a site
- Understand who the stakeholders are and what their role is in terms of the site's overall goals
- Create a chart describing the structure of your site
- Learn about hierarchical, linear, hub or star structures and other visual organization methods

SITE DESIGN

The design of the site structure and information architecture is probably one of the most important steps in Web design and the step most often skipped as well. Planning is not the most fun part of Website design, but even a little forethought can save you much time later on down the line.

One accepted idea about Web development and design over traditional print design is that it resembles software development more in some ways than it resembles traditional design. It is also accepted that there are some specialized tasks in Web development and that it might be beneficial to have more than a single person working on a project. In traditional print design, the designer is often the client contact, the technical specialist, and the artist. Often, the more people there are, the easier it is to plan and brainstorm.

Poorly thought out sites are hard to navigate, difficult to keep up, and often costly. Your clients certainly aren't going to want any of those qualities for their site, so take the time up front to think about the structure and navigability of the sites that you design. Create a visual map that will show you and the client how the pages will link together and what potential problems might occur. You should be able to determine problems in navigation and in organization long before you type an HTML tag!

THE TEAM IN A NUTSHELL

The Web team can be organized in a number of ways. First, you could organize your team by skill category into the administrative, technical, and artistic divisions. You could also organize them by importance into the primary, secondary, and tertiary members; primary team members are crucial to the process, secondary team members are part of a wish list (but secondary jobs could be handled by others already on the primary team), and tertiary team members are specialists that are hired from outside or, in large development companies, float from project to project on an as-needed basis. We have tried to indicate which job goes where for both ways of looking at these team members.

Manager

The manager of a project is part of the administrative team. This is a primary team member who manages all aspects of the project including but not limited to the schedule, budget, production, client contact, and milestone deliverables and, in the absence of an account manager, handles client management/client satisfaction. The manager of a Web project intercedes as needed in personnel issues that arise or with delicate political situations. This person should have excellent people skills, have working knowledge of project management software (Gantt and Pert charts), and have at least a basic understanding of the artistic and technical needs of a Web project. This person might be compared to a film or theater producer.

Sales Account Manager

As an extension of the manager, this secondary team member would alleviate administrative duties that might have to do with the client. The sales account manager would be a liaison between the development firm and the client. This position might also have contact with the chief artistic personnel.

Chief Technician

This primary team member oversees the project from a technical point of view. The chief technician works with the manager in the creation of a sound technical strategy for a Web development project. This person is the manager of additional programmers who might be involved in a project. The chief technician might also be the person who hires tertiary team members with expertise in security, database programming, *JavaScript*, and so on.

Computer Programmer

If the budget will allow, the hiring of programmers to support a project as secondary team members is a good use of resources. Programmers can assist with the HTML layout, construct the *site architecture,* and develop applications for the project (CGI scripts, Java applets, and so on). They are managed by the chief technician.

Networking Specialist

This technical secondary team member is responsible for setting up and configuring the Web server. The networking specialist may in turn be responsible for domain name registration and for setting up email servers as well. This person might have a direct counterpart in the client's organization who facilitates site setup within the client organization.

Internet Security Specialist

Though this job often falls to the networking specialist, the chief technician, or some other programmer, if the budget will allow this tertiary team member to exist, this person can concentrate solely on Internet security strategies for a project. This is especially helpful on an e-business project where potential sensitive information, such as credit card numbers is being transmitted via the Web. This person at the very least should have set up sites using encryption technologies.

HTML Specialist

This primary team member is a technical necessity these days when developing a Website. This person oversees and integrates the site using HTML/XHTML/ DHTML or some other suitable markup language. This person, who is often a programmer but could be a technical artist, is responsible for the implementation of the site when it is time to go online. The HTML specialist should be the person who develops the technical style guide for the site and confers with the artistic team members on how best to achieve the goals of the site artistically and technically.

Art Director/Principal Creative

Unless your technical team also has extensive visual design experience, this primary team member is a creative must-have. The art director is responsible for developing the *concept* and is responsible for the site's design. This person may do all the work themselves if the team is small or may manage a creative group. This person would be on the same level as the chief technician and would interact with the project manager, keeping them apprised of the creative aspects of a project. This person should be technically savvy in order to meet with the chief technician and the HTML specialists in determining what is technically possible.

Production Artist

Unless your art director is going to do all the creative work, these primary team members will be responsible for creating the look and feel of the site. The production artists will take the concept that is put forth by the creative lead and produce all final graphics in the correct file format and appropriate palettes for use in a Web project. Graphic designers working on the Web must understand how images are prepared for the Web and that it is very different from print! Production artists must consider compression technology and its effect on Web graphics. Production people report to the art director or principal creative.

Content Provider

This secondary team member would be great to have. The content provider should be an excellent wordsmith, tweaking the textual content or creating it from scratch as needed. This person could act as an editor for content provided by the client.

Usability Tester

This person seems to end up on the most-expendable list for Web development when in fact this team member can be the most crucial. This person must have a combination of administrative, artistic, and technical skills and should not be a member of any of those teams. The tester needs to be objective. This person comes late in the process and should be responsible for seeing that what is delivered is what the client ordered. This person develops the testing measures by which the prototype site is evaluated and carries out the testing, reporting problems to the various teams as they are encountered. Each bug fix suggestion must be followed up on and re-tested as needed.

The following team members are primarily technical and tertiary. They are often third-party vendors for hire, doing a very specific task relating to Web technologies.

Web Audio and Video Specialists

These people specialize in delivering audio and video via Websites. They do streaming audio/video, are Webcast specialists, or just specialize in creating audio and video for the Web.

3-D Modeler

This person has expertise in building 3-D models and 3-D Web technology. The modeler may be a content provider or a solution/implementation specialist.

SITE DEVELOPMENT/PLANNING

Define the Project

Every instructor of every course ever taken for every paper and every project ever assigned has said, "Make an outline!" This is the advice most often ignored by every student in the world. Then, as employees at corporations, we again ignore this advice. Well we are here to tell you that there is a direct correlation between the success of a Web project and the amount of time spent planning prior to implementation. All of the major successful sites had a plan before they ever started coding. Many opinions were sought, considered, digested, and revised well before any HTML editor was ever fired up. Sketches were made and diagrams tweaked and refined and changed and argued over. But even major planning starts with small steps. The definition of a project can be arrived at fairly quickly and simply. The first steps are related to that old journalistic cliché: Who, What, Where, Why, and When—the "Five Ws."

Mission Objectives Statement

One initial step in project definition is to develop a *mission objective statement* (MOS). This will assist you in ferreting out what specifically the site can and will do. It will allow you and your design team to ignore possible distractions along the way and focus your efforts on the necessary parts. There is much literature in the business discipline about writing mission statements, and it might be helpful to look at some of that work. A project's mission objective statement isn't that dissimilar to a corporate mission statement.

Identify Specific Results

A mission objective statement should clarify what the expected results of the project may be and how to identify when those results have been achieved. You should be able to articulate how you will assess the results' success or failure, and some time frame should be identified for when those results are to be achieved or reformulated.

The following URLs are some places to go to look at mission statements. Refine this information to best suit your purposes. Most universities and colleges have mission statements. Perhaps you can find your school's mission statement and use it as a starting point.

- http://www.digital-women.com/howto11a.htm
- http://www.tgci.com/publications/98fall/MissionStatement.html
- http://www.businessplansoftware.org/advice_mission.asp

The Stakeholders in a Project

In addition to you and your team brainstorming about the goals of a site, you need to pay careful attention to the *stakeholders* in a project. The stakeholders are the people who sign off on the money and the ideas in a corporation. Generally, you need to pay attention to the organizational chart of the company for whom you are designing the project. Identify early on the person in the organization who has the veto power, and that will be the chief person to assist you either directly or indirectly with the goals of the site and how they relate to the other goals the company has set. This person is known as "the major stakeholder." You may be very thorough and interview everyone in a company who has any stake in the project, but their ideas may run counter to the major stakeholder's; you will have to decide whether you want to act as the middleman and clear all those other ideas with the major stakeholder. Everyone needs to work together in this process, assisting the major stakeholder and facilitating his or her satisfaction that the company's needs are being met by the objectives of this specific project. It will be helpful to obtain written documentation from the corporation detailing their mission statement. This can be a good place to begin discussion.

Ultimately, the hope is to identify things like:

- To sell more product
- To assist our customers better
- To increase consumer awareness of our brand identity
- To educate our customers about our products

Using the infinitive form of active verbs, as shown above, is a good way to construct a goal, objective, or result. Your goals should be active, not passive, direct and not convoluted. Simplicity is the key.

Working with the stakeholders, both major and minor, becomes a process of educating the client as you go. Good planning and documentation of the process will contribute greatly to the education process. Most stakeholders might have a general idea of what the Web can and can't do for them, but you will have to spend some time up front detailing the specifics of how the project can be achieved, what is possible, and what is not. You will need to be sensitive to the client's level of knowledge, neither condescending to nor speaking above the client's level of understanding. The project manager of the team needs to be a real "people person," not only so that egos aren't trampled, but also so that the project isn't held up by a lack of understanding on the client's part.

Take the time to make periodic presentations to the client. Set dates where you and/or members of your team take the time to report on progress and share information with the client. It goes a long way toward facilitating the client's "buying into the project" if the client feels a part of the communication loop. Even small amounts of information received by other means, such as email or phone, can assist with the forward progression of a project. These reports are in addition to formal "sign off" meetings where a client actually agrees to portions of the project with a signature.

Target Audience

An MOS should identify who is the *target audience*. Whom you are trying to reach will greatly influence "the what" of the *content* and "the how" of the delivery medium. Who is it that the site is trying to attract or service? Is there more than one kind of audience member? Are you appealing to a particular age group? Targeting a specific income bracket? Are there stylistic considerations to pay attention to for particular groups of people?

Brainstorming on this aspect of the design can be time well spent. Identifying and servicing disparate groups of people can be a daunting task. By spending time figuring out the make-up of each group, you might find a tie that binds them together and weight your design and content decisions toward that end. You might also discover that you need to organize your site content differently for each individual group that accesses your site—perhaps even including access to sections that are identified clearly for each group at a common gateway.

Enlist the help of your major and secondary stakeholders in determining who their audience might be. They should have either market research or some other data that can greatly help you in refining who the targets are for a particular site. They might also be trying to attract a group they have not previously appealed to, and you definitely need to know this before you begin.

Often times the major stakeholders wish a Website to be both an external resource for customers as well as an internal site for their current employees. Many universities use this approach since both audience groups utilize much of the same information. It takes some care, though, to properly organize information without reproducing it in its entirety for both groups. Be aware when this situation arises or if it presents itself as a solution for a project.

Whatever methods you use, finding out about your audience before you take the time creating content, navigation, and structure can be a time-saver.

Determining "The What": Content

Once you have identified your goals and objectives, written your mission statements, and identified and met with your stakeholders, you should have a pretty good idea about what content needs to be included. You may be generating the content or just organizing and reworking content provided by the stakeholder, but you will need to be refining this content as it relates to the mission objective statement and the determined target audience. Content at this point has to be filtered through the idea of "How does this help us meet our goal and communicate with our target audience?" This way of working will help to reduce "fluff" content and to reduce site bloat.

Your online content may exactly duplicate a client's pre-existing *print collateral material,* which is okay. Sometimes, if that material is working, duplicating it online is a good place to start. You certainly should have read and examined all the printed pieces that the current marketing department utilizes. This is especially true if the Website goals are aligned with the marketing goals that already exist. Also, even if you retool existing material, it is still a time-saver for you and your team. Remember, though, that one aspect of the Web that doesn't exist in print is the interactive aspect. As you rework existing material, be looking for ways or areas that can be exploited or enhanced with the interactive aspect of the Web. Incorporating hyperlinks within documents that take you to supporting documents and the like is a chief reason why you would want to build a Web presence at all.

You also need to decide what form this content needs to take. Will it be all text? What portion of it needs to be supported visually with graphics? Can you deliver audio successfully? Is there room and need for video? These questions need to be carefully considered. It is all too easy to be seduced by the "eye candy" that seems to be popping up all over the Web these days. You must keep in mind that one question about your target audience needs to address their technological capability. What is the speed of their connection to the Web? Most likely, you can count on your general audience connecting at 28.8 or 56K, but not much more. Your university audience has at least DSL or ISDN, if not T-1. Your corporate audiences might have a fast intranet but be slow on the external connection. So be aware of the technological side of content and its delivery. Choose your delivery methods wisely. Don't be seduced by the "flashy side."

It's hard to separate content needs from the actual structure, so though we aren't talking about the specifics of site structure yet, you need to keep in mind that specific content pieces might be added or subtracted from your content list depending on how the site begins to take shape. In your site plan, you might have an introduction section that in previously existing materials doesn't exist, so that content will have to be created. You might have a price list as a piece of printed collateral that you end up not using in your Website. So be aware that the inventory of content pieces will change as the site structure begins to develop.

You should make a list of every type of content that you think might be included in the site. You should assign a task for how that content is to be obtained, whether it will be delivered in an electronic form from the client, or whether you will scan it in for placement. Keep a checklist as to whether or not the task is complete or outstanding. This way, you will always have knowledge about the state of the content for the site and know what still needs to be completed.

Scope: How Big Is It Really?

Scope is the big picture, which isn't always obvious once you are immersed in the whole—sort of a "you can't see the forest for the trees" kind of thing. Scope creep, however, can overwhelm a project and create potential difficulties if you agree to something and then it gets bigger than you imagined. Assessing the scope of a project is important before agreeing to anything with the client. Once the needs analysis has been done and the site structure plan is created and refined, you can then begin to assess the actual scope of a project. There will always be a little creep, but you need to be very up front with the client that adding anything to a project will increase costs and time for implementation. There is no getting around it. All additions will affect deadlines and cost more. You can't afford to give your time and talent away, and there isn't any way to do more work or to work faster without adding team members or taking more time.

Again, keeping the client informed at every step in the project is very important. Once you've built trust with the client, it is easier to say things like, "Okay, if we add this flashy aspect, what don't you want us to do?" Then you can arrive at a compromise or decision that is objective and on par with the project parameters.

Skills Assessment: What Is Required of Your Team? HTML, Flash, ASP...

Once you have assessed the project and refined the requirements of who the audience is, who the decision makers are, what the content needs to include, and how you are going to deliver the content, you need to do some self-reflection and decide on what is required of you and your team.

Are there any specialized tasks that need to be considered? Do you need not only programmers, but also graphic/information designers? Are you in need of someone who can write JavaScript? Will active server pages (ASP) technology be a part of the site? These questions are part of the process in assembling a project team to meet the requirements of the outlined site. You need to pick team members who cover all your needs or who have multiple talents to contribute to the project. Some expertise areas to be aware of are:

- *Technical writer*
- Flash/JavaScript programmer
- Database programmer
- *Graphic designer*
- GUI (graphical user interface) designer
- HCI (human/computer interface) expert
- Audio/Video specialist
- Photographer: traditional and digital
- Security expert
- 3-D modeler

Whatever the project, make sure you have the ability and expertise to deliver what the client has been promised.

SITE STRUCTURING/SITE ARCHITECTURE

The early planning is complete, and now it's time to begin to make it happen. Actually, some of this portion of a project might need to happen simultaneously with the brainstorming and preplanning stages, but we've separated it out here to focus on it.

Organizing Content

You have gathered all the possible content (even though you know there will be more) and now it is time to allow it to assist you with your site structure. Begin by compiling a list of content types. For www.larkinstudio.com, there was content that related to:

- fine art
- portraits
- illustration
- pastels
- oils
- watercolor
- lithography
- custom frames
- biographical information
- other artists

It was apparent that some of the categories could be combined, so the first three categories (which were based on how the artist viewed his marketability) were selected and the medium type (how the artist produced the work) became a subcategory of fine art, illustration, and portraits. The biographical information was kept as a separate section. Other artists' information was also placed on the biography page. The custom frames information related more to the artist than to his other art, so it went on the artist information page as well. This is a simple site, but the process of analyzing the content and its possible place in a site is the same for a 10-page site as for a 1,000-page site. Some people work in piles, some people work in lists. Some projects use thousands of 3x5 cards tacked up on a wall to chart the site structure. The cards are shuffled around to tweak the site, and it is fairly easy to move a card from one category to another. You can always see the width and depth of the site, though, and know if one section is becoming overwhelmingly information heavy. Whatever method you choose, choose one and use it.

Schematics, Flow Charts, and Storyboards

Once the content has been organized, you can begin to sketch the actual layout of the site in terms of pages and links to pages. This site map will give you an idea of how the site will be constructed and how the navigation will work in the context of a Website. Most Web designers at this point use *flow charts, schematics,* or *storyboards.* Each term basically means the same thing; each is a visual representation of the structure of the site and how the pages are linked together via HTML.

Structure in General

There are as many opinions about Website structure as there are Websites. There are many successful sites that break all the rules detailed in this text.

Basically, there are two choices at first in terms of structure: vertical (deep) or horizontal (shallow). Both have advantages and disadvantages. Horizontal sites have lots of stuff right up front, presenting the user with the optimum number of options right off the bat. Vertical sites are layered so that the general information is nearer the top and specific information is below waiting to be unearthed. Lots of options can overwhelm a user, and having to dig deep can frustrate a user. Some people like to know all that is available as soon as they arrive, and others enjoy the hunt for buried information.

Most sites have what is referred to as a home page; from that home page, the rest of the site is accessed in two to three basic structural patterns. Depending on the kinds of information being conveyed, the target audience, and the goals of the site, one of these structures might be more conducive to your project than another. Make this decision part of your planning sessions and allow the content and goals to guide you in your choice of structure.

Linear

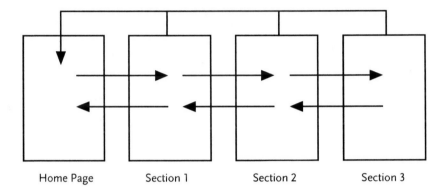

| Home Page | Section 1 | Section 2 | Section 3 |

FIGURE 4.1: AN EXAMPLE OF A LINEAR SITE STRUCTURE

A linear site basically follows the idea that first there is one page and then the next choice is obviously the second page and so on. Most of the activity is between the sections, with each section having direct access back to the home page. There might be links off of the section pages for additional information, but the site is generally read like a book from one page to the next. Other times, this structure will appear as part of a larger site where you want to lead the user through a logical progression and not let them stray. There is ultimate control of the user's experience in a linear site.

Hierarchical

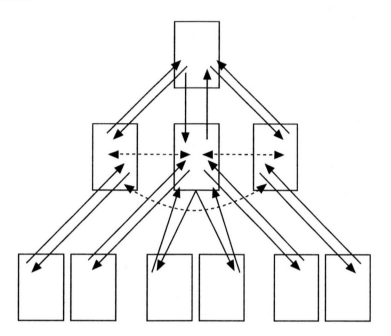

FIGURE 4.2: AN EXAMPLE OF A HIERARCHICAL OR PYRAMID STRUCTURE

A *hierarchical* structure is sometimes called a pyramid structure. Though our example only shows three tiers, it could be a lot more complex. Obviously, this is more complex than a linear site structure. Usually, the information is organized with a main or home page detailing some general categories, and each general category has subcategories associated with it. Some branches of the pyramid can be deeper than others, depending on the topics and content.

The dotted line above shows a common adaptation of this structure, which allows the level-one sections to have links that allow travel between these sections, so the user doesn't have to go all the way back to the home page in order to traverse down another branch of the site. There are many ways that a site can be adapted. Choosing a site structure should help in the organization of the information; it shouldn't lock it up tight. As the site evolves, it may soon represent something other than the beginning structure, but that should be okay. The Web is an evolving medium, and change is constant.

Hub

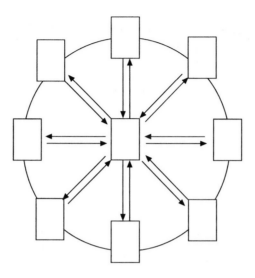

FIGURE 4.3: AN EXAMPLE OF A HUB STRUCTURED SITE

The *hub* or spoke structure is like a wagon wheel, with the home page at the center and all the other pages radiating from it like spokes. There is also interaction between the pages that are at the outside of the wheel. Generally, the idea is that users start and return to the hub after each interaction.

Using these basic structures as your beginning point, the structure of your site can take any shape that visually graphs the relationship of the supporting pages to the home page and the resource pages to the support pages. What is important to remember in Website design is to chart the structure before you begin storyboarding what the interface is to look like. There may be things about the structure that influence the look and feel of the interface. As you can probably tell, the planning of a Website is an activity where one aspect builds on and uses the information from the previous step. Skipping ahead is not a good idea because you won't have the firm foundation of exploration on which to continue your plan.

Linking Strategies

There are some common ideas that have developed in Website design. They are not hard and fast rules, but most designers try to adhere to them. They relate to user expectation, user satisfaction, and user retention. Try to make as much of your site accessible within three to five clicks. This way, the user isn't spending precious time (and on the Web, that can be seconds) hunting for what they need. Keep your links per page to fewer than nine. This way, your layers aren't too thick. If you begin to find yourself doing more than nine, you should consider breaking the site into more pieces so that each of the sections adheres to this practice.

METAPHOR/CONCEPT/PERSONALITY/STYLE

Branding and Consistency

The middle ground of a site is everything we talked about so far—purpose, goals, audience, content, and organization. The face that a site puts to the world is the next step. Often, this face is the unifying element in a Website, its *personality* that is presented to the viewing public. This is the experience that the user has at your site. It is essential to choose an appropriate theme or *metaphor* for your site. It too should be related to the goals and objectives set in the planning stages of the project. All the visual information, navigation controls, and such should support and clarify the communicative goals of the site and appeal to the target audience based on the assessment done regarding the target audience. In addition, your interface design should be intriguing, usable, and a joy to experience. This will keep people coming back again and again. There are sites that exist that have the essential information that people need, but because the experience is so poor, people don't come back.

One way of involving an audience member in your Web experience is to use a metaphor for your interface design. Use one thing, usually a recognizable item, to represent something completely different. A common metaphor used in interactive multimedia is the VCR controls metaphor (this was probably once the cassette player metaphor, but that would be a while ago). Most people are familiar with the "play," "forward," and "reverse" buttons on a VCR, so a Website could employ the VCR metaphor as a navigation experience. To advance forward a page, you click the > arrow. To go back a page, you click the < button.

Often, the metaphors used on the Web are extremely elaborate whole environments, where recognizable icons are used to assist the user in getting around and using the site. Common metaphors on the Web revolve around home appliances like the VCR; virtual rooms with doors, windows, and furniture; books; and then what I call the "vending machine" metaphor, which has clearly labeled buttons somewhere on the screen that present the choices (like D1 for gum) as we would expect.

The key to any metaphor's success is *consistency*. Users get really upset if you change or abandon your metaphor part way through their journey. Even if you modify or simplify the metaphor, as long as you continue to use the rules you set up at the beginning, the user is pretty willing to go along. If you, however, go too far in a different direction, they can become confused and lost, and then they become resentful and unwilling to remain at your site. Remember, any user of your site is just a single click away from your competitor's site.

The other thing to consider about your interface design, whether it is a complex environment or a straightforward interface, is to keep the user apprised of where they are at all times. Whether you use color-coding to identify which part of the map a user is on and where they have been or some other visual feedback to the user, do something. We have all had the experience where we get so deep into a site and then suddenly can't remember what the page we came from was called or what part of the large support site we are on. A simple listing of the links back to the main section title is all it takes. Then users can find their way back or jump to some portion of the site that they visited previously. You should be able to get anywhere from anywhere in a Website. The easiest way to do this is a simple text-based menu at the bottom of each page that transports the user to the beginning of major sections. The more elegant way is to have a changing interface that changes as the user moves through the site.

Look at the following sites to see examples of *branding* and visual and navigational consistency.

- http://www.apple.com — It even looks like its own operating system interface.
- http://www.toyota.com — Toyota's site. Wow!
- http://www.bosch.com — Bosch International.
- http://www.discovery.com — The Discovery Channel's site is one of the best sites for this concept. Definite branding; compare it to the TV counterpart.

It should be noted here that the process of design and implementation should also be one of constant evaluation and refinement. At each phase of the process, there should be at least a self-assessment of what has been done and what is still to be done. It should be compared with the goals and objectives. If it is determined that parts of the project have strayed from their original goals, then it should be decided how to get it back on track or whether the information is really necessary. It is hard to plan just what this evaluation might reveal, but it is important to take the time to step back from the process and look at the bigger picture.

Usability testing is a formative approach used once a full prototype is developed.

USABILITY AND ACCESSIBILITY

Usability

The recognized expert in Web *usability* and Web usability testing is Jakob Nielsen. His Website at http://www.useit.com is an excellent resource for the student interested in usability. We will attempt to summarize the process here, but as it is a huge subject, further exploration outside this text will be necessary. Nielsen has two excellent books, *Designing Web Usability: The Practice of Simplicity*, published by New Riders, and *Usability Engineering*, published by Morgan Kaufmann, that should also be consulted.

Usability refers to the ease of use with which visitors to a Website can access the information they are seeking or how easily and quickly they can complete tasks such as online purchasing. The idea of usability testing is not new; it has its origins in industrial and product design. When a prototype was developed, usability testers (sometimes they were just randomly selected consumers) were given products to use. Teams of experts observed and evaluated their behavior and assessed whether a redesign was needed. Often, tasks were developed (such as finding the windshield wiper on/off switch or locating the rear defrost button), and users were timed to see how long these tasks took to accomplish.

The idea is similar in Web design. Once a prototype of the site is developed and working, it is an excellent idea to take it to a cross-section of your audience and watch them use it. The Web development team should devise tasks prior to that time that will honestly and accurately allow them to assess whether the site is meeting its goals as set forth in the planning documentation and by the client. From the planning stage, the team should know what it is the client thinks the customer wants, and the tests should reflect that.

Observations should note how difficult it is to find links. Watch users work and look for and understand their confusions and frustrations. So often decisions about user interface designs are made solely on aesthetics and not on use (as in USE-ability—the ability to use a product). Listening to users is good, but observing them is best. Don't necessarily believe their explanations for not being able to perform a task. This kind of anecdotal evidence doesn't really assist you in the assessment of a site. A user who misses the button that is crucial to perform a task might rationalize the behavior by suggesting that if it had been a different color, it would have been more visible. Only take the result, the user didn't find the button, as data! Changing the color of the button and retesting is the only way to know if this indeed was a factor. It is human nature to fudge and prevaricate, so we cannot take people at their words — we can only observe their actions.

Accessibility

Accessibility is related to usability but specifically focuses on the needs of handicapped people. The *Americans with Disabilities Act (ADA)* mandates the accessibility of Web pages for publicly funded sites. Including all persons, enabled or otherwise, is a good idea. The *World Wide Web Consortium (W3C)* has set forth some guidelines on its Website at http://www.w3c.org/WAI/. WAI stands for Web Accessibility Initiative. This is a working document and is constantly under revision. The current guidelines in effect are the Web Content Accessibility Guidelines 1.0 (May 1999), which can be found at http://www.w3.org/TR/WCAG10/ and are summarized below. Full explanations for each point are detailed on the W3C Website.

1. Provide equivalent alternatives to auditory and visual content.
2. Don't rely on color alone.
3. Use markup and style sheets and do so properly.
4. Clarify natural language usage.
5. Create tables that transform gracefully.
6. Ensure that pages featuring new technologies transform gracefully.
7. Ensure user control of time-sensitive content changes.

8. Ensure direct accessibility of embedded user interfaces.
9. Design for device-independence.
10. Use interim solutions.
11. Use W3C technologies and guidelines.
12. Provide context and orientation information.
13. Provide clear navigation mechanisms.
14. Ensure that documents are clear and simple.

The newer guidelines (Web Content Accessibility Guidelines 2.0, January 2001), as of this writing, appear to be much more in-depth and extensive. The W3C Website provides HTML examples of how to implement their suggestions.

CHAPTER SUMMARY

In this chapter, we learned who the Web team members are. We learned it is essential to plan a Website first, before you ever type one line of HTML code. Planning allows you to see how the goals affect the assumptions about the user and how the anticipated user affects the goals. Planning allows for the client or stakeholder to have input and allows the content to be considered. These items contribute to the physical structure and site architecture and help to refine the linking strategies. The nature of Web design is that integral parts of the process cannot be skipped or removed or the foundation for the whole project is weakened, which could be disastrous and possibly costly to the developer. We also touched on usability and usability testing as well as accessibility and Web Content Accessibility Guidelines to ensure access for handicapped Web surfers.

KEY TERMS

mission objective statement
stakeholder
target audience
brainstorming
content
print collateral material
technical writer
JavaScript
graphic designer
site architecture
schematics
flow charts
storyboards

hierarchical
hub
concept
branding
consistency
usability
accessibility
Americans with Disabilities Act
   (ADA)
World Wide Web Consortium
   (W3C)
personality
metaphor

REVIEW QUESTIONS

1. What are the things a mission objective statement should do?
2. Who are all the possible primary team members on a Web development team?
3. What are the three structures illustrated in the chapter?
4. Users prefer sites that have a metaphoric, navigational, and conceptual

   _____.

5. True or false: Usability testing was developed specifically for Web development.
6. Who is a recognized expert on usability testing?
7. Which group has a document detailing the guidelines for Web content accessibility?

EXERCISES

1. Choose a Website that you think is a good example of an easy-to-use, well-structured site. Using a flow-charting software package, an illustration software package, or the drawing tools in your word processor, chart that site.

2. Choose a Website that you think is a poor example of site structure, one that you found difficult to use, and chart that site. How might it be improved? Chart that idea.

3. Brainstorm on the idea of your family and a Website for them. Go back two generations. What would the goals of a site like this be? Who might be your potential audience? Who are the stakeholders? What does the content inventory consist of for this site? What is the content organization for this site? What structure will you use to pursue this site for publication on the Web? What metaphor or concept will you use to produce this site? What other metaphors exist for this type of site beyond the obvious one?

4. Find a small business in need of a Website, or have your instructor assign you one, and go through the process of a needs analysis for the business as it pertains to a possible Website. Document everything and collate it in a three-ring binder. Share it with the class as the project progresses.

5. Read at least two articles from Jakob Nielsen's www.useit.com site. Summarize your findings and report back to the class.

6. Pick a site that you think exhibits high usability and devise a simple usability seek-and-find test for some page, information, or task. Observe either a classmate or friend attempting to carry out your test and discuss your findings with the class.

7. How might you test whether the placement of a link is a successful choice? What are some expectations that users have developed since the Web became popular? How can you use this information?

8. What are some of the possible challenges someone with a disability might face in navigating and interacting with a Website? What are some ways to overcome these challenges?

9. Read the W3C guidelines in more depth and then pick a Website and evaluate it based on the guidelines (either 1.0 or the proposed 2.0). What recommendations would you give the creators of the Website to enhance their site for persons with disabilities?

PROJECT

Now that we have an idea of who our audience is and what their environment is, as well as a justification for developing the site, we need to turn our attention toward making the client's vision a reality. The client likes the efficiency of portal sites. Do the following:

- Analyze some of the major portal sites and determine what qualities make them efficient. Make sure to consider both the graphical layout of each page and how those pages are interconnected.

- Based on your analysis, create four different sample home pages for your site. Each page should strive to meet your client's vision of efficiency but should be different enough to provide your client with some choices. Have your instructor or an associate critique your work and select one of samples.

At this point, we have a preliminary audience analysis and even a preliminary page design. Now we need to take our client's mandate and turn it into a functional site. The focus at this stage of the game is not on developing entire pages but instead on developing an informational structure that will facilitate communication. Do the following:

- Create two different site-design diagrams that account for our client's vision. Make sure to address the events, classifieds, and events areas. Your diagram should show how all of the pages are interrelated and the information that should be displayed on each page. Have your instructor or an associate critique your work and select one of the charts.

REFERENCES

Burdman, Jessica. 1999. *Collaborative Web Development*. Reading, MA: Addison-Wesley.

Davis, Jack and Merritt, Susan. 1998. *The Web Design Wow Book*. Berkeley, CA: Peachpit Press.

Kristof, Ray and Satran, Amy. 1995. *Interactivity by Design*. Mountainview, CA: Adobe Press.

Nielsen, Jakob. 2000. *Designing Web Usability*. Indianapolis, IN: New Riders, 2000.

Weinman, Lynda. 1999. *Designing Web Graphics.3*. Indianapolis, IN: New Riders.

Weinman, Lynda. 1999. *Coloring Web Graphics*. Indianapolis, IN: New Riders.

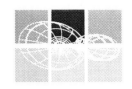

chapter 5
page design

CHAPTER OVERVIEW

This chapter will look at the structure of the home page and the layout of a design using grids. Also discussed in this chapter are browser-safe colors and choosing and notating them in XHTML. Lastly, the chapter will include a short discussion on using navigational elements on a page to assist users with keeping track of their whereabouts in a site.

CHAPTER OBJECTIVES

- Learn home.html and index.html dos and don'ts
- Use grids and their use as a layout tool
- Understand Web-safe colors
- Understand RGB and hexadecimal color
- Use the navigational elements to keep track of a user's position in a site

PAGE DESIGN

As we can see from the chapter on design principles, what often looks arbitrary in terms of design actually has a fairly complex structure underneath. As you explored the design principles, hopefully you began to dissect each piece of visual design information you came across to learn its structure. By trying to identify the various principles and rules used on good and bad design, you begin to develop your own eye for design. Layout is something that many people spend a lifetime studying and getting right. If you are serious about design, you should find at least a semester-long course that deals with nothing but design and layout in order to better appreciate and more effectively lay out print or Web publications.

There are some things about Web page design that can be considered fairly common and necessary. Then there are some rules that should be followed but can be broken if it fits the needs of the site concept and the navigational needs of the site. Mostly what is presented in this chapter are suggestions for how to construct Web pages that ultimately should lead you to make discoveries on your own. As you look at sites on the Web, you will see that many designers are successful by doing the same basic grid in each site and letting the content elements be dynamic. Other designers go out of their way to alter, modify, and invent new ways to present information in a Web page.

THE HOME PAGE OR INDEX

The home page in a Website (*home.html* or *index.html*) is the entryway or gateway to a much larger body of information. It is the first piece of visual information from which a user forms an impression of the person, company, product, or service for which the Website provides information and access. It is similar to the table of contents in a book. It gives general overviews about what lies ahead and may actually have links to each of those subsequent sections. Your home page should be attractively laid out in such a way that the user gets information as quickly as possible. At the very best, a Website has 30 seconds or fewer to persuade a user to stay. If you haven't given them a reason within that time, they will leave. You should think of a home page as a magazine cover or book cover. On the rack, they are all competing for the reader's attention. The same is true for the Web. There are millions of pages out there. What is it that makes your site different? Exploit that fact to capture users.

Sometimes, the home page is preceded by what is called a *splash page*. The splash page (from comic book parlance) is a very clever and dynamic, often animated, introductory page that either automatically moves to the home page or, with a single click, allows users to go to the home page. Many splash pages these days use Flash technology for animating page elements so that many Websites have little movies that play when a user arrives at the site. It is important to note that if you use this kind of device, you should give users a way to opt out of it. Either provide a skip intro *link* that moves you to the real information or some other way for the user to avoid your splash page. Users might not have appropriate plug-ins, the download time may be long, or they may have too little patience to want to enjoy your splash page. Never hold a user hostage. They will resent it and leave your site as quickly as they can.

Some Elements to Include on the Home Page

You should have access to as much of the major site structure as possible on the home page. Users should be able to get almost anywhere from the home page. Whether this becomes a major design element or just simple text links is up to you, but you should offer up some quick and expedient ways to get into the site without having to wait for graphics to download. Plan for one click to major site divisions (primary level information) and no more than three to five clicks to get to the bottom of what you are presenting (secondary and tertiary information).

Include an email link on the home page so that if there is a problem or users have feedback, they don't have to hunt through the entire site to find a human contact.

You should also include alternate *contact information* on the home page. Not all users set up their browsers to allow the mailto:// function to be enabled. The name and telephone number, at the very least, should be available, and you should probably include an address as well. Remember, the more helpful you are up front, the more likely users stick with you even if you don't have what they are looking for.

A successful photographer and Website designer, Gary Mills (www.garymills.com), says that "Home page design should be "above the fold." That's an old-time newspaper term I've (re)-interpreted for the Web . . . no scrolling on the home page to see all the vital information." This is so true. Home pages should be of the smallest screen size and have everything visible up front. Once you have hooked users, they are more willing to explore, but until you have them on the line, you can't expect them to do things like scroll to find important information. Designers should design for 13-inch monitors. There are still many of them in use today. So the screen size is *640×480 pixels*. Twenty pixels are used for the menu bar display, so the usable screen real estate is 640×460 pixels. Home pages, if not all pages, should be designed horizontally. The monitor is built that way, and this is the framal reference of each and every Web page. Rather than fight it, you should design for it as a given.

You can orient the home page grid (more later on grids) one way that suits the needs of the information being presented, and you can have a totally separate grid layout for succeeding pages that is different, and people will accept it. But once into a site, each section should look and behave consistently relative to the other pages in that section of the site. Changes should only be made at major (primary level) junctures, if they are made at all. Carrying over the home page look and feel will almost always be the most consistent and predictable winner in terms of user success.

There are successful sites that don't heed the advice given here, but on closer inspection, those sites might benefit from some alterations in the direction of cleaner design.

GRIDS

Grids, whether formal or casual, linear or free-form, shown or hidden, are the structure providers for visual information designers. Even a designer who doesn't start out using a grid more often than not ends up defining a grid at some point in the creative process, either consciously or unconsciously. For beginners, grids are essential. They provide an organization, a set of rules that are to be followed and/or broken. Mostly, they are the impetus for the design to begin. It is recommended that all beginning visual designers consider the creation of a grid for every project or composition they create until the idea of the grid is an engrained and intuitive tool. After using them for a while, you begin to get quite adept at seeing them behind the elements you are arranging. You begin to see the relationships when they are not unified, and you begin to make adjustments to strengthen your composition in terms of grid unification. Until such a time, *use a grid!* Even if you design it yourself and it is far out there, at least you will have defined your starting point. Sometimes, in visual design, that is half the battle. What follows are some simple ideas for grids and layouts of Web pages. They are a beginning and should be used as jumping off points and discussion/idea starters for your own designs. In HTML layout, creating a grid through the use of a table is a recommended practice. Remember that users have control over much of what the browser does, and if you don't protect your layout, their choice to use a larger font may throw your exquisite layout right out the window. Tables assist in keeping things aligned properly. There are many ways to do this, as you will discover in future chapters.

Page Structure

Currently, the printed page and the screen page still have a lot in common. Grids are used in the print design world all the time. The grids basically describe the possible places and relationships for elements on a page. They help determine things like the size of a graphic element. They assist us in determining where repeating elements might go. There is really no mystery behind a grid. They assist in giving the page or screen an overall unified and cohesive appearance. They also assist in group design projects because once a grid is developed and agreed upon for a particular project, then all the people involved can follow that structure.

Grids are often defined in terms of *columns*, which relates back to their print origins. On screen, we can use columns, but instead of the usual terms of measurement from print, points and picas, we use pixels. *Pixels* (from "picture element") are the smallest onscreen elements. Although we generally specify our type in terms of points, ultimately we are using a bitmapped version of the type, which relates back to the pixel. Type size in XHTML can be determined in pixels. This is helpful because one of the things the grid allows us to do is design with proportions in mind. We tend to see unity in proportion. If something is one half the size of something else, we perceive that relationship and are at ease with it. If things are arbitrarily sized in relation to each other, it creates feelings of unease in the viewer.

As a designer of pages, whether printed or displayed, we are constantly trying to make educated guesses as to how our designs will be used. One thing about the Internet is that it has made the use of lengthy text documents popular again. Newspapers often put more text in their online stories than is printed in the paper delivered to your door. So, you as a designer need to consider how the information is going to be used: Will it only be read online, or will the user be printing it? In the case of a lengthy article, it is often better to design a page whose structure is very long and to include an index and index markers. This makes navigating through the article easier, and if a user should want to print it, one print command sends the whole thing to the printer. Breaking up a long document into bite size chunks for people who will be printing means that every page has to accessed and printed separately. Not good. Very frustrating. Keep in mind how the user, not you the designer, will utilize the information you provide. Sometimes it is unavoidable and necessary to chop something up, but make sure it is the best choice for the site.

Grid Types

There are conceivably as many grids as a designer's imagination can generate. There are, however, some standard grids that can get you started. In the previous chapter, you created some of your own grids for the recomposition project and for the grid-coloring composition. You should feel free to sketch your own grids or dissect a Website that you like to discover the grid that designer used.

One-column Grid with Display Headings

A one-column grid is a single column of text with average-sized margins. Generally, a one-column grid has some sort of display heading to it that might be a company logo or some sort of masthead or banner. Graphics inserted into a one-column structure are either justified *left*, *right*, or *centered*, with *text wrapped* around the graphic.

Three ways in which a one-column grid with display headings can be used: without graphics, a graphic either right or left justified, and a graphic centered in the space.

FIGURE 5.1

One Narrow, One Wide

Some people would call this a two-column grid, others a modified one-column. Nonetheless, as it is defined, it has a narrow column on the left side with a wide column stretching to the right margin. The left column isn't wide enough for great amounts of text, but it is good for navigational items such as links. This grid can be right-handed as well as left-handed.

These examples show the one narrow, one wide format of a page. The narrow column is reserved for bulleted items, a table of contents, or, in the case of a Web page, links

FIGURE 5.2

TWO-COLUMN GRIDS

Generally, these grids have two equal columns amounting to half the screen space each (about 300 pixels wide each). Two-column grids have a formality about them and are best for text-heavy sites. Graphics are usually placed squarely in one column or the other and are sized to be the width of the column. The other place for a graphic is straddling both columns. The graphic should still be equal in width to the column size. These layouts have a symmetry and balance to them.

These two-column grids are shown with a graphic in the column and spanning both columns. This proportional relationship should be maintained with this format.

FIGURE 5.3

MULTI-UNIT GRIDS

Grids can be 3, 4, or 12 columns across. Whatever number you choose, let the grid guide you as to where text goes. Graphics should span a column, one and a half columns, two columns, and so forth. Using whole and half units lends a consistency to the layout. You can break your grid up into multiple shapes and columns if you like, as long as your purpose for doing so is to lend some sort of structure to the overall design. Below are some examples of multi-unit (more than two) grids.

The grid in Figure 5.4 is a three-column grid with a graphic that spans one and a half columns. The banner at the top spans all three columns. Conceivably, the banner could be one, two, or three columns wide or some other combination of whole and half units. Again, you can break the rules, but do so consciously and for a reason. Span one and a quarter columns, and that might work, but know that you are doing it for a reason that facilitates, clarifies, or strengthens the overall design of the page.

Three-column format. Very common in print publishing and Internet publishing.

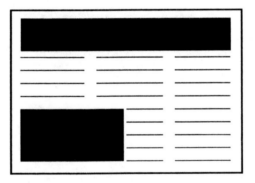

FIGURE 5.4

This flexibility makes this grid a very easy one to use.

The grid in Figure 5.5 is a 12-unit grid. It can be utilized horizontally and vertically in many different combinations. Graphics can be the size of one unit or span multiple units. Text can be in blocks or columns. There is infinite flexibility in a multi-unit grid, but this flexibility lends a great amount of unification to the overall design.

This is a 12-unit grid. The number of columns can be more than this, but the column size determines
the smallest visual unit on the page. Time magazine uses a 12-column format.

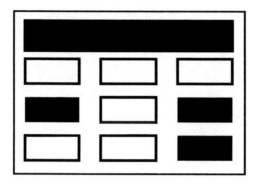

FIGURE 5.5

Most page layout, illustration, and Web design software has a snap-to-grid feature. This invisible internal grid can be set and sized to be the equivalent of your design grid if you want. Otherwise, a sketch and some calculations as to the size of columns and such will be enough to keep you organized. Below are some other common Web page grid formats. As you surf the Web, see if you can identify the underlying structure of the pages you see.

COMMON WEB GRID FORMATS

The L and Inverted L Grid

The L-shaped grid is probably the most common grid used on the Web today. It is, as its name suggests, shaped like an L. It has navigation organized vertically along the left-hand side of the page and additional *navigation* on the bottom of the page. This type of grid, like the one narrow, one wide, is good for text-dominated sites.

The inverted L grid has a horizontal section that dominates the top of the page with vertical navigational elements on the left as in the L grid. The relationship of these two elements pushes the eye into the center of the page and makes it an ideal layout for graphic-intensive sites.

The bottom of the L grid would contain the textual navigation links commonly found on the Web today. Iconographic links might go up the left-hand side. The inverted L has navigation across the top and alternate or additional navigation down the side.

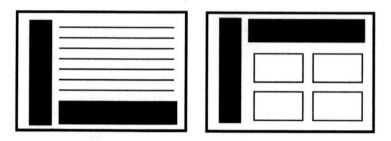

FIGURE 5.6

TWO NARROW, ONE WIDE

One prevalent grid design in use today is the two narrow, one wide grid that puts the navigation down both the left and the right margins. Though many sites use it, it is not a recommended design choice. It generally is used when there are more than seven navigational choices on the home page. It crowds other information into the center, which can make it hard to digest. We would suggest a serious redesign/reorganization of the information if your site begins to go toward a design such as this. There has to be some other organizational method to tame that much information.

The two narrow, one wide is common on the Web today, but is not a very good choice. It is for crowded sites that have many links. These sites could do with a redesign or reorganization of information.

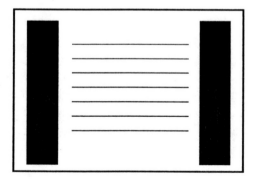

FIGURE 5.7

Most often, the grid on a page is an invisible structure beneath the page elements. However, a strong design choice can be to reveal the whole or part of the grid itself. Experiment with different combinations and see which ones appeal to you and which ones strengthen the communication and objectives of the site, and then you'll be ready to go.

THE LOOK AND FEEL OF THE USER INTERFACE: IDEAS FOR HELPING USERS FIND THEIR WAY

Lots of the whiz bang things a Web page can do are clever and novel, but ultimately they don't assist the user in how to function in the world of your Website. KISS, "Keep It So Simple," was advice given to a student by a mentor, and it is a good axiom for Web design. Less is still more, and simple can most often be the best choice.

Since this is not a tutorial on "How to Make Buttons and Such for a Web Page," we won't be describing in depth the process of making these elements, but we will talk about how they can be used to increase user satisfaction with your Website. Users don't like getting lost, not understanding where they are, or being confused about how to operate a Website. These are feelings that will ensure that a user will not stay at your site. A designer must make every attempt at meeting user expectations.

Users expect that they will be able to know where to click on a Website in order to elicit some response. They know that when the cursor changes, this indicates that there is interactivity available at the point where the cursor is located. If you decide not to use this built-in feedback function, you must let the user know in some way how to recognize links. You could use rollovers to signal a clickable spot. Mostly, teach the user simply and quickly how to use your site.

In addition to adhering to good design principles, navigational elements (this includes buttons, links, image maps, graphics, and whatever else a user can click on) should aid users in understanding where in the site structure they are in relation to where they have been and where else they can go.

There is a joke about asking directions when in the back country of the state of Maine. No matter where you want to go, the Maine native's answer is, "You can't get there from here." The motto of the Web designer should be "You can get anywhere from anywhere." In whatever method of navigation you decide on, you should include the ability to at least get back to the home page, so users can then go down another branch of the site. A stronger choice at this stage of the Web game is to allow users to jump from branch to branch freely in order to continue their journey and exploration. If navigation is an impedance to the users' expected experience, they will leave you as soon as look at you.

At the very least, navigational graphics should clearly denote what section of the site a user is currently at. This can be done with color changes of navigational elements. If, on the home page, a link is one color, once a user lands in that section, the color could change to signify that this is where the user is now. It could be a sort of "You are here" marker.

In the site for artist Alan Larkin (www.larkinstudio.com), the designer created little banners for each section of the site: fine art, portraits, and illustration. When users land on the thumbnail page, they know to which section of the site they have arrived. This banner also serves as the way to take them back to the home page in order to get to a different section of the site. These mini-banners are similar to the home page banner, utilizing the idea of repetition and consistency to assist users in feeling secure about their experience of the site.

The human mind is an amazing thing, and one thing it does well is recognize patterns. It uses this recognition to organize and catalog the information that it observes. Employing the idea of proximity and grouping navigational elements that perform similarly together creates these organizational patterns and associations that assist the user in understanding the navigation of a site. A repeated item should always be found in the same place from page to page. Moving repeated items creates confusion in the user because it appears as if the function is changing when you change the location.

In addition to proximity, use similarity to cement the relationships. Similarity of color, shape, texture, and such are all visual clues that will assist visitors in navigating your site.

These choices aren't made by chance; they are planned in the early stages of the design process. The more pre-planning you engage in, the more solid your design choices will be and the better the experience for the user. This user-centric design approach is critical in Web and interactive media design.

Label the sections of your site. Don't ever leave users hanging as to where they are. Put it right up front. If you don't label, then use the navigation buttons as tabular markers to indicate where a user is. Amazon.com uses this method quite successfully on its site. Amazon.com also uses color coding to indicate which section of the site you are currently visiting. These are two fairly simple but strong ways to help users keep track of their journey.

Once you establish a route from one link to its destination, don't create some other similar way of getting from the current screen to the same place. In Web page design, often there are two ways from each screen to another screen. One way is through the established visual metaphor or concept. The second is a very simple text-based clickable link usually found at the bottom of the Web page. More than this, and things can get confusing. In interactive media design, the rule is to use one and only one route to avoid confusion.

Be sure users can go back, either through the use of the browser's back button or through a link on the destination page that returns them to where they came from. Within reason, "anywhere from everywhere" should be the motto of a well-designed site.

Consult the W3C's Website for information on how your Web pages should be designed to adhere to the Web Content Accessibility Guidelines currently in effect.

COLOR

Color to designers is a wonderful thing, but its use comes with a responsibility. Used correctly, it can hammer home the concept, metaphor, meaning, and focus of a graphic communication. Used incorrectly, it can turn people away in droves. For Web color information, there is no better reference than Lynda Weinman's *Coloring Web Graphics*. This is the quintessential book on color graphics and the Web. We will touch on some of the technical aspects of Web color and briefly mention some of the aesthetic issues on color, but we recommend additional reading in the area. Review the "Using Color/The Aesthetics of Color," section in Chapter 3 before moving on to color and the computer.

Color and the Computer

Most of us learned color from our crayon boxes. Color names are some of the first words some of us spoke. For years, we knew that red, blue, and yellow were the primary colors. We knew that combining blue and yellow would make green, that blue and red made purple, and that red and yellow made orange. These were the primary and secondary colors of our world. We personally knew Roy G. Biv, that purveyor of color that came with every rainbow. These rules were hard and fast. Then along came the computer (actually the television was doing it too, but most of us weren't in television production so we didn't learn it) and the idea that there was another set of primary colors—*RGB* or red, green, and blue. Rather than combining to make black, these colors combined and made white light. This process, known as additive color mixing, is the basis of all color display in the computer world.

Now that you are thoroughly confused, let's sort it all out. We are concerned here with color for display on computer monitors. So we won't deal with our crayon colors. We are not concerned with print for the most part, so we won't deal with CMYK (which is actually just a modified red, blue, and yellow pigment system). We will, however, be talking about RGB color, how it's used in the Web page design process, and how XHTML deals with and understands RGB color.

Monitors and Color

One of the things that people notice right off the bat is that the color of an image on their monitor is never the same as the color on their friend's monitor, even if both monitors are the same make and model. This variance can be the single biggest headache in a Web designer's career. Color shifting is part of the deal. There are some things that are contributing to this shift that need mentioning.

Gamma

Gamma is the thing that controls the brightness and *contrast* of the display. Though there are standards (Macintosh gamma is 1.8 and PC gamma is 2.2), there is still a wide margin of error. For the most part, gamma cannot be controlled.

Calibration

You can recalibrate your monitor to compensate for gamma inconsistencies, but it is difficult to settle on an average or safe setting. Sometimes it is best to leave the default alone and to live with what you are given. Hopefully, the hardware industry will come up with a better standard, now that the accuracy of information on the screen is becoming a more important part of visual communication technology. In general, PC monitors tend to be much darker than Macintosh monitors, so compensate accordingly and view your work on both platforms.

Resolution

The average computer screen display *resolution* is 72 pixels per inch (72ppi). This is the highest it can go, so images prepared for viewing on the Web should always be at this screen resolution. Sometimes this is mistakenly indicated as 72 dpi (dots per inch), but that is a print term. Always work in pixels per inch when preparing graphics for the Web.

Computers

Computers don't understand color in the descriptive and visual way that we do. Perhaps they never had access to a box of 64 Crayola crayons. Computers understand color using *hexadecimal* notation.

Hexadecimal is the base-16 number system that consists of 16 values instead of 10 as in the decimal system. These values are the numbers 0 to 9 and the letters A to F. The number 12 in hexadecimal would be represented by the value C, 15 would be F. The hexadecimal system can represent each byte (or 8 bits) as two consecutive hexadecimal digits.

The hexadecimal values we are concerned with as Web designers are 00, 33, 66, 99, CC, and FF. These six values, in combinations of three pairs, represent all of the available colors that a Web browser recognizes. These colors have come to be known as the *Web-safe color* palette.

Web-safe Color

Browsers handle only 8-bit (2^8) color (256 colors). This limitation is because HTML caters to the simplicity of information exchange. In the late 1980s and early 1990s, *8-bit color* cards were the default standard on most systems. Many (more than we would like to admit) are still in use today. So, in order for color depth not to be an issue, browser technology standardized on 8-bit color. In the future, of course, when the majority of the world has moved up to 16-bit or even 32-bit color (most kids have better color options on their Nintendos and PlayStation 2s than we do on our computers), we won't even have to talk about a limited, "browser-safe" palette. For now, Web designers should still utilize the browser-safe palette in their designs.

Hexadecimal	RGB Value	Percentage
00	0	0
33	51	20
66	102	40
99	153	60
CC	204	80
FF	255	100

A further limitation of the browser palette is that, of the 256 colors recognized, 40 are reserved for the operating system of the platform on which the browser is functioning. So, there are 40 colors given over to Windows and

Macintosh operating systems. If you only want consistency on a single platform, then you have 40 additional colors to use, but for the most part, stick with the 216.

The *216-color palette* also was not decided upon by a designer. It was created mathematically. There are some predictable aspects of the color system that actually make choosing a browser-safe color fairly easy whether in an HTML editor or some graphics editor like FreeHand or Photoshop.

The 216 colors are derived from six shades of red, six shades of green, and six shades of blue. As mentioned before, there are six hexadecimal values for HTML color: 00, 33, 66, 99, CC, and FF. Normally, RGB color is specified on a 0 to 255 (=256) scale. The previous hexadecimal values represent the following on the RGB scale: 00=00, 33=51, 66=102, 99=153, CC=204, and FF=255. As you can see, the RGB values have a pattern as well. They go from 0 to 255 in increments of 51. Thus, when you are faced with an RGB color selector, all you have to do is put in one of the numbers from the pattern here and you will know that your color choice is browser-safe. There is also one other way that RGB color is sometimes specified. Often color is specified in percentages from 0 to 100 percent—100 percent red, 20 percent green, and 60 percent blue, for example. Those percentage values that start at 0 percent and go up in increments of 20 are also the browser-safe colors. The chart on the previous page shows the correlation between hexadecimal, RGB values, and percentages.

Most image creation programs allow you to load Web-safe palettes right into the application itself, so choosing colors when creating images is fairly easy. If you don't load an already created palette, sticking with the values above will always be browser-safe.

What happens if you include artwork that doesn't have browser-safe colors in it? Well, the browser converts the color to the nearest browser-safe equivalent. In some cases, this might not be too bad, but in other cases it can be disastrous. Your text color could shift so far as to be the same color as your background, and then it would be lost!

If you use browser-safe colors for your background color, text color, link color, and line art images that have large areas of a single color (like your navigational images, usually saved in the .gif format), then you should be fine. JPEG images (photographs and continuous tone images) should never be converted to browser-safe colors. The JPEGs format handles color differently, and they are usually not prone to too large a color shift when displayed.

There is a standard set of colors that correspond to the set of *VGA colors* on a PC. These colors are defined by name in the HTML 3 and 4 standards. They certainly will display properly on a PC and can actually be specified in HTML code by using the label name instead of a hexadecimal number. However, of the 16 VGA colors, only seven are truly browser-safe and will dis-

VGA Color	Hexadecimal Number	Browser Safe
Black	000000	Yes
White	FFFFFF	Yes
Red	FF0000	Yes
Lime (Green)	00FF00	Yes
Blue	0000FF	Yes
Aqua (Cyan)	00FFFF	Yes
Fuchsia (Magenta)	FF00FF	Yes
Yellow	FFFF00	Yes
Green	008000	No
SilverGray	C0C0C0	No
Grey	808080	No
Olive	808000	No
Maroon	800000	No
Navy	000080	No
Purple	800080	No
Teal	008080	No

play properly across both platforms. The colors are indicated in the accompanying table.

Notice that the colors that are browser-safe correspond to black and white plus the primary and secondary colors of light: RGB as primary and CMY as secondary!

Background Color

Though some people will try to prescribe formulaic approaches to choosing colors in a design, the ultimate proof of the choices is in the finished design. The rules above are but jumping-off points for choices that can be made. Other choices that fly in the face of any "theory" also work. It is suggested that you stick to the rules to either get you started or to unstick you in a creative block as you go about creating Web pages.

Your background color should be a color that is not too overpowering in relation to the other elements that will appear in the frame of reference. The background color should be a color that unifies and ties together the elements in the frame. Subtler is probably better than garish, but distinct and dynamic backgrounds have also been successful on the Web. The color choices for your background should strengthen and promote the communicational goals of the site. To reiterate: Lynda Weinman's book, *Coloring Web Graphics*, is an excellent resource that shows most of the possible color combinations. She has done an extraordinary job with palette choices, and her book and Website should be consulted when choosing Web colors. Appendix C lists URLs for sites where you can try out color combinations.

Text Color

Readability should be the number one goal of text on a Web page. Whether it is HTML text or text in a graphic, the communication value should remain high. Text effects, that is text used as an abstract design element as opposed to an informational element, can be an exception, but wherever information is given textually, keep the readability as most important. High-contrast color choice with the background color is key to readability. Choose carefully what your text color is and what your visited link color will be.

The text should always remain readable in each of those varied states a link can possess. Certainly, one of the most readable combinations of text and background is black text on white. This should be your benchmark. As you stray from this, the attempt should be to keep the contrast at a similar value to black on white.

As your background value passes the halfway mark on the value scale (white to black), then your text color needs to switch from dark to light or from black to white with the other end of the scale being white text on a black background. Keep in mind also that the darker backgrounds tend to make text appear smaller than it is, so you will need to increase the size of light text on a dark background by a point or two.

Remember also that often the background color is omitted in printing. Therefore, if you use white or light text on a dark background and you expect the user to print that page, the text will not print on white paper. Keep this in mind as you design.

CHAPTER SUMMARY

Utilizing grids to shape the design of a page can be a time-saver. Grids allow you to not leave any element's location and relationship to the design to chance. They can assist in defining the proximity of elements on a page, which aid in creating a unified and consistent design. Web color can be a tricky and difficult thing to tame, but understanding the limitations of color on the Web and how it is determined make its use that much easier. The same can be said for type on the Web. Embracing the limitations and exploiting them can only help strengthen a designer's choices. Making good choices with color, type, backgrounds, and navigational elements provide a user with a sense of certainty about what to expect from your Website. User satisfaction is directly proportional to interface consistency, navigability, and feedback to the user about where in the site a user is located. The whole should be greater than the sum of the parts!

KEY TERMS

8-bit color
216-color palette
640x480 pixels
centered
color
column
contact information
contrast
gamma
grid
hexadecimal
home.html

index.html
left justified
link
navigation
pixel
resolution
RGB
right justified
splash page
text wrap
VGA colors
Web-safe color

REVIEW QUESTIONS

1. The first page in a Website is often called the home page or the _____ page.
2. Contact information on the home page should include:_____, _____, _____, and _____.
3. The home page should be sized to be _____ pixels by _____ pixels so that all of the information fits on a 13-inch screen.
4. Designers use a _____ to aid them in laying out a page.

5. In a two-column grid design, graphics can be fit inside one column, the other column, or _____.

6. The two narrow, one wide grid shouldn't be used because it _____ information into the _____ of the page.

7. Monitors and display devices use the _____ color system.

8. The six hexadecimal values that are part of the Web-safe palette are _____, _____, _____, _____, _____, and _____.

9. Using an RGB color selector that specifies values from 0 to 255, we can always determine if a color is Web-safe because it will be some number that is incremented by _____.

10. Using percentages in an RGB color selector, Web-safe colors will land on _____, _____, _____, _____, _____, and _____.

11. True or false: You should use as many colors as you can in the overall design of your pages and site. Explain.

12. Some of the ways to organize your color in a site are _____, _____, _____, and _____.

13. You should use _____ type for headlines and _____ for body text.

14. From any page in a site, you should be able to get _____ in the site.

EXERCISES

1. Search the Web or go to one of your favorite Websites and assess these sites relative to their layout and page design. How well do they present the information? Is there a logical flow to the page and how the information is presented? Are there any usability or accessibility (see Chapter 4) issues that you wish to comment on? Summarize your findings in a short paper or an email that is then shared with the class.

2. Place your summaries from Exercise 1 and the URL on a Web page that is then published for your class to share. Choose two other student commentaries, read them, visit those sites, and assess for yourself whether the comments are justified.

3. Choose a grid or define your own and create a small informational site about yourself. This can be a work résumé, skills page, hobbies, or family information page. It should include at least one graphic image and text—both body and headline type. Decide on your palette prior to beginning, and use traditional tools (pencil and paper) to sketch out your grid and the information placement. Use colored pencils or markers to denote your palette and colors on your sketch. Once this has been discussed with your instructor, use XHTML to create your home page. Include at least one link to another page that uses either the same grid or a different one. If you choose to do a different grid on the second page, make sure to include it in your preliminary sketch phase for your instructor to okay.

4. Visit at least one of the color sites that deals with choosing Web colors that are listed in Appendix C. Attempt to assemble a Web palette that is made up of two primary hues, one that is a primary and its complement, and then a palette that is monochromatic (as opposed to achromatic, which is black, white, and gray). Write down the hexadecimal notations for the colors you select. Create a simple page of text on a colored background using the three palettes you assembled.

PROJECT

Now that we have an idea of what information should be displayed on each page, we need to focus on making our pages communicative. The site diagram is great for making the site work as a whole, but we still need to make sure that each page is organized in a way that maximizes communication. Do the following:

- Create mock pages of at least four different pages in your site diagram. The pages should have a unified look and feel. Have your instructor or an associate critique your work.

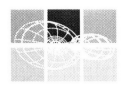

introduction to XHTML

CHAPTER OVERVIEW

This chapter introduces the basic building blocks that will enable you to write well-formed XHTML documents. We start by looking at how we present information in a document by using tags and attributes. The process of writing XHTML starts by using the proper document structure and structure/syntax of elements and tags. This chapter presents elements that deal with how the document is rendered by the browser. In this chapter, XHTML block-level elements are used to organize or group text into easily understandable blocks of text. Once block-level elements have been covered, the chapter presents XHTML inline elements which are used to control specific formatting changes to text within block-level elements.

CHAPTER OBJECTIVES

- Create well-formed XHTML documents
- Create XHTML documents using an editor
- Use proper XHTML syntax
- Use comments to explain XHTML documents
- Use block elements to structure an XHTML document
- Format text using inline logical elements
- Format text using inline physical elements
- Create lists using XHTML list elements

BASICS OF XHTML

In Chapter 2, we learned about the tools that were available to aid in the creation of an XHTML document. Now that we know how to create an XHTML document, we will start to learn the basics: tag structure and syntax, document structure, formatting of text with block elements, formatting of text with logical and physical elements, and using lists. So let's get started.

STRUCTURE/SYNTAX OF ELEMENTS AND TAGS

An *element* is the fundamental structural component of an XHTML document. Elements are made up of tags, and it is these tags that enable the browser to distinguish between the content of the Web page and the instructions specifying how that content is to be rendered (displayed) on the screen. Tags can be used to identify structural elements of the XHTML document as well as to control the appearance or format.

XHTML elements have three parts: opening tags, element content, and closing tags. For example, look at the following heading element:

```
<h1>This is the largest heading</h1>
```

The opening tag for a level-one heading is <h1>. Notice that the element name is enclosed in angle braces. The closing tag </h1> is also enclosed in angle braces, but the element name is preceded by a forward slash (/), which tells the browser that this is the end. The element content is contained between the opening and closing tags. Anything between the two tags will be marked up in the manner specified by the tag. These tags are often referred to as container tags, meaning that they have a paired starting and ending tag.

Some tags, such as line break <br> and horizontal rule <hr>, are single tags and have no ending tag. These tags are often referred to as stand-alone tags, meaning that they have no ending tag. Although HTML does not require ending tags, in XHTML, the ending tag is an absolute requirement. This requirement is met by placing a forward slash (/) after the element. For example, the line *break element*
 would be ended in the following manner:

```
<br />
```

Don't forget to leave a space between the element name and the forward slash.

Many tags can contain optional or required attributes. An attribute is part of a tag that further specifies how the tag is to be processed by the browser. For example, in order to put a picture (graphical image) on a page, we use an image tag with an attribute specifying where the actual graphic file is located. For example:

```
<img src="image source" />
```

The src attribute is required, but many attributes are optional and may have a default value. Notice that the <img> tag does not have a closing tag. In XHTML, the closing tag requirement is met by placing a forward slash (/) before the ending brace.

> tip: Tags that are not understood by a particular browser are simply ignored.

As you begin creating your Web pages in this chapter, you will learn much more about different kinds of tags and how they are used. Although many Web development tools automatically take care of the tags for you, it is important that you know and understand how tags work.

XHTML DOCUMENT STRUCTURE

There are three main parts associated with the XHTML document structure that we should define before actually creating an XHTML document. The following are the main document parts:

- *Document information*
- *Document header*
- Document body

This basic document structure is illustrated by the following XHTML code:

```
<?xml version="1.0" encoding="UTF-8"?>
<!DOCTYPE html PUBLIC "-//W3C//DTD/XHTML 1.0 Transitional//EN"
"http://www.w3.org/TR/xhtml1/DTD/xhtml1-transitional.dtd">
<html xmlns="http://www.w3.org/1999/xhtml" xml:lang="en" lang="en">
<head>
<title>Basic XHTML Document Structure</title>
</head>
<body>
</body>
</html>
```

Let's take a closer look at the document structure by looking at each part.

DOCUMENT INFORMATION

The document information part consists of a version declaration and document type definition. The version declaration indicates what version of the XML standard is being used. This XML declaration is not required to be included in an XHTML document, but it is highly recommended by the XHTML 1.0 standard. The XML version declaration is as follows:

```
<?xml version="1.0" encoding="UTF-8"?>
```

The declaration also could include an encoding attribute, which identifies the character sets used in the document. The UTF-8 encoding is the default value in the version declaration, but it is recommend that the encoding attribute be included. Some other common character set encodings includes UTF-16 and ISO-8859-1. XML parsers are only required to recognize UTF-8 and UTF-16, which should handle any language commonly used.

The *document type definition (DTD)* is next and looks like

```
<!DOCTYPE html PUBLIC "-//W3C//DTD/XHTML 1.0 Transitional//EN"
"http://www.w3.org/TR/xhtml1/DTD/xhtml1-transitional.dtd">
```

In the previous chapter, we discussed the various DTDs and what they are used for. Let's take a closer look at what the DTD is telling us. The <!DOCTYPE> element indicates what DTD the document is validated against. The <!DOCTYPE> element contains the following parts:

- html—indicates that <html> is the root element and will contain all other elements within the document.
- PUBLIC—identifies the name of the DTD. In this case it is "-//W3C//DTD/ XHTML 1.0 Transitional//EN". The EN at the end of the name indicates that the DTD is written in English.
- The URL—indicates where the browser can locate the DTD.

THE <HTML> ELEMENT

The html tags, <html> and </html>, are used to indicate that the XHTML document content is written using the HTML language. The <html> element will be the container for the entire XHTML document. The following is the <html> element from our basic document:

```
<html xmlns="http://www.w3.org/1999/xhtml" xml:lang="en" lang="en">
<head>
</head>
<body>
</body>
</html>
```

Notice that the </html> tag must be the last tag in the document. Looking at the <html> element, notice that it has three attributes:

- xmlns—identifies the XML namespace, which was discussed in the last chapter.
- xml:lang="en"—indicates that English is the language of the document when used as an XML document.
- lang="en"—indicates that English is the language of the document when used as an HTML document.

The <html> element also contains two very important container elements, <head> and <body>, which will make up the rest of our document structure.

DOCUMENT HEADER

The header portion of the document contains information about the page that is used by the browser and the Web server. This part of the document is enclosed within the <head> and </head> tags.

THE <HEAD> ELEMENT

The <head> </head> element is a container element that will contain several other elements used to describe the Web page. The information contained within the <head> element is usually not displayed as Web page content. These elements include:

- <title>
- <script>
- <link>
- <meta>
- <style>
- <base>

ADDING A DOCUMENT TITLE, THE <TITLE> ELEMENT

All XHTML documents should have a title; it is really a must for a proper document. The <title> and </title> tags are used to add a title to your XHTML document by placing text between the two tags. The following is an example from our basic structure:

```
<title>Basic XHTML Document Structure</title>
```

The text between the tags will usually be displayed in the browser title bar and be stored as the "bookmark" in most browsers. The title also serves another important function; it allows World Wide Web search engines to use keywords from the title to refer to the page. Figure 6.1 shows how the document's title is displayed in the browser.

> tip: The title text should be descriptive and relatively short.

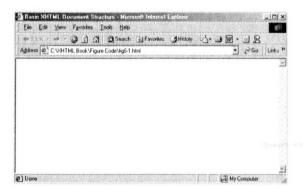

FIGURE 6.1: TITLE IN BROWSER TITLE BAR

THE <SCRIPT> ELEMENT

The <script> element is used to embed scripts written in JavaScript or VBScript into an XHTML document. This element is usually included within the *head element,* but is included in the body of the document when it needs to

> tip: If your Web page only displays a title and no content, check to make sure that you have not forgotten to include a closing tag for the <head> </head> element.

interact with the Web page. The <script> element will be discussed in more detail in Chapter 14.

THE <LINK> ELEMENT

The <link> element is used to provide information about the relationship of the current document with other documents. The information that the link element would provide to the browser would include where the document can be found and the type of document that it is. The <link> element would be used in the <head> element when specifying an external style sheet. This element does not contain any content, but it still must be properly terminated in XHTML. This element will be discussed further in Chapter 12. The following is an example of using the <link> element:

```
<link rel="stylesheet" href="extstyle.css" />
```

THE <BASE> ELEMENT

The <base> element is used to specify a base URL for all hyperlinks used in the document. This element does not have a closing tag, so it should be closed by using a forward slash before the closing angle bracket. The <base> element is used only in the <head> element and has two attributes:

- href—the URL to be used as the base hyperlink. This attribute is required.
- target—provides the name of the target frame where all links will open.

THE <STYLE> ELEMENT

The <style> element is used to create styles for an entire Web page. Cascading style sheets can be either external or embedded. Style sheets are covered in Chapter 12.

THE <META> ELEMENT

The <meta> element provides information about the content of a document, which can be used by Internet search engines to index the Web pages. XHTML documents can contain multiple <meta> elements. The attributes of the <meta> element include: name, content, and http-equiv.

tip: Although you can use any value for the name attribute, it is recommended that you use one of the predefined values.

The name Attribute
This is a required attribute of the <meta> element but can be omitted if the http-equiv attribute is used. The name attribute is listed first within the <meta> element. This attribute has some predefined values, such as:

- Author
- Keywords
- Description
- Generator
- Formatter
- Copyright

The content Attribute
This is a required attribute of the <meta> element. This attribute contains the information that is associated with the name.

Examples of the <meta> Element
```
<meta name="keywords" content="Antique Cars, Ford, Model T, Model
A, Chalmers" />

<meta name="description" content="Using XHTML to design and create
Web pages. Visual Design techniques are discussed." />

<meta name="generator" content="Microsoft FrontPage 4.0" />

<meta name="author" content="Jeff Griffin" />

<meta name="copyright" content"&copy; 2001 Jeff Griffin" />
```

Example of the http-equiv Attribute
```
<meta http-equiv="Content-Type" content="text/html;
charset=windows-1252">
```

DOCUMENT BODY
The body portion of the document is the largest part and contains the content that will be displayed by the browser. This part of the document is enclosed within the <body> and </body> tags.

THE <BODY> ELEMENT
The <body> </body> element is a container element that contains several other elements used to describe the content of the Web page. The rest of the chapter is devoted to the elements that can be used to format text in an XHTML document.

CREATING A BASIC XHTML DOCUMENT

Let's use what we have talked about so far to create a basic XHTML document.

1. Using your choice of editor, open a new file.
2. Enter the XML version information.

```
<?xml version="1.0" encoding="UTF-8"?>
```

3. Enter a transitional document type definition (DTD).

```
<!DOCTYPE html PUBLIC "-//W3C//DTD/XHTML 1.0 Transitional//EN"
        "http://www.w3.org/TR/xhtml1/DTD/xhtml1-transitional.dtd">
```

4. Next, add an opening <html> and closing </html> tag. Remember to include the namespace information in the opening <html> tag. Leave some space between the opening and closing tags.

```
<html xmlns="http://www.w3.org/1999/xhtml" xml:lang="en" lang="en">
</html>
```

5. Next, add the head container element to the document. Also add a document title by using the title element.

```
<head>
<title> A Basic XHTML Document </title>
</head>
```

6. To complete our basic XHTML document, add the *body element* between the closing </head> tag and closing </html> tag.

```
<html xmlns="http://www.w3.org/1999/xhtml" xml:lang="en" lang="en">
<head>
<title> A Basic XHTML Document </title>
</head>
<body>
</body>
</html>
```

7. Your completed XHTML code should resemble what is seen in Notepad in Figure 6.2.

FIGURE 6.2: BASIC XHTML DOCUMENT IN NOTEPAD

8. Save the document as basicdoc.html.

9. In the browser, select Open from the File menu to open basicdoc.html. Your screen should resemble Figure 6.3.

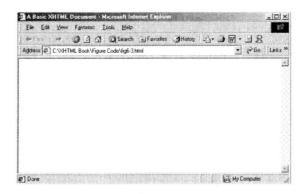

FIGURE 6.3: BASIC XHTML DOCUMENT OPENED IN BROWSER

ADDING COMMENTS

Comments can be used to help organize or clarify parts of an XHTML document. *Comments* are notes placed within the document by the author to himself or herself or to someone else working on the document. These comments might identify the intent of the entire document, who created it, what a specific group of elements accomplishes, or the purpose of a single line. Comments are not displayed and have no impact on the functioning of the document.

The comment tag in XHTML has the following syntax:

```
<!-- comment goes here -- >
```

The comment starts with a less-than sign followed by an exclamation point and two dashes; it ends with two dashes and a greater-than sign. The exclamation point indicates to the browser that what follows is to be ignored until an end comment tag is reached. Comments can be used anywhere in the document.

Going back to the basic XHTML document that we created, add comments that will identify the document and the different sections. The result might resemble the following:

tip: The browser may not display comments, but they are not totally hidden from someone's view. Anyone could view your source code and read your comments. So don't put anything in the comments you would not want your mother to read.

note: The syntax for a comment is the same for XHTML, XML, HTML, and SGML documents.

```
<!-- Author: Joe Designer -- >
<!-- Purpose: Demonstrate Basic XHTML Document -- >
<!-- Last Update: May 1, 2002 -- >
<?xml version="1.0" encoding="UTF-8"?>
<!DOCTYPE html PUBLIC "-//W3C//DTD/XHTML 1.0 Transitional//EN"
"http://www.w3.org/TR/xhtml1/DTD/xhtml1-transitional.dtd">
<html xmlns="http://www.w3.org/1999/xhtml" xml:lang="en" lang="en">
<head>
<title> A Basic XHTML Document </title>
</head>
<!-- Document Body Starts Here -- >
<body>
</body>
</html>
```

USING BLOCK ELEMENTS TO STRUCTURE A DOCUMENT

Block-level elements are used to organize or group text into easily understandable blocks of text. These elements add structure by creating headings, line breaks, paragraphs, or special text formatting. If we did not use these block-level elements to add structure, the browser would ignore any formatting done

without these elements and just display the text in one long paragraph, making it difficult to read. Remember, people have a short attention span when viewing Web pages, so it is important to make the text easy to navigate and understand.

The following are block elements that can be used to add structure to an XHTML document:

- Paragraph
- Heading
- Division
- Blockquote
- Preformatted
- Line break
- Horizontal rule

PARAGRAPHS, THE \<P\> ELEMENT

The \<p\> \</p\> element is a container element that will enclose a block of text that is to be treated as a paragraph. Unlike a word processor, a browser ignores blank lines, carriage returns, and indentations in the source text. Let's look at the following XHTML code that includes two paragraphs but does not use the *paragraph element:*

```
<?xml version="1.0" encoding="UTF-8"?>
<!DOCTYPE html PUBLIC "-//W3C//DTD/XHTML 1.0 Transitional//EN"
"http://www.w3.org/TR/xhtml1/DTD/xhtml1-transitional.dtd">
<html xmlns="http://www.w3.org/1999/xhtml" xml:lang="en" lang="en">
<head>
<title> Using Paragraphs </title>
</head>
<body>
    This is a basic XHTML document that has two paragraphs.
    They may be simple, but I think they will get the point
    across. This is the first paragraph.

    This is the second paragraph of our document. It has one
    blank line before it starts. I also included carriage returns,
    blank lines, and indentations.
</body>
</html>
```

At first glance, the XHTML looks formatted very well. Will this XHTML document display the two paragraphs the way we have formatted them? If you answered no, you are correct. The result of the XHTML as displayed by the browser can be seen in Figure 6.4.

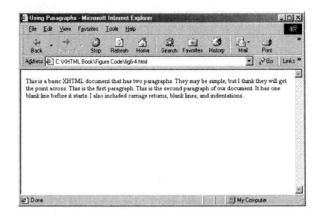

FIGURE 6.4: BASIC XHTML DOCUMENT WITHOUT PARAGRAPH ELEMENTS

Let's fix the problem by adding the paragraph elements in the appropriate places. The XHTML would look like the following:

```
<?xml version="1.0" encoding="UTF-8"?>
<!DOCTYPE html PUBLIC "-//W3C//DTD/XHTML 1.0 Transitional//EN"
"http://www.w3.org/TR/xhtml1/DTD/xhtml1-transitional.dtd">
<html xmlns="http://www.w3.org/1999/xhtml" xml:lang="en" lang="en">
<head>
<title> Using Paragraphs </title>
</head>
<body>
    <p>
    This is a basic XHTML document that has two paragraphs.
    They may be simple, but I think they will get the point
    across. This is the first paragraph.
    </p>
    <p>
    This is the second paragraph of our document. It has one
    blank line before it starts. I also included carriage returns,
    blank lines, and indentations.
    </p>
</body>
</html>
```

The results of the above XHTML are in Figure 6.5.

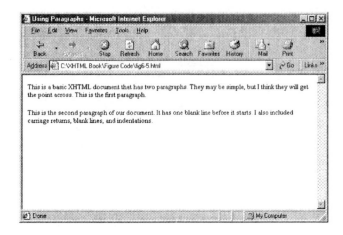

FIGURE 6.5: BASIC XHTML DOCUMENT USING PARAGRAPH ELEMENTS

Notice that, by using the <p> element, a blank line was placed before and after the paragraph. The indentation in the second paragraph is still ignored.

THE <P> TAG ATTRIBUTE

We might want to control where on the browser page our paragraph is located. Let's look at the align attribute.

The Paragraph Align Attribute

By default, a paragraph is aligned with the left margin of the page. This can be changed by using the <p> tag's align attribute. For example, if you wanted to center your paragraph, you would use the following:

```
<p align = "center">
```

The possible values for the align attribute, when used with the <p> tag, are left, center, right, or justify. Figure 6.6 illustrates the use of the *paragraph align attribute*.

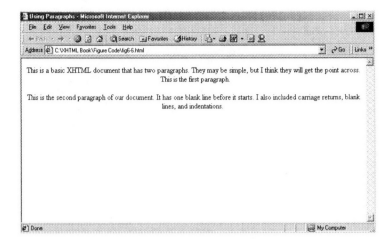

FIGURE 6.6: BASIC XHTML DOCUMENT USING PARAGRAPH ALIGNMENT

HEADINGS, THE <H1>...<H6> ELEMENTS

Headings can also be used to add structure to a page. The heading element is a container element that encloses text used for document headings. XHTML allows six levels of headings numbered 1 through 6 and has the following syntax:

```
<hx>This is a heading in XHTML </hx>
```

The "x" could be any number between 1 and 6 to indicate the level of the heading. The following XHTML illustrates the use of the heading element:

```
<?xml version="1.0" encoding="UTF-8"?>
<!DOCTYPE html PUBLIC "-//W3C//DTD/XHTML 1.0 Transitional//EN"
"http://www.w3.org/TR/xhtml1/DTD/xhtml1-transitional.dtd">
<html xmlns="http://www.w3.org/1999/xhtml" xml:lang="en" lang="en">
<head>
<title> Using Headings </title>
</head>
<body>
    <h1>Level 1 headings are the Largest</h1>
    <h2>Level 2 heading</h2>
    <h3>Level 3 heading</h3>
    <h4>Level 4 heading</h4>
    <h5>Level 5 heading</h5>
    <h6>Level 6 headings are the Smallest</h6>
</body>
</html>
```

The results of the above XHTML are in Figure 6.7.

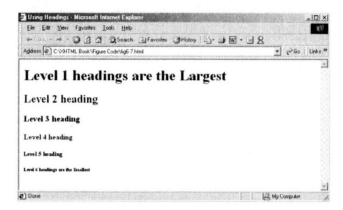

FIGURE 6.7: BASIC XHTML DOCUMENT USING HEADING ELEMENTS

DIVIDING SECTIONS, THE <DIV> ELEMENT

The <div> </div> element is used to divide an XHTML document into sections and allow information within that section to be aligned. The <div> element is very useful when using style sheets, but it is also is an effective way to handle a block of text when not using style sheets. The <div> element allows for aligning entire sections of text as well as adding a style to the same. Let's look at the following XHTML code that uses the <div> element:

```
<?xml version="1.0" encoding="UTF-8"?>
<!DOCTYPE html PUBLIC "-//W3C//DTD/XHTML 1.0 Transitional//EN"
"http://www.w3.org/TR/xhtml1/DTD/xhtml1-transitional.dtd">
<html xmlns="http://www.w3.org/1999/xhtml" xml:lang="en" lang="en">
<head>
<title> Using the div Element </title>
</head>
<body>
   <p>
      This is a basic XHTML document that has one paragraph and
      multiple divisions. They may be simple, but I think they
      will get the point across. This is the first paragraph.
   </p>
   <div align = "center" style = "color: blue; font-style: italic">
      This book is a practical approach to web design and coding.
      We believe that a person should have a good understanding
      of the basic concepts of design and a basic understanding
      of the language before using a WYSIWYG application to
```

```
      develop web pages. By developing this understanding of these
      concepts, you will be able to use your skill and creativity
      to control your designs. The best way to learn these basic
      concepts is by doing. If you want to keep up with current
      standards, you have to understand the code.
    </div>
    <div>
      This is the second division.
    </div>
    <div>
      This is the third division.
    </div>
  </body>
</html>
```

The results of the above XHTML are in Figure 6.8. Notice the space between the paragraph and the first <div>. Also, there is no space between the divisions.

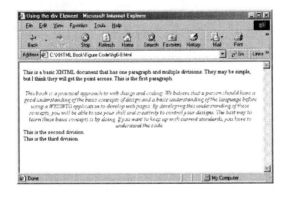

FIGURE 6.8: BASIC XHTML DOCUMENT USING <DIV> ELEMENTS

BLOCK QUOTES, THE <BLOCKQUOTE> ELEMENT

The <blockquote> </blockquote> element is a container element that encloses a block of text that is to be treated as a quote. Let's look at the following XHTML code that includes a <blockquote> element:

```
<?xml version="1.0" encoding="UTF-8"?>
<!DOCTYPE html PUBLIC "-//W3C//DTD/XHTML 1.0 Transitional//EN"
"http://www.w3.org/TR/xhtml1/DTD/xhtml1-transitional.dtd">
<html xmlns="http://www.w3.org/1999/xhtml" xml:lang="en" lang="en">
<head>
<title> Using the blockquote Element </title>
</head>
```

```
<body>
  <blockquote>
     "The Surgeon General of the United States has determined
     that the consumption of alcoholic beverages impairs your
     ability to drive a car or operate machinery, and may
     cause health problems"
  </blockquote>
  <p>
  Does that warning also apply to writing XHTML?
  </p>
</body>
</html>
```

The results of the above XHTML are in Figure 6.9. Notice the left and right margin indentation.

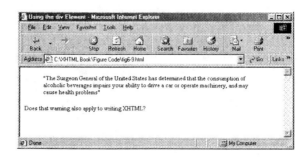

FIGURE 6.9: BASIC XHTML DOCUMENT USING <BLOCKQUOTE> ELEMENT

PREFORMATTED TEXT, THE <PRE> ELEMENT

The <pre> </pre> element is a container element that encloses a block of text that is preformatted. The <pre> tag identifies the text as preformatted and instructs the browser that it should be displayed as entered.

> tip: Use tabs in your preformatted text with caution since the number of characters for tab stops varies between browsers.

It is often used to display program listings or columnar data. Preformatted text is usually rendered in a monospaced font such as Courier. Let's look at the following XHTML code that includes a <pre> element:

```
<?xml version="1.0" encoding="UTF-8"?>
<!DOCTYPE html PUBLIC "-//W3C//DTD/XHTML 1.0 Transitional//EN"
```

```
"http://www.w3.org/TR/xhtml1/DTD/xhtml1-transitional.dtd">
<html xmlns="http://www.w3.org/1999/xhtml" xml:lang="en" lang="en">
<head>
<title> Using The pre Element </title>
</head>
<body>
   <pre>
                    M E M O R A N D U M


   Date       January 9, 2001
   To         CPT 250 Class
   From       Jeff Griffin, Computer Technology Department
   Subject    Activities for Lab 1 on Thursday January 11, 2001

   </pre>
</body>
</html>
```

The results of the above XHTML are in Figure 6.10.

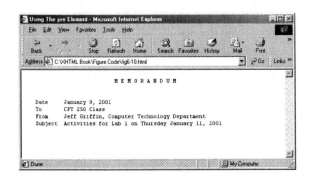

FIGURE 6.10: BASIC XHTML DOCUMENT USING THE <PRE> ELEMENT

LINE BREAKS, THE
 ELEMENT

The <br /> element is an empty element used to end a line of text and restarts after the tag beginning at the left margin. The <br /> element will also not include an extra space before or after the new line. It can be placed at any point within a line of text, and the break

tip: Since <br /> is an empty element and does not have a closing tag, it must be terminated properly by adding a space and a slash.

occurs when the tag is encountered. The following XHTML uses the <br> element in the paragraph example shown earlier to control the line breaks instead of leaving it up to the browser:

```
<?xml version="1.0" encoding="UTF-8"?>
<!DOCTYPE html PUBLIC "-//W3C//DTD/XHTML 1.0 Transitional//EN"
"http://www.w3.org/TR/xhtml1/DTD/xhtml1-transitional.dtd">
<html xmlns="http://www.w3.org/1999/xhtml" xml:lang="en" lang="en">
<head>
<title> Using Line Breaks </title>
</head>
<body>
    <p>
    This is a basic XHTML document that has two paragraphs.<br />
    They may be simple, but I think they will get the point
    across.<br />  This is the first paragraph.
    </p>
    <p>
    This is the second paragraph of our document. It has one
    blank line before it starts. I also included carriage returns,
    and blank lines.
    </p>
</body>
</html>
```

The results of the above XHTML are in Figure 6.11.

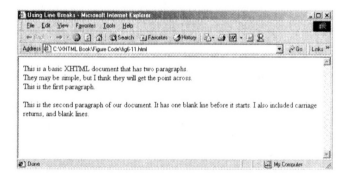

FIGURE 6.11: BASIC XHTML DOCUMENT USING LINE BREAKS

HORIZONTAL RULES, THE <HR> ELEMENT

The <hr /> element is an empty element used to draw horizontal lines to vertically separate sections of the document. The rule size, width, and alignment can also be controlled using different attributes. The following demonstrates using the <hr> element with various attributes:

```
<?xml version="1.0" encoding="UTF-8"?>
<!DOCTYPE html PUBLIC "-//W3C//DTD/XHTML 1.0 Transitional//EN"
"http://www.w3.org/TR/xhtml1/DTD/xhtml1-transitional.dtd">
<html xmlns="http://www.w3.org/1999/xhtml" xml:lang="en" lang="en">
<head>
<title> Using Horizontal Rules </title>
</head>
<body>
   <h3 align="center">Changing Width</h3>
   <hr align="center" size="1" width="10%" />
   <hr align="center" size="1" width="25%" />
   <hr align="center" size="1" width="50%" />
   <hr align="center" size="1" width="100%" />
   <h3 align="center">Changing Size</h3>
   <hr align="center" size="1" width="10%" />
   <hr align="center" size="5" width="25%" />
   <hr align="center" size="10" width="50%" />
   <hr align="center" size="15" width="100%" />
   <h3 align="center">Changing Alignment</h3>
   <hr align="left" size="1" width="10%" />
   <hr align="left" size="1" width="25%" />
   <hr align="right" size="1" width="50%" />
   <hr align="right" size="1" width="75%" />
   <h3 align="center">Two-dimensional</h3>
   <hr align="center" size="15" width="100%" noshade="noshade" />
</body>
</html>
```

The results of the above XHTML are in Figure 6.12.

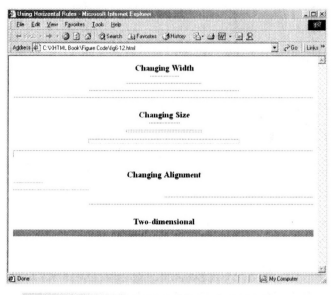

FIGURE 6.12: BASIC XHTML DOCUMENT USING HORIZONTAL RULES

FORMATTING TEXT WITH XHTML INLINE ELEMENTS

XHTML inline elements are used within the block-level elements that we have just finished discussing. The inline elements provide the ability to control specific formatting changes to text within the block-level elements. In XHTML, there are two types of inline elements:

- logical
- physical

LOGICAL STYLES

Logical style elements are used to describe how the text is used, not how it will be displayed. These elements allow the browser to determine the appearance of the text. The logical style elements are introduced below, and an example of their use can be seen in Figure 6.13.

ABBREVIATION, THE <ABBR> ELEMENT

The <abbr> </abbr> element is a descriptive element that indicates the abbreviation of a word. The text used with this element is usually rendered as italics or plain text. This element would be used as follows:

```
<abbr>IN</abbr>
```

ACRONYM, THE <ACRONYM> ELEMENT

The <acronym> </acronym> element is a descriptive element that indicates a word that is formed by using the initial letters of several words. The text used with this element is usually rendered as italics or plain text. This element would be used as follows:

```
<acronym>PDLC</acronym>
```

CITATION, THE <CITE> ELEMENT

The <cite> </cite> element is used to indicate a quotation or citation. The text used with this element is usually rendered as italics. This element would be used as follows:

```
<cite>Jeff Griffin</cite> was one of the authors who wrote the
second edition of the Web Page Workbook.
```

CODE, THE <CODE> ELEMENT

The <code> </code> element is a descriptive element that is used to indicate programming code. The text used with this element is usually rendered as a monospaced font. This element would be used as follows:

```
<code>If ( a == b)</code>
```

EMPHASIS, THE <EM> ELEMENT

The <em> </em> element is used to indicate that some text is to be emphasized. The text used with this element is usually rendered as italics. This element would be used as follows:

```
<p>Let's emphasize <em>XHTML</em>.</p>
```

STRONG, THE <STRONG> ELEMENT

The <strong> </strong> element is used to indicate that some text is to be emphasized more strongly than <em>. The text used with this element is usually rendered as bold. This element would be used as follows:

```
<p>Let's emphasize <em>XHTML</em>a little and <strong>XML</strong>
even more.</p>
```

SAMPLE, THE <SAMP> ELEMENT

The <samp> </samp> element is used to indicate sample text. The text used with this element is usually rendered as a monospaced font.

VARIABLE, THE <VAR> ELEMENT

The <var> </var> element is used to indicate a variable name that is to be replaced with some value. The text used with this element is usually rendered as italics.

Let's look at some XHTML and see how the logical style elements work. For example:

```
<?xml version="1.0" encoding="UTF-8"?>
<!DOCTYPE html PUBLIC "-//W3C//DTD/XHTML 1.0 Transitional//EN"
"http://www.w3.org/TR/xhtml1/DTD/xhtml1-transitional.dtd">
<html xmlns="http://www.w3.org/1999/xhtml" xml:lang="en" lang="en">
<head>
<title> Using Logical Style </title>
</head>
<body>
    <h1>Logical Styles</h1>
    <div>This is the <abbr>abbreviation</abbr> style.</div>
    <div>This is the <acronym>acronym</acronym> style.</div>
    <div>This is the <cite>citation</cite> style.</div>
    <div>This is the <code>code</code> style.</div>
    <div>This is the <em>emphasis</em> style.</div>
    <div>This is the <strong>strong</strong> style.</div>
    <div>This is the <samp>sample</sample> style.</div>
    <div>This is the <var>variable</var> style.</div>
</body>
</html>
```

The results of the above XHTML are in Figure 6.13.

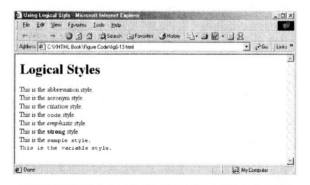

FIGURE 6.13: BASIC XHTML DOCUMENT USING LOGICAL STYLES

PHYSICAL STYLES

Physical style elements are used to specify exactly how the browser will display the text. These elements are fairly self-explanatory, so let's just see how they would be used in an XHTML document. For example:

```
<?xml version="1.0" encoding="UTF-8"?>
<!DOCTYPE html PUBLIC "-//W3C//DTD/XHTML 1.0 Transitional//EN"
"http://www.w3.org/TR/xhtml1/DTD/xhtml1-transitional.dtd">
<html xmlns="http://www.w3.org/1999/xhtml" xml:lang="en" lang="en">
<head>
<title> Using Physical Style </title>
</head>
<body>
   <h1>Physical Styles</h1>
   <div>This is the <big>big</big> style.</div>
   <div>This is the <b>bold</b> style.</div>
   <div>This is the <i>italic</i> style.</div>
   <div>This is the <u>underline</u> style.</div>
   <div>This is the <small>small</small> style.</div>
   <div>This is the <strike>strikethrough</strike> style.</div>
   <div>This is the <sub>subscript</sub> style.</div>
   <div>This is the <sup>superscript</sup> style.
</div>
   <div>This is the <tt>true type</tt> style.</div>
</body>
</html>
```

The results of the above XHTML are in Figure 6.14.

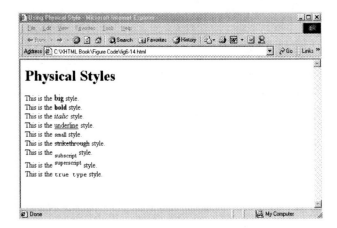

FIGURE 6.14: BASIC XHTML DOCUMENT USING PHYSICAL STYLES

USING LIST ELEMENTS TO FORMAT DOCUMENT TEXT

Lists are used in all forms of communication to add clarity and to draw attention to important information quickly. We use lists every day to keep track of things to do, a shopping list, or instructions on how to make something. Lists can also be created in XHTML by using list elements, which are used to organize, or logically group text into easily understandable lists. Remember, people have a short attention span when viewing Web pages, so it is important to make the text easy to navigate and understand. We can add this clarity and logical order by using lists.

In an XHTML document, three types of lists are available:

- Ordered lists
- Unordered lists
- Definition lists

Let's start by looking at the <li> element, which is common to creating both ordered and unordered lists.

LIST ITEM, THE <LI> ELEMENT

The <li> </li> element is a container element that will enclose text that is to be treated as a list item in either an ordered or unordered list. The following is an example of how the <li> element would be used:

```
<li>Analyze the problem</li>
<li>Design the logic</li>
<li>Code the program</li>
<li>Test and Debug program</li>
<li>Create program documentation</li>
```

Before we can display this list, we must combine the <li> element with the ordered list or unordered list element.

ORDERED LISTS, THE <OL> ELEMENT

The <ol> </ol> element is a container element that will enclose a block of text that is to be treated as a list. Ordered lists are sometimes referred to as numbered lists. An ordered list is used to display ordered items or sequential steps. Each item represents a

> tip: Since items in an ordered list are going to be numbered sequentially, it is important that they be listed in the correct order.

step in a given operation or procedure. Each item in an ordered list is typically labeled with numbers, but it could also be labeled with letters or Roman numerals. Let's look at the following XHTML code that includes the <li> and <ol> elements to create an ordered list:

```
<?xml version="1.0" encoding="UTF-8"?>
<!DOCTYPE html PUBLIC "-//W3C//DTD/XHTML 1.0 Transitional//EN"
"http://www.w3.org/TR/xhtml1/DTD/xhtml1-transitional.dtd">
<html xmlns="http://www.w3.org/1999/xhtml" xml:lang="en" lang="en">
<head>
<title> Using Ordered Lists </title>
</head>
<body>
    <h3>Program Development Life Cycle</h3>
    <ol>
       <li>Analyze the problem</li>
       <li>Design the logic</li>
       <li>Code the program</li>
       <li>Test and Debug program</li>
       <li>Create program documentation</li>
    </ol>
</body>
</html>
```

The results of the above XHTML are in Figure 6.15.

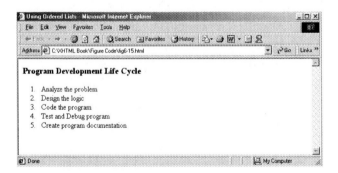

FIGURE 6.15: BASIC XHTML DOCUMENT USING AN ORDERED LIST

The Ordered List type Attribute

By default, the label for each item in an ordered list is a standard Arabic numeral. This can be changed by using the <ol> tag's type attribute. For example, if you wanted each item labeled with Roman numerals, you would use the following:

```
<ol type = "I">
```

There are five possible values for the *type attribute* to define what type of numbering to use on an ordered list. They are

- Arabic numerals is the default (numbers a list 1, 2, 3, and so on)
- "I" to specify uppercase Roman numerals (numbers a list I, II, III, IV, and so on)
- "i" to specify lowercase Roman numerals (numbers a list i, ii, iii, iv, and so on)
- "a" to specify lowercase letters (numbers a list a, b, c, d, e, and so on)
- "A" to specify uppercase letters (numbers a list A, B, C, D, E, and so on

Let's look at the following XHTML code to create three ordered lists using different type values:

```
<?xml version="1.0" encoding="UTF-8"?>
<!DOCTYPE html PUBLIC "-//W3C//DTD/XHTML 1.0 Transitional//EN"
"http://www.w3.org/TR/xhtml1/DTD/xhtml1-transitional.dtd">
<html xmlns="http://www.w3.org/1999/xhtml" xml:lang="en" lang="en">
<head>
<title> Using Ordered Lists </title>
</head>
<body>
    <p>Ordered List Using Arabic Numerals</p>
    <ol>
        <li>Analyze the problem</li>
        <li>Design the logic</li>
        <li>Code the program</li>
        <li>Test and Debug program</li>
        <li>Create program documentation</li>
    </ol>
    <p>Ordered List Using Roman Numerals</p>
    <ol type = "I">
        <li>Analyze the problem</li>
        <li>Design the logic</li>
        <li>Code the program</li>
        <li>Test and Debug program</li>
        <li>Create program documentation</li>
    </ol>
    <p>Ordered List Using Letters</p>
    <ol type = "A">
        <li>Analyze the problem</li>
        <li>Design the logic</li>
        <li>Code the program</li>
        <li>Test and Debug program</li>
        <li>Create program documentation</li>
```

```
    </ol>
  </body>
</html>
```

The results of the above XHTML are in Figure 6.16.

UNORDERED LISTS, THE <UL> ELEMENT

The <ul> </ul> element is a container element that will enclose a block of text that is to be treated as an unordered list. Unordered lists are sometimes referred to as bulleted lists. An unordered list is used to provide logical organization for the displayed text; in other words, the order is not significant. Each item in an unordered list is typically labeled with a bullet (disc), but this could be changed to a circle or square. Let's look at the following XHTML code that includes the <li> and <ul> elements to create an unordered list:

note: When using strict XHTML 1.0, the type attribute is replaced with style sheets. Cascading style sheets are covered in Chapter 12.

```
<?xml version="1.0" encoding="UTF-8"?>
<!DOCTYPE html PUBLIC "-//W3C//DTD/XHTML 1.0 Transitional//EN"
"http://www.w3.org/TR/xhtml1/DTD/xhtml1-transitional.dtd">
<html xmlns="http://www.w3.org/1999/xhtml" xml:lang="en" lang="en">
<head>
<title> Using Unordered Lists </title>
</head>
<body>
    <h3>My Antique Cars</h3>
    <ul>
        <li>1911 Ford Model T</li>
        <li>1913 Chalmers Torpedo Model 30</li>
    </ul>
</body>
</html>
```

The results of the above XHTML are in Figure 6.17.

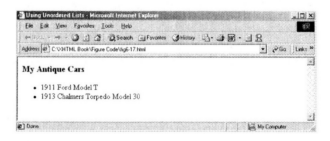

FIGURE 6.17: BASIC XHTML DOCUMENT USING AN UNORDERED LIST

The Unordered List type Attribute

By default, the label for each item in an ordered list is a standard bullet or disc. This can be changed by using the <ul> tag's type attribute. For example, if you wanted each item labeled with a square, you would use the following:

```
<ul type = "square">
```

There are three possible values for the type attribute to define what type of bullet to use on an unordered list. They are

- solid disc, which is the default
- "square" to specify that a square is used
- "circle" to specify that a circle is used

Let's look at the following XHTML code to create three unordered lists using different type values:

```
<?xml version="1.0" encoding="UTF-8"?>
<!DOCTYPE html PUBLIC "-//W3C//DTD/XHTML 1.0 Transitional//EN"
"http://www.w3.org/TR/xhtml1/DTD/xhtml1-transitional.dtd">
<html xmlns="http://www.w3.org/1999/xhtml" xml:lang="en" lang="en">
<head>
<title> Using Unordered Lists </title>
</head>
<body>
   <p>Unordered List Using Disc</p>
   <ul>
       <li>Oranges</li>
       <li>Apples</li>
       <li>Banana</li>
       <li>Strawberry</li>
   </ul>
<p>Unordered List Using Square</p>
   <ul type = "square">
       <li>Oranges</li>
       <li>Apples</li>
       <li>Banana</li>
       <li>Strawberry</li>
   </ul>
<p>Unordered List Using Circle</p>
   <ul type = "circle">
       <li>Oranges</li>
       <li>Apples</li>
       <li>Banana</li>
       <li>Strawberry</li>
   </ul>
</body>
</html>
```

The results of the above XHTML are in Figure 6.18.

FIGURE 6.18: BASIC XHTML DOCUMENT USING DIFFERENT TYPE ATTRIBUTE VALUES

NESTING LISTS

A list could also contain another list within it; this is referred to as "nesting." We refer to the first list as the outer list and the *nested list* as the inner list, which should help us keep things straight. By nesting a list structure within another, the nested list becomes an item of the outer list and will be indented from the other parts of the list. It is also possible to nest different types of lists. Let's look at the following XHTML code that includes an ordered nested list within an ordered list:

note: When using strict XHTML 1.0, the type attribute is replaced with style sheets. Cascading style sheets are covered in Chapter 12.

tip: Remember to close the inner list with the appropriate closing tag before closing the outer list.

```
<?xml version="1.0" encoding="UTF-8"?>
<!DOCTYPE html PUBLIC "-//W3C//DTD/XHTML 1.0 Transitional//EN"
"http://www.w3.org/TR/xhtml1/DTD/xhtml1-transitional.dtd">
<html xmlns="http://www.w3.org/1999/xhtml" xml:lang="en" lang="en">
```

```
<head>
<title> Using Nested Ordered Lists </title>
</head>
<body>
   <h3>This is a nested ordered list</h3>
       <ol>
           <li>First item outer list</li>
           <li>Second item outer list has a nested list </li>
           <ol>
               <li>First item inner list</li>
               <li>Second item inner list</li>
               <li>Third item inner list</li>
           </ol>
           <li>Third item outer list</li>
           <li>Fourth item outer list</li>
       </ol>
</body>
</html>
```

The results of the above XHTML are in Figure 6.19.

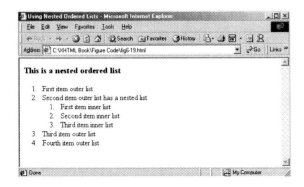

FIGURE 6.19: BASIC XHTML DOCUMENT WITH NESTED ORDERED LISTS

Next, let's take a look at what a nested unordered list would look like.

```
<?xml version="1.0" encoding="UTF-8"?>
<!DOCTYPE html PUBLIC "-//W3C//DTD/XHTML 1.0 Transitional//EN"
"http://www.w3.org/TR/xhtml1/DTD/xhtml1-transitional.dtd">
<html xmlns="http://www.w3.org/1999/xhtml" xml:lang="en" lang="en">
<head>
<title> Using Nested Unordered Lists </title>
</head>
<body>
   <h3>This is a nested unordered list</h3>
       <ul>
```

```
            <li>First item outer list</li>
            <li>Second item outer list has a nested list </li>
              <ul>
                  <li>First item inner list</li>
                  <li>Second item inner list</li>
                  <li>Third item inner list</li>
              </ul>
            <li>Third item outer list</li>
            <li>Fourth item outer list</li>
        </ul>
</body>
</html>
```

The results of the above XHTML are in Figure 6.20.

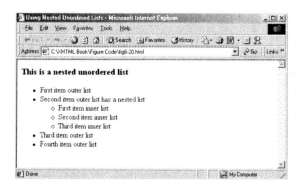

FIGURE 6.20: BASIC XHTML DOCUMENT WITH NESTED UNORDERED LISTS

Notice that the item label for the outer list is a solid disc and for the inner list it is a circle. What would happen to the label if we added another list to the inner list? Let's see by running the following XHTML:

```
<?xml version="1.0" encoding="UTF-8"?>
<!DOCTYPE html PUBLIC "-//W3C//DTD/XHTML 1.0 Transitional//EN"
"http://www.w3.org/TR/xhtml1/DTD/xhtml1-transitional.dtd">
<html xmlns="http://www.w3.org/1999/xhtml" xml:lang="en" lang="en">
<head>
<title> Using Nested Unordered Lists </title>
</head>
<body>
    <h3>This is a nested unordered list</h3>
        <ul>
            <li>First item outer list</li>
            <li>Second item outer list has a nested list </li>
              <ul>
```

```
                <li>First item inner list</li>
                <li>Second item inner list</li>
                <li>Third item inner list</li>
                  <ul>
                        <li>First item in nested inner list</li>
                        <li>Second item in nested inner list</li>
             </ul>   </ul>
          <li>Third item outer list</li>
          <li>Fourth item outer list</li>
        </ul>
</body>
</html>
```

The results of the above XHTML are in Figure 6.21. The item label for the third list is a square.

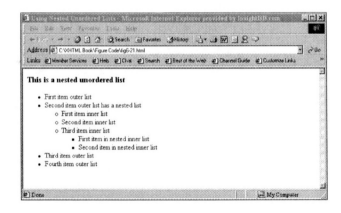

FIGURE 6.21: BASIC XHTML DOCUMENT WITH TWO NESTED UNORDERED LISTS

DEFINITION LISTS

Finally, let's look at the last of the list types, the definition list. As the name implies, it is used to display a term and its definition. Definition lists are unordered lists and are useful to display information in a dictionary-like style. The definition list has two parts, which are enclosed within the <dl> element, a definition term and a definition description.

note: When nesting either ordered or unordered lists, the nested list will be indented.

DEFINITION LIST, THE <DL> ELEMENT

The <dl> </dl> element is a container element that will enclose a block of text that is formatted with the <dt> and <dd> elements. The <dl> element creates the list.

DEFINITION TERM, THE <DT> ELEMENT

The <dt> </dt> element is a container element that will enclose text that is to be treated as the term to be defined. The following is an example of how the <dt> element would be used:

```
<dt>Analyze the problem</dt>
```

DEFINITION DESCRIPTION, THE <DD> ELEMENT

The <dd> </dd> element is a container element that will enclose text that is to be treated as the definition of the term. The following is an example of how the <dd> element would be used:

```
<dd>Analyze the problem</dd>
```

The following XHTML combines these three elements to create a definition list:

```
<?xml version="1.0" encoding="UTF-8"?>
<!DOCTYPE html PUBLIC "-//W3C//DTD/XHTML 1.0 Transitional//EN"
"http://www.w3.org/TR/xhtml1/DTD/xhtml1-transitional.dtd">
<html xmlns="http://www.w3.org/1999/xhtml" xml:lang="en" lang="en">
<head>
<title> Using Definition Lists </title>
</head>
<body>
    <p>Here is a definition list</p>
    <dl>
        <dt>Orange</dt>
          <dd>Juicy citrus fruit with reddish yellow rind</dd>
        <dt>Apple</dt>
          <dd>A rounded fruit with firm white flesh</dd>
        <dt>Banana</dt>
          <dd>A yellow or reddish finger-shaped fruit</dd>
    </dl>
</body>
</html>
```

The results of the above XHTML are in Figure 6.22. Notice how the definition term is placed on its own line and aligned at the left margin, while the definition description is placed on the next line indented.

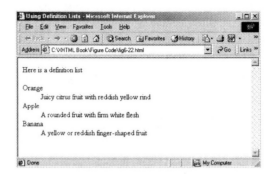

FIGURE 6.22: BASIC XHTML DOCUMENT USING A DEFINITION LIST

CHAPTER SUMMARY

In this chapter, we learned how to create well-formed XHTML documents using the correct document structure and element syntax. This chapter introduced XHTML elements that controlled how the browser would render text on the screen. We learned how to apply block-level elements to create paragraphs, divisions, horizontal rules, and line breaks to separate sections of the XHTML document.

When formatting XHTML documents, inline elements are used to control specific formatting changes to text within block-level elements. This chapter discussed two types of inline elements, logical and physical. Logical style elements are used to describe how the text is used, not how it will be displayed. Physical style elements are used to specify exactly how the browser will display the text. We also learned how lists could be used within an XHTML document to add clarity and draw attention to important information quickly.

KEY TERMS

body element	lists
break element	logical styles
comments	nested lists
document header	paragraph align attribute
document information	paragraph element
document type definition (DTD)	physical styles
element	type attribute
head element	XHTML element

XHTML TABLE TAG SUMMARY

Tag	Attribute(s)	Use/Values
\<html\>	xmlns	= url—Identifies the xml namespace
	xml:lang	= en—Indicates language when used as an XHTML document
	lang	= en—Indicates language when used as a HTML document
\<head\>		Contains elements that provide information about the page
\<title\>		Provides a title to the XHTML document
\<script\>		Embeds scripts into XHTML documents
\<link\>	rel	
	href	
\<base\>	href	
	target	

<style>		Creates styles for entire Web page
<meta>	name	= author, keywords, description, generator, formatter, copyright
	content	Information associated with name attribute
	http-equiv	
<body>		Document body
<p>	align	left, center, right, justify
<hr>	align	left, center, right
	size	
	width	=n%, width in percentage of screen
<hx>..<hx>		x could be any number between 1 and 6 to indicate the level of the heading
<ol>	type	= "1" i—Arabic numerals is the default (numbers a list 1, 2, 3, and so on)
		= "I"—Specifies uppercase Roman numerals (numbers a list I, II, III, IV and so on)
		= "i"—Specifies lowercase Roman numerals (numbers a list i, ii, iii, iv and so on)
		= "a"—Specifies lowercase letters (numbers a list a, b, c, d, e and so on)
		= "A"—Specifies uppercase letters (numbers a list A, B, C, D, and so on)
<ul>	type	No type—solid disc, which is the default
		= "square"—Specifies that a square is used
		= "circle"—Specifies that a circle is used
<div>		Divides document into sections
<!-- -->		Adds comments to clarify parts of document

REVIEW QUESTIONS

1. What can be used to edit an XHTML document?
2. What XHTML element is used to insert a line across a Web page?
3. What is the basic structure of an XHTML element?
4. List and explain the three XHTML elements that define the overall structure of an XHTML document.
5. How many levels of headings are supported in XHTML?
6. What is the <pre> element used for?
7. What is the difference between physical and logical styles?
8. What is the syntax for inserting a horizontal rule across the entire Web page?
9. What XHTML element defines a paragraph?
10. What is the difference between a block element and an inline element?

EXERCISES

1. Create an XHTML document that is your résumé. It should include sections for objectives, education, employment, and references. Use the following elements:
   - Headings
   - Paragraphs
   - Horizontal rules
   - Unordered lists
2. Using the preface of this book, create a Web page using XHTML that would tell the reader what this book is about. This page should also include a list of chapters and what they are about.
3. Create a personal Web page that utilizes the elements discussed in this chapter. This page should include sections that tell the reader about your
   - Family
   - Life before college
   - Life in college

   Utilize the following XHTML elements:
   - Headings
   - Paragraphs
   - Lists
   - Horizontal rules

- Block quote
- Logical styles—emphasis
- Physical styles—bold, and underline

4. Using the text found below, create a Web page that utilizes the elements discussed in this chapter. Be creative, using the following elements:
    - Headings
    - Paragraphs
    - Lists
    - Horizontal rules
    - Block Quote
    - Logical Styles—emphasis
    - Physical Styles—bold, and underline
    - The following text:

Mary Ellen's Flower Garden

Mary Ellen's Flower Garden is set on the side of a mostly shaded hill. Filled with perennials, the garden boasts blooming flowers of one kind or another from early April through September. The earliest blooms are the bulbs that greet spring. Brightly colored tulips, hyacinths, and crocuses dot the hillside as the last flakes of winter melt away.

The highest corner of the hillside enjoys the most sun being warmed by the early morning rays and again with the last sun of the evening. It is on this spot that the Fiesta daisies have found their home, spreading wherever they want, crowding out the Black-Eyed Susans they now surround.

The foxgloves grow taller before opening their throaty flowers, which provide a safe haven for fat bumblebees seeking their sweet nectar. And scattered up and down the hill are the carefree daylilies whose blooms follow the sun as it moves encircling the hill each day.

Sloping down the hill into the shade, the delicate columbine have long since bloomed and turned to seed. Still deeper into the shade are the dark purple irises with their long, slender green foliage framing their beauty.

Columbine
Black-Eyed Susan
Iris

Columbine
This easy-to-grow perennial is loved by hummingbirds. Plant in full sun or partial shade for blooms in May and June.

Black-Eyed Susan
Orange coneflowers that grow on 2- to 3-foot stems; these do best in full sun. These are great flowers for the wild garden, producing blooms through July and August.

Iris
There are more than 200 species available in a vast array of colors. Irises are easy to grow and most need sunlight. Plant the rhizomes in the fall for blooms in early May.

PROJECT

At this point, we need to begin the construction of each of the pages on our site diagram. We need to make sure that each of the pages we construct follows the organizational structure we developed in Chapter 5:

- Create each page on your site diagram. Make sure to follow the structure developed in Chapter 5. Make sure to enter all textual content.

ADDITIONAL REFERENCES

XHTMLguru.com, http://www.xhtmlguru.com
W3Schools.com—XHTML, http://www.w3schools.com/xhtml
HTML compendium.org, http://www.htmlcompendium.org
HTML Home Page, http://www.w3.org/MarkUp

chapter 7
hypertext links

CHAPTER OVERVIEW

In this chapter, we will learn how to add hypertext links to our Web pages. Hypertext links are what makes accessing other documents or another section of the same document from our Web pages possible. Without links, the Web would be just a collection of documents. It is this linking of documents in a non-linear fashion that provides the real power of the Web. Although links provide users easy access to other documents, correctly implementing them can be a source of frustration. Only one element is required to add a hypertext link to a Web page and one attribute to enable the link to function properly. We will discuss the use and difference between absolute and relative linking.

CHAPTER OBJECTIVES

- Understand what absolute links are and how they work
- Understand what relative links are and how they work
- Link to other sections of the same document
- Understand the different parts of a Uniform Resource Locator (URL)

HYPERTEXT LINKS

What's a hypertext link and why should we use one? Quite simply, a *hypertext link* is a connection between one resource and another. It enables users to easily navigate a document or be taken to related documents by clicking a word or phrase. These links are commonplace; people know that when they see the familiar blue underlined text, they can click on it and be taken somewhere else in the document or to another document altogether. Once the link has been followed, the link text will appear as a light purple color. The color of hypertext links can be customized, but remember that everyone who is familiar with the Web recognizes that the default blue underlined text will take them somewhere.

Hypertext links can lead to resources in various locations:

- Documents on different servers
- Documents within the same directory
- Documents in a different directory
- Locations within the same document

This chapter will explore how to create links that will cover all of the above situations. Figure 7.1 illustrates what a hypertext link looks like within a simple paragraph.

Creating hypertext links in XHTML uses one element and two different attributes and sometimes both attributes together. There are also other optional attributes, but they are seldom used. Links can sometimes be complicated and confusing. What do you need to

FIGURE 7.1: SIMPLE HYPERTEXT LINK

know before you can create a hypertext link? You need two things: the location of the file you want to link to and instructions for how the link actually works. So, let's keep it simple and start by looking at the anchor element, which is used to actually create the hypertext link and its two common attributes.

CREATING A HYPERTEXT LINK, THE <A> ELEMENT

In order to create a link, the anchor tags, <a> and </a>, are used. All attributes are contained within this element. The anchor element allows an XHTML document to attach or anchor itself to another document in the various locations discussed earlier. The text that is between the opening <a> tag and the closing </a> tag is the link that will be highlighted and underlined for the user to click. The simplest use of the anchor element is

```
<a>Previous Page</a>
```

Will this create a link for us? No, the above XHTML will not create a link, but it will also not cause an error. The words "Previous Page" will be displayed by the browser but will not have the familiar blue color or underline. In order for a link to function properly, the anchor element must include either an "href" or a "name" attribute, and it might even need both attributes. The anchor element can be either the source or the target of a link. Let's look into how these attributes will allow us to complete the creation of our link.

href Attribute

The *href attribute* stands for **h**ypertext **ref**erence; to put it in simpler terms, it is the location of the document that is to be linked to. The value of the href attribute is usually a *Uniform Resource Locator (URL)*, which would be the location of the document that is to be linked. For example, if you wanted to provide a link on a page to the publisher of this book, you would use the following:

> tip: Always use double-quotes around the URL.

```
<a href = "http://www.fbeedle.com">Click for the FBA home page.</a>
```

name Attribute

The *name attribute* is used to identify certain points within a document that are available to be used as targets of links. This attribute can be used to provide users a way to easily navigate large Web pages. Providing users with an index that includes hyperlinks enables them to move to various parts of the document. We will see how to use this attribute later in the chapter.

RELATIVE VS. ABSOLUTE LINKS

Relative and absolute links are two types of links that can be created in XHTML documents.

ABSOLUTE LINKS

The *absolute link* is the most common link and is used when we want to load a document that is located on a different server. The complete address to the destination must be provided. The link could also be absolute even if the documents are located on the same server. It will depend on how complete the address is that is provided for the href attribute.

> tip: When the protocol is not included in the hyperlink's URL, the server will assume it is a relative link.

The following XHTML illustrates the use of an absolute link:

```
<?xml version="1.0" encoding="UTF-8"?>
<!DOCTYPE html PUBLIC "-//W3C//DTD/XHTML 1.0 Transitional//EN"
"http://www.w3.org/TR/xhtml1/DTD/xhtml1-transitional.dtd">
<html xmlns="http://www.w3.org/1999/xhtml" xml:lang="en" lang="en">
<head>
<title> A Basic Absolute Link </title>
</head>
<body>
<a href="http://www.fbeedle.com">Click here for the FBA home
page</a>
</body>
</html>
```

The results of the above XHTML are in Figure 7.2. Notice that the text between the tags is what is displayed and is highlighted and underlined. I have also placed the cursor over the link; notice that by doing so, the address for the link is displayed in the browser status bar. If this link were clicked, it would take you to the Franklin, Beedle & Associates Website.

RELATIVE LINKING

The *relative link* is used when we want to load a document that is located on the same server. These documents could be in the same folder or in different folders. The address is relative to the document that contains the link.

When working with relative links, it is important to understand the directory (folder) structure we are working with. You may already know some of these terms, but let's review. The top-level directory of a disk is referred to as the root directory. This directory can also contain subdirectories. The terms *parent* and *child* directories are often used to describe the relationship between directories.

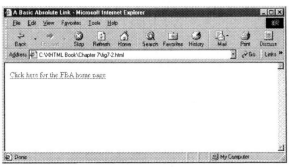

FIGURE 7.2: USING AN ABSOLUTE LINK

tip: The Uniform Resource Locator (URL) can be the address of any available resource on the Web.

To locate a file using a relative link, we must navigate the directory structure, which is referred to as a *path*. For example, Figure 7.3 illustrates a directory structure.

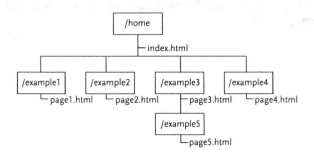

FIGURE 7.3: A DIRECTORY STRUCTURE

When using relative links, the path name is specified using the Unix style. In Unix, directories are separated using a *forward slash (/)*, not a *backslash (\)* as used in Windows. The two periods (..) could also be used as part of the path name to refer to the directory before the current one.

Using the directory structure in Figure 7.3, let's look at some examples of what path would be used in the href attribute for a given situation, if the current directory was example5:

```
href ="page5.html"
```

The referenced file is in the current directory.

```
href="../page3.html"
```

The referenced file is located one level above the current directory.

```
href="../../index.html"
```

The referenced file is located two levels above the current directory.

```
href="../example1/page1.html"
```

The referenced file is located in the directory example1 and one level above the current directory.

Let's try some relative links.

LINKING USING FILES IN THE SAME FOLDER

We will use the anchor element and attributes to create a relative link using files that are located in the same folder. The href attribute will be supplied with the name of the file that is to be loaded. No other directory information is supplied with the file name. When no directory information is supplied with the file name, the browser knows to look for the file in the same directory as the source page.

1. Type the following using your choice of editor and save it as linkpage1.html. We will add a link in the next step.

```
<?xml version="1.0" encoding="UTF-8"?>
<!DOCTYPE html PUBLIC "-//W3C//DTD/XHTML 1.0 Transitional//EN"
"http://www.w3.org/TR/xhtml1/DTD/xhtml1-transitional.dtd">
<html xmlns="http://www.w3.org/1999/xhtml" xml:lang="en" lang="en">
<head>
<title> Relative Link - Same Folder </title>
</head>
<body>
   <h2 align="center">This is Page 1</h2>
</body>
</html>
```

2. Next, add a paragraph to our document by placing a <p> element below the <h2> element. This indicates to the browser that a paragraph will begin. Place a </p> tag above the </body> tag to close the paragraph. Add some text to the paragraph, so it looks like the following:

```
<p>
    This is page one using a relative link. We can link to page
    two to find out more about the flower columbine.
</p>
```

3. Now we can add the link to page two using the <a> element and the attribute href, which is placed inside the <p> element. Add the anchor element as follows:

```
<p>
    This is page one using a relative link. We can
    link to page two to find out more about the flower
    <a href="linkpage2.html">columbine.</a>
</p>
```

Before we go to the next step, make sure that you save your work!

4. Next, open the file linkpage1.html and save it as linkpage2.html. Make the following changes to linkpage2.html:

```
<h2 align="center">This is Page 2</h2>

<p>
    Columbine: This easy-to-grow perennial is loved by
    hummingbirds. Plant in full sun or partial shade for blooms
    in May and June.
</p>
```

5. Let's add another link on page two that will take us back to page one. Add the following to linkpage2.html:

```
<p>
    Go back to <a href="linkpage1.html">page one.</a>
</p>
```

6. Save the document linkpage2.html.
7. The completed XHTML documents should resemble the following:

XHTML for page one:

```
<?xml version="1.0" encoding="UTF-8"?>
<!DOCTYPE html PUBLIC "-//W3C//DTD/XHTML 1.0 Transitional//EN"
"http://www.w3.org/TR/xhtml1/DTD/xhtml1-transitional.dtd">
<html xmlns="http://www.w3.org/1999/xhtml" xml:lang="en" lang="en">
<head>
<title> Relative Link - Same Folder </title>
</head>
<body>
    <h2 align="center">This is Page 1</h2>
    <p>
      This is page one using a relative link. We can
      link to page two to find out more about the flower
      <a href="linkpage2.html">columbine.</a>
    </p>
</body>
</html>
```

XHTML for page two:

```
<?xml version="1.0" encoding="UTF-8"?>
<!DOCTYPE html PUBLIC "-//W3C//DTD/XHTML 1.0 Transitional//EN"
"http://www.w3.org/TR/xhtml1/DTD/xhtml1-transitional.dtd">
<html xmlns="http://www.w3.org/1999/xhtml" xml:lang="en" lang="en">
<head>
<title> Relative Link - Same Folder </title>
</head>
<body>
    <h2 align="center">This is Page 2</h2>
    <p>
      Columbine: This easy-to-grow perennial is loved by
      hummingbirds. Plant in full sun or partial shade for blooms
      in May and June.
    </p>
    <p>
      Go back to <a href="linkpage1.html">page one.</a>
    </p>
</body>
</html>
```

8. In the browser, select Open from the File menu to open linkpage1.html. Your screen should resemble Figure 7.4. You will notice that the name of the flower is highlighted and underlined.

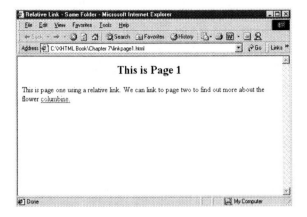

FIGURE 7.4: RELATIVE LINK WITH FILES IN SAME FOLDER—PAGE ONE

9. Click on the underlined name of the flower, and linkpage2 will be loaded and displayed. Your screen should resemble Figure 7.5.

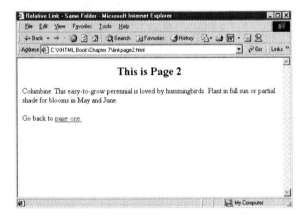

FIGURE 7.5: RELATIVE LINK WITH FILES IN SAME FOLDER—PAGE TWO

10. On page two where it says "Go back to page one," click on the highlighted and underlined words "page one" and you will go back to page one.

Notice that when you return to page one that the color of the link has changed to a lighter color. What happens if the browser cannot find the linked file? Figure 7.6 shows what your screen might look like.

LINKING USING FILES IN DIFFERENT FOLDERS

We will use the anchor element and attributes to create a relative link using files that are located in different folders.

1. On your computer, create a directory called home. Within the home directory, create a subdirectory called flowers.

2. Type the following using your choice of editor and save it as index.html in the home directory. We will add a link in the next steps.

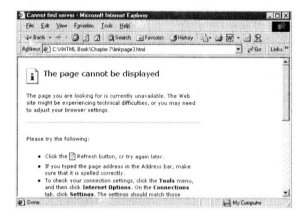

FIGURE 7.6: RELATIVE LINK WITH FILE NOT FOUND

```
<?xml version="1.0" encoding="UTF-8"?>
<!DOCTYPE html PUBLIC "-//W3C//DTD/XHTML 1.0 Transitional//EN"
"http://www.w3.org/TR/xhtml1/DTD/xhtml1-transitional.dtd">
<html xmlns="http://www.w3.org/1999/xhtml" xml:lang="en" lang="en">
<head>
<title> Relative Link - Different Folders </title>
</head>
<body>
   <h2 align="center">Mary Ellen's Flower Garden</h2>
</body>
</html>
```

3. Next, add a paragraph to our document by placing a <p> element below the <h2> element. Place a </p> tag above the </body> tag to close the paragraph. Let's make this interesting; place an unordered list of flower names after the paragraph. Your XHTML should look like the following:

```
<p>
     Please select the flower you wish to know more about.
```

```
</p>
<ul>
  <li>Columbine</li>
  <li>Black-Eyed Susan</li>
  <li>Iris</li>
  <li>Daylily</li>
  <li>Foxglove</li>
</ul>
```

4. Now we can add the link to the flower pages using the <a> element and the attribute href. Add the anchor element as follows:

```
<ul>
  <li><a href="../flowers/columbine.html">Columbine</a></li>
  <li><a href="../flowers/black.html">Black-Eyed Susan</a></li>
  <li><a href="../flowers/iris.html">Iris</a></li>
  <li><a href="../flowers/day.html">Daylily</a></li>
  <li><a href="../flowers/fox.html">Foxglove</a></li>
</ul>
```

Before we go to the next step, make sure that you save your work!

5. Next, type the following using your choice of editor and save it as columbine.html in the flowers directory.

```
<?xml version="1.0" encoding="UTF-8"?>
<!DOCTYPE html PUBLIC "-//W3C//DTD/XHTML 1.0 Transitional//EN"
"http://www.w3.org/TR/xhtml1/DTD/xhtml1-transitional.dtd">
<html xmlns="http://www.w3.org/1999/xhtml" xml:lang="en" lang="en">
<head>
<title> Relative Link - Flowers Folder </title>
</head>
<body>
   <p>
     Columbine: This easy-to-grow perennial is loved by
     hummingbirds. Plant in full sun or partial shade for blooms
     in May and June.
   </p>
   <p>
     Go back to the <a href="../index.html">flower list.</a>
   </p>
</body>
</html>
```

6. If you want all of the links to work, repeat step 5 using the following information and save with the appropriate file names:

black.html

Black-Eyed Susan: Orange coneflowers that grow on 2- to 3-foot stems do best in full sun. These are great flowers for the wild garden, producing blooms through July and August.

iris.html

Iris: There are more than 200 species available in a vast array of colors. Irises are easy to grow, and most need sunlight. Plant the rhizomes in the fall for blooms in early May.

day.html

Daylily: Daylilies are perennials that earned their name because each bloom opens, matures, and withers in 24 hours or less. Daylilies do well in partial shade and require little care.

fox.html

Foxglove: Most foxglove are biennials that grow on tall, strong stems in partial shade. They are easy to care for and flower during May and June.

7. The completed XHTML document index.html should resemble the following:

```
<?xml version="1.0" encoding="UTF-8"?>
<!DOCTYPE html PUBLIC "-//W3C//DTD/XHTML 1.0 Transitional//EN"
"http://www.w3.org/TR/xhtml1/DTD/xhtml1-transitional.dtd">
<html xmlns="http://www.w3.org/1999/xhtml" xml:lang="en" lang="en">
<head>
<title> Relative Link - Different Folders </title>
</head>
<body>
  <h2 align="center">Mary Ellen's Flower Garden</h2>
  <p>
    Please select the flower you wish to know more about.
  </p>
  <ul>
   <li><a href="../flowers/columbine.html">Columbine</a></li>
   <li><a href="../flowers/black.html">Black-Eyed Susan</a></li>
   <li><a href="../flowers/iris.html">Iris</a></li>
   <li><a href="../flowers/day.html">Daylily</a></li>
   <li><a href="../flowers/fox.html">Foxglove</a></li>
  </ul>
</body>
</html>
```

8. In the browser, select Open from the File menu to open index.html in the home directory. Your screen should resemble Figure 7.7. You will notice that the name of each flower in the list is highlighted and underlined.

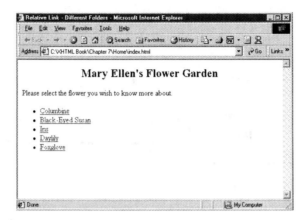

FIGURE 7.7: RELATIVE LINK; FILES IN DIFFERENT FOLDERS—INDEX PAGE

9. Click on the flower columbine, and this flower's page will be loaded and displayed. Your screen should resemble Figure 7.8.

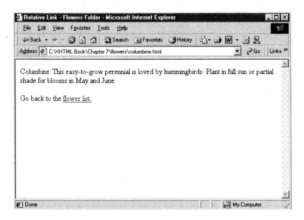

FIGURE 7.8: RELATIVE LINK; FILES IN DIFFERENT FOLDERS—COLUMBINE PAGE

10. On the place where it says "Go back to the flower list," click on the highlighted and underlined words "flower list" and you will go back to the index page.

LINKING TO LOCATIONS WITHIN THE SAME DOCUMENT

This is sometimes referred to as *intra-page linking*. This method of linking provides users with an easy way to navigate large pages, so they do not have to scroll through the entire page to get to a specific section. We will use the anchor element as a destination, which will allow us to point to that specific location by using what we have already learned about linking. This destination is referred to as a *named anchor* or *named target*.

When we want to link to another section of our document, we must create somewhere to link to. This is accomplished using the anchor element along with the id and name attributes. This will give a name to a particular section of our document. The *id attribute* is used in XHTML to create a named *anchor*; in HTML, the name attribute was used for this same purpose. So why use both? In XHTML, the name attribute has been deprecated and will be removed in later versions, but some browsers do not support the id attribute, so we need to use both for now.

The following is the proper syntax for creating a named anchor:

```
<a id="columbine" name="columbine">The flower columbine</a>
```

Now that I have created an anchor with the name "columbine," I can now refer to that section using a link. Here is how we could use the *anchor element* to link to the columbine section:

```
<a href="#columbine">columbine</a>
```

Notice anything different? For the most part, it looks like the relative links that we have already created except for the *hash mark (#)*, also known as a pound sign. The hash mark is followed by the name or id, which is used to identify and point to the destination. Use both id and name attributes for compatibility.

Let's give this a try by creating a document that uses intra-page linking.

1. Type the following using your choice of editor and save it as interlink.html.

```
<?xml version="1.0" encoding="UTF-8"?>
<!DOCTYPE html PUBLIC "-//W3C//DTD/XHTML 1.0 Transitional//EN"
"http://www.w3.org/TR/xhtml1/DTD/xhtml1-transitional.dtd">
<html xmlns="http://www.w3.org/1999/xhtml" xml:lang="en" lang="en">
<head>
<title> Relative Link - Same Document </title>
```

```
</head>
<body>
   <h1 align="center">Mary Ellen's Flower Garden</h1>
</body>
</html>
```

2. Next, add the following paragraphs to our document by placing the first
   <p> element below the <h1> element. The last </p> tag should be above
   the </body> tag. Add some text to the paragraphs, so it looks like the
   following:

```
<p>
   Mary Ellen's Flower Garden is set on the side of a mostly
   shaded hill. Filled with perennials, the garden boasts blooming
   flowers of one kind or another from early April through
   September. The earliest blooms are the bulbs that greet spring.
   Brightly colored tulips, hyacinths, and crocuses dot the
   hillside as the last flakes of winter melt away.
</p>
<p>
   The highest corner of the hillside enjoys the most sun, being
   warmed by the early morning rays and again with the last sun
   of the evening. It is on this spot that the Fiesta daisies have
   found their home, spreading wherever they want, crowding out the
   Black-Eyed Susans they now surround.
</p>
<p>
   The foxgloves grow taller before opening their throaty flowers,
   which provide a safe haven for fat bumblebees seeking their
   sweet nectar. And scattered up and down the hill are the
   carefree daylilies whose blooms follow the sun as it moves
   encircling the hill each day.
</p>
<p>
   Sloping down the hill into the shade, the delicate columbine
   have long since bloomed and turned to seed. Still deeper into
   the shade are the dark purple irises with their long, slender,
   green foliage framing their beauty.
</p>
<p>
   Select the flower you wish to know more about:
</p>
<ul>
   <li>Columbine</li>
   <li>Black-Eyed Susan</li>
   <li>Iris</li>
</ul>
```

3. Next, add the paragraphs that will become the target of the links as follows:

```
<h3>Columbine</h3>
<p>
    This easy-to-grow perennial is loved by hummingbirds. Plant in
    full sun or partial shade for blooms in May and June.
</p>
<h3>Black-Eyed Susan</h3>
<p>
    Orange coneflowers that grow on 2- to 3-foot stems do best in
    full sun. These are great flowers for the wild garden, producing
    blooms through July and August.
</p>
<h3>Iris</h3>
<p>
    There are more than 200 species available in a vast array of
    colors. Irises are easy to grow, and most need sunlight. Plant
    the rhizomes in the fall for blooms in early May.
</p>
```

Before we go to the next step, make sure that you save your work!

4. Next, create named targets by modifying the headings created in the previous step:

```
<h3><a id="columbine" name="columbine">Columbine</a></h3>

<h3><a id="black" name="black">Black-Eyed Susan</a></h3>

<h3><a id="iris" name="iris">Iris</a></h3>
```

5. Let's finish this by adding links in the unordered list to the named targets that we just created.

```
<ul>
  <li><a href="#columbine">Columbine</a></li>
  <li><a href="#black">Black-Eyed Susan</a></li>
  <li><a href="#iris">Iris</a></li>
</ul>
```

6. Save the document interlink.html.

7. The completed XHTML document should resemble the following:

```
<?xml version="1.0" encoding="UTF-8"?>
<!DOCTYPE html PUBLIC "-//W3C//DTD/XHTML 1.0 Transitional//EN"
"http://www.w3.org/TR/xhtml1/DTD/xhtml1-transitional.dtd">
```

```
<html xmlns="http://www.w3.org/1999/xhtml" xml:lang="en" lang="en">
<head>
<title> Relative Link - Same Document </title>
</head>
<body>
   <h1 align="center">Mary Ellen's Flower Garden</h1>
   <p>
      Mary Ellen's Flower Garden is set on the side of a mostly
      shaded hill. Filled with perennials, the garden boasts
      blooming flowers of one kind or another from early April
      through September. The earliest blooms are the bulbs that
      greet spring. Brightly colored tulips, hyacinths, and
      crocuses dot the hillside as the last flakes of winter
      melt away.
   </p>
   <p>
      The highest corner of the hillside enjoys the most sun,
      being warmed by the early morning rays and again with the
      last sun of the evening. It is on this spot that the
      Fiesta daisies have found their home, spreading wherever
      they want, crowding out the Black-Eyed Susans they now
      surround.
   </p>
   <p>
      The foxgloves grow taller before opening their throaty
      flowers, which provide a safe haven for fat bumblebees
      seeking their sweet nectar. And scattered up and down the
      hill are the carefree daylilies whose blooms follow the sun
      as it moves encircling the hill each day.
   </p>
   <p>
      Sloping down the hill into the shade, the delicate columbine
      have long since bloomed and turned to seed. Still deeper
      into the shade are the dark purple irises with their long,
      slender, green foliage framing their beauty.
   </p>
   <p>
   Select the flower you wish to know more about:
   </p>
   <ul>
     <li><a href="#columbine">Columbine</a></li>
     <li><a href="#black">Black-Eyed Susan</a></li>
     <li><a href="#iris">Iris</a></li>
   </ul>
   <h3><a id="columbine" name="columbine">Columbine</a></h3>
   <p>
      This easy-to-grow perennial is loved by hummingbirds. Plant
      in full sun or partial shade for blooms in May and June.
```

```
    </p>
    <h3><a id="black" name="black">Black-Eyed Susan</a></h3>
    <p>
        Orange coneflowers that grow on 2- to 3-foot stems do best
        in full sun. These are great flowers for the wild garden,
        producing blooms through July and August.
    </p>
    <h3><a id="iris" name="iris">Iris</a></h3>
    <p>
        There are more than 200 species available in a vast array
        of colors. Irises are easy to grow, and most need sunlight.
        Plant the rhizomes in the fall for blooms in early May.
    </p>
</body>
</html>
```

8. In the browser, select Open from the File menu to open interlink.html. Your screen should resemble Figure 7.9.

FIGURE 7.9: RELATIVE LINK—INTRA-PAGE

9. Click on the underlined name of the flower iris. Your screen should resemble Figure 7.10.

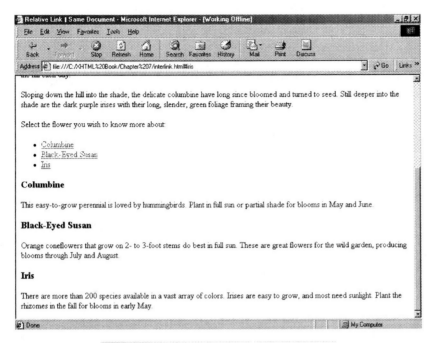

FIGURE 7.10: RELATIVE LINK—USING INTRA-PAGE LINK

LINKING TO A SPECIFIC LOCATION IN A DIFFERENT DOCUMENT

This technique of intra-page linking can also be combined with the other relative links. Let's modify the previous example to see how this works.

1. Type the following using your choice of editor and save it as specificlink.html.

```
<?xml version="1.0" encoding="UTF-8"?>
<!DOCTYPE html PUBLIC "-//W3C//DTD/XHTML 1.0 Transitional//EN"
"http://www.w3.org/TR/xhtml1/DTD/xhtml1-transitional.dtd">
<html xmlns="http://www.w3.org/1999/xhtml" xml:lang="en" lang="en">
<head>
<title> Relative Link - Specific Location Different File </title>
</head>
<body>
    <h1 align="center">Mary Ellen's Flower Garden</h1>
<p>
    Select the flower you wish to know more about:
</p>
<ul>
```

```
    <li><a href="#columbine">Columbine</a></li>
    <li><a href="#black">Black-Eyed Susan</a></li>
    <li><a href="#iris">Iris</a></li>
</ul>
</body>
</html>
```

2. Type the following and save it as specific2.html.

```
<?xml version="1.0" encoding="UTF-8"?>
<!DOCTYPE html PUBLIC "-//W3C//DTD/XHTML 1.0 Transitional//EN"
"http://www.w3.org/TR/xhtml1/DTD/xhtml1-transitional.dtd">
<html xmlns="http://www.w3.org/1999/xhtml" xml:lang="en" lang="en">
<head>
<title> Relative Link - Specific Location Different File </title>
</head>
<body>
<h3><a id="columbine" name="columbine">Columbine</a></h3>
<p>
    This easy-to-grow perennial is loved by hummingbirds. Plant in
    full sun or partial shade for blooms in May and June.
</p>
<h3><a id="black" name="black">Black-Eyed Susan</a></h3>
<p>
    Orange coneflowers that grow on 2- to 3-foot stems do best in
    full sun. These are great flowers for the wild garden, producing
    blooms through July and August.
</p>
<h3><a id="iris" name="iris">Iris</a></h3>
<p>
    There are more than 200 species available in a vast array of
    colors. Irises are easy to grow, and most need sunlight. Plant
    the rhizomes in the fall for blooms in early May.
</p>
</body>
</html>
```

3. Next, in the specificlink.html file, change the anchor element to include the file name where the targets are located.

```
<ul>
    <li><a href="specific2.html#columbine">Columbine</a></li>
    <li><a href="specific2.html#black">Black-Eyed Susan</a></li>
    <li><a href="specific2.html#iris">Iris</a></li>
</ul>
```

4. Save both documents.
5. In the browser, select Open from the File menu to open specificlink.html. Your screen should resemble Figure 7.11.

FIGURE 7.11: RELATIVE LINK—NAMED TARGETS IN DIFFERENT FILES

6. Click on the underlined name of the flower iris. Your screen should resemble Figure 7.12.

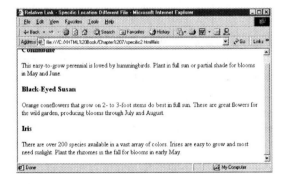

FIGURE 7.12: RELATIVE LINK—USING NAMED TARGETS IN DIFFERENT FILE

USING A MAILTO LINK

You have probably used this type of link before and never realized how it was accomplished. Sometimes you notice a person's email address at the bottom of a Web page. When it is clicked, the system's email client will be opened. This is accomplished with the use of a mailto link. Let's look at how to add this link to a document.

1. Type the following using your choice of editor and save it as mail.html.

```
<?xml version="1.0" encoding="UTF-8"?>
<!DOCTYPE html PUBLIC "-//W3C//DTD/XHTML 1.0 Transitional//EN"
"http://www.w3.org/TR/xhtml1/DTD/xhtml1-transitional.dtd">
<html xmlns="http://www.w3.org/1999/xhtml" xml:lang="en" lang="en">
<head>
<title> Using the Mailto Link </title>
</head>
<body>
  <a href="mailto:sales@cars.org">Click here if you would like more
information</a>
</body>
</html>
```

2. Save the document.
3. In the browser, select Open from the File menu to open mail.html.
4. Click on the link. Your screen should resemble Figure 7.13. It will depend on what mail client your system uses.

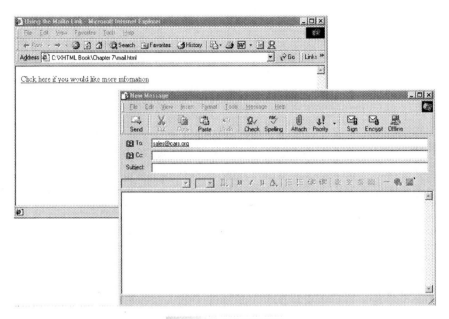

FIGURE 7.13: MAILTO LINK

CHAPTER SUMMARY

In this chapter, we learned how to use absolute and relative links on our Web pages. We learned that without links, the Web would just be a collection of unrelated documents. We saw how the relative link could be used to link documents in the same directory, different directories, or even different sections of the same document.

KEY TERMS

absolute link	id attribute
anchor	intra-page
anchor element	linking
backslash (\\)	name attribute
child directory	named anchor
forward slash (/)	named target
hash mark (#)	path
href attribute	relative link
hypertext link	Uniform Resource Locator (URL)

XHTML LINK TAG SUMMARY

Tag	Attribute(s)	Use/Values
<a>	href	Location (URL) of the target document
	name	Specifies an anchor name
	id	A unique identifier used to create anchors

REVIEW QUESTIONS

1. What is the difference between absolute and relative links? *link on a different server* *link on same server*
2. What are the advantages of using relative links?
3. What does the href attribute do? *Hypertext Reference*
4. What does href stand for? *Great hyperlink*
5. How are hypertext links displayed in an XHTML document? *blue underline*
6. How can you tell if a hypertext link has been used? *turns purple*
7. What is the difference between the id and name attributes? *Id = XHTML to create a named anchor* *name = HTML to create a named anchor*
8. What special character is used in the href attribute when linking to a named target? *#*
9. What is a URL? *uniform resource locator*
10. What are the different parts of a URL?

EXERCISES

1. Complete the intra-page linking example by adding two more flowers to the list and linking them to the following paragraphs:

   Daylily
   Daylilies are perennials that earned their name because each bloom opens, matures, and withers in 24 hours or less. Daylilies do well in partial shade and require little care.

   Foxglove
   Most foxglove are biennials which grow on tall, strong stems in partial shade. They are easy to care for and flower during May and June.

2. Add an anchor to the intra-page linking document created in Exercise 1 that will allow the user to return to the list from the various sections.

3. Given the following paragraph, create links for the highlighted words to pages about each flower. The user should be able to click on the highlighted word and be taken to the appropriate page. The descriptions about each flower are included in the chapter examples.

Mary Ellen's Flower Garden is set on the side of a mostly shaded hill. Filled with perennials, the garden boasts blooming flowers of one kind or another from early April through September. The earliest blooms are the bulbs that greet spring. Brightly colored tulips, hyacinths, and crocuses dot the hillside as the last flakes of winter melt away.

The highest corner of the hillside enjoys the most sun, being warmed by the early morning rays and again with the last sun of the evening. It is on this spot that the Fiesta daisies have found their home, spreading wherever they want and crowding out the **Black-Eyed Susans** they now surround.

The **foxgloves** grow taller before opening their throaty flowers, which provide a safe haven for fat bumblebees seeking their sweet nectar. And scattered up and down the hill are the carefree **daylilies** whose blooms follow the sun as it moves encircling the hill each day.

Sloping down the hill into the shade, the delicate **columbine** have long since bloomed and turned to seed. Still deeper into the shade are the dark purple **irises** with their long, slender, green foliage framing their beauty.

4. Create a Web page about your state and add three absolute links to interesting places.

5. Create a resume Web page for yourself. Provide an absolute link to your school and relative links within the document for work experience, education, and references.

PROJECT

With each page created, we can now turn our attention towards interlinking the pages through the construction of hyperlinks. Do the following:

- Create all of the necessary hyperlinks to interconnect your pages. Make sure to use relative links.

REFERENCES

HTML Body: Hyperlinks or Anchors, http://www.wdvl.com/Authoring/HTML/Links

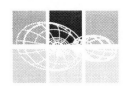

chapter 8
tables

CHAPTER OVERVIEW

Tables are a popular way to organize data and are surprisingly easy to do. This chapter will present tables, which are a very useful method of displaying data. We will discuss the difference between table structure and style (table presentation). The structure topics will include elements for table creation, captions, cell widths, and spanning rows and columns. The style topics will include borders, frames, and rules.

CHAPTER OBJECTIVES

- Create a table with rows, columns, and cells, and fill the cells with data
- Add headings and a title to our table
- Control the width, alignment, and borders of our table
- Adjust the amount of space between cells, borders, and cell contents
- Control the height, width, and alignment of rows and cells
- Spread table cells across several columns or rows (spanning)
- Nest a table inside another table
- Align text with tables
- Group/align rows and columns

TABLES

What's a table and why should we use one? Quite simply, a *table* is a group of information that is organized into *rows* (horizontal) and *columns* (vertical). Why? Because all of the information in the table is related in some way, and a table allows us to quickly and easily locate and compare information. Where a row and a column meet is called a *cell*, the part of the table that actually contains the information.

Tables were first introduced in early 1995 as a Netscape extension supported only by that browser. Tables were such a popular way to display data in a tabular form that they were rapidly included in the official HTML language specification as defined by the World Wide Web Consortium (W3C).

Today, the strict interpretation of the XHTML standard recommends that use of tables to display data in tabular form be discontinued. Why? Because the use of absolute positioning with cascading style sheets allows more control of objects on a Web page. In reality, because of the number of pages still using tables and the fact that so many people are still using browsers that don't support the use of cascading style sheets, tables are still a good option to display data in tabular form.

TABLE STRUCTURE

There are various terms associated with the table structure that we should define before actually creating a table using XHTML. Almost all tables will consist of the following parts:

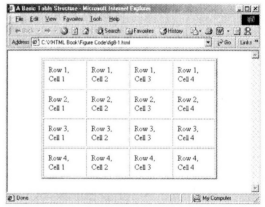

FIGURE 8.1: THE STRUCTURE OF A TABLE

- Caption—indicate the contents or purpose of the table.
- Table headings—provide a label for each column. They are usually in a different font or emphasized to distinguish them from the rest of the table.
- Table cells—the individual squares, which could contain the table data or headings.

Figure 8.1 illustrates the structure of a typical table.

BASIC TABLES

Creating tables in XHTML can use 10 different elements and 10 different attributes and can be complicated and confusing. So, let's keep it simple. A basic table can be created using just three elements and no attributes. We will learn about the other elements and attributes once we understand how to create a simple table.

CREATING A TABLE, THE <TABLE> ELEMENT

In order to create a table, the *table element*, <table> </table>, is used. All other table tags and attributes are contained within this element. Several optional attributes of the table element allow us to control the way the table looks. These attributes will be discussed in detail later in this chapter.

CREATING ROWS IN THE TABLE, THE <TR> ELEMENT

Once the table has been defined, the data that the table is to contain is placed in rows, just like in a spreadsheet. In order to begin a new row, the *table row element,* <tr> </tr>, is used.

> tip: Determining the number of rows that a table contains is as easy as counting the number of <tr> elements.

INSERTING DATA INTO THE TABLE CELLS, THE <TD> ELEMENT

There are two ways to define individual cells that hold the data in the rows of a table. The first and most common way is the *table data element*, <td> </td>. The table data element has many different attributes to control how the cell looks and we will explore them later. Figure 8.2 shows our basic table.

> tip: Determining the number of columns that a table contains is as easy as counting the number of <td> elements in a row.

CREATING A BASIC TABLE

We will use the table elements introduced above to create a basic table.

1. Type the following using your choice of editor and save it as basictable1.html. We will add a basic table in the next steps.

```
<?xml version="1.0" encoding="UTF-8"?>
<!DOCTYPE html PUBLIC "-//W3C//DTD/XHTML 1.0 Transitional//EN"
"http://www.w3.org/TR/xhtml1/DTD/xhtml1-transitional.dtd">
<html xmlns="http://www.w3.org/1999/xhtml" xml:lang="en" lang="en">
<head>
<title> A Basic Table </title>
</head>
<body>
</body>
</html>
```

2. Next, add a <table > element below the <body> element. This indicates to the browser that a table will begin. Place a </table> tag above the </body> tag to close the table.

3. Now we can build the table row by row using the <tr> element, which is placed inside the <table> element.

```
<table>
    <tr>

    </tr>
</table>
```

4. Using the <td> element, data can be placed into each cell of the table.

```
<table>
    <tr>
            <td>Mercury</td>
            <td>0.387</td>
            <td>57,910</td>
            <td>4,879</td>
    </tr>
</table>
```

5. Add three more rows of data to the table by using the information provided in Step 6.

6. Your completed XHTML code should resemble the following:

```
<?xml version="1.0" encoding="UTF-8"?>
<!DOCTYPE html PUBLIC "-//W3C//DTD/XHTML 1.0 Transitional//EN"
    "http://www.w3.org/TR/xhtml1/DTD/xhtml1-transitional.dtd">
```

```
<html xmlns="http://www.w3.org/1999/xhtml" xml:lang="en" lang="en">
<head>
<title> A Basic Table </title>
</head>
<body>
   <table>
          <tr>
                  <td>Mercury</td>
                  <td>0.387</td>
                  <td>57,910</td>
                  <td>4,879</td>
          </tr>
          <tr>
                  <td>Venus</td>
                  <td>0.723</td>
                  <td>108,200</td>
                  <td>12,104</td>
          </tr>
          <tr>
                  <td>Earth</td>
                  <td>1.000</td>
                  <td>149,597</td>
                  <td>12,756</td>
          </tr>
          <tr>
                  <td>Mars</td>
                  <td>1.524</td>
                  <td>227,940</td>
                  <td>6,794</td>
          </tr>
   </table>
</body>
</html>
```

7. Save the document as basictable1.html.

8. In the browser, select Open from the File menu to open basictable1.html. Your screen

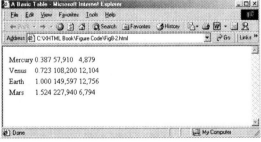

FIGURE 8.2: A BASIC TABLE OF PLANETS

should resemble Figure 8.2. This is an example of a four-row by four-column table. You will notice that tables have no border by default.

ADDING HEADINGS TO COLUMNS, THE <TH> ELEMENT

The second way to define a cell of a table is with the *table header element,*
<th> </th>. What's the difference between the table data and the table header
element? A table header element is automatically formatted as boldfaced and
centered to set it apart from other table cells in that column.

ADDING A TITLE TO THE TABLE, THE <CAPTION> ELEMENT

In addition to labeling each column of data in our table, we may want to add
a title to the entire table. We can do this by using the *table caption element,*
<caption> </caption>. The caption element specifies a title for the table and
will be centered either above or below the table, depending upon the align attribute. The possible values for the align attribute of the caption tag are top and
bottom, with the default usually
being top. So, if you want a caption below your table, use <cap-
tion align="bottom">. The basic
table we used earlier has been
modified in Figure 8.3 to include
table headers and a table caption.

> warning: When using the <caption> ele-
> ment, it must be the first element
> within the table element.

ADDING COLUMN HEADINGS AND A CAPTION

In the previous example, we created a basic table of data. The data is of little
meaning if user does not understand what the table contains, so we will add a
caption and column headers to it.

1. Using your choice of editor, open the file basictable1.html.

2. Next, change the title of the document as follows:

```
<title> A Basic Table using a Caption and Headings </title>
```

3. Add five more rows of data to the table as follows:

```
<tr>
<td>Jupiter</td>
<td>5.203</td>
<td>778,330</td>
<td>142,984</td>
</tr>

<tr>
<td>Saturn</td>
```

```
<td>9.569</td>
<td>1,429,400</td>
<td>120,536</td>
</tr>

<tr>
<td>Uranus</td>
<td>19,309</td>
<td>2,870,900</td>
<td>51,118</td>
</tr>

<tr>
<td>Neptune</td>
<td>30,284</td>
<td>4,504,300</td>
<td>49,572</td>
</tr>

<tr>
<td>Pluto</td>
<td>39,781</td>
<td>5,913,520</td>
<td>2,320</td>
</tr>
```

4. Using the <caption> element gives the user a better idea what the table contains. Place the <caption> element after the <table> element.

```
<table>
<caption> PLANETS </caption>
    .
    .
    .
</table>
```

5. Finally, add column headings to the table by using the <th> element. This element is placed within a <tr> element. The column headings should be placed after the <caption> element.

```
<tr>
    <th>Name</th>
    <th>Ast. Units</th>
    <th>Distance (000 km)</th>
    <th>Diameter (km)</th>
</tr>
```

6. Save the document as basictable1.html.

7. In the browser, select Open from the File menu to open basictable1.html. Your screen should resemble Figure 8.3. This is an example of a four-row by four-column table. You will notice that tables have no border by default.

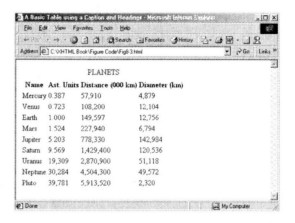

FIGURE 8.3: THE BASIC PLANET TABLE WITH TABLE HEADERS AND A CAPTION

TABLE ATTRIBUTES

Now that we know how to build a simple table, let's look at how we can control how the table looks. We will start by looking at the five attributes that may be used with the <table> tag. They are align, width, border, cellspacing, and cellpadding. The table attributes frame and rules will be covered later in the chapter after row grouping has been discussed.

tip: When you decide to use a table, it is helpful to sketch your table first. This will make the writing of the XHTML easier by enabling you to see how the rows and columns will fall and see which cells may span multiple columns.

<TABLE> TAG ATTRIBUTES

First, we might want to control where on the browser page our table is located. Let's look at the align attribute.

Table align Attribute

By default, a table is aligned with the left margin of the page. This can be changed by using the *table align attribute* with the *table tag*. For example, if you wanted to center your table, you would use the following:

```
<table align = "center">
```

The possible values for the align attribute when used with the table tag are left, center, or right.

Table width Attribute

If the width of a table is not specified, the browser will automatically define the width based upon the contents of the cells. If you want to control the width of your table, you can specify the width using the *table width attribute,* either as an absolute value in pixels or as a percentage of the space between the left and right margins of the browser page. For example, if you want a table that is exactly 400 pixels wide, you would use the following:

```
<table width = "400">
```

If you wanted your table to occupy 75 percent of the space between the left and right margins, you would use the following:

```
<table width = "75%">
```

Table border Attribute

By default, a table has no border. This is the same as specifying a table with a border of zero. The *table border attribute* represents the width (in pixels) of the border of the table. So if you wanted a table with a border width of three pixels, you would use the following tag:

```
<table border = "3">
```

Figure 8.4 illustrates differences in border widths.

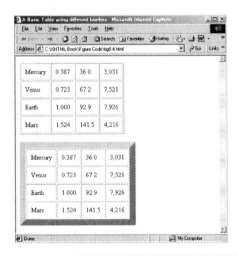

FIGURE 8.4: BASIC TABLES WITH DIFFERENT BORDER WIDTHS

Now, try adding the three attributes we just talked about to the <table> tag. The table in Figure 8.5 shows a table using the three attributes align, width, and border.

tip: Although borders can help define your table, they should be used sparingly so that they do not clutter the page.

1. Using your choice of editor, open the file basictable1.html.
2. Next, make the following changes to the <table> tag:

```
<table align = "center" width = "75%" border = "3">
```

3. Save the document as basictable2.html.
4. In the browser, select Open from the File menu to open basictable2.html. Your screen should resemble Figure 8.5.

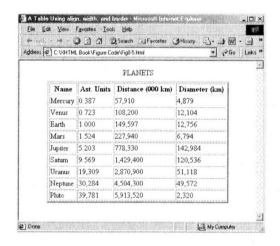

FIGURE 8.5: THE PLANET TABLE USING TABLE ALIGN, WIDTH, AND BORDER ATTRIBUTES

Table cellpadding Attribute

The *table cell padding attribute* controls the amount of space (in pixels) between the border of each table cell and the contents of that cell. For example, if you wanted to leave three pixels of space between the border of each cell and its contents, you would use the following:

```
<table cellpadding = "3">
```

Figure 8.6 shows an example of changing the cellpadding attribute to 10 pixels. By comparing the results with those of Figure 8.5, you will notice the change in space between the contents of the cell and the border.

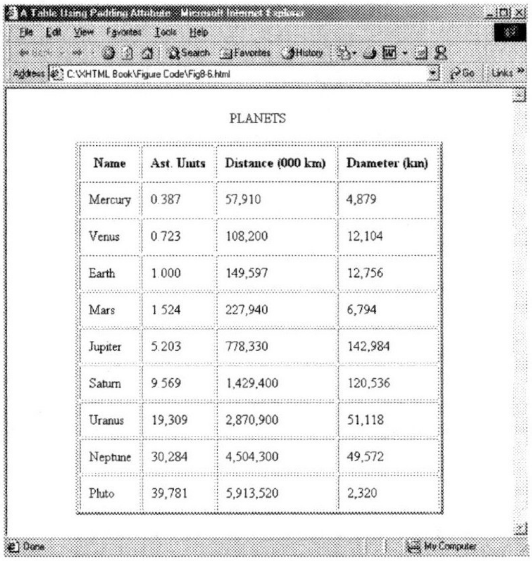

Name	Ast. Units	Distance (000 km)	Diameter (km)
Mercury	0.387	57,910	4,879
Venus	0.723	108,200	12,104
Earth	1.000	149,597	12,756
Mars	1.524	227,940	6,794
Jupiter	5.203	778,330	142,984
Saturn	9.569	1,429,400	120,536
Uranus	19,309	2,870,900	51,118
Neptune	30,284	4,504,300	49,572
Pluto	39,781	5,913,520	2,320

FIGURE 8.6: THE PLANET TABLE INCREASING THE CELL PADDING

Table cellspacing Attribute

The *table cellspacing attribute* is used to specify the amount of separation (in pixels) between the border of one cell and the border of the adjacent cells. Unlike many spreadsheet applications where adjacent cells share a common border, in XHTML, each table cell has its own border. An easy way to think about cell spacing is to think of it as the width of the gridlines inside the table. So, if you wanted each cell of your table to be separated from all other cells by five pixels, you would use the following:

```
<table cellspacing = "5">
```

Figure 8.7 shows an example of changing the cellspacing attribute to five pixels. As you can see by comparing the results to Figure 8.6, the space between the cells changed.

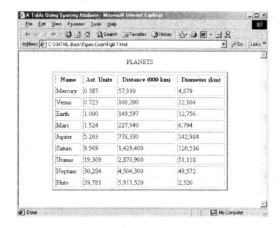

FIGURE 8.7: THE PLANET TABLE INCREASING THE CELLSPACING

Now try modifying the planet table using the cellpadding and cellspacing attributes. Figure 8.8 shows the effects of modifying the table with these attributes.

1. Using your choice of editor, open the file basictable2.html.
2. Next, make the following changes to the <table> tag:

```
<table align = "center" width = "75%" border = "3" cellspacing =
"5" cellpadding = "10">
```

3. Save the document as basictable3.html.
4. In the browser, select Open from the File menu to open basictable3.html. Your screen should resemble Figure 8.8.

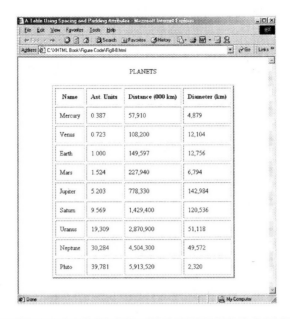

FIGURE 8.8: THE PLANET TABLE WITH CELLSPACING AND CELLPADDING

TABLE ROW, TABLE DATA, AND TABLE HEADER TAG ATTRIBUTES

The attributes that we just learned are all attributes of the <table> tag only. The next group of attributes may be used with the table row <tr> tag and/or the table data <td> and table header <th> tags. Once we have aligned and formatted the table,

note: With the introduction of cascading style sheets, the align attribute for the <table> element has been deprecated, but not for <th> or <td>.

we might want to control how the contents of whole rows of cells appear or just control individual cells. The next group of attributes allows us to specify the alignment of rows and cells.

Row and Cell Alignment Attributes

There are two alignment attributes, align and valign. Either (or both) may be applied to whole rows and/or individual cells. If either align or valign is applied to both a row and a cell in that row, the value applied to that cell will override the value applied to the row. First, we will look at the way the contents of a cell or row are aligned horizontally.

Horizontal Alignment (align attribute)

The horizontal alignment of the contents of either a particular cell or a whole row of cells can be controlled by using the *align attribute*. The align attribute has three possible values, left, center, and right. The default value depends upon the tag. The *table data tag* has a default horizontal alignment of left, but the default horizontal alignment for the *table header tag* is center. If the align attribute is specified for both the table row and a specific table cell, the alignment specified for the particular cell overrides the value specified for the row. If we wanted the contents of a whole row of cells to be center aligned, we would use

```
<tr align = "center">
```

If we wanted a particular cell within that row to be right-aligned, we would have to add the following:

```
<td align = "right">
```

The following is an example of aligning cell data to the center, right, and left.

```
<table align = "center" width = 50% border = "3" cellpadding =
"10">
<caption> HORIZONTAL ALIGNMENT </caption>
<tr>
<th>LEFT</th>
<th>CENTER</th>
<th>RIGHT</th>
</tr>
<tr>
<td align = "left">Cell 1</td>
<td align = "center">Cell 2 </td>
<td align = "right">Cell 3</td>
</tr>
</table>
```

The results of the above XHTML are in Figure 8.9.

Vertical Alignment (valign attribute)

The vertical alignment of the contents of either a particular cell or a whole row of cells can be controlled by using the *valign attribute*. The valign attribute can be set to three possible values: top, middle, and bottom. The default value of the vertical alignment attribute is middle. Again, if the valign attribute is specified for both the table row and a specific table cell, the vertical alignment specified for the particular cell overrides the value specified for the row. If we wanted the contents of a whole row of cells to be vertically aligned at the top, we would use

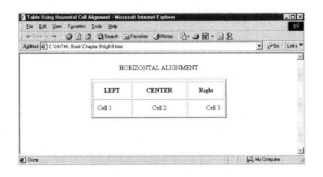

FIGURE 8.9: CELL DATA ALIGNED HORIZONTALLY

```
<tr valign = "top">
```

If we wanted a particular cell within that row tó be vertically aligned at the bottom, we would have to add:

```
<td valign = "bottom">
```

The following is an example of aligning cell data to the center, right, and left.

```
<table align = "center" width = 50% border = "2" height = "200">
<caption> VERTICAL ALIGNMENT </caption>
<tr>
    <th>TOP</th>
    <th>MIDDLE</th>
    <th>BOTTOM</th>
</tr>
<tr>
    <td valign = "top">Cell 1</td>
    <td valign = "middle">Cell 2 </td>
    <td valign = "bottom">Cell 3</td>
</tr>
</table>
```

The results of the above XHTML are in Figure 8.10.

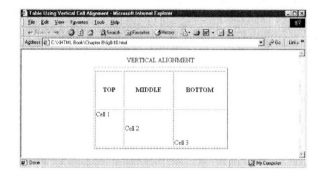

FIGURE 8.10: CELL DATA ALIGNED VERTICALLY

The use of the attributes align and valign together is demonstrated using the following XHTML:

```
<table align = "center" width = 85% border = "2" height = "200">
<caption> HORIZONTAL AND VERTICAL ALIGNMENT </caption>
<tr>
    <th></th>
    <th>Left Aligned Column</th>
    <th>Center Aligned Column</th>
    <th>Right Aligned Column</th>
</tr>
<tr valign = "top">
    <th>Top Aligned Row</th>
    <td>Top-Left</td>
    <td align = "center">Top-Center</td>
    <td align = "right">Top-Right</td>
</tr>
<tr valign = "middle">
    <th>Middle Aligned Row</th>
    <td>Middle-Left</td>
    <td align = "center">Middle-Center</td>
    <td align = "right">Middle-Right</td>
</tr>
<tr valign = "bottom">
    <th>Bottom Aligned Row</th>
    <td>Bottom-Left</td>
    <td align = "center">Bottom-Center</td>
    <td align = "right">Bottom-Right</td>
</tr>
</table>
```

The results of this XHTML can be seen in Figure 8.11.

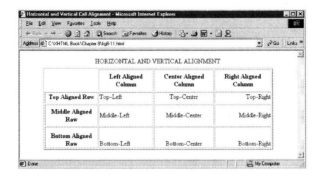

FIGURE 8.11: A TABLE USING HORIZONTAL AND VERTICAL ALIGNMENT

CELL FORMAT ATTRIBUTES

Now that we have aligned our rows and cells in order to make the table look the way we want it to, we might want to change the height or width of rows or cells using the height and width attributes. Also, we can control how cell contents appear using the nowrap attribute, which will disable automatic text wrapping for a given cell. These attributes can be used only with the <td> and <th> tags.

width Attribute

The *width attribute* can be specified for either the table data or the table header tags. It is used to specify the width (in pixels) of the cell, excluding any cell padding. This attribute may be ignored if any other cells in that same column have greater specified widths. If we wanted to create a column of cells whose width was 25 pixels, we would use the following:

```
<td width = "25">
```

height Attribute

The *height attribute* can also be specified for either the table data or the table header tags. It is used to specify the height (in pixels) of the cell, excluding any cell padding. This attribute may be ignored if any other cells in that same row have greater specified heights. If we wanted to create a row of cells whose height was 40 pixels, we would use the following:

```
<th height = "40">
```

nowrap Attribute

The *nowrap attribute,* used with either the table data or the table header tags, is used to disable automatic word wrapping within the contents of a cell. As such, it is equivalent to using the non-breaking space entity ( ). This attribute is useful when you want the contents of a cell to remain together on the same line rather than being broken into two or more lines. The use of the last three attributes is demonstrated using the following XHTML:

```
<table width = "75%" border = "1">
<tr>
<th>
</th>
<th width=150>Width 150</th>
<th width=80>Width 80</th>
<th width="100">Width 100 (about 250)</th>
</tr>

<tr>
<th height="75">Height 75</th>
<td>A</td>
<td>medium</td>
<td>row</td

<tr>
<th height="150">Height 150</th>
<td> A tall row</td>
<td>This cell is automatically wrapped</td>
<td nowrap>This cell is wider because of NOWRAP</td>
    </tr>

    <tr>
<th height="30">Height 30</th>
<td>A</td>
<td>short</td>
<td>row</td>
</tr>
</table>
```

The results of this XHTML can be seen in Figure 8.12.

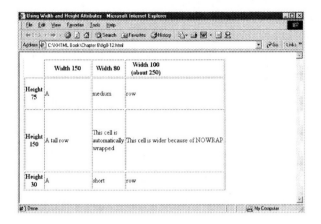

FIGURE 8.12: A TABLE USING HEIGHT, WIDTH, AND NOWRAP

CELL SPANNING ATTRIBUTES

Sometimes, we might want the contents of one cell to extend across several columns or rows of our table. This is called spanning. This is particularly useful if the contents of the cell are being used as a heading to describe or categorize the data in several other columns or rows. The two spanning attributes are colspan and rowspan. The attributes can only be used with the <td> and <th> tags, not with <tr>.

note: With the introduction of cascading style sheets, the nowrap attribute has been deprecated.

Spanning Columns (colspan attribute)

In order to do this, we use a *colspan attribute*. This attribute may be used with either the table data <td> tag or the table header <th> tag. For example, if we wanted a table cell to span across three columns in the table, we would use

tip: Sometimes text in a cell can be too long. If this is the case, you can add a line break by using the <br /> element.

```
<td colspan="3">
```

Spanning Rows (rowspan attribute)

Just as we might want to spread a cell across several columns, we might also want to span a cell across multiple rows. Spanning a cell across several rows is accomplished by the *rowspan attribute*. Again, it may be applied to either the table data or the table header tags. If we wanted a table cell to span across two rows, we would use

```
<th rowspan="2">
```

Now try modifying the planet table using the colspan and rowspan attributes. Figure 8.13 shows the effects of modifying the table with these attributes.

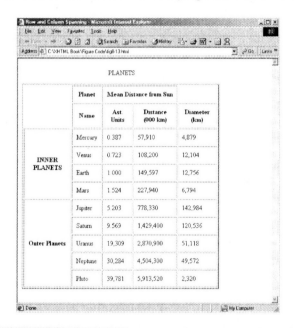

FIGURE 8.13: OUR PLANET TABLE WITH ROW AND COLUMN SPANNING

1. Using your choice of editor, open the file basictable3.html.
2. Next, add the following table row after the caption tag.

```
<tr>
<th></th>
<th>Planet</th>
<th colspan="2">Mean Distance from Sun</th>
</tr>
```

3. In the first row that contains the column headings, add an empty cell before the <th>Name</th>.

```
<th></th>
```

4. In the row that contains the data for Mercury, add the following before the first <td>:

```
<th rowspan="4">INNER PLANETS</th>
```

5. In the row that contains the data for Jupiter , add the following before the first <td>:

```
<th rowspan="5">Outer Planets</th>
```

6. Save the document as basictable4.html.
7. In the browser, select Open from the File menu to open basictable4.html. Your screen should resemble Figure 8.13. This illustrates the use of both the colspan and rowspan attributes.

The XHTML used to produce Figure 8.13 should now look like this:

```
<table width = 80% border = "3" cellpadding = "10">
<caption> PLANETS </caption>
   <tr>
     <th></th>
     <th>Planet</th>
     <th colspan="2">Mean Distance from Sun</th>
    </tr>
   <tr>
     <th></th>
     <th>Name</th>
     <th>Ast. Units</th>
     <th>Distance (000 km) </th>
     <th>Diameter (km)</th>
   </tr>
   <tr>
     <th rowspan="4">INNER PLANETS</th>
     <td>Mercury</td>
     <td>0.387</td>
     <td>57,910</td>
     <td>4,879</td>
   </tr>
   <tr>
     <td>Venus</td>
     <td>0.723</td>
     <td>108,200</td>
     <td>12,104</td>
```

```
      </tr>
      <tr>
        <td>Earth</td>
        <td>1.000</td>
        <td>149,597</td>
        <td>12,756</td>
      </tr>
      <tr>
        <td>Mars</td>
        <td>1.524</td>
        <td>227,940</td>
        <td>6,794</td>
      </tr>
      <tr>
        <th rowspan="5">Outer Planets</th>
        <td>Jupiter</td>
        <td>5.203</td>
        <td>778,330</td>
        <td>142,984</td>
      </tr>
      <tr>
        <td>Saturn</td>
        <td>9.569</td>
        <td>1,429,400</td>
        <td>120,536</td>
      </tr>
      <tr>
        <td>Uranus</td>
        <td>19,309</td>
        <td>2,870,900</td>
        <td>51,118</td>
      </tr>
      <tr>
        <td>Neptune</td>
        <td>30,284</td>
        <td>4,504,300</td>
        <td>49,572</td>
      </tr>
      <tr>
        <td>Pluto</td>
        <td>39,781</td>
        <td>5,913,520</td>
        <td>2,320</td>
      </tr>
    </table>
```

NESTED TABLES

Can we put a table inside another table? Sure! Although the reasons for wanting to do that may not be clear, any valid XHTML code may be placed inside the cells of a table, including images, links, and other tables. (That should give you some neat ideas to try!) Suppose we wanted to create a table that had a cell containing a second table. The use of a *nested table* is demonstrated using the following XHTML:

```
<table border="2" cellpadding="5" cellspacing="5">
      <tr>
<td>T1, R1, C1</td>
<td>T1, R1, C2</td>
<td>T1, R1, C3</td>
      </tr>
      <tr>
<td>T1, R2, C1</td>
<td>T1, R2, C2</td>
<td>T1, R2, C3</td>
      </tr>
      <tr>
<td>T1, R3, C1</td>
<td>
      <table border="1" cellpadding="5" cellspacing="5">
<tr>
      <td>T2, R1, C1</td>
      <td>T2, R1, C2</td>
</tr>
<tr><td>T2, R2, C1</td>
      <td>T2, R2, C2</td>
</tr>
      </table>
<td>T1, R3, C3</td>
      </tr>
</table>
```

The results of this XHTML can be seen in Figure 8.14.

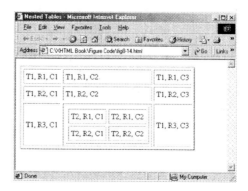

FIGURE 8.14: A NESTED TABLE

SETTING COLORS

bgcolor Attribute

This attribute is used to control a background color for the table. The color value may be in either a hexadecimal color code in the form #RRGGBB or one of the 16 predefined color names. The 16 predefined colors include white, black, green, silver, lime, gray, olive, yellow, maroon, navy, red, blue, purple, teal, fuchsia, and aqua. Background colors will override the color of an enclosing element. For example, a row's background color will override that of a table's. The use of the bgcolor attribute is demonstrated using the following XHTML:

```
<?xml version="1.0" encoding="UTF-8"?>
<!DOCTYPE html PUBLIC "-//W3C//DTD/XHTML 1.0 Transitional//EN"
"http://www.w3.org/TR/xhtml1/DTD/xhtml1-transitional.dtd">
<html xmlns="http://www.w3.org/1999/xhtml" xml:lang="en" lang="en">
<head>
<title> Example of Using Color </title>
</head>
<body>
<table border="2" align = "center" width = 85% height = "200">
<caption> USING COLORS </caption>
<tr bgcolor="aqua">
```

```
  <th>Column 1</th>
  <th>Column 2</th>
  <th>Column 3</th>
</tr>
<tr>
  <td bgcolor="yellow"> YELLOW </td>
  <td bgcolor="teal"> TEAL </td>
  <td bgcolor="green"> GREEN </td>
</tr>
<tr>
  <td bgcolor="FF0000"> RED </td>
  <td bgcolor="FFFFFF"> WHITE </td>
  <td bgcolor="00FFFF"> AQUA </td>
</tr>
</table>
</body>
</html>
```

The results of this XHTML can be seen in Figure 8.15.

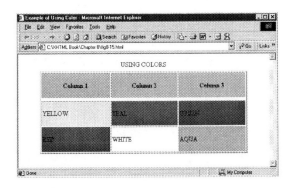

FIGURE 8.15: A TABLE USING COLOR

ALIGNING TEXT WITH TABLES

By default tables are displayed on the left side of the page, with text being placed before or after the table.

Figure 8.16 shows an example of text being displayed with a table using the default alignment. The text can also wrap around the table by setting the table's alignment attribute to left or right.

note: With the introduction of cascading style sheets, the bgcolor attribute of the <table>, <tr>, <th>, and <td> elements has been deprecated.

Figure 8.17 shows an example of a table being aligned right with text wrapping around.

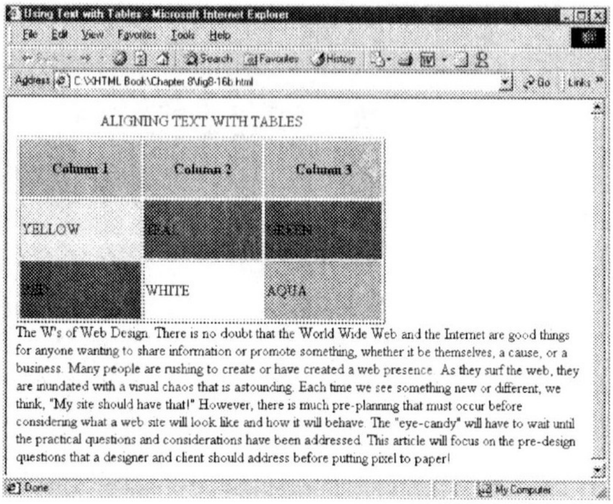

FIGURE 8.16: ALIGNING TEXT WITH TABLES USING NO ALIGNMENT

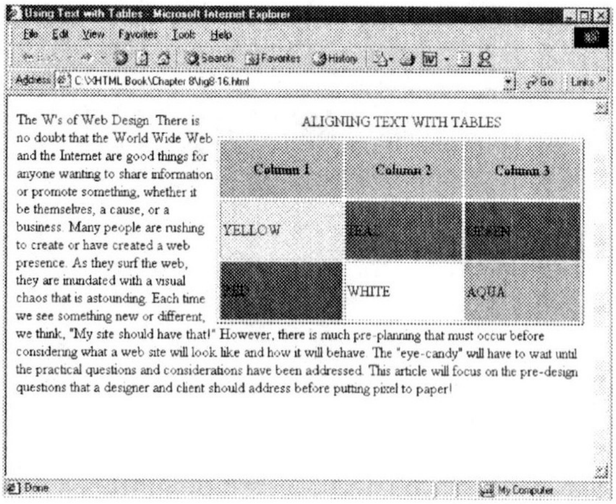

FIGURE 8.17: ALIGNING TEXT WITH TABLES USING ALIGNMENT

TABLE STRUCTURE ENHANCEMENTS

Up to this point, we have worked with the basic structural elements of a table. We can add some complexity to the table structure by:

■ Grouping and aligning columns
■ Grouping and aligning rows

GROUPING AND ALIGNING COLUMNS

These table enhancements enable the browser to load and display large tables incrementally. This is accomplished by creating structural divisions using the <colgroup> and <col> elements. These elements allow for the formatting of entire columns within a group.

Creating Column Groups, Using the <colgroup> and <col> Tags
In order to create column groups, the *column group tags,* <colgroup> and </colgroup> are used. Several optional attributes of the table tag allow us to control the format of the columns. These attributes include span, width, align, and valign. These attributes function the same as previously discussed; please refer back to previous paragraphs for their function. Let's create a table with four columns of equal width. We can use the following element:

```
<colgroup span = "4" width="25%"></colgroup>
```

This is fine if we want all of our columns to have the same width, but what if we want them to have different widths? Say we wanted our first column to have a width of 10 percent, the remaining three to have a width of 30 percent, and centered text in those columns. We would use the following elements:

```
<colgroup width="10%"></colgroup>
<colgroup span = "3" width="30%" align="center"></colgroup>
```

We can further define the column structure by using the <col /> tag. This tag will allow us to define the structure within a <colgroup> element. This will allow us to format individual columns of a group. In the previous example, we used the align attribute to align the text in those columns. What if we wanted to align the columns using left, center, and right? We would use the following:

```
<colgroup width="10%"></colgroup>
<colgroup width="30%">
   <col align="left" />
   <col align="center" />
   <col align="right" />
</colgroup>
```

What if we wanted each column in the column group to have a different width? The following code would be used:

```
<colgroup width="10%"></colgroup>
<colgroup span="3">
   <col align="left" width="20%"/>
   <col align="center" width="30%"/>
   <col align="right" width="40%"/>
</colgroup>
```

These elements can provide us with some powerful tools to format columns in a table and can be enhanced through the use of style sheets.

Now let's apply these new elements by creating a table.

1. Type the following using your choice of editor and save it as tablecol.html. We will create a table using column groups in the next steps.

```
<?xml version="1.0" encoding="UTF-8"?>
<!DOCTYPE html PUBLIC "-//W3C//DTD/XHTML 1.0 Transitional//EN"
"http://www.w3.org/TR/xhtml1/DTD/xhtml1-transitional.dtd">
<html xmlns="http://www.w3.org/1999/xhtml" xml:lang="en" lang="en">
<head>
<title> Example of Column Groups </title>
</head>
<body>
</body>
</html>
```

2. Next, add a <table > element and <caption> below the <body> element that looks like the following:

```
<table align = "center" width = 85% border = "2" height = "200">
<caption> CREATING COLUMN GROUPS </caption>
```

Place a </table> tag above the </body> tag to close the table.

3. Next, we define the column groups within the table. By using the following:

```
<colgroup width="10%"></colgroup>
<colgroup>
    <col align="left" width="30%"/>
    <col align="center" width="30%"/>
    <col align="right" width="30%"/>
</colgroup>
```

4. Now we can build the table row by row using the <tr> element and adding data to each cell using the <td> element. Build the rows by using the following:

```
<tr>
    <th>Row Number</th>
    <th>Left Aligned Column</th>
    <th>Center Aligned Column</th>
    <th>Right Aligned Column</th>
</tr>
<tr>
    <th> 1 </th>
    <td>Top-Left</td>
    <td>Top-Center</td>
    <td>Top-Right</td>
</tr>
<tr>
    <th> 2 </th>
    <td>Middle-Left</td>
    <td>Middle-Center</td>
    <td>Middle-Right</td>
</tr>
<tr>
    <th> 3 </th>
    <td>Bottom-Left</td>
    <td>Bottom-Center</td>
    <td>Bottom-Right</td>
</tr>
```

5. Save the document as tablecol.html.

6. In the browser, select Open from the File menu to open tablecol.html. Your screen should resemble Figure 8.18. This illustrates the use of both the <colgroup> and <col> elements.

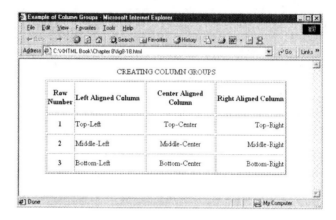

FIGURE 8.18: CREATING COLUMN GROUPS

GROUPING AND ALIGNING ROWS

We can organize table rows by adding structural divisions us ing the XHTML elements: <thead>, <tbody>, and <tfoot>. The advantage of using these tags becomes apparent with large tables. These elements allow the body of the table to scroll while the header and footer remain in place.

Using the <thead> Element

The <thead> and </thead> elements are used to create a header for the table. Typically, it is the same information that you place in the header cells to describe the columns using the <th> elements. The <thead> element is placed immediately after the <table> element or after the <colgroup> elements if they are present. It also must contain a minimum of one row. The <thead> elements are used in the following:

```
<table align = "center" width = 85% border = "2" height = "200">
<caption> CREATING ROW GROUPS </caption>
<colgroup width="10%"></colgroup>
<colgroup>
    <col width="30%"/>
    <col width="30%"/>
    <col width="30%"/>
```

```
</colgroup>
<thead bgcolor = "blue">
<tr>
   <th>Row Number</th>
   <th>Column 1</th>
   <th>Column 2</th>
   <th>Column 3</th>
</tr>
</thead>
```

Using the <tfoot> Element

The <tfoot> and </tfoot> elements are used to create a table footer when rows are being grouped. The table footer will typically contain column totals or provide a description about all the columns. The <tfoot> element is placed immediately after the </thead> element and before the <tbody> element. It also must contain a minimum of one row. The <tfoot> elements are used in the following example:

```
<tfoot>
<tr>
   <td colspan="4" align="center"> THIS IS THE FOOTER </td>
</tr>
</tfoot>
```

Using the <tbody> Element

The <tbody> and </tbody> elements are used to create a table body. The <tbody> elements define the row groups, and a table can have any number of these elements. The <tbody> elements are placed immediately after the </foot> element. The placement of the <tbody> may seem a little odd, but by using this structure, the browser can render the footer of the table while it is receiving all the data for the table body. The following example demonstrates two table bodies, with one consisting of two rows and the other of just one row. The <tbody> elements are used in the following example:

note: A table can have only one <thead> and one <tfoot> element.

```
<tbody>
<tr>
   <th> ROW 1 </th>
   <td> ROW 1, COL 1</td>
   <td> ROW 1, COL 2</td>
   <td> ROW 1, COL 3</td>
```

```
</tr>
<tr>
   <th> ROW 2 </th>
   <td> ROW 2, COL 1</td>
   <td> ROW 2, COL 2</td>
   <td> ROW 2, COL 3</td>
</tr>
</tbody>
<tbody>
<tr>
   <th> ROW 3 </th>
   <td> ROW 3, COL 1</td>
   <td> ROW 3, COL 2</td>
   <td> ROW 3, COL 3</td>
</tr>
</tbody>
```

Putting the <thead>, <tfoot>, and <tbody> elements above together would produce Figure 8.19.

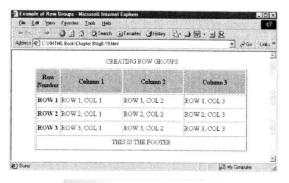

FIGURE 8.19: CREATING ROW GROUPS

By looking at the table produced, it is easy to see that the table has a head and footer. Can you see any row groups? We can use two additional attributes of the <table> element to visually enhance the table's border display. Remember from earlier in the chapter we introduced the border attribute, which could be used to set the thickness of the border. The table attributes frame and rules can be used to provide more control of the border.

warning: When using the <thead>, <tfoot>, and <tbody> elements, you must use them in that order.

Table frame Attribute

The *table frame attribute* will allow us to decide where the external border will be displayed. The frame attribute can have one of the following values:

- void   No frame will be drawn. This is also the default value.
- above   Only the top border will be displayed.
- below   Only the bottom border will be displayed.
- hsides   The top and bottom borders will be displayed.
- vsides   The left and right borders will be displayed.
- lhs   Only the left side border will be displayed.
- rhs   Only the right side border will be displayed.
- box   Displays a border on all four sides.
- border   Displays a border on all four sides. This is also the default value.

So if you wanted a table with a border width of three pixels and only top and bottom borders, you would use the following :

```
<table border = "3" frame="hsides">
```

Table rules Attribute

The *table rules attribute* defines how the dividing lines between cells will be drawn. The rules attribute can have one of the following values:

- none   No interior borders displayed.
- groups   Borders will be displayed between row groups and column groups as defined by <thead>, <tfoot>, <tbody>, <colgroup>, and <col>.
- rows   Borders will be displayed between rows.
- cols   Borders will be displayed between individual columns.
- all   Borders will be displayed around every cell.

So if you wanted a table with a border width of three pixels, only top and bottom borders, and group borders, you would use the following:

```
<table border = "2" frame="hsides" rules="groups">
```

Let's apply frame and rules attributes to the XHTML used to create Figure 8.19 using the following:

```
<table borders="2" align = "center" width = 85% height = "200"
frame="hsides" rules="groups">
```

This change would produce Figure 8.20.

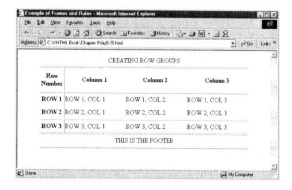

FIGURE 8.20: USING FRAMES AND RULES ATTRIBUTES

USING TABLES FOR PAGE LAYOUT

Tables can be used for more than just displaying tabular information. Many people use tables to control the layout of whole Web pages. Using tables for layout can provide the Web developer with additional flexibility, such as placement of graphics and control of margins. One benefit of using tables for layout is being able to control the formatting of the cells using the attributes we have discussed up to this point. Figure 8.21 is an example of using a header and a fixed left margin as a navigation area. This is of one of the most popular layouts using tables. You may notice that it looks very much like a page layout using frames, which will be discussed in the next chapter.

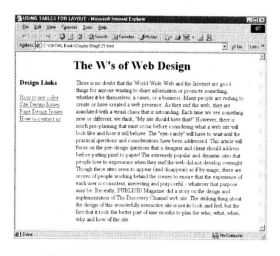

FIGURE 8.21: USING TABLES FOR PAGE LAYOUT

The following XHTML was used to produce Figure 8.21:

```
<?xml version="1.0" encoding="UTF-8"?>
<!DOCTYPE html PUBLIC "-//W3C//DTD/XHTML 1.0 Transitional//EN"
"http://www.w3.org/TR/xhtml1/DTD/xhtml1-transitional.dtd">
<html xmlns="http://www.w3.org/1999/xhtml" xml:lang="en" lang="en">
<head>
<title> USING TABLES FOR LAYOUT </title>
</head>
<body>
<table border="0" width = 95% cellpadding="0" cellspacing="0">
<tr>
<td colspan="2"> <h1 align="center"> The W's of Web Design
</h1></td>
</tr>
<tr>
<td width="25%" valign="top">
<h3> Design Links </h1>
<a href="color.html">How to use color</a> <br/>
<a href="site.html">Site Design Issues</a> <br/>
<a href="page.html">Page Design Issues</a> <br/>
<a href="contact.html">How to contact us</a> <br/>
</td>
<td width="75%" valign="top">

There is no doubt that the World Wide Web and the Internet are good
things for anyone wanting to share information or promote something,
whether it be themselves, a cause, or a business. Many people are
rushing to create or have created a web presence. As they surf the
web, they are inundated with a visual chaos that is astounding.
Each time we see something new or different, we think, "My site
should have that!" However, there is much pre-planning that must
occur before considering what a web site will look like and how it
will behave. The "eye-candy" will have to wait until the practical
questions and considerations have been addressed. This article will
focus on the pre-design questions that a designer and client should
address before putting pixel to paper! The extremely popular and
dynamic sites that people love to experience when they surf the web
did not develop overnight. Though these sites seem to appear (and
disappear) as if by magic, there are scores of people working behind
the scenes to ensure that the experience of each user is consistent,
interesting and purposeful - whatever that purpose may be.
Recently, PUBLISH! Magazine did a story on the design and
implementation of The Discovery Channel web site. The striking thing
about the design of this wonderfully interactive site is not its
look and feel, but the fact that it took the better part of nine
months to plan the who, what, when, why and how of the site.
</td>
```

```
    </tr>
    </table>
    </body>
    </html>
```

USING STYLE SHEETS TO FORMAT TABLES

Cascading style sheets (CSS) can be used to define the formatting of a table. Cascading style sheets will be covered in detail in Chapter 12, when we look at style sheets and their impact on table style.

CHAPTER SUMMARY

In this chapter, we learned how to build tables. We learned how to build a basic table with rows and cells, how to add a column heading and a table caption. We also learned how to control the width, alignment, and border of the table and how to adjust the amount of space between cells and between cell borders and cell contents. We saw how to control the height, width, and alignment of rows and cells and how to span table cells across several columns or rows. This chapter showed how to nest a table inside another table. The table structure enhancements of grouping and aligning columns and rows can be used to load and display large tables incrementally. This chapter also introduced the concept of using tables for page layout.

KEY TERMS

align attribute	table cellpadding attribute
cell	table cellspacing attribute
colspan attribute	table data element
column	table data tag
column group tag	table element
height attribute	table frame attribute
nested tables	table header element
nowrap attribute	table header tag
row	table row element
rowspan attribute	table rules attribute
table	table tag
table align attribute	table width attribute
table border attribute	valign attribute
table caption element	width attribute

XHTML TABLE TAG SUMMARY

Tag	Attribute(s)	Use/Values
<table>	align	left, center, right
	border	= n, width of border in pixels
	cellspacing	= n, pixels between border and cell contents
	cellpadding	= n, pixels between cell borders
	width	= n or m%, width in pixels or percentage of screen
	bgcolor	
<tr>	align	left, center, right
	valign	top, middle, bottom
<td>	align	left, center, right
	valign	top, middle, bottom
	colspan	= n, number of columns to span
	rowspan	= n, number of rows to span
	nowrap	
	height	= n, cell height in pixels
	width	= n, cell width in pixels
<th>	align, valign, colspan, rowspan, nowrap, height, width	(same as above)
<caption>	align	top, bottom

REVIEW QUESTIONS

1. List the three tags that must be used in order to create a table. *<table> <td> <tr>*
2. What two tags can be used to create a table cell? How are they different?
3. What tag can be used to create a title for a table? Where can the title be placed? Where is the default location?
4. List and explain the five attributes for the <table> tag.
5. Explain the difference between cell padding and cell spacing.
6. How can the width of a table column be controlled? How can the width of the entire table be controlled?
7. How is a border added to a table? What is the default border?
8. What is the difference between the align and the valign attribute? What is the default alignment for a <td> cell? A <th> cell?

9. Explain the use of the nowrap, height, and width attributes.

10. How can data in a table be spread across several columns? Several rows?

11. Can one table be placed inside another? How?

EXERCISES

1. Create a simple table of radio frequencies. The table should have three columns and nine rows. The data for the table is given below.

Extremely low frequency	ELF	below 3 kilohertz
Very low frequency	VLF	3 to 30 kilohertz
Low frequency	LF	30 to 300 kilohertz
Medium frequency	MF	300 to 3,000 kilohertz
High frequency	HF	3 to 30 megahertz
Very high frequency	VHF	30 to 300 megahertz
Ultrahigh frequency	UHF	300 to 3,000 megahertz
Superhigh frequency	SHF	3 to 30 gigahertz
Extremely high frequency	EHF	30 to 300 gigahertz

2. Modify the table created in Exercise 1 by adding the caption "RADIO FRE-QUENCIES" below the table. Also, add table headers for each column, in order: "Class," "Abbreviation," and "Range."

3. Create a four-column, seven-row, partial periodic table. The table should have a border width of three pixels. The table should have cell spacing of 10 pixels and cell padding of five pixels. The table should have a caption below it, "PERIODIC TABLE." Each column should have a table header, in order: "Atomic #," "Element," "Atomic Weight," and "Symbol." The data for the table is given below.

18	Argon	39.948	Ar
4	Beryllium	9.01218	Be
55	Cesium	132.9054	Cs
66	Dysprosium	162.5	Dy
68	Erbium	167.26	Er
9	Flourine	18.9984	F
31	Gallium	69.72	Ga
2	Helium	4.0026	He
77	Iridium	192.22	Ir

4. Modify the table created in Exercise 3. Column 1 and column 3 should be aligned right. Column 4 should be centered. Rows 3, 6, and 9 should

have heights of 75 pixels. Column 2 should have a width of 100 pixels. Column 3 should have a width of 50 pixels. Vertically align row 3 at the top, row 6 in the middle, and row 9 at the bottom.

5. Create a five-column, 15-row, beaufort scale table. The first row should be spanned across all five columns and contain "BEAUFORT SCALE." The first cell of the second row should be blank, the second cell spanned across two columns and contain "Beaufort," the fourth column "Miles," and the fifth column blank. The first cell of the third row should be blank, the second should "#," the third "Name," the fourth "Per Hour," and the fifth "Description." The word "BREEZE" in column one should be rowspanned five rows starting with row six. The word "GALE" in column 1 should be spanned across four rows starting in row 11. All of the preceding cells should be created using the table header tag. (Empty cells have been shaded.) The data for the table is given below.

BEAUFORT SCALE

	Beaufort		Miles	
	#	Name	Per Hour	Description
	0	calm	< 1	calm; smoke rises vertically
	1	light air	1 - 3	direction of wind shown by smoke but not wind vanes
	2	light breeze	4 - 7	wind felt on face; leaves rustle
	3	gentle breeze	8 - 12	leaves and small twigs in constant motion; wind extends light flag
BREEZE	4	moderate breeze	13 - 18	raises dust and loose paper; small branches moved
	5	fresh breeze	19 - 24	small trees sway; crested wavelets form
	6	strong breeze	25 - 31	large branches in motion; umbrella use difficult
	7	moderate gale	32 - 38	whole trees in motion; inconvenience walking against the wind
	8	fresh gale	39 - 46	breaks twigs off trees; impedes progress
GALE	9	strong gale	47 - 54	slight structural damage
	10	whole gale	55 - 63	trees uprooted; considerable structural damage
	11	storm	64 - 72	very rarely experienced; widespread damage
	12	hurricane	73 - 136	devastation occurs

6. Create a table that contains two nested tables. The first table should have three rows and three columns with a border of five pixels, and a caption of "The Greek Alphabet." The first cell of that table should contain the first nested table; no border, two rows, and two columns. The last cell of the table should contain another nested table; border of one pixel, three rows, and three columns. The data for the tables is given below.

Main Table

(first nested table)	epsilon	zeta
Eta	theta	iota
Kappa	lambda	(second nested table)

First Nested Table

alpha	beta
gamma	delta

Second Nested Table

mu	nu	xi
omicron	pi	rho
sigma	tau	upsilon

PROJECT

Now that we have all our pages interconnected, we can focus on making sure each page is as communicative as possible. We should use tables to organize any repeating information such as our list of events. Do the following:

- Create tables on any of the pages that show repeating information. For example, the page that lists events or items for sale in the classifieds section has information that repeats, such as dates, item names, and so on. Place this information in a table.

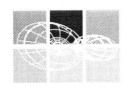

frames

CHAPTER OVERVIEW

Frames were an exciting feature in the HTML 4 standard and can be used in XHTML using the frameset DTD. Using frames, you can enhance the navigational possibilities and achieve layout control over Web pages. This feature is controversial among Web designers because it divides the available space, which is already in short supply. It also causes the browser to load more than one XHTML file, which may result in a delay for the user. This chapter will cover the following frame topics: creation, elements, nesting, and the use of frames.

CHAPTER OBJECTIVES

- Understand terminology related to frames
- Know what a frame is and how it can be used
- Know how to create a basic framed page
- Controlthe appearance of frames
- Create nested frames
- Create inline/floating frames

FRAMES

What are frames and why should we use them? The use of frames is a powerful feature in XHTML programming that provides a way to divide the browser window so it can hold more than one page. Why? By using frames, you can enhance the navigational possibilities and achieve layout control over Web pages. Although this feature is powerful, it is controversial among Web designers because it divides the available space, which is already in short supply. Web designers also dislike frames because they require them to write more code for the individual frames and can be difficult to code. They also causes the browser to load more than one XHTML file, which may result in a delay for the user. Because frames are difficult to use, Web designers must have a strong understanding of frame coding and design to enable them to integrate frames well into the site design.

They also are a source of frustration for users because of problems in bookmarking pages within the site, using a URL to refer to a specific page in a framed structure, and poorly designed frames that cause information to be partially displayed.

Even though they may be controversial, they still have their advantages. Frames can be useful in providing a static navigation area or devoting a portion of the screen to a constantly displaying message area. The decision to use or not to use frames should be made very carefully. A Web designer should not use frames simply because it can be done or it looks good. Using frames should be part of the design decision, which would include such things as the needs of the particular Website and accessibility issues. Keep in mind that even though both Netscape and Internet Explorer support frames, some browsers do not; let's not forget those PDAs and cell phones.

Frames were first introduced in Netscape 2.0 and Internet Explorer 3. They are included in the official XHTML 1.0 language specification as defined by the World Wide Web Consortium (W3C).

FRAME STRUCTURE

Frames divide the available browser space into rectangular areas. These frames can be arranged in *columns* (vertically), *rows* (horizontally), or a combination of both. Each frame in the browser window can display an independent document. Figure 9.1 illustrates the creation of *vertical frames* by dividing the browser window into three equal parts.

Figure 9.2 illustrates the creation of *horizontal frames* by dividing the browser window into three equal horizontal parts.

One of the most common ways to divide the browser window is with a combination of one horizontal and two vertical frames. This is a little more complex and involves nesting frameset elements. This technique will be discussed later in the chapter. Figure 9.3 illustrates the combination of vertical and horizontal frames.

FIGURE 9.1: THE BROWSER DIVIDED INTO VERTICAL FRAMES

BASIC FRAMES

The creation of frames in XHTML is accomplished by using three elements and several different attributes, and can be complicated and confusing. So, let's keep it simple. We will learn about the various attributes that can be used to control the frames once we understand how to create a simple framed page.

FIGURE 9.2: THE BROWSER DIVIDED INTO HORIZONTAL FRAMES

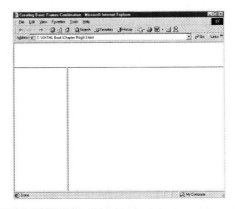

FIGURE 9.3: COMBINATION OF VERTICAL AND HORIZONTAL FRAMES

CREATING A FRAMESET, THE <FRAMESET> ELEMENT

A framed Web page is organized in a standard XHTML document called a frameset, which has a different format than an XHTML document that does not include frames. In order to create the frame structure, the *frameset elements,* <frameset> and </frameset>, are used. These elements will replace the <body> </body> elements of a nonframed page. The frameset document will determine the frame structure, the number and the size of the frames, and what will be displayed in each frame. A document can contain an unlimited number of frameset elements. The frameset element uses the rows and cols attributes to determine the number and size of the vertical and horizontal frames. These attributes and three others will be discussed later in the chapter.

INSERTING CONTENT INTO THE FRAMES, THE <FRAME> ELEMENT

The *frame element,* <frame>, follows the frameset element and establishes the source, or location, of the frame's contents. The src attribute of this element specifies the source URL of the document that will become the content of the frame. The frame element has many different attributes to control the frame's look and behavior. We will explore the other attributes later.

note: The frame element has no closing element </frame>. All information is contained inside the element and is considered closed when the "/>" is encountered.

HANDLING BROWSERS WITHOUT FRAME SUPPORT: THE <NOFRAMES> ELEMENT

The *noframes element,* <noframes> and </noframes>, follows the frame elements. The noframes element will provide an alternative for browsers that are not capable of displaying frames. Frame-capable browsers ignore these elements. This element is used to specify what is to be displayed when a browser is not capable of displaying frames. Refer to the next section, "Creating a Framed Page." It will demonstrate how to use this element to give users the opportunity to view a non-framed version of your page.

Let's start with something simple by dividing the browser window into three vertical frames.

CREATING A FRAMED PAGE

We will use the frame elements introduced above to create a basic framed page.

1. Type the following using your choice of editor and save it as basicfram.html. This will create our frameset document. Remember that the frameset element replaces the <body> tag.

```
<?xml version="1.0" encoding="UTF-8"?>
<!DOCTYPE html PUBLIC "-//W3C//DTD/XHTML 1.0 Frameset//EN"
"http://www.w3.org/TR/xhtml1/DTD/xhtml1-frameset.dtd">
<html xmlns="http://www.w3.org/1999/xhtml" xml:lang="en" lang="en">
<head>
<title>  Creating Basic Frames  </title>
</head>
<frameset cols="33%,33%,34%">
   <frame src="frame1.html"/>
   <frame src="frame2.html"/>
   <frame src="frame3.html"/>
   <noframes>
   <p> Your browser does not support frames!  You can view our
   non-framed version by clicking <a href="main.html"> here</a>
   </p>
   </noframes>
</frameset>
</html>
```

2. Next, we can create the first content file. Type the following and save it as frame1.html. This is what will be the content of the first frame.

note: The XHTML 1.0 frameset DTD must be used to enable frames to be displayed. The XHTML 1.0 strict DTD does not support the elements <frameset>, <frame>, <noframes>, and <iframe>. The XHTML 1.0 transitional DTD only supports <noframes> and <iframe>.

```
<?xml version="1.0" encoding="UTF-8"?>
<!DOCTYPE html PUBLIC "-//W3C//DTD/XHTML 1.0 Transitional//EN"
"http://www.w3.org/TR/xhtml1/DTD/xhtml1-transitional.dtd">
<html xmlns="http://www.w3.org/1999/xhtml" xml:lang="en" lang="en">
<head>
<title>  Frame File 1  </title>
</head>
<body>
  <p> This is frame 1 </p>
</body>
</html>
```

3. Now create the content files for the other two frames. Change the <title> and <p> tags appropriately. Save the files as frame2.html and frame3.html.

note: Since frame1.html will be the contents for a frame and not contain frames itself, use the XHTML 1.0 transitional DTD.

4. In the browser, select Open from the File menu to open basicfram.html. Your screen should resemble Figure 9.4. This is an example of a browser window divided into three vertical frames. You will notice that frames have a border between them by default.

Now let's modify the frameset that we created above to have three horizontal frames.

5. Open the frameset document basicfram.html previously created using your editor of choice and save it as rowframe.html. Make the following changes to the frameset element that will create horizontal frames.

```
<frameset rows="33%,33%,34%">
```

6. Save the document as rowframe.html.

FIGURE 9.4: THREE VERTICAL FRAMES   FIGURE 9.5: THREE HORIZONTAL FRAMES

7. In the browser, select Open from the File menu to open rowframe.html. Your screen should resemble Figure 9.5. This is an example of a browser window divided into three horizontal frames.

note: The content is not changing, just the orientation of the frames. The frameset document is the only one changed.

<FRAMESET> ELEMENT ATTRIBUTES

Now that we know how to build a simple frameset document, let's look at how we can control the size and orientation of the frames. We will start by looking at the two special attributes, rows and cols, that are used with the frameset element. The attributes frameborder and framespacing are extensions provided by the two main browsers to alter the borders that surround the frames in a given frameset. To learn more about these attributes, refer to Appendix A.

Frameset rows and cols Attributes

The frameset element requires rows or cols attributes, which are used to determine the number and size of the size of the vertical and/or horizontal frames. The values for both of these attributes are enclosed in quotes and are separated by a comma. These values specify the height of horizontal frames or width of vertical frames and are defined by using pixels, percentages, or ratios. For example, look at what we used earlier:

```
<frameset cols="33%,33%,34%">
```

This creates three columns of frames by using *relative frame measurements*. When using relative measurements, the frame size is expressed as a percentage of the browser window. We could have also used a wildcard (*) in place of the third value. The asterisk (*) instructs the browser to use the remaining space for the column or row. For example:

```
<frameset cols="33%, 33%,*">
```

In this three-column frameset, the remaining 34 percent of the browser's window will be allocated to the third frame.

The following frameset would provide three equal columns:

```
<frameset cols="*,*,*">
```

Let's experiment with percentages. Suppose we were to change the frameset to

```
<frameset rows="10%,50%,10%">
```

What would the results be? Figure 9.6 shows the results you should see. Is it what you expected? When percentages do not add up to 100 percent, they are treated as ratios.

Another form of relative measurement that can be used to express frame size is a ratio. A ratio is an integer value followed by an asterisk (*). It would be specified as follows:

```
<frameset rows="1*,5*,1*">
```

Figure 9.7 shows what the browser looks like when these ratios are used. Does it look like Figure 9.6 when the percentages did not add up to 100?

Let's take a closer look at ratios using columns this time. We will use the following:

```
<frameset cols="1*,2*,3*">
```

What are the integer proportions 1, 2, and 3 telling us? They indicate that column 2 is two times as wide as column 1, and column 3 is three times as wide as column 1. This is illustrated in Figure 9.8.

FIGURE 9.6: PERCENTAGES THAT DO NOT ADD UP TO 100

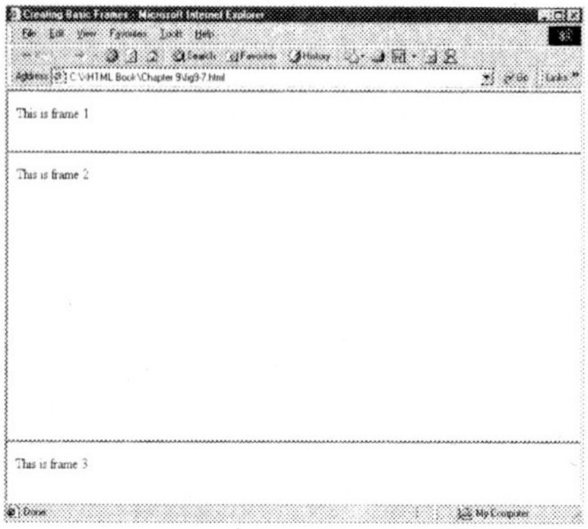

FIGURE 9.7: RATIOS USED AS RELATIVE MEASUREMENTS

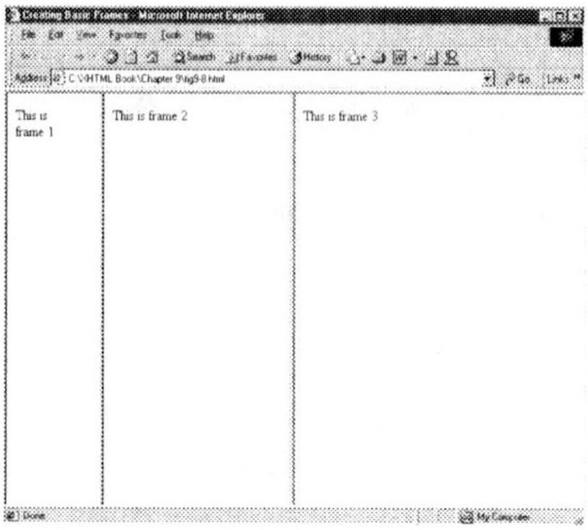

FIGURE 9.8: FRAMES USING RATIOS

note: When using relative measurements for frame size, the proportions will be maintained no matter what the size of the browser window is.

FIGURE 9.9: FRAMES USING ABSOLUTE VALUES

The third way to express frame size is with an absolute value in pixels. An integer is used to represent the value. The following is an example of using absolute values to create frames:

```
<frameset cols="100, 200, *">
```

This would produce the result in Figure 9.9. What happens if we make the following change:

```
<frameset cols="100,200,100">
```

FIGURE 9.10: FRAMES USING THREE ABSOLUTE VALUES

We would expect that it would give us three frames that were precisely 100, 200, and 100 pixels. Well, it will not provide the frames in those proportions; this is illustrated in Figure 9.10. Instead, the browser will interpret the pixel values as a set of

tip: To better understand how to use the different values of the cols and rows attributes, take some time to experiment with different values and combinations to see what effect they would have on the browser window.

ratios. When using absolute values, you must leave one frame size open and use the asterisk (*) for the value.

<FRAME> ELEMENT ATTRIBUTES

Now that we know how to control the size of our frames using the <frameset> attributes, let's look at how we can control the content and look of the frames. The <element> has the following attributes: src, id, name, scrolling, noresize, frameborder, marginheight, and marginwidth. We will start by looking at the important attributes src, name, and id, which are used with the frame element.

Frame src Attribute

The src ("source") *attribute* specifies the source URL of the document that will become the content of the frame. This document may be any type that the browser support, such as image, text, XHTML, and multimedia files. The following is from our basic frames example and illustrates the use of this attribute:

```
<frame src="frame1.html"/>
```

Frame id Attribute

The *id attribute* is used to define a name for an individual frame. This name can be used as a *target* of hyperlinks in the <a>, <form>, <area>, and <base> elements. Targeting allows the contents of a frame to be changed using a link in another frame. Targeting will be discussed in more detail later in the chapter. Here is an example of using the id attribute:

warning: The name attribute has been deprecated for frames, but some browsers (such as Netscape) do not support the frame attribute id. For compatibility, use both id and name attributes (see the name example).

```
<frame src="toc.html" id="toc_menu" />
```

Frame name Attribute

The *name attribute* provides the same function as the id attribute discussed above. Both attributes can be used (see the warning above). For example:

tip: Use descriptive names for the id and name attributes to help identify the frame's content.

```
<frame src="toc.html" id="toc_menu" name="toc_menu" />
```

Frame noresize Attribute

The user can manually resize the dimensions of the frames set in the frameset element by using the mouse to click and drag the frame's border. By using the *noresize attribute*, the user will not be allowed to alter the frame size. This attribute takes its own name as a value. For example:

```
<frame src="toc.html" noresize="noresize" />
```

Now try adding the nore-size attribute we just talked about to the frame element.

> **warning:** Using the noresize attribute could make some of the frame content inaccessible.

1. Using your choice of editor, open the file basicfram.html.
2. Next, add a noresize attribute to the first frame element. The frameset should now look like the following:

```
<frameset cols="33%,33%,34%">
    <frame src="frame1.htm" noresize="noresize"/>
    <frame src="frame2.html"/>
    <frame src="frame3.html"/>
    <noframes>
    <p> Your browser does not support frames!</p>
    </noframes>
</frameset>
```

3. Save the document as basicfram.html.
4. In the browser, select Open from the File menu to open basicfram.html. Your screen should still resemble Figure 9.4 because we did not make any structural changes to the <frameset>.
5. Try to resize the border of frame 1 manually by clicking and dragging. Can it be done? Try to resize frame 2 by doing the same. You should not be able to manually resize frame 1, but you should be able to resize frame 2.

Frame scrolling Attribute

By default, browsers display scrollbars for frames when their content exceeds the allotted space. The *scrolling attribute* will give you control over the appearance of scrollbars for each frame. This attribute has three possible values: yes, no, and auto. The default value is auto and gives control to the browser to determine when a scrollbar is needed. The yes value will always place a scrollbar in the frame, and a no value will prevent a scrollbar from appearing in the frame. The following illustrates the use of this attribute:

```
<frame src="toc.html" scrolling="yes" />
<frame src="toc.html" scrolling="no" />
```

Now try adding the scrolling attribute we just talked about to the frame element.

1. Using your choice of editor, open the file basicfram.html.
2. Next, add a scrolling attribute with a yes value to the second frame element. The frameset should now look like the following:

```
<frameset cols="33%,33%,34%">
    <frame src="frame1.htm"noresize="noresize"/>
    <frame src="frame2.html"scrolling="yes"/>
    <frame src="frame3.html"/>
    <noframes>
    <p> Your browser does
    not support frames!</p>
    </noframes>
</frameset>
```

3. Save the document as basicfram.html.
4. In the browser, select Open from the File menu to open basicfram.html. Your screen should still resemble Figure 9.11, with a scrollbar always visible on frame 2.

FIGURE 9.11:: FRAMES USING THE SCROLLING ATTRIBUTE

> **warning:** Using a scrolling value of no could make some of the frame's content unviewable.

Frame marginheight and marginwidth Attributes

The *marginheight* and *marginwidth attributes* are used to specify the amount of separation (in pixels) between the border of a frame and the frame's content. When marginheight is used, the white space around any content will be at the top and the bottom. When marginwidth is used, the white space around the content will be on the sides.

> **tip:** The value supplied for marginheight and marginwidth cannot be less than one pixel. If the requested value cannot be displayed, the attribute is ignored.

The following are examples of these attributes set to five pixels:

```
<frame src="frame1.htm"noresize="noresize" marginheight="5"/>
<frame src="frame2.html"scrolling="yes" marginwidth="5"/>
```

COMBINING HORIZONTAL AND VERTICAL FRAMES

One of the most common ways to divide the browser window is with one horizontal frame and two vertical frames. The horizontal frame across the top usually contains information such as a company name, advertisements, or the site name. This frame usually remains static no matter what is done with the main frame. The left vertical frame usually contains navigational tools and is the smaller of the two. The right vertical frame is the main frame, which contains the content. Figure 9.12 illustrates the combination of vertical and horizontal frames.

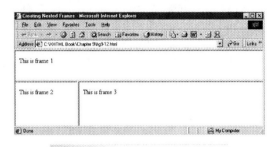

FIGURE 9.12: A COMBINATION OF FRAMES

This layout is accomplished by nesting frameset elements. The use of a *nested frameset* is demonstrated using the following XHTML:

```
<?xml version="1.0" encoding="UTF-8"?>
<!DOCTYPE html PUBLIC "-//W3C//DTD/XHTML 1.0 Frameset//EN"
"http://www.w3.org/TR/xhtml1/DTD/xhtml1-frameset.dtd">
<html xmlns="http://www.w3.org/1999/xhtml" xml:lang="en" lang="en">
<head>
<title>  Creating Nested Frames  </title>
</head>
<frameset rows="75, *">
   <frame src="frame1.html" />
   <frameset cols="25%,75%">
      <frame src="frame2.html" />
      <frame src="frame3.html" />
   </frameset>
</frameset>
</html>
```

The initial (outer) frameset element creates a framed document with two rows. The second row can be subdivided into two columns by nesting another frameset element. You may notice that it looks very much like a page layout using tables, which we discussed at the end of the previous chapter.

TARGETING FRAMES

When the id and name attributes of the frame element have been given a name, that frame can be a target of a hyperlink. In order to use our frame to enhance navigation, we must first review the behavior of a hyperlink.

Normally, when a hyperlink is clicked, the new file will be loaded into the frame that contains the hyperlink. By using the target attribute of hyperlinks in the <a>, <form>, <area>, and <base> elements, the hyperlink document can be displayed in another frame.

The value of the target attribute should be the id or name of the frame that is to be updated. For example:

```
<frame src="home.html" id="main" name="main" />
<a href="color.html" target="main">How to use color</a>
```

In this example, the name of the frame to be updated is "main." When the user clicks on the hyperlink "How to use color," color.html will be loaded into the frame named "main."

There are also four predefined target names that can be assigned to the target attribute. They are sometimes referred to as magic tags and are used to ensure that pages are displayed where intended. These predefined targets begin with the underline character (_). They are

_blank   This attribute opens the selected file in a new browser window.

_self   This attribute instructs the browser to open the selected file in the current frame.

_parent   This attribute instructs the browser to replace the current document (frameset) with the new file.

_top   This attribute instructs the browser to clear all current frames and load the new page into the main browser window.

Let's take what we have learned so far about nested frames and targeted frames to create a page with the following features: a title across the top, a navigation area on the left, and a main display area on the right.

note: If the hyperlink specified does not exist, a new browser window will be opened to display the page.

1. Type the following using your choice of editor and save it as menu.html. This will be used to create the menu in the left frame.

```
<?xml version="1.0" encoding="UTF-8"?>
<!DOCTYPE html PUBLIC "-//W3C//DTD/XHTML 1.0 Transitional//EN"
"http://www.w3.org/TR/xhtml1/DTD/xhtml1-transitional.dtd">
<html xmlns="http://www.w3.org/1999/xhtml" xml:lang="en" lang="en">
<head>
<title>Menu</title>
</head>
<body>
    <p><a href="chapter1.html" target="main">CHAPTER 1 </a></p>
    <p><a href="chapter2.html" target="main">CHAPTER 2 </a></p>
    <p><a href="chapter3.html" target="main">CHAPTER 3 </a></p>
</body>
</html>
```

2. Type the following to create a header in the top frame. Save it as head.html.

```
<?xml version="1.0" encoding="UTF-8"?>
<!DOCTYPE html PUBLIC "-//W3C//DTD/XHTML 1.0 Transitional//EN"
"http://www.w3.org/TR/xhtml1/DTD/xhtml1-transitional.dtd">
<html xmlns="http://www.w3.org/1999/xhtml" xml:lang="en" lang="en">
<head>
<title>Page Heading</title>
</head>
<body>
<div align="center">
    <h1> TABLE OF CONTENTS OVERVIEW </h1>
</div>
</body>
</html>
```

3. Enter the following to create an initial home page display. Save it as home.html.

```
<?xml version="1.0" encoding="UTF-8"?>
<!DOCTYPE html PUBLIC "-//W3C//DTD/XHTML 1.0 Transitional//EN"
"http://www.w3.org/TR/xhtml1/DTD/xhtml1-transitional.dtd">
<html xmlns="http://www.w3.org/1999/xhtml" xml:lang="en" lang="en">
<head>
<title>Page Heading</title>
</head>
<body>
<div align="center">
    <h1> Welcome to XHTML</h1>
</div>
</body>
</html>
```

4. Now, create a simple XHTML file for the Chapter 1 link by entering the following. Save it as chapter1.html.

```
<?xml version="1.0" encoding="UTF-8"?>
<!DOCTYPE html PUBLIC "-//W3C//DTD/XHTML 1.0 Transitional//EN"
"http://www.w3.org/TR/xhtml1/DTD/xhtml1-transitional.dtd">
<html xmlns="http://www.w3.org/1999/xhtml" xml:lang="en" lang="en">
<head>
<title>Chapter 1</title>
</head>
<body>
<p> History, philosophy and the practical aspects of the Internet as
a community and as a series of machines physically linked together.
This chapter will focus on the beginnings from ARPANET to Tim
Berners-Lee to  e-commerce today. It will also include explanations
on the physical setup of the machines and nodes that make up the
Internet as well as the philosophies that are driving the World Wide
Web's rapid growth. </p>
</body>
</html>
```

5. Create the XHTML file for the Chapter 2 link. Enter and save the following as chapter2.html.

```
<?xml version="1.0" encoding="UTF-8"?>
<!DOCTYPE html PUBLIC "-//W3C//DTD/XHTML 1.0 Transitional//EN"
"http://www.w3.org/TR/xhtml1/DTD/xhtml1-transitional.dtd">
<html xmlns="http://www.w3.org/1999/xhtml" xml:lang="en" lang="en">
<head>
<title>Chapter 2</title>
</head>
<body>
<p> This chapter will focus on an introduction to the vocabulary
and principles of visual design based on the Gestalt Theories of
Information Perception pioneered by Max Wertheimer. Additionally,
the exploration of the interrelationships of forms utilizing Boolean
operations: union, difference, and intersection. This hands-on
exploration will include design exercises and projects that stimu-
late the imagination and will lead to strengthening the visualiza-
tion skills of the student. The techniques and theories discussed
in this chapter will lead directly to the student's own Web page
designs.</p>
</body>
</html>
```

6. Create the XHTML file for the Chapter 3 link. Enter and save the following as chapter3.html.

```
<?xml version="1.0" encoding="UTF-8"?>
<!DOCTYPE html PUBLIC "-//W3C//DTD/XHTML 1.0 Transitional//EN"
"http://www.w3.org/TR/xhtml1/DTD/xhtml1-transitional.dtd">
<html xmlns="http://www.w3.org/1999/xhtml" xml:lang="en" lang="en">
<head>
<title>Chapter 3</title>
</head>
<body>
<p> This chapter will focus on the concepts necessary to
build effective Websites. Before getting into the nuts-and-bolts
development of your Website, it's important to think about its
overall organization. In previous chapters, design considerations
have been focused on individual pages, but these pages are just
part of a Website. How will the pages relate to each other?  This
is one of many questions that will be explored in this chapter
along with: concepts of good site design, site structure, planning,
content, and management.</p>
</body>
</html>
```

7. Now it's time to create the frameset using nested framesets. Enter the following and save it as overview.html.

```
<?xml version="1.0" encoding="UTF-8"?>
<!DOCTYPE html PUBLIC "-//W3C//DTD/XHTML 1.0 Frameset//EN"
"http://www.w3.org/TR/xhtml1/DTD/xhtml1-frameset.dtd">
<html xmlns="http://www.w3.org/1999/xhtml" xml:lang="en" lang="en">
<head>
<title>TOC Overview</title>
</head>
<frameset rows="75, *">
   <frame src="head.html" id="head"name="head" scrolling="no" />
   <frameset cols="25%,75%">
     <frame src="menu.html" id="menu" name="menu" />
     <frame src="home.html" id="main" name="main"/>
   </frameset>
</frameset>
</html>
```

8. In the browser, select Open from the File menu to open overview.html. Your screen should resemble Figure 9.13. Go ahead and try your links.

FIGURE 9.13: A FRAMED PAGE USING A NESTED FRAMESET

CREATING INLINE FRAMES, THE <IFRAME> ELEMENT

A frame can also be added to a regular XHTML document, one without a frameset, by using the *iframe element*. These inline or floating frames can appear any place that you want and are displayed as part of the document's text. The most common attributes used with the iframe element are src, height, and width. These attributes provide the same function as they did with the frame element. The following XHTML illustrates the use of inline frames:

```
<?xml version="1.0" encoding="UTF-8"?>
<!DOCTYPE html PUBLIC "-//W3C//DTD/XHTML 1.0 Transitional//EN"
"http://www.w3.org/TR/xhtml1/DTD/xhtml1-transitional.dtd">
<html xmlns="http://www.w3.org/1999/xhtml" xml:lang="en" lang="en">
<head>
<title>Inline Frames Example</title>
</head>
<body>
<h1>Inline Frames</h1>
<p>This is an example of how to use basic inline frames. In the
inline frame you will see a chapter overview. </p>
<iframe src="chapter3.html" height="300" width="300">
</iframe>
</body>
</html>
```

This would produce the result shown in Figure 9.14.

Some browsers do not support frames, and some browsers do not support inline frames. Internet Explorer 5 and Netscape Navigator 6 support inline frames. An alternate presentation should be included when using the iframe element. Use the content of the iframe element to provide information to the user indicating the problem. If the browser supports the iframe element, the content information will be ignored. If the browser does not support the iframe element, the elements will be ignored. The following XHTML is an example with the alternate processing included.

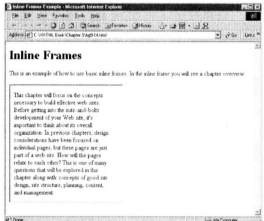

FIGURE 9.14: BASIC INLINE FRAME

```
<?xml version="1.0" encoding="UTF-8"?>
<!DOCTYPE html PUBLIC "-//W3C//DTD/XHTML 1.0 Transitional//EN"
"http://www.w3.org/TR/xhtml1/DTD/xhtml1-transitional.dtd">
<html xmlns="http://www.w3.org/1999/xhtml" xml:lang="en" lang="en">
<head>
<title>Inline Frames Example</title>
</head>
<body>
<h1>Inline Frames</h1>
<p>This is an example of how to use basic inline frames. In the
inline frame, you will see a chapter overview. </p>
<iframe src="chapter3.html" height="300" width="300">
<p>This does not support the inline frames feature.</p>
</iframe>
</body>
</html>
```

You can include as much text in the iframe element as you want. You could also include the target document that you were placing in the frame.

CHAPTER SUMMARY

This chapter demonstrated the power of frames by showing how to divide the browser window into multiple sections, with each one holding a separate document. The use of frames can enhance the navigational possibilities and achieve more layout control over Web pages. Although frames provide many benefits, they are also a source of considerable frustration for Web designers because they are difficult to code.

In this chapter, we learned how to build a Web page with frames. We learned how to build basic horizontal and vertical frames. Various methods of controlling the size of each frame were introduced. This chapter also demonstrated how horizontal and vertical frames could be combined to provide a page title, static navigation area, and an information display area. Frames can also be added to a document that does not have a frameset element by using inline frames. We learned how to handle browsers that do not support frames by using the noframes element.

KEY TERMS

column	iframe element
frame element	id attribute
frameset element	marginheight attribute
horizontal frame	marginwidth attribute

name attribute
nested frameset
noframes element
noresize attribute
relative frame measurement

row
scrolling attribute
src attribute
target
vertical frame

XHTML TABLE TAG SUMMARY

Tag	Attribute(s)	Use/Values
<frameset>	rows	=n%, frame size as percentage of browser window
	cols	= n, frame size in pixels
		= n*, frame size relative to other frames
<frame>	src	Document URL
	id	Anchor name
	name	
	noresize	noresize, disable resizing of frame by users
	scrolling	yes/no, enables/disables scrollbars
	marginheight	=n, pixels between frame and contents, top and bottom
	marginwidth	=n, pixels between frame and contents, on sides
<noframes>		Allows browser not capable of displaying frames to give user a message and options
<iframe>	src	Document URL
	height	=n, frame height in pixels
	width	=n, frame width in pixels

REVIEW QUESTIONS

1. What tag set holds the structure for a framed Web page?
2. What attribute of the frame element is used to locate a frame's content?
3. What attribute of the frameset element is used to divide a Web page into horizontal frames?
4. What attribute of the frameset element is used to divide a Web page into vertical frames?
5. What element is replaced in a document when the <frameset> element is used?
6. What attribute of the frame element is used to define the XHTML docu-

ment that loads into the frameset?

7. What attribute is used to direct linked pages to load into a frame?
8. What is the purpose of the noframes element?
9. What attribute of the frame element is used to prevent the user from changing the size of a frame?
10. Does using the <iframe> element require a frameset element?
11. Can one frameset be nested inside another? How?

EXERCISES

1. Create a Web page that consists of four equal horizontal frames. Once you have the correct structure, create an XHTML document that can be loaded into each frame.
2. Create a Web page that consists of four vertical frames each taking up 25 percent of the browser window. Create at least two different <frameset> declarations that will have the same result.
3. Given the following table definition, create a Web page using frames that is identical in layout.

```
<table>
<tr>
<td rowspan="2">CELL1</td>
<td>CELL2</td>
</tr>
<tr>
<td rowspan="2">CELL3</td>
</tr>
<tr>
<td rowspan="2">CELL4</td>
</tr>
<tr>
<td>CELL5</td>
</table>
```

4. Using the Web page shown in Figure 9.13, modify the navigation frame, so that when the hyperlink for Chapter 2 is clicked, it opens it in a new browser window to display the linked document.
5. Create a simple framed paged that will provide descriptions of flowers. The layout should have three frames: a header frame that displays "The Flower Garden," a navigation frame that contains the hyperlinks for each flower, and a main display frame that displays the information about the flower when the hyperlink is clicked. The Web layout should be similar to the one created in Figure 9.13. The data is given below.

Columbine
Columbine: This easy-to-grow perennial is loved by hummingbirds. Plant in full sun or partial shade for blooms in May and June.

Black-Eyed Susan
Black-Eyed Susan: Orange coneflowers that grow on 2- to 3-foot stems do best in full sun. These are great flowers for the wild garden producing blooms through July and August.

Iris
Iris: There are over 200 species available in a vast array of colors. Irises are easy to grow and most need sunlight. Plant the rhizomes in the fall for blooms in early May.

Daylily
Daylily: Daylilies are perennials that earned their name because each bloom opens, matures, and withers in 24 hours or less. Daylilies do well in partial shade and require little care.

Foxglove
Foxglove: Most foxgloves are biennials which grow on tall, strong stems in partial shade. They are easy to care for and flower during May and June.

PROJECT

Continue using the project created in the previous chapters. Frames are a great way to minimize bandwidth requirements. By putting any information that remains the same from page to page into a frame, we only need to load it once. This reduces the amount of information that we need to send to the user. Do the following:

- Create a frameset and the appropriate pages necessary to create a text-based navigational bar at the bottom of each page. Make the frames invisible.

REFERENCES

Frames: An Introduction,
http://home.netscape.com/assist/net_sites/frames.html
Frames, http://www.w3.org/TR/REC-html40/present/frames.html
Authoring Frames, http://hotwired.lycos.com/webmonkey/authoring/frames

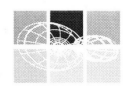

working with images and multimedia

CHAPTER OVERVIEW

In this chapter, we will learn how to add images to our Web pages. Images, in one form or another, are what make our Web pages really attractive. Most images on the Web today are one of only three common types of graphic file formats. Only one element is required to add an image to a Web page, but 10 attributes allow us to control exactly how that image appears. We will also learn about image compression and using image maps instead of ordinary hyperlinks.

CHAPTER OBJECTIVES

- Add an image to a Web page and specify a textual alternative to the picture
- Control the size of the displayed image and the flow of the text around it
- Put a border around our image and use it as an image map
- Perform image compression and control palette colors and graphics file size
- Choose between various graphics file formats for different applications

IMAGES

What would a Web page be without some type of graphic? Today, graphics are an integral part of the content of almost every Web page. They may be used to catch the user's attention, deliver information, or even aid in site navigation. Images can make our Web pages really attractive, or they can have a negative effect by their overuse. So we must learn to use images effectively; this means more than just being able to add images to our pages. You must also understand file formats, compression techniques, file size considerations, and image maps. Images can be either inline or external. Browsers display inline images as part of the Web page along with text. External images are not displayed as part of a Web page and are loaded only when requested, which is usually accomplished through the use of a link.

So let's get started by discussing the only element that is required to add an inline image to a Web page and the several attributes used to control how the image appears.

ADDING AN INLINE IMAGE, THE <IMG> ELEMENT

The *img element* is an empty element used to specify the image that is to be inserted into the Web page. Since <img> is an empty element and does not have a closing tag, it must be terminated properly in XHTML by adding a space and a slash before the closing angle bracket, as follows:

```
<img />
```

The img element has two required attributes, src and alt.

src Attribute

The *src attribute* is the most important of the attributes; without it, no image is displayed. Src stands for "source" and directs the browser to get the file at the specified location. The value of the attribute is the address of the image and could be

- a file name if the file is located in the same directory
- a relative path name
- an absolute URL

The use of the src attribute should look familiar to you; it is identical to how the href attribute is used in the anchor element.

alt Attribute

The *alt attribute* stands for "alternate." The value of this attribute is a text description of the image. This text is displayed when an image is encountered by a non-graphical browser or a browser that has graphics disabled.

> tip: Describe the image. Don't just use the image file name, which is usually not very descriptive.

The syntax of the img element is:

```
<img src="image address" alt="text describing image" />
```

Let's take a look at an XHTML document that includes an image. The following XHTML includes the img element to add an inline image to a Web page:

```
<?xml version="1.0" encoding="UTF-8"?>
<!DOCTYPE html PUBLIC "-//W3C//DTD/XHTML 1.0 Transitional//EN"
"http://www.w3.org/TR/xhtml1/DTD/xhtml1-transitional.dtd">
<html xmlns="http://www.w3.org/1999/xhtml" xml:lang="en" lang="en">
<head>
<title> Inline Image </title>
</head>
<body>
    <h2 align="center">1913 Chalmers</h2>
    <img src="dsc00023d.jpg" alt="1913 Chalmers" />
</body>
</html>
```

The results of the above XHTML are in Figure 10.1.

FIGURE 10.1: XHTML DOCUMENT WITH INLINE IMAGE

Notice the position of the image on the page; the default setting for the browser places the image on the left side of the page. When the cursor is placed on the image, the value in the alt attribute is displayed. What happens if the browser cannot find the image requested? Figure 10.2 shows what the Web page would look like if the browser could not find the image in the XHTML document used in the previous example.

FIGURE 10.2: XHTML DOCUMENT WITH INLINE IMAGE NOT FOUND

Image width and height Attributes

The *width* and *height attributes* tell the browser how much space to set aside on the page for a given image. The values of these two attributes are provided in pixels. When the browser is able to allocate the correct image size on the page, it will not have to rearrange other elements to accommodate the image as it is downloaded. The syntax of the img element, using the width and height attributes, is as follows:

```
<img src="image address" alt="text describing image"
width="in pixels" height="in pixels" />
```

Figure 10.3 illustrates the use of the img element with width and height attributes.

FIGURE 10.3: IMAGE USING WIDTH AND HEIGHT ATTRIBUTES

The width and height values can be determined by opening the image in a graphics program or in Internet Explorer by right-clicking on the image to check the image properties. See Figure 10.4 for an example.

FIGURE 10.4: USING PROPERTIES TO DETERMINE WIDTH AND HEIGHT

When the width and height attributes are used, the browser displays a box on the page while the image loads. What happens when the width and height values do not exactly match the size of the image? The browser will stretch or squeeze the image into the allotted space. Figure 10.5 shows how an image is altered to fit the available space.

FIGURE 10.5: IMAGE DISPLAYED WITH DIFFERENT WIDTH AND HEIGHT VALUES

Notice how the images are displayed (left to right):

- the first one has correct width and height
- the second has larger width and height
- the third has smaller width and height
- the fourth has not loaded but is correct size
- the fifth has no width and height; note that the browser has allocated the default space

IMAGE ALIGNMENT

There are several options when it comes to aligning images. The images can be aligned with text, or they can be entirely separate and then aligned to the middle, left, right, top, or bottom.

Image align Attribute

The *align attribute* has been deprecated and is not available in the XHTML 1.0 strict DTD. This attribute can still be used in the XHTML 1.0 transitional DTD, and we will discuss its use here since it is so widely used. Image alignment can also be accomplished

tip: *Always* include width and height attributes. The loading time for the Web page can be reduced when these attributes are used correctly.

through the use of style sheets and style attributes, which is the preferred method.

Images can be aligned either horizontally or vertically using one of the following values: left, right, top, middle, or bottom. When these values are used, they will allow text to be aligned with the image and wrap text around the image. The default alignment for an image is left. Figure 10.6 illustrates the default alignment of an image.

FIGURE 10.6: IMAGE DISPLAYED WITH DEFAULT ALIGNMENT

Horizontal Alignment

- right – Image is placed on the right margin, and any text will wrap around the left margin of the image.
- left – Image is placed on the left margin, and any text will wrap around the right margin of the image.

Figure 10.7 illustrates using the align attribute to horizontally align an image with text and how text wraps around an image.

FIGURE 10.7: IMAGE DISPLAYED WITH LEFT AND RIGHT ALIGNMENT

Vertical Alignment

To understand how text is aligned with images, we must have a reference. When dealing with text, this reference is called the baseline. If you were to draw an imaginary horizontal line across the bottom of the text, this would identify the baseline.

- top – The image will be aligned with the top of the text. Think of an imaginary line across the top of the text.
- middle – The vertical center of the image is aligned with the baseline of the text.
- bottom – The bottom of an image is aligned with the baseline of the text. This is the default, and the same results would be achieved by not specifying an align attribute value.

The following XHTML is an example of how the align attributes are used with text:

```
<?xml version="1.0" encoding="UTF-8"?>
<!DOCTYPE html PUBLIC "-//W3C//DTD/XHTML 1.0 Transitional//EN"
"http://www.w3.org/TR/xhtml1/DTD/xhtml1-transitional.dtd">
<html xmlns="http://www.w3.org/1999/xhtml" xml:lang="en" lang="en">
<head>
<title> Text and Image Alignment </title>
</head>
```

```
<body>
   <h2 align="center">Text and Image Alignment</h2>
   <div>
<img src="FlagsEagle.jpg" alt="American Flags and Eagle" align="bottom" />
   Here the align attribute is set to "bottom."  The bottom of the
   image is aligned with the text baseline.
   </div>
   <div>
<img src="FlagsEagle.jpg" alt="American Flags and Eagle" align="middle"
/>
   Here the align attribute is set to "middle."  The center of the image
is aligned with the text baseline.
   </div>
   <div>
<img src="FlagsEagle.jpg" alt="American Flags and Eagle" align="top"/>
   Here the align attribute is set to "top."  The top of the image is
aligned with the top of the text.
   </div>
</body>
</html>
```

The results of this XHTML document are shown in Figure 10.8.

Give it a try yourself:

1. Type the XHTML used to create Figure 10.8 using your choice of editor and save it as vertalign.html.

2. Copy the graphic from the CD or one of your choosing to the directory where you saved the XHTML document.

3. Open the document in your browser. Did you achieve the same results?

FIGURE 10.8: VERTICAL IMAGE ALIGNMENT WITH TEXT

Adding Horizontal and Vertical Space Around Images

In Figure 10.9, there are three images placed horizontally. Notice that there is a thin line of space between each image. What if we wanted more? We could use the hspace and vspace attributes.

The hspace and vspace attributes have been deprecated and are not available in the XHTML 1.0 strict DTD. These attributes can still be used in the

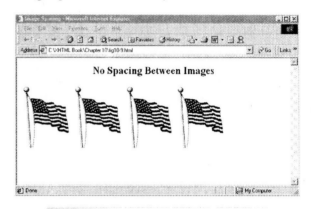

FIGURE 10.9: HORIZONTAL IMAGES WITH NO SPACE

XHTML 1.0 transitional DTD, and we will discuss their use here since they are so widely used. Image alignment can also be accomplished through the use of style sheets and style attributes, which are the preferred methods.

hspace Attribute

The *hspace attribute* can be used to add horizontal space between the images. The value of this attribute is stated in pixels and indicates the amount of space on either side of the image. For example:

```
hspace = "10"
```

This would indicate that 10 pixels of space would be on each side of the image.

vspace Attribute

The *vspace attribute* can be used to add vertical space between the images. The value of this attribute is stated in pixels and indicates the amount of space above and below the image. For example:

```
vspace = "10"
```

This would indicate that 10 pixels of space would be above and below the image.

The following XHTML is an example of how to set the horizontal and vertical space between images and text.

```
<?xml version="1.0" encoding="UTF-8"?>
<!DOCTYPE html PUBLIC "-//W3C//DTD/XHTML 1.0 Transitional//EN"
"http://www.w3.org/TR/xhtml1/DTD/xhtml1-transitional.dtd">
<html xmlns="http://www.w3.org/1999/xhtml" xml:lang="en" lang="en">
<head>
<title> Image Spacing </title>
</head>
<body>
   <h2 align="center">Spacing Between Images</h2>
   <img src="American_Flag_2.jpg" alt="American Flag" width="117"
   height="150" hspace="15" vspace="15" />
   <img src="American_Flag_2.jpg" alt="American Flag" width="117"
   height="150" hspace="15" vspace="15"/>
   <img src="American_Flag_2.jpg" alt="American Flag" width="117"
   height="150" hspace="15" vspace="15"/>
   <img src="American_Flag_2.jpg" alt="American Flag" width="117"
   height="150" hspace="15" vspace="15"/>
</body>
</html>
```

The results of the XHTML document are shown in Figure 10.10.

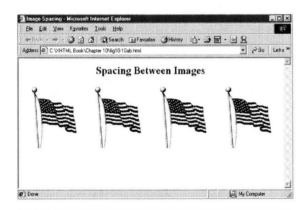

FIGURE 10.10: HORIZONTAL AND VERTICAL SPACE ATTRIBUTES

IMAGE BORDERS

Currently, the image defaults to having no border unless it is a link, which
would have a border the same color as a link. A border is just a line that
is placed around the edge of the image. A border can be intentionally placed
around the image by using the border attribute.

Image border Attribute

The *border attribute* has been deprecated and is not available in the XHTML 1.0 strict DTD. This attribute can still be used in the XHTML 1.0 transitional DTD, and we will discuss its use here.

The border attribute is used to add borders around images. The thickness of the border can vary and is changed by supplying a value in pixels. The default color of the border is the same as the text on the page, or in the case of a linked image, it defaults to the link color. Here is an example of using the border element:

```
<img border = "10" />
```

This would place a 10-pixel border around the image. The following XHTML is an example of how to add a border to an image.

```
<?xml version="1.0" encoding="UTF-8"?>
<!DOCTYPE html PUBLIC "-//W3C//DTD/XHTML 1.0 Transitional//EN"
"http://www.w3.org/TR/xhtml1/DTD/xhtml1-transitional.dtd">
<html xmlns="http://www.w3.org/1999/xhtml" xml:lang="en" lang="en">
<head>
<title> Image Borders </title>
</head>
<body>
   <h2 align="center">Images With Borders</h2>
   <img src="FlagsEagle.jpg" alt="American Flags and Eagle"
   width="225" height="191" border="10" />
</body>
</html>
```

The results of this XHTML document are shown in Figure 10.11.

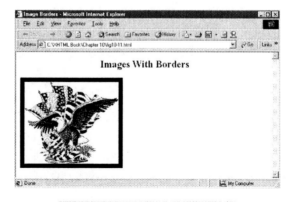

FIGURE 10.11: IMAGE BORDER ATTRIBUTE

IMAGE COMPRESSION TECHNIQUES

Since graphics play an important part in the design of our Web pages, we must consider the issues of download time, storage, and quality. All these can be linked to the actual size of the image file and need to be considered. Think about how many times you sat there waiting for an image to download on a Web page. What did you do? You probably did what many other people do and went to another Web page. So remember, just because your graphics are cool or great looking, if nobody ever sees them, does it matter how great they are?

The file format of the image has a great deal of impact on appearance, quality, and download time. The file type can impact both of these factors by how it reduces the size of the file through compression. There are two common compression techniques: lossless and lossy.

Lossless compression allows an image file to be compressed, and when it is later decompressed, there is no loss of data. This means that the decompressed file is identical to the original.

Lossy compression eliminates information that is unimportant when the file is compressed. This means that the decompressed file will not be identical to the original. This is accomplished in such a way that the loss of data will not be noticed.

IMAGE FILE FORMATS

There are many different kinds of graphic file formats currently available for use on the Web. Fortunately for us, there are only three commonly used formats:

- GIF
- JPG
- PNG

GRAPHIC INTERCHANGE FORMAT (GIF)

Before we actually start talking about GIF files, we should discuss the issue of pronunciation. Some people pronounce the "G" as a "J," which then sounds like "JIF." I prefer using the hard "G" pronunciation; it comes down to a personal preference.

The *GIF* standard was released by CompuServe in 1987 and uses the lossless compression algorithm called LZW. The LZW compression algorithm is named after its inventors Lempel, Ziv, and Welch. Without getting into a lot of detail, Unisys Corporation holds the patent on LZW compression. So software that creates or displays LZW-compressed files should be licensed by Unisys.

Because the GIF compression algorithm is lossless, it will not cause any loss of image quality when saved. This algorithm does its work by figuring out which areas of the image have identically colored pixels and then replaces them with a numeric pattern. This compression scheme limits GIF files to 256 colors, which is the number that can be represented with eight bits. The GIF format is best used with line drawings or images with a limited number of colors.

The types of GIF images are

- Animated
- Interlaced
- Transparent

Animated GIF Images

One of the most popular uses of GIF images is to create animated GIFs, which sometimes appear to be small video clips. The effect of animation is achieved by simply displaying a series of images in rapid succession. Maybe you have played with or seen a cartoon flip-book where each page has an image that varies slightly from the previous one. When the pages are viewed by flipping the pages, the image appears animated. The animated GIF works in a similar way.

The animated GIF file is composed of a series of images called frames. You can create these frames with an image-editing program. But to create the animated GIF file, you will need special software to put the frames together into a single GIF file. This special software allows you to have control over the speed of the animation and the number of times it is repeated before it stops. The animated GIF can be included in an XHTML document the same way any other image is with the img element.

Interlaced GIF Images

Images are usually stored one line at a time and when the image is loaded, it is drawn one line at a time from top to bottom. With an interlaced GIF, a whole image appears initially, but it is rough and seems to be out of focus. As the download process continues, the image becomes clearer. Using an interlaced GIF allows an image to be seen before the download is complete. The term interlaced refers to how the image file has been saved by the image editing software.

Transparent GIF Images

The GIF89a specification provides the ability to create transparent colors. This transparent color is not displayed when the image appears on the Web page, and this gives the appearance of a floating image. Image-editing software allows the selection of a particular color of the image to be transparent. The background color of the image is usually selected to be the transparent color, but care should be taken because the color chosen will be transparent throughout the entire image. Figure 10.12 shows an example of a GIF file with transparency and one without.

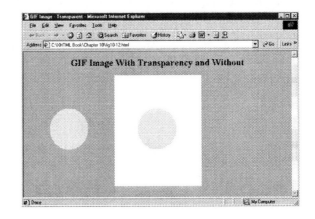

FIGURE 10.12: GIF FILE WITH TRANSPARENCY AND WITHOUT

JOINT PHOTOGRAPHIC EXPERT GROUP (JPEG)

This format gets its name from the organization that created the standard, the Joint Photographic Expert Group. The *JPEG* format was designed to store photo-like images containing a large number of colors. This format uses 24 bits per pixel to store color information, which would allow for over 16.7 million different colors. JPEG images are identified by the file extension .jpg. Images saved in this format are compressed using a lossy compression scheme, which means that some information is lost when the image is saved. You are probably asking yourself, if image information is thrown away, will image quality be affected? The answer is yes, but image information is removed in such a way that it is hardly noticeable, and the disk space that is saved is significant.

The JPEG compression algorithm removes color information where it is hard for the human eye to perceive any color difference. JPEG compression is accomplished using a mathematical technique called Adaptive Discrete Cosine Transformation.

One thing to remember when working with JPEG images is every time the image is saved, it is compressed again. The gradual loss of image detail will occur from repeated compression. Each time the image is saved, it is like making a copy of a copy. You have probably seen this same concept if you have ever made repeated photocopies of a document. The quality of the copy gets worse with each copy that is made.

Most image editing tools allow you to select the amount of compression to apply to a particular image when it is saved.

PORTABLE NETWORK GRAPHICS (PNG)

The Portable Network Graphics format or *PNG*, which is pronounced as "ping," is the newest image format. PNG images are identified by the file extension .png. PNG was developed as a royalty-free replacement for the GIF format. Just like the GIF format, images saved in the PNG format are compressed using a lossless compression scheme, which means there will be no loss of image quality when saved. This format provides flexibility by supporting 24-bit and 48-bit images, which allows more color information to be stored, unlike the GIF format, which uses only eight bits. Since PNG files have a higher bit depth and use lossless compression, images saved in this format have a larger file size.

The advantages of the PNG format include

- Full color support
- No loss of image quality
- Royalty-free use

The disadvantage:

- Not supported by all browsers

LINKING WITH IMAGES

Images can also be combined with links to provide navigational icons that look like buttons. To make an image into a link, simply place the img element in between the opening and closing tags of the anchor element. The following XHTML is an example of how to create a link with an image.

```
<?xml version="1.0" encoding="UTF-8"?>
<!DOCTYPE html PUBLIC "-//W3C//DTD/XHTML 1.0 Transitional//EN"
"http://www.w3.org/TR/xhtml1/DTD/xhtml1-transitional.dtd">
<html xmlns="http://www.w3.org/1999/xhtml" xml:lang="en" lang="en">
<head>
```

```
<title>  Creating A Link With An Image  </title>
</head>
<body>
<a href = "http://www.fbeedle.com"><img src="arrow2.gif"
alt="Click the arrow to go back" /></a>
</body>
</html>
```

IMAGE MAPS

Images not only make our Web pages look good, they can also make our pages more interactive by acting as graphical navigation aids. This navigation is accomplished through the use of image maps. An image map is a single image that has been divided into multiple regions of various shapes known as hotspots. Each one of the image's hotspots is clickable and acts as a hyperlink. The hotspot boundaries are defined

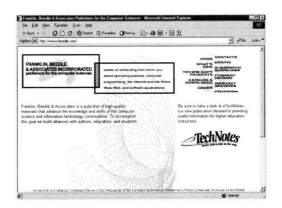

FIGURE 10.13: FRANKLIN, BEEDLE & ASSOCIATES HOME PAGE

using x and y coordinates and are listed in the image map. When a user clicks within a hotspot's boundary, the associated hyperlink is activated. Image maps don't have to be geographical maps, pictures, or drawings; they could also be menu bars. Look at Figure 10.13, the Franklin, Beedle & Associates home page.

In the upper-right corner of the Web page is an image used for navigating the site. This image has been divided into 11 hotspots, with each one providing a link to another page. The following XHTML created the image map:

```
<map name="navbar2Map23">
    <area shape="rect" coords="110,121,190,135"
        href="technote/03-01/03-01.html"
        alt="View the latest edition of eTechNotes" />
    <area shape="rect" coords="108,96,186,118" href="webcast.html"
        alt="Download files from our webcasts" />
    <area shape="rect" coords="109,71,183,91" href="history.html"
        alt="Read our company history" />
```

```
<area shape="rect" coords="109,46,198,66" href="submit.html"
    alt="Guidelines for prospective authors" />
<area shape="rect" coords="110,28,169,40" href="errata.html"
    alt="Get the latest updates for our books" />
<area shape="rect" coords="109,12,188,25" href="contacts.html"
    alt="Contact your representative" />
<area shape="rect" coords="51,110,105,122" href="order.html"
    alt="How to order" />
<area shape="rect" coords="8,85,104,103" href="products.html"
    alt="Download sample chapters and request review copies" />
<area shape="rect" coords="6,60,104,80" href="review.html"
    alt="Request review copies of our books" />
<area shape="rect" coords="48,34,102,53" href="news.html"
    alt="Find out what's new at Franklin, Beedle" />
<area shape="rect" coords="59,18,105,31" href="index.html"
    alt="The Franklin, Beedle home page" />
</map>
<img src="art/navbar2.gif" width="205" height="140" align="bottom"
  border="0" usemap="#navbar2Map23" />
```

We will see how to create our own image maps shortly. There are two types of image maps: server-side and client-side.

Server-side Image Maps

Server-side image maps are the older type and are supported by most browsers. This type of image map requires the server and browser to work together. When the user clicks on a hotspot, a connection is made to the server and the appropriate x and y coordinates are sent to a server program to be translated into a URL using a map file. The server uses the URL to retrieve the requested information and sends the contents back to the browser. This process is repeated each time a hotspot on the image map is clicked. This method of image mapping requires the server to do a lot of work, resulting in delays in accessing information. The creation of this type of image map can be complicated and sometimes confusing.

Client-side Image Maps

The client-side image map is the preferred method of creating image maps. This method has all of the hotspot information included as part of the XHTML document. Since all of the map information is stored and processed locally, client-side image maps tend to be faster.

Creating Client-side Image Maps

There are many great tools available to create image maps automatically, but we feel that it is important to understand the concepts involved, so we will show how to hand-code simple image maps. The creation of a client-side image map requires the use of three XHTML elements. The first element, <img>, was introduced earlier in the chapter. The other two required elements are: <map> and <area>. We will discuss the new elements later in the creation process. The process of creating an image map can be broken down into the following steps:

1. Selecting the image
2. Defining the map areas
3. Making the connection between image and map information

Selecting the Image

This may seem kind of obvious, but there are some things that you should keep in mind. The image selected for mapping should be appropriate for this function, which means the image

- has distinct areas
- is easily recognized by the user

Line drawings or images with distinct shapes tend to make better image maps than photographs.

Defining the Map Areas

Once the image has been selected, the areas that will be the hotspots need to be defined using coordinates and various shapes. The shapes are used to describe the boundary of the hotspot. There are three possible shapes: rectangle, circle, and polygon. The x and y coordinates are then determined for the shape being used. In computer imaging, zero for both the x and y axes starts in the upper-left corner of the image. The x axis increases horizontally (to the right), and the y axis increases vertically (down) from the upper-left corner. Each set of coordinates consists of an x and y value expressed in pixels. The coordinates used to describe the various shapes are determined as follows:

- Rectangle—The coordinates of the top-left and bottom-right corners
- Circle—The coordinates of the center of the circle and the radius
- Polygons—The coordinates of each corner of the shape used

To determine the x and y coordinates, the image can be opened in an image-editing program. These programs will display the coordinates of the cursor when it is placed on a particular point. A program as simple as Windows Paint shows the coordinates of the cursor. Figure 10.14 shows an image that contains the three shapes. Let's determine the x and y coordinates required to make each one a hotspot. Notice in the status bar the x and y coordinates of where the cursor is located.

The rectangle shape coordinates are upper left (52, 54) and bottom right (196, 126).

The circular shape coordinates for the center are (217, 238). But for the circular shape, we also need the radius. The radius can be determined

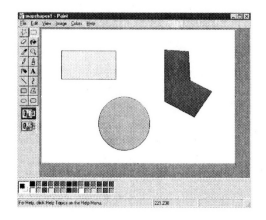

FIGURE 10.14: SHAPES IMAGE OPENED IN PAINT

by subtracting the center x axis from the right border x axis (287 - 217).

The polygon shape requires coordinates from each point. Let's start in the upper left: (326, 52), (326, 182), (404, 222), (450, 157), (393, 129), and (389, 55).

Now that we have all the coordinates, we can use them to create hotspots on our image. To create our image map, we use the <map>, <area>, and <img> elements.

Creating an Image Map, the <map> Element

The map element is used to create the map specification and will enclose the area elements. It also defines the map name, which is used by the img element. The map name is set using the id attribute, which is the only one required. Since some browsers do not yet support the id attribute, the name attribute should also be used. The name/id value must be unique within the XHTML document. The syntax of the map element is:

```
<map id="map identifier" name="map identifier">
</map>
```

When the map element is used, it must contain at least one area element.

Creating Hotspots in Image Maps, the <area> Element

The <area> element is an empty element used to specify the hotspot of a client-side image map. Since <area> is an empty element and does not have a closing tag, it must be terminated properly in XHTML by adding a space and a slash before the closing angle bracket, as follows:

```
<area  />
```

The area element uses four attributes: shape, coords, href, and alt. The syntax of the area element is:

```
<area shape="shape name" coords="coordinate values" href="link"
alt="description of hotspot" />
```

shape Attribute

The shape attribute is used to specify the shape of the mapped area. If no shape attribute is given, the default value will be rect. The possible values of the shape attribute are rect, circle, poly, and default. The default is any area not covered by another area element. When an area is set up using the default shape, any time the user clicks outside of one of the hotspots, the user activates the URL setup for the default.

coords Attribute

The coords attribute is used to specify the coordinates of the hotspot. The values of this attribute depend on the value used for the shape attribute. Coordinates are expressed in pixels and are listed separated by commas.

href Attribute

The href attribute stands for **h**ypertext **ref**erence; to put it in simpler terms, it is the location of the document that is to be linked to for display. The value of the href attribute is the hyperlink target that is to be displayed when the associated hotspot is clicked.

alt Attribute

The alt attribute stands for "alternate." The value of this attribute is a text description of the defined hotspot. This text is displayed when an image is encountered by a non-graphical browser or a browser that has graphics disabled.

Now that we know how to use the map and area elements, use the coordinates that were determined for the hotspots in Figure 10.14. The XHTML for the image map would look like the following:

```
<map id="shapes"name="shapes">
   <area shape="rect" coords="52,54,196,126"
      href="rectangle.html" alt="rectangle hotspot" />
   <area shape="poly"
coords="326,52,326,182,404,222,450,157,393,129,389,55"
href="polygon.html" alt="polygon hotspot" />
```

```
<area shape="circle" coords="217,238,70" href="circle.html"
    alt="circle hotspot" />
</map>
```

It's time to move on to the last step in the map creation process, making the connection between the image and the map information.

Making the Connection Between Image and Map Information

The connection between the image and the map is done with the img element. It uses the same attributes as discussed earlier in the chapter. The *usemap attribute* is used to connect the image with the map information. The following is an example of the img element that would be used to connect the shapes image with the map information that was just created:

```
<img src="mapshpapes1.gif" width="510" height="339" border="0"
usemap="#shapes" />
```

Notice the hash symbol (#) used in front of the map name. This indicates that the map file is located in the current XHTML document. It is also possible to reference another document by using its path.

Let's take a look at an XHTML document that includes a client-side image map for the shapes image:

```
<?xml version="1.0" encoding="UTF-8"?>
<!DOCTYPE html PUBLIC "-//W3C//DTD/XHTML 1.0 Transitional//EN"
"http://www.w3.org/TR/xhtml1/DTD/xhtml1-transitional.dtd">
<html xmlns="http://www.w3.org/1999/xhtml" xml:lang="en" lang="en">
<head>
<title> Client-Side Image Map </title>
</head>
<body>
   <h2 align="center">A Simple Client-Side Image Map</h2>
   <map id="shapes"name="shapes">
     <area shape="rect" coords="52,54,196,126"
       href="rectangle.html" alt="rectangle hotspot" />
     <area shape="poly"
   coords="326,52,326,182,404,222,450,157,393,129,389,55"
   href="polygon.html" alt="polygon hotspot" />
     <area shape="circle" coords="217,238,70" href="circle.html"
       alt="circle hotspot" />
   </map>
   <img src="mapshapes1.gif" width="510" height="339" border="0"
   usemap="#shapes" />
</body>
</html>
```

The results of the above XHTML are in Figure 10.15.

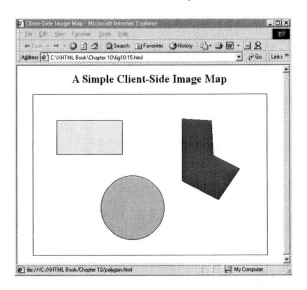

FIGURE 10.15: XHTML DOCUMENT WITH A SIMPLE IMAGE MAP

When the cursor is placed over a hotspot, a pop-up box appears with the alt text displayed and indicates that this part of the image is a hotspot.

USING IMAGES EFFECTIVELY

Images are used to enhance visual appearance and convey information. On the other hand, they can also detract from the overall purpose by cluttering and increasing the download time of the page. There are no concrete rules for using images on Web pages, but as a general rule, the total amount of images on a given page should not be more than 50K. The following are guidelines to aid you in the effective use of images:

1. Determine the appropriate image file format.

   When working with images for the Web, this choice comes down to GIF or JPEG. Use the GIF file format for
   - Line drawings
   - Text images
   - Images with less than 256 colors
   - Animated images
   - When transparency is needed

Use the JPEG file format for
* Images with more than 256 colors
* Displaying photographs
* File size reduc-
  tion through
  the use of com-
  pression

2. Reduce the size
   of images.

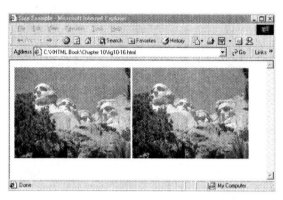

FIGURE 10.16: RESIZING IMAGES

You are probably
thinking why not
just use the img
elements width
and height attri-
butes that we
talked about ear-
lier in the chapter to control the size of the image? Nice idea, but that only
changes the size of the displayed image, not the size of the image that is
downloaded. So no time will be saved, and this will make the browser fit
the image into the available space. Figure 10.16 illustrates this by showing
two images that appear to be the same size. The image on the left is only
80k, and the one on the right is 376k. The following shows the image size
and the approximate download time at various speeds:

File Size	Download Speed (kbps)	Time (seconds)
80k	14.4	55.2
	28.8	27.6
	56.6	14.0
376k	14.4	243.0
	28.8	122.0
	56.6	62.0

It is important to know the intended audience for your image so it
can be properly sized. Reducing the size of the image decreases download
time.

3. Reduce the number of colors in the image.

Reducing the number of possible colors in a GIF file will result in a reduction in file size. The amount of color reduction that can be used depends on the image and at what point the image quality begins to suffer. Below are sample images where the number of colors has been reduced. To see the examples in color, check the CD that accompanies this book:

Colors: 256, Image Size: 25k

Colors: 128, Image Size: 20k

Colors: 64, Image Size: 16k

Colors: 32, Image Size: 11k

Colors: 16, Image Size: 8k

Colors: 4, Image Size: 4k

Notice that the image quality does not start to suffer until the number of colors reaches 16.

4. Increase image compression.

The JPEG file format allows for different levels of compression, which will result in a decrease in the file size. As the level of compression increases, the quality of the image decreases. The images below illustrates the effects of various amounts of compression. To see these images in color, check the CD that accompanies this book:

Compression: low, File Size: 12k

Compression: moderate, File Size: 7k

Compression: medium, File Size: 4k

Compression: high, File Size: 3k

By looking at the images, you can see that as the compression ratio increases, the quality decreases.

5. Reuse images.

When creating multiple-page Websites, consider using images on more than one page. This will decrease the image load time on subsequent uses of an image because it is held in cache memory.

MULTIMEDIA

So far, we have seen how the effective use of images can enhance a Web page's delivery of information. Multimedia can also be used in the same manner as images while adding an interactive element to the Web page. When we use the term multimedia, we are referring to the integration of text, images, audio, and video on a Web page.

The rest of this chapter will introduce how to include audio and video files on your Web pages. The inclusion of audio and video on a Web page should not be rushed into without careful thought and planning. Just as easily as multimedia can attract users to your Web page by adding interactivity, it can also drive visitors away if done poorly. The biggest concern when using audio and video files is bandwidth because of the size of these types of files. In simple terms, bandwidth refers to the carrying capacity of a connection.

Let's see how to add audio and video to our Web pages.

AUDIO

The use of audio on a Web page has become very popular either as background sounds or by providing information where text or graphics may not have the same impact. Audio files are available in a number of formats. Some of the more common formats are

U-Law
- file extension .au
- developed by Sun Microsystems
- 8-bit sound
- poor sound quality

AIFF (Audio Interchange File Format)
- file extensions .aiff or .aif
- developed by Apple Computer
- mainly used by Macintosh

MIDI (Musical Instrument Digital Interface)
- file extensions .midi or .mid
- uses digitized sounds

MPEG

- file extension .mp3
- developed by the International Standard Organizations Moving Picture Expert Group
- very popular format
- high compression provides small file size
- high-quality audio

Real Audio

- file extensions .ra or .ram
- developed by Real Audio
- lower quality sound
- allows audio to be streamed in real time

WAV

- file extension .wav
- developed by Microsoft and IBM
- commonly used on the Windows platform

VIDEO

Video can also be used to provide additional information where text or graphic content may not have the same impact. Video files are available in a number of formats. Some of the more common formats are

AVI (Audio-Video Interleaved)

- file extension .avi
- developed by Microsoft
- commonly used on the Windows platform

MPEG

- file extensions .mpeg or .mpg
- developed by the International Standard Organizations Moving Picture Expert Group
- very popular format
- high compression with good quality

QuickTime

- file extensions .qt or .mov
- developed by Apple Computer
- can be used on Macintosh and Windows platforms

ADDING AUDIO AND VIDEO TO XHTML DOCUMENTS

Audio and video can be included in an XHTML document by using either the inline or external method. The inline method completely downloads the multimedia file as part of the XHTML document while the user waits. Once the page has loaded, an external application is launched to play the file. A hyperlink to an external multimedia file can also be used to include multimedia files with an XHTML document. This allows the user to click on the hyperlink to download the file and launch the application to play it. Some examples of external applications that may be used to view multimedia files are Windows Media Player, Real Player, and QuickTime.

Linking to External Audio and Video Files

Sometimes multimedia files can be very large, and if they were added to the XHTML document using the inline method, they would cause the user to wait for the download to complete. Instead of having a user wait to see your page, a hyperlink could be used to control when the file is downloaded. Since we already know how to use hyperlinks, let's give this a try.

In this example, you can use your own multimedia files or the ones provided on the CD. We have created a temp directory on our C drive to save the XHTML and multimedia files since they may be too large to fit on a diskette. You may also be using a directory on a network drive to complete your work, so make the necessary changes to make the links function properly.

1. Type the following using your choice of editor and save it as extmulti.html. We will add a link in the next steps.

```
<?xml version="1.0" encoding="UTF-8"?>
<!DOCTYPE html PUBLIC "-//W3C//DTD/XHTML 1.0 Transitional//EN"
"http://www.w3.org/TR/xhtml1/DTD/xhtml1-transitional.dtd">
<html xmlns="http://www.w3.org/1999/xhtml" xml:lang="en" lang="en">
<head>
<title> Linking External Multimedia Files </title>
</head>
<body>
   <h2 align="center"> External Multimedia Files </h2>
</body>
</html>
```

2. Next, add a paragraph to our document by placing a <p> element below the <h2> element. Place a </p> tag above the </body> tag to close the paragraph. Let's make this interesting—place an unordered list of multimedia files after the paragraph. Your XHTML should look like the following:

```
<p>
    Please select the multimedia file you wish to play.
</p>
<ul>
  <li>Play audio WAV file</li>
  <li>Play audio MIDI file</li>
  <li>Play video AVI file </li>
  <li>Play video MPEG file</li>
</ul>
```

3. Now we can add the link to the external multimedia files using the <a> element and the href attribute. Add the anchor element as follows:

```
<ul>
  <li><a href="testwav.wav">Play audio WAV file </a></li>
  <li><a href="testmidi.midi">Play audio MIDI file </a></li>
  <li><a href="testavi.avi">Play video AVI file </a></li>
  <li><a href="testmpeg.mpeg">Play video MPEG file </a></li>
</ul>
```

Before we go to the next step, make sure that you save your work!

4. The completed XHTML document extmulti.html should resemble the following:

```
<?xml version="1.0" encoding="UTF-8"?>
<!DOCTYPE html PUBLIC "-//W3C//DTD/XHTML 1.0 Transitional//EN"
"http://www.w3.org/TR/xhtml1/DTD/xhtml1-transitional.dtd">
<html xmlns="http://www.w3.org/1999/xhtml" xml:lang="en" lang="en">
<head>
<title> Linking External Multimedia Files </title>
</head>
<body>
  <h2 align="center"> External Multimedia Files </h2>
  <p>
    Please select the multimedia file you wish to play.
  </p>
  <ul>
  <li><a href="testwav.wav">Play audio WAV file </a></li>
  <li><a href="testmidi.midi">Play audio MIDI file </a></li>
  <li><a href="testavi.avi">Play video AVI file </a></li>
```

```
   <li><a href="testmpeg.mpeg">Play video MPEG file </a></li>
   </ul>
</body>
</html>
```

5. In the browser, select Open from the File menu to open extmulti.html. Your screen should resemble Figure 10.17.

FIGURE 10.17: RELATIVE LINKS TO MULTIMEDIA FILES

6. Click on the link for the WAV file; the player will load and start playing the file. Your screen should resemble Figure 10.18. After the multimedia file has played, close the player.

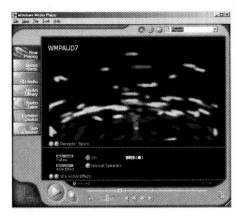

FIGURE 10.18: WAV FILE RELATIVE LINK, PLAYER LAUNCHED

7. Click on the link for the MPEG file; the player will load and start playing the file. Your screen should resemble Figure 10.19. After the multimedia file has played, close the player.

FIGURE 10.19: MPEG FILE RELATIVE LINK, PLAYER LAUNCHED

When the hyperlink is clicked, the browser locates the file and determines what type of file it is. Once the file type is known, the browser can then determine if it can handle the file or if it needs to launch an external application.

Including Audio and Video Files Inline

After seeing how simple it was to add multimedia files to our Web page using hyperlinks, why would we want to do it any other way? Simply put, using the hyperlink doesn't integrate the multimedia element into your Web page. By including the multimedia file inline, the player can be embedded inside the XHTML document and not just be a window that pops up. The two elements that could be used to include multimedia players in an XHTML document are <embed> and <object>. The embed element is not part of the HTML or XHTML standards as put forth by the World Wide Web Consortium (W3C). The current standards recommend the use of the object element, but because the object element is not fully supported, it is recommended that you continue to use the embed element.

ADDING INLINE AUDIO AND VIDEO, THE <EMBED> ELEMENT

The embed element is an empty element that allows a plug-in to be embedded into an XHTML document to play audio and video files. Since <embed> is an empty element and does not have a closing tag, it must be terminated properly in XHTML by adding a space and a slash before the closing angle bracket as follows:

```
<embed />
```

The embed element has many attributes and, depending on the plug-in application, different ones may be used. However, there are four attributes that are supported by the common plug-in players. These include src, width, height, and autostart.

src Attribute

The src attribute is the most important of the attributes; without it, no image is displayed. Src stands for "source" and directs the browser to get the file at the specified location. The value of the attribute is the address of the image and could be

- a file name if the file is located in the same directory
- a relative path name
- an absolute URL

The use of the src attribute should look familiar to you; it is identical to how the attribute is used in the img element.

height Attribute

The height attribute is used to specify the height of the embedded element. The value of this attribute is expressed in pixels or as a percentage.

width Attribute

The width attribute is used to specify the width of the embedded element. The value of this attribute is expressed in pixels or as a percentage.

autostart Attribute

The *autostart attribute* is used to specify if the multimedia file should be played immediately upon loading. The syntax of the embed element is:

```
<embed src="" height="" width="" autostart="" />
```

Let's take a look at an XHTML document that includes a multimedia file. The following XHTML includes the embed element to add an inline video to a Web page:

```
<?xml version="1.0" encoding="UTF-8"?>
<!DOCTYPE html PUBLIC "-//W3C//DTD/XHTML 1.0 Transitional//EN"
"http://www.w3.org/TR/xhtml1/DTD/xhtml1-transitional.dtd">
<html xmlns="http://www.w3.org/1999/xhtml" xml:lang="en" lang="en">
<head>
<title> Inline Video </title>
</head>
<body>
    <h2 align="center">Inline Video </h2>
    <embed src="testmpeg.mpeg" height="400" width="400"
autostart="false" />
</body>
</html>
```

The results of the above XHTML are shown in Figure 10.20.

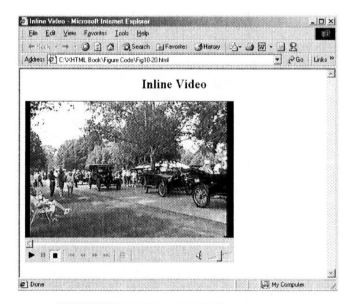

FIGURE 10.20 INLINE VIDEO USING THE EMBED ELEMENT

CHAPTER SUMMARY

In this chapter, we learned how to use images on our Web pages. We learned why it is important to always provide an alternate textual description for all graphics and that we can control the size of the graphic image on the page. We saw how the alignment of the graphic could be adjusted and the flow of the text around the image modified. We learned how to create image maps, and we learned some of the advantages and disadvantages of the three common graphic file types. We also saw how two different types of compression affect the resulting file size and image quality. This chapter demonstrated how multimedia elements could be added to a Web page inline or by linking to external files.

KEY TERMS

align attribute	JPEG
alt attribute	lossless compression
autostart attribute	lossy compression
border attribute	PNG
GIF	src attribute
height attribute	usemap attribute
hspace attribute	vspace attribute
img element	width attribute

XHTML IMAGE TAG SUMMARY

Tag	Attribute(s)	Use/Values
<img>	src	=path and graphic file name
	alt	=text describing image
	align	top, middle, bottom, left, right
	width	=w; desired width of image in pixels
	height	=h; desired height of the image in pixels
	border	=b; width of border in pixels
	hspace	=hs; white space (in pixels) left and right
	vspace	=vs; white space (in pixels) above and below
	usemap	=map name; for client-side image maps
	ismap	For server-side image maps

REVIEW QUESTIONS

1. What does the alt attribute of the img element do? Why is it important to use that attribute for all images?
2. What are the advantages and disadvantages of using the height and width attributes?
3. What does the border attribute do? What are the default values for the border attribute?
4. Explain the use of the hspace and vspace attributes.
5. What is the difference between a client-side image map and a server-side image map?
6. Identify three types of graphic file formats. List two advantages and disadvantages of each format.
7. Explain the relationship between pixel depth and the number of palette colors available in a particular graphic.
8. Identify and explain the difference between the two types of compression.
9. What does the src attribute of the img element do?
10. List the five possible values for the align attribute of the img element. How does the use of the align attribute affect the flow of text around an image?

EXERCISES

1. Create a professional resume Web page that includes an image of you.
2. Create a Web page, including images and text, that demonstrates the use of the img element's align attribute.
3. Create a Web page about your state and add three photos of interesting places.
4. Create a Web page that demonstrates the use of the hspace and vspace attributes.
5. Create a Web page about your state that includes an image map of the state. On the image map, make hotspots for your school's location, the state capital, a special place of interest, and your hometown. When one of the hotspots is clicked, a page should load that provides information about that particular location. Use images on each of the pages.
6. Create a Web page that contains four images, demonstrating the use of the img element's border attribute.
7. Create a Web page that contains an image map of the United States, which includes hotspots for Washington D.C., your hometown, Florida, and Kansas. Each hotspot should take the user to a Web page that describes that particular place. The following image can be found on the CD.

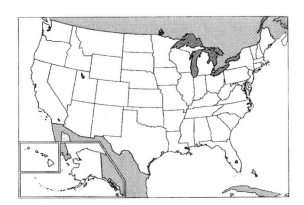

PROJECT

At this point, we should focus on improving the look of our pages through the inclusion of images and other multimedia assets. While it would be possible for us to include music and even digital video on our pages, we need to follow our client's mandates—a fast-loading portal site. Because of this, we should restrict our media selection to images. Do the following:

- Create a banner for your site using your image-editing program of choice and place it on the home page. Make sure to use the alt tag to enter a description of the image.
- Create a smaller version of the banner and place it on other pages.
- Create images for any buttons on your pages.

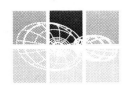

chapter 11
forms

CHAPTER OVERVIEW

Forms are the foundation for bi-directional, Web-based communications. By utilizing forms in combination with server-side information processing, we can create Websites that react and interface with the user. This chapter covers how to create forms and their elements. Common data fields such as text boxes, radio buttons, check boxes, and selection boxes are presented. The chapter also covers form attributes and explores server-side form processing using ASP.

CHAPTER OBJECTIVES

- Explore relationships between forms and their processing
- Use GET and POST transfer methods for posting form data
- Create forms
- Utilize common form input elements such as text fields, password fields, hidden fields, radio buttons, text areas, check boxes, and drop-down selection boxes
- Create an ASP-based form handler

FORMS

When the Web made its widespread public debut in the early 1990s, people followed a one-way mass-communications paradigm. Companies and organizations would put their print-based materials online, add a few hyperlinks, and that was about it. As the Web gained more popularity, it became apparent that a mechanism was needed for users to send information back to the server. Forms and their accompanying programs came into existence for this purpose.

With the advent of *forms*, it became possible for users to sign guest books, register for information, and order merchandise online. For a long time, the design of the forms, or the "front end", was the domain of Web designers. Programmers with expertise in writing *Common Gateway Interface (CGI)* programs usually did the processing of the form information.

Today, it is no longer necessary to be fluent in C or Perl to write form-processing modules. Early Web servers did not have internal facilities for doing anything other than serving Web pages. In order to handle any incoming form data, they had to pass the information to an outside program using a protocol called the Common Gateway Interface. The external program would accomplish its task and pass the results back to the Web server to send to the original user. These external programs became known as CGI programs.

Today's major Web servers have facilities for handling incoming form data without having to resort to using CGI programs. The net result is that it is now infinitely easier to handle forms using technologies like ASP, JSP, or PHP. But the ease of processing forms using the scripting facilities of today's servers comes at the price of portability. Because CGI programs are fully executable stand-alone programs, they work with just about any server. ASP, JSP, or PHP form-handling modules only run on the server running that scripting engine. ASP code only runs on Microsoft's Internet Information Server. JSP only runs on Java-based servers, and PHP only runs on Apache. And while there are third-party products to bridge these gaps, we need to realize the limitations these form-processing tools can impose on us before undertaking a project.

STATELESS PROTOCOL

Forms can be thought of as serving two primary functions. The first, and most obvious, is that of allowing users to transfer information to the server. This function allows users to fill out registration forms, sign guest books, select recipes, and so on.

The second function is to allow the server to track the user from page to page. The Web uses a protocol called HTTP to transfer pages. This is a *stateless protocol*. In other words, each time a user requests a Web document from a Web server, he or she must create a connection to the server, open that connection, retrieve the document, close the connection, and finally destroy the connection. Each time this happens, the server forgets all of the information about the user. For example, if a user fills out an online order for a set of music CDs and then goes to another page to pay for those CDs, the Web server will have forgotten the order.

In order to create shopping carts or any other Web experience where it is important to keep track of user information across more than one page, we can use forms to transfer this information. In the example above, we could use forms to tell the server, "I'm Carlos Morales, and I ordered CDs 1290, 1293, and 1932," when we go to check out.

Thus, forms have two functions. One is to allow the user to send information to the server, and the second is to allow the server to track the user.

THE FRONT END

In isolation, forms do nothing. It is the combination of the forms on the front end and the processing program on the back end or server that allows us to implement some functionality. Let's examine how we can handle the front end.

Placing fields on a Web page using field tags creates forms. When the user hits the submit button, the information is sent to the server. In Figure 11.1, we have the splash page for a portal site. On the upper right part of the page, there is a small

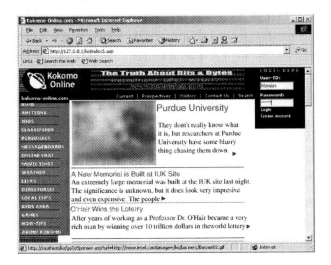

FIGURE 11.1: SAMPLE FORM

form that allows the user to log in to the site. This particular form consists of two text fields and one submit button implemented as an image. When the user hits submit, the server retrieves the information in the fields and checks to see if the user is allowed into the site.

As you see, a form does not necessarily need to be a stand-alone Web document. Let's build a form as an isolated document. Type the following using your choice of editor.

1. We'll start by adding our XHTML headers. Here we define the document that conforms to the transitional HTML 4.0 standard as defined by the W3C.

```
<!doctype html public "-//w3c//dtd html 4.0 transitional//en">
```

2. Now we define the content as text/html. This is not necessary with most Web servers because they automatically add this header. But we have elected to add it anyway to ensure that our page works with all Web servers.

```
<html><head>
<meta http-equiv=content-type content="text/html; charset=unicode">
</head>
```

3. Now we display the phrase "People Searcher" in a font size of five.

```
<body>
<p><b><font size=5>People Searcher</font></b></p>
<br/>
```

4. Here we add our form. While there are numerous attributes that can be set on a form, we have elected to only set the most important three. The title is used to differentiate among other forms on the same page. We set the action to search_act.asp. The action attribute holds the name of the document that will process this form when it is submitted. The action always indicates the destination for the information our form is submitting. We also set the method to GET. We will explore the differences between GET and POST in the next section.

```
<form title="searchForm" method="get" action="search_act.asp">
```

5. Now we add two text input fields. Note that we have set the type to text. The name attribute has also been set for each of the fields. It is in using

the name attribute that we will reference these fields when it comes time to process the form.

```
First name: <input type="text" name="first">
<br/>
Last name: <input type="text" name="last">
<br/>
```

6. Now we add a submit button. We declare it by using the input attribute and setting the type to "submit." Clicking on the submit button causes the form to be submitted to the action page that we identified in the form tag. If a form does not have a submit button, it is essentially useless.

```
<input type="submit" value="Find Them" name="submit">
```

7. Now we close the form.

```
</form>
```

8. Finally, we close the page.

```
</p></body></html>
```

The completed code should look like Figure 11.2.

```
<!doctype html public "-//w3c//dtd html 4.0 transitional//en">
<html><head>
<meta http-equiv=content-type content="text/html; charset=unicode">
</head>
<body>
<p><b><font size=5>People Searcher</font></b></p>
<br/>

<form title="searchForm" method="get" action="search_act.asp">
First name: <input type="text" name="first">
<br/>
Last name: <input type="text" name="last">
<br/>
<input type="submit" value="Find Them" name="submit">
</form>
</p></body></html>
```

FIGURE 11.2: PEOPLE SEARCH COMPLETED CODE

Now open your Web browser and view the document we just created. It should look similar to the document in Figure 11.3.

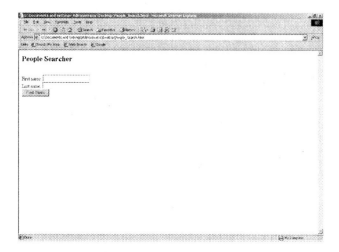

FIGURE 11.3: PEOPLE SEARCH FORM

SUBMISSION METHODS: GET VS. POST

In the document we just created, we set the method to GET. There are two methods available for transferring form data to the server. The first one is called *GET.* Using this method causes the browser to encode all of the information into the query string. In other words, the information is just added to the end of the URL indicated by the action parameter. When the user hits the submit button, the URL in the browser address field will change to something similar to

```
http://localhost/search_act.asp?first=John&last=Smith&submit1=Find+Them
```

Notice that all of the information we passed is clearly visible in the URL. We can tell the form that submitted this query string had a total of two fields. One was a field named first, which had the contents John. The format for this query string is always the same. First, we have the address to the page of the destination page, in this case, http://localhost/search_act.asp. This is followed by a question mark. Then we have the name of each field and the contents of those fields separated by equal signs.

The second method for submitting form data is to use the *POST* method. The POST method transfers the form information in the HTTP header. Every time a Web page is transferred, two main portions of information are sent. First, the server and the client exchange the HTTP header. This contains information about the type of file that is to follow, the IP address of the server, and a few other things. This information is not meant for the user to see directly. The second part is the body information, which contains the content. The POST method sends the form information in the header.

Both methods have advantages and disadvantages. The GET method provides a way to bookmark a form because all of the information is available in the URL. When we go the Weather Channel's page and put in our zip code, we can bookmark the resulting page and simulate the submittal of that form each time we recall that URL from our bookmarks. The disadvantage is that the information is clearly visible and that there is a size limitation using this method. It would not be good to use this method for exchanging username/password information. The POST method hides the information transferred and has no size limitation, but it cannot be bookmarked.

From a pragmatic perspective, it is preferable to use the POST method. We can pass both textual and binary information to the server using POST and not have to worry about size limitations. The GET method is almost always used when we would like to give the user the capability of bookmarking the information they would like to send to a form or when we would like our site to fake a form post through the construction of a URL link. For example, when we construct a listing of results from a query, we need to provide the user with a method for submitting his selection to the next page. Each selection we put on the screen for the user must allow him to be passed form information to the subsequent page. An easy way to accomplish this is through the use of the GET method.

TEXT FIELDS

Getting back to the code we typed earlier, on lines 9 and 11, we find two text fields that can be used for data entry. *Text fields* are created using the <input> tag. The type parameter indicates whether this will be a regular text field, where the user can see what he or she is typing; a *password text field*, where the information is displayed as asterisks; or a *hidden text field*, where the user cannot see or type into the field. Hidden fields are useful for tracking information from page to page. For example, we could place the user's name into a hidden text field on each page visited. This would allow our site to access the user's name any time it was needed. Try changing line 9 to:

```
First name: <input type="Password" name="first">
```

Now reload the page. Notice that when you type into the first name field, asterisks are displayed instead of your text. When you hit the submit button, look at the URL. It contains the information you put into the first name field even though it showed up as asterisks.

Each field name must have a unique name. This is how the server-side script that will process the form identifies the content. The field on line 9 has the name " first," and the field on line 11 has the name "last." When the server-side program receives the contents from this form, it will ask for the contents of the fields" first," and "last." The two must match exactly. The last element on this form is a submit button created on line 13. When the user clicks on this button, the browser will send the information to the address indicated on the form action. It is common for beginners to put the action parameter on the button because they think that clicking it starts the form submittal. This does not work.

FIELD VALUE PARAMETER

The value parameter of a form element performs one of two actions. In most cases, it designates the contents of a field. Thus, by putting something into this parameter, we can assign a default value to a field. For example, if we had typed

```
<input type="text" value="hello there" name="greeting">
```

we would have created a field named greeting whose content would be "hello there." The user would have the option of either leaving the values in the field or overwriting them. The second function that can be performed by changing the value parameter is to change the labels on the submit and reset buttons. Let's see both of these in operation.

1. Create an XHTML document with the proper headers and title.

```
<!doctype html public "-//w3c//dtd html 4.0 transitional//en">
<html><head>
<meta http-equiv=content-type content="text/html; charset=unicode">
</head>
<body>
<p><b><font size=5>People Searcher</font></b></p>
<br/>
```

2. Create a form.

```
<form title="searchForm" method="get" action="search_act.asp">
```

3. Create two form fields. Note that we have specified a value parameter. When we load our form into a browser, these fields should reflect the values we have specified.

```
First name: <input type="text" value="type here" name="first">
<br/>
Last name: <input type="text" value="here too" name="last">
<br/>
```

4. We have also changed the value for the submit button. When we view our document, our button should be labeled "Go."

```
<input type="submit" value="Go" name="submit">
```

5. Now we close the form and the page.

```
</form>
</p></body></html>
```

The completed code should look like Figure 11.4.

```
<!doctype html public "-//w3c//dtd html 4.0 transitional//en">
<html><head>
<meta http-equiv=content-type content="text/html; charset=unicode">
</head>
<body>
<p><b><font size=5>People Searcher</font></b></p>
<br/>

<form title="searchForm" method="get" action="search_act.asp">
First name: <input type="text" value="type here" name="first">
<br/>
Last name: <input type="text" value="here too" name="last">
<br/>
<input type="submit" value="Go" name="submit">
</form>

</p></body></html>
```

FIGURE 11.4: FORM WITH VALUE PARAMETERS SPECIFIED

When you reload the document, you will notice that both fields already have text in them and the label on the button has changed to "Go." This was a direct result of adding the value parameter to the field elements. Using this method, we can indicate default values or even add instructions, such as "type here." See Figure 11.5.

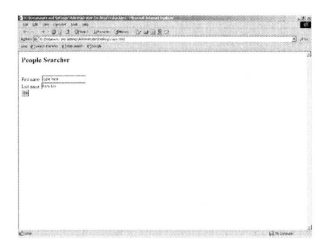

FIGURE 11.5: VALUE PARAMETER CHANGED

In addition to text fields, we have a variety of other data-entry mechanisms such as radio buttons, check boxes, and drop-down menus. Let's create a more complete People Search form that utilizes the other options we have available.

The new form will be more complex. We'll use text fields like we have done in our examples thus far. We will also add radio buttons, check boxes, selection boxes, and finally text areas. We'll expand the form that we created in the last section to include these new features.

Type the following using your choice of editor and save it when you are done.

1. Create an XHTML document with the proper headers and title. We will expand on the form that we built in the last section.

```
<!doctype html public "-//w3c//dtd html 4.0 transitional//en">
<html><head>
<meta http-equiv=content-type content="text/html; charset=unicode">
</head>
<body>
<p><b><font size=5>People Searcher</font></b></p>
<br />
```

2. Create the form. Note that we have kept everything the same as in the last section. We can add as many fields as we like to any form without having to change its declaration.

```
<form title="searchForm" method="get" action="search_act.asp">
```

3. Create two form fields. Note that we have specified a value parameter. We have deleted the value parameter we had in the last section because we do not want to specify default values for these fields.

```
First name: <input type="text" name="first">
<br/>
Last name: <input type="text " name="last">
<br/>
```

4. Add a series of radio buttons to allow the user to select a sex.

```
<b>Sex:</b>
<br/>
<input type="radio" value="M" name="sex" />Male
<br/>
<input type="radio" value="F" name="sex" />Female
<br/>
<br/>
```

Radio Buttons

We have a set of radio buttons that asks the user to select the sex of the person. *Radio buttons* will allow the user to select only from the available choices. To construct these, we use the input tag but set the type to "radio." We then set the value parameter to the value that we would like to pass to the server if that choice is selected. If the user selects male, the server will receive the value "M." This occurs because we set the value parameter to "M." Notice that both input tags have the same name. This is how we associate these two radio buttons as belonging to the same group. The browser will only allow one selection per group.

5. Now we add a select box for the user to select a favorite color.

```
<b>Favorite Color</b>
<select name="Favorite_Color">
   <option value="R">Red</option>
   <option value="G">Green</option>
   <option value="B">Blue</option>
</select>
<br/>
<br />
```

Selection Boxes

We create a drop-down *selection box*. We start by using the <select> tag to
create the selection box and then use the <option> tag to populate the box with
choices. Note that unlike radio buttons, which name each choice, the selection
box has a name that applies to the entire box. In our case, it is called "Favorite
Color." Each of the choices uses the value tag to indicate the value we would
like to pass to the server. If the user selects the color red, the form will pass the
server a field named "Favorite_Color" with a value of R.

6. Now we add some check boxes for the user to select favorite foods.

```
<b>Food He/She Likes</b>
<br />
<input type="checkbox" name="Pizza" value="PZ" checked /> Pizza<br />
<input type="checkbox" name="Burger" value="BG" /> Burger<br />
<input type="checkbox" name="Steak" value="SK" /> Steak<br />
<br/>
<br/>
```

Check Boxes

We create a menu of choices to allow the user to select from a variety of food.
Because we would like the user to be able to select more than one choice, we
have elected to use check boxes instead of radio buttons. We create *check boxes*
by using the <input> tag and then setting the type to "checkbox." Notice that
each check box has its own name. If a check box is selected, it passes its value to
the server. If it is not selected, it passes nothing. This is an important point that
escapes many budding Web developers. Many expect the unselected choices to
be passed as empty fields. This is not the case. Only those selected are reflected
in the data passed.

7. We also add a text area.

```
<b>What are they like?</b>
<textarea rows=5 cols=20 name="Description">
</textarea>
<br/>
<br/>
```

Text Areas

Text areas are a good choice when the user needs to input multiple lines of text.
A text area is declared by using the <textarea> tag. We assign name and default

values in the same manner as other form fields. We can also set the physical size of the box by using the row and column parameters.

8. Now we add a submit button and a reset button.

```
<input type="reset" value="Oops" id=reset1 name=reset1 />
<input type="submit" value="Go" name="submit" />
```

9. Finally, we close the form and the page.

```
</form>
</p></body></html>
```

Your final code should look similar to Figure 11.6, and it should render like Figure 11.7.

```
<!doctype html public "-//w3c//dtd html 4.0 transitional//en">
<html><head>
<meta http-equiv=content-type content="text/html; charset=unicode">
</head>
<body>
<p><b><font size=5>People Searcher</font></b></p>
<br/>

<form title="searchForm" method="get" action="search_act.asp">
First name: <input type="text" name="first">
<br/>
Last name: <input type="text" name="last">
<br/>
<br/>

<b>Sex:</b>
<br/>
<input type="radio" value="M" name="sex" />Male
<br/>
<input type="radio" value="F" name="sex" />Female
<br/>
<br/>

<b>Favorite Color</b>
<select name="Favorite_Color">
    <option value="R">Red</option>
    <option value="G">Green</option>
    <option value="B">Blue</option>
</select>
<br/>
<br/>
```

```
<b>Food He/She Likes</b>
<br />
<input type="checkbox" name="Pizza" value="PZ" checked /> Pizza<br>
<input type="checkbox" name="Burger" value="BG" /> Burger<br>
<input type="checkbox" name="Steak" value="SK" /> Steak<br>
<br/>
<br/>

<b>What are they like?</b>
<textarea rows=5 cols=20 name="Description" />
</textarea>
<br/>
<br/>

<input type="reset" value="Oops" id=reset1 name=reset1 />
<input type="submit" value="Go" name="submit" />

</form></p></body></html>
```

FIGURE 11.6: SOURCE FOR COMPLEX SEARCH FORM

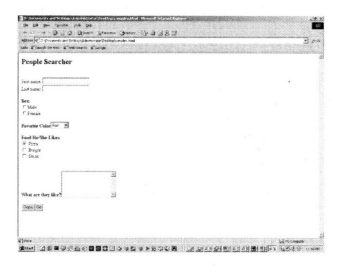

FIGURE 11.7: RENDERING OF COMPLEX SEARCH FORM

That is all there is to forms. All forms are some combination of the elements that we examined in this section.

VALIDATION

Any forms that we develop will eventually pass information back to our server. In our last example, the form would pass back the information about a particular person we were searching for. While we have not developed the server-based program that would process this information, we can be assured that it requires a minimum set of information to be effective. For example, if we were searching for a person, we would at least need the first and last names. Without that information, there is no way the server would be able to accomplish its task.

From a practical point of view, it makes sense to check if the user has provided the information requested on our form. We can also check if the user has provided the information in the requested format. This process is called form validation and is best accomplished using JavaScript. We will explore this issue further in Chapter 15. Change your form to read as shown below. Notice that we have instructed the form to pass the form data to the JavaScript function validateForm(). We then check to see if the first name or the last name fields are blank. If they are blank, we set the variable go to false. Then we check if the variable go contains the value true. If it does, then we submit the form.

```
<html><head>
<meta http-equiv=content-type content="text/html; charset=unicode">
<script language="javaScriptJavaScript">

  var go=true
  if (document.searchForm.first.value=="") {
    go=false
    alert("The First Name Field is required")
    document.searchForm.userName.focus()
  }

  if (document.searchForm.last.value=="") {
    go=false
    alert("The Last Name Field is required")
    document.searchForm.userName.focus()
  }

  if (okSoFar==true) {
    document.searchForm.submit()
    alert ("Thank you.")
    location.href=history.back()
  }
}
</script>
</head>
<body>
```

```
<p><b><font size=5>People Searcher</font></b></p>
<br/>

<form title="searchForm" method="get" action="search_act.asp">
First name: <input type="text" name="first">
<br/>
Last name: <input type="text" name="last">
<br/>
<br/>

<b>Sex:</b>
<br/>
<input type="radio" value="M" name="sex" />Male
<br/>
<input type="radio" value="F" name="sex" />Female
<br/>
<br/>

<b>Favorite Color</b>
<select name="Favorite_Color">
   <option value="R">Red</option>
   <option value="G">Green</option>
   <option value="B">Blue</option>
</select>
<br/>
<br/>

<b>Food He/She Likes</b>
<br />
<input type="checkbox" name="Pizza" value="PZ" checked /> Pizza<br>
<input type="checkbox" name="Burger" value="BG" /> Burger<br>
<input type="checkbox" name="Steak" value="SK" /> Steak<br>
<br/>
<br/>

<b>What are they like?</b>
<textarea rows=5 cols=20 name="Description" />
</textarea>
<br/>
<br/>

<input type="reset" value="Oops" id=reset1 name=reset1 />
<input type="button" value="Go" onclick="validateForm()" />

</form></p></body></html>
```

FIGURE 11.8: SOURCE FOR COMPLEX SEARCH FORM WITH VALIDATION

THE BACK END

Now that we have looked at how to create forms, let's focus on how to handle the information once it gets to the server. As we discussed in the beginning of this chapter, there are numerous technologies that allow the processing of form data on the server. Some, like those based on CGI, will run on just about any server, but are difficult for beginners to master. Others like ASP, JSP, or PHP are easier to learn but run only on specific servers. Microsoft's Active Server Pages (ASP) allow the execution of programs on Microsoft servers. Java Server Pages also allow us to write *server-side programs*, but they execute on Java-based servers. PHP is a server-side scripting technology that runs on Apache servers and is based on Perl.

In Chapter 16, we will look at ASP in great detail, but no chapter on forms is complete without addressing how we use the data once it arrives at the server. In all of our examples in this chapter, we have set the action attribute of our form to search_act.asp. Let's create this document. You will need access to a machine running Microsoft Internet Information Server 4.0 (IIS) or Personal Web Server (PWS) for this to work. If you do not have access to this software, you can download it for free from Microsoft. See Chapter 16 for more information on implementing ASP.

1. Create a directory called ASP_Form in the IIS WWWROOT folder. Copy the form you created earlier into this directory.
2. Type the following using your choice of editor and name it search_act.asp. Save it in the ASP_Form directory you just created. Do not type in the numbers in the left-hand column. These will be used for us to discuss the code.

```
1:   <%@ Language="VbScript" %>
2:
3:   <%
4:
5:   'Let's Pull the variables out of the form
6:   p_name= Request("first")
7:   p_last= Request("last")
8:   p_Pizza= Request("Pizza")
9:   p_Burger= Request("Burger")
10: p_Steak=Request("Steak")
11: p_description=Request("Description")
12:
13: Response.Write ("<h1> Here is what you entered </h1>")
```

```
14: Response.Write ("<br/><b>First name:</b> "&p_name)
15: Response.Write ("<br/><b>Last name:</b> "&p_last)
16: Response.Write ("<br/><b>Pizza:</b> "&p_pizza)
17:
18: If p_Burger="BG" then
19:     Response.Write ("<br/><p><H2>I like burgers too!!</H2>>")
20: end if
21: %>
```

In Chapter 16, we will look at what all of this code means. For right now, we will focus only on those portions that handle the form data we submitted. Lines 6 through 11 retrieve the information that we passed by using the ASP's Request statement. Specifically on line 6, we are reading what our form passed in a field called "first" into a variable called p_name. The name inside of the Request statement must match the name we assigned the fields.

To verify that the information arrived, we use the Response.Write statement on lines 13 through 16 to write out the information we loaded into our variables in lines 6 through 11. Restating the information entered back to the user is not the only thing that we can do. On line 18, we test to see if the person selected the check box entitled Burger by checking to see if it contains the value BG. If it does, then we write out, "I like burgers too!!"

As you can see, the combination of forms and server-side scripting provides us with the capability of interacting with the user in a very dynamic manner.

CHAPTER SUMMARY

In this chapter, we learned how to create forms that used a variety of different fields. We learned how to use text fields, hidden text fields, password fields, text areas, check boxes, and radio buttons. We learned the differences between using GET and POST for sending form information to the server. We explored the advantages and disadvantages of the available techniques for processing form information on the server. Finally, we implemented a simple form processor using ASP technology.

KEY TERMS

check boxes

Common Gateway Interface (CGI)

form

GET

hidden text field

password text field

POST

radio button

selection box

server-side programs

stateless protocol

text field

REVIEW QUESTIONS

1. List the different types of form input elements that are available to us and the tags needed to implement them.
2. List the advantages of using the POST and GET methods for processing forms.
3. Under what conditions is it more beneficial to use check boxes over radio buttons?
4. Under what conditions would it be beneficial to use hidden form fields?
5. What is the significance of the Web being a stateless protocol to us as Web designers when constructing forms?
6. How do we associate radio buttons to be part of the same group?
7. What function does the value parameter of a text box serve?
8. How about on a submit button—what function does the value parameter serve?
9. How can we place a default value on a check box?
10. Why do we need a server-side program to handle form input?

EXERCISES

1. Create a form that could be used by a local pizza ordering company to take online orders. Include text fields for demographic information (name, telephone, street, and so on) and check boxes for toppings (pepperoni, ham, onions, and so on).
2. Modify the form to include the direction "Fill in your name here" as a default value on the last name field.
3. Add a set of radio buttons to the form to allow the user to select one of the following methods of payment: "check," "cash," and "credit."
4. Now add a text area for the customer to specify any "special delivery instructions."

PROJECT

Based on our client's instructions, we need to allow users to place and search for events on our site. This will require the user to send information to our site using forms. The same will be needed for the classifieds section. Do not worry at this point about processing the forms. Do the following:

- Create a form to allow the user to search for upcoming events.
- Create a form to allow the user to enter an event.
- Create a form to allow the user to post an item into the classifieds section.
- Create a form to allow the user to search for items in the classifieds.

REFERENCES

- Baatsee, M., Blair, R., et. al. 2000. *ASP XML*. Birmingham, U.K.: Wrox Press.
- Liberty, J., Kraley, M. 2000. *XML Web Document from Scratch*. Indianapolis: QUE Publishing.
- Marchal, B. (2000). *XML by Example*. Indianapolis: QUE Publishing.
- 4 Guys from Rolla.com, www.4GuysFromRolla.com
- ASP 101, www.ASP101.com

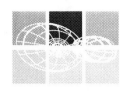

chapter 12
cascading style sheets

CHAPTER OVERVIEW

In this chapter, we will learn how to create simple style sheets in a language called CSS (cascading style sheets) and use them with XHTML documents. CSS can be used to control the design aspects (style) of a page such as colors, fonts, and the positions of objects. The syntax of the CSS language will be discussed, along with the three ways a style sheet can be applied to an XHTML document.

CHAPTER OBJECTIVES

- Understand the advantages of using style sheets
- Understand the basic syntax of the CSS language
- Understand how to embed and link style sheets
- Understand how to control fonts with style sheets
- Understand how to control colors with style sheets
- Understand how to control white space with style sheets
- Create XHTML documents using style sheets

INTRODUCTION

Style sheets can be used to control the style of an XHTML document without affecting its structure. The *style* of the document would consist of design elements such as colors, fonts, and the positions of objects. The structure of a document refers to the formatting or layout of a page and would consist of paragraphs, the document body, divisions, headers, and lists. It is important to remember that the developers of HTML, and now XHTML, intended these languages to be used only for the formatting of documents. As the Web became more popular in the mid-1990s, designers wanted more control over the style of a page. During this time, browsers added HTML tags and attributes that provided control over the style of HTML documents. These style changes were used so extensively with the layout elements that it was hard to separate one from the other.

CASCADING STYLE SHEETS

To bring back the separation of style and structure, in 1996 the World Wide Web Consortium (W3C) released the cascading style sheet language known as CSS1. In 1998, the current specification, CSS2, was released. When working with CSS, keep in mind that Netscape Navigator and Internet Explorer do not fully support the CSS specifications.

Cascading style sheets (CSS) contain rules that define the appearance of elements within an XHTML document. Even though cascading style sheets tell the browsers how to display the XHTML document, they are not XHTML. There are three ways of using cascading style sheets in XHTML documents:

- Inline styles
- Embedded style sheets
- External style sheets

The use of these three types of style sheets will be discussed later in the chapter.

Why are they called "cascading style sheets" and not just style sheets? Since it is possible to use more than one style sheet with a document, the term "cascading" refers to how these various style sheets affect a document. In order for there to be no conflict between multiple style sheets, the CSS specification defines a precedence order for how the browser interprets multiple style sheets. The browser will interpret and apply style sheet information in the following order:

1. Inline styles, which will override any other style
2. Embedded style sheets
3. Linked style sheets

If the browser does not find any of the above or does not know how a particular element should be displayed, the browser's default style sheet will be used to display the element or document.

Another important style sheet concept is "inheritance." Elements at some time will be placed within other elements. The outer element is referred to as the parent, and the embedded elements are referred to as child elements. These embedded or child elements will inherit the properties of the parent element. For example in the following XHTML,

```
<body>
  <p>
    <em>This paragraph is part of a basic <strong>XHTML</strong>
        document.  This may be a simple paragraph, but I think
        it will get the point across.
    </em>
  </p>
</body>
```

the <strong> element is a child of the <em> element, which is a child of the <p> element. So when dealing with style inheritance, any style created for a parent will be inherited by the child element. If we were to create a CSS that sets the color of the paragraph to red, that style would also be inherited by any element it contained. In the case of the above XHTML, the text would be red with parts marked up as <em> and <strong>.

By understanding how inheritance works, you will be able to format your documents at the highest level.

CSS SYNTAX

Since the CSS language is different from XHTML, it has a vocabulary all its own. Cascading style sheets contain rules that define the appearance of elements within an XHTML document. The rules are composed of the following parts:

■ *Selectors* identify the XHTML element that is to be linked to the style being defined, such as a header or paragraph. The selector could also identify a class to which the rule is to apply.

- The *property* indicates the style that is to be applied to the XHTML element identified by the selector. A style sheet can contain many properties to define a particular selector. Properties include attributes such as color, margins, or fonts.
- The *value* describes how that property is to be displayed.

The combination of properties and values is referred to as a declaration. A CSS rule consists of a selector and one or more declarations. The following illustrates the basic syntax of a CSS rule:

```
h1{
   font-style: italic;
   color: blue
   }
```

The CSS rule syntax requires specific punctuation. In the above example, "h1" is the selector, which is followed by curly brackets that enclose the two declarations "font-style: italic" and "color: blue." Each property in the declarations is separated from its value by a colon (:). When the rule contains multiple declarations, a semicolon (;) is used to separate each individual declaration. Notice that the last declaration, "color: blue," does not end with a semicolon. When there is only one declaration, a semicolon is not necessary, but it is a good practice to use one.

CSS rules are not case-sensitive. That means that a rule can be written in different ways and still have the same effect on the XHTML document. The following rules all are functionally the same:

```
h1{
   font-style: italic;
   color: blue;
   }

h1{font-style: ITALIC; color: blue;}

h1{FONT-STYLE: italic; color: BLUE;}
```

We prefer to write our rules using the first method. Let's apply our sample CSS rule to the following basic XHTML document:

```
<?xml version="1.0" encoding="UTF-8"?>
<!DOCTYPE html PUBLIC "-//W3C//DTD/XHTML 1.0 Transitional//EN"
"http://www.w3.org/TR/xhtml1/DTD/xhtml1-transitional.dtd">
<html xmlns="http://www.w3.org/1999/xhtml" xml:lang="en" lang="en">
<head>
```

```
<title>Simple XHTML Document</title>
</head>
<body>
  <h1>Hello XHTML World</h1>
    <p>This is our first XHTML document that includes cascading
       style sheets.  Don't worry, we will see how it is done
       real soon.
    </p>
</body>
</html>
```

Figure 12.1 shows the results of the above XHTML without using a style sheet, and Figure 12.2 shows the results applying the sample style sheet. Can you see the difference?

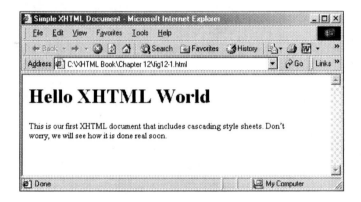

FIGURE 12.1: SIMPLE XHTML DOCUMENT WITHOUT STYLE SHEET

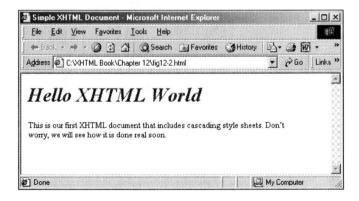

FIGURE 12.2: SIMPLE XHTML DOCUMENT WITH STYLE SHEET

Note

When the value consists of multiple words, it must be enclosed in quotes. For example:

```
h1{
    font-family: "sans serif";
    }
```

Punctuation is very important when writing CSS rules; a small error can cause the properties to be ignored. A common problem is to forget to include the semicolon (;) between properties. In the example, if the semicolon is not included between the properties, the document will be rendered as if it did not include a cascading style sheet.

Properties can also be grouped together. For example, look at the following CSS rule, which has declarations for various levels of headings:

```
h1{
    font-style: italic;
    color: blue;
    }

h2{
    font-style: italic;
    color: blue;
    }

h3{
    font-style: italic;
    color: blue;
    }
```

Since the same style will be applied to all three elements, they can be grouped by placing the selectors in a list separated by commas. The grouped declaration would be as follows:

```
h1,h2,h3{
        font-style: italic;
        color: blue;
        }
```

tip: Grouping can help avoid errors by decreasing repetitive statements.

STYLE SHEET COMMENTS

Just as comments can be added to an XHTML document, they can also be inserted into CSS code. Comments help explain the intention of the code when it is edited at a later date. The syntax of CSS comments is different from that of

XHTML comments. A CSS comment starts with a /* followed by the comment text and then ends with a */. For example:

```
/*This is a Comment for the CSS Language */
h1{
    font-style: italic;
    color: blue;
    }
```

STYLE SHEET TYPES

Now that we understand the basic syntax of CSS, let's look at how to use them. There are three ways of using styles in XHTML:

- Inline styles
- Embedded style sheets
- External style sheets

INLINE STYLES

There may be times when you want to add styles directly to individual elements within an XHTML document. This style will only affect the particular element that it has been added to. This method provides for maximum control of element display by allowing for the brief deviation of other defined styles. *Inline* style is accomplished by adding the style attribute to an XHTML element, which includes elements such as paragraphs, headers, anchors, tables, and horizontal rules. If an XHTML element is used to display something on a page, it probably supports the style attribute. Some of the XHTML elements that cannot use the style attribute include <base>, <basefont>, <head>, <html>, <meta>, <script>, <style>, and <title>. The style attribute can be very useful and is preferred over the use of the font element. Its use does not let us achieve the separation of style from the document, which is a benefit of style sheets.

The following is the syntax for the use of the style attribute:

```
<element style="declaration">
```

The declaration consists of a property and value that is to be applied to the element. The CSS punctuation rules on use of colons and semicolons apply to the declaration. The entire declaration is enclosed in quotes.

The following is an example of a paragraph element using the style attribute:

```
<p style = "color: blue; font-style: italic">
  This is a basic XHTML document that has multiple paragraphs.
  They may be simple, but I think they will get the point across.
  This is the first paragraph.
</p>
```

Let's start our style sheet adventure by creating an XHTML document that uses inline styles.

USING INLINE STYLES

We will use the style attribute introduced above to create a basic page that uses inline styles.

1. Type the following using your choice of editor and save it as instyle1.html.

```
<?xml version="1.0" encoding="UTF-8"?>
<!DOCTYPE html PUBLIC "-//W3C//DTD/XHTML 1.0 Transitional//EN"
"http://www.w3.org/TR/xhtml1/DTD/xhtml1-transitional.dtd">
<html xmlns="http://www.w3.org/1999/xhtml" xml:lang="en" lang="en">
<head>
<title>  Using Inline Styles </title>
</head>
<body>
  <p>
     This is a basic XHTML document that has three paragraphs.
     They may be simple, but I think they will get the point
     across. This is the first paragraph.
  </p>
  <p>
     This is the second paragraph in our inline style adventure.
  </p>
  <p>
     This is the third paragraph in our inline style adventure.
  </p>
</body>
</html>
```

2. Using the style attribute, modify the <p> element of the first paragraph so it uses the following properties and values:

color:	red
font-family:	sans-serif
font-style:	italic

3. Using the style attribute, modify the <p> element of the second paragraph so it uses the following properties and values:

      color: blue
      font-family: arial
      font-style: bold

4. Using the style attribute, modify the <p> element of the third paragraph so it uses the following properties and values:

      color: black
      font-family: Times New Roman
      font-size: 200%

5. Save the document as instyle1.html.

6. In the browser, select Open from the File menu to open instyle1.html. Your screen should resemble Figure 12.3.

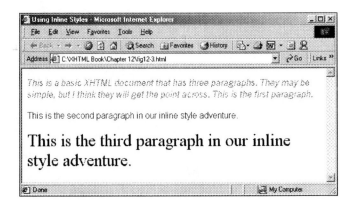

FIGURE 12.3: BASIC XHTML DOCUMENT USING INLINE STYLES

If you have problems with your display, a common problem is with punctuation. Check the colons and semicolons; if these are missing, the browser may not render the page correctly.

Your paragraph elements with the style changes made should resemble the following:

```
<p style="color:red; font-family:sans-serif; font-style:italic">
     This is a basic XHTML document that has three paragraphs.
     They may be simple, but I think they will get the point
     across. This is the first paragraph.
</p>
<p style="color:blue; font-family:arial; font-style:bold">
     This is the second paragraph in our inline style adventure.
</p>
<p style="color:black; font-family:Times New Roman; font-size:200%">
```

```
        This is the third paragraph in our inline style adventure.
</p>
```

USING THE <SPAN> ELEMENT WITH THE STYLE ATTRIBUTE

<span> is an inline element that is used to select a portion of inline text and apply a style to that part. The style will override the default settings. The following is an example of using the <span> element:

```
<p>
        This is a basic XHTML document that uses the span
element to change the font size of the second sentence.  <span
style="font-size:200%;">It may be simple, but I think you will get
the idea.</span> The font size is now back to normal for the
remainder of the paragraph.
</p>
```

Figure 12.4 shows the results of the above paragraph when placed in a simple XHTML document.

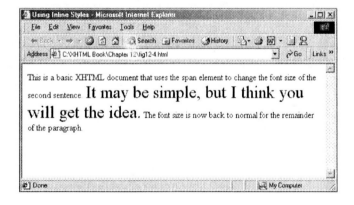

FIGURE 12.4: SIMPLE XHTML DOCUMENT USING SPAN ELEMENT

The opening <span> tag causes a new style to take effect until the ending </span> tag is reached, which turns off the new style. The style will override the default settings. Multiple properties can also be used. For example:

```
<span style="font-size:200%; color:red;">
```

USING THE <DIV> ELEMENT WITH THE STYLE ATTRIBUTE

The <div> </div> element is a *block-level element*, which means that it can contain other XHTML elements. This element is used to divide an XHTML document into sections and allows whatever information is within that section to have styles applied. Let's look at the following XHTML code that uses the <div> element:

```
<?xml version="1.0" encoding="UTF-8"?>
<!DOCTYPE html PUBLIC "-//W3C//DTD/XHTML 1.0 Transitional//EN"
"http://www.w3.org/TR/xhtml1/DTD/xhtml1-transitional.dtd">
<html xmlns="http://www.w3.org/1999/xhtml" xml:lang="en" lang="en">
<head>
<title> Using The div Element With Styles </title>
</head>
<body>
    <div align = "center" style = "color: blue; font-style: italic">
    <p>
        This is a basic XHTML document that has one division and
        multiple paragraphs. They may be simple, but I think they
        will get the point across. This is the first paragraph.
    </p>
    <p>
        This book is a practical approach to web design and coding.
        We believe that a person should have a good understanding
        of the basic concepts of design and a basic understanding
        of the language before using a WYSIWYG application
        to develop web pages.  By developing this understanding of
        these concepts, you will be able to use your skill and
        creativity to control your designs.  The best way to learn
        these basic concepts is by doing. If you want to keep up
        with current standards, you have to understand the code.
    </p>
    </div>
    <p>
        This paragraph is outside of the division and has default
        styles.
    </p>
</body>
</html>
```

The results of the above XHTML are shown in Figure 12.5.

FIGURE 12.5: BASIC XHTML DOCUMENT USING <DIV> ELEMENT AND STYLE ATTRIBUTE

Notice the two paragraphs that were enclosed within the division; both had the styles of the division applied.

EMBEDDED STYLE SHEETS

Embedded style sheets are part of the XHTML document and contain the style rules. They are used to apply styles to the entire document. Embedded styles are placed within the head section of the document by using the <style> element. Since the style rules are placed within the XHTML document, are we really achieving the separation of style and content? Yes, they are separate because the rules are placed in the head section before the document content.

APPLYING EMBEDDED STYLES, THE <STYLE> ELEMENT

The <style> </style> element is used to create styles within a single document. It contains the rules that the browser will use to render the document. The syntax for these rules was discussed earlier in the chapter. The basic syntax for using the style element is

```
<style type="text/css">

        The style rules are placed here

</style>
```

The style element's type attribute specifies the media type, which is *text/css* when using cascading style sheets. Since older browsers may not recognize the style element, it is necessary to hide the embedded style from the browser. This is accomplished by enclosing the contents of the style element within the XHTML comments. Why is this necessary? When a browser does not recognize a specific tag, it just displays its content. The syntax for the style element including the comment is

```
<style type="text/css">
<!--
      The style rules are placed here
-->
</style>
```

The opening comment tag is placed directly after the opening <style> tag, and the closing comment tag is placed before the closing </style> tag.

USING EMBEDDED STYLE SHEETS

We will use the style element introduced above to create a basic page that uses an embedded style sheet.

1. Type the following using your choice of editor and save it as embedstyle1.html.

```
<?xml version="1.0" encoding="UTF-8"?>
<!DOCTYPE html PUBLIC "-//W3C//DTD/XHTML 1.0 Transitional//EN"
"http://www.w3.org/TR/xhtml1/DTD/xhtml1-transitional.dtd">
<html xmlns="http://www.w3.org/1999/xhtml" xml:lang="en" lang="en">
<head>
<title>  Using Embedded Style Sheet </title>
</head>
<body>
    <h1>Paragraph One</h1>
    <p>
      This is a basic XHTML document that has three paragraphs.
      This is the first paragraph, which has a level one heading
      that is red. The font for every paragraph is: sans-serif.
    </p>
    <h3>Paragraph Two</h3>
    <p>
      This is the second paragraph in our embedded style example.
      It has a level three heading that is blue and italic.
    </p>
    <h6>Paragraph Three</h6>
    <p>
      This is the third paragraph in our embedded style example.
      It has a level six heading that is aqua.
    </p>
```

```
</body>
</html>
```

2. Add the style element by placing it after the </title> tag.

```
<style type="text/css">
<!--

-->
</style>
```

3. Next, add the style rules for the three different levels of headings.

```
h1{
    color: red;
    }

h3{
    font-style: italic;
    color: blue;
    }

h6{
    color: aqua;
    }
```

4. Add the style rule for paragraphs within the document.

```
p{
    font-family: sans-serif;
    color: black;
    }
```

5. Save the document as embedstyle1.html.
6. The completed style element should look like

```
<style type="text/css">
<!--
  h1{
      color: red;
      }

  h3{
      font-style: italic;
      color: blue;
      }

  h6{
      color: aqua;
```

```
    }
 p{
    font-family: sans-serif;
    color: black;
    }
-->
</style>
```

7. In the browser, select Open from the File menu to open
   embedstyle1.html. Your screen should resemble Figure 12.6.

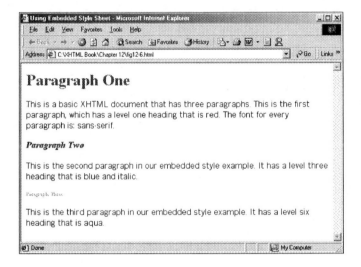

FIGURE 12.6: BASIC XHTML DOCUMENT USING EMBEDDED STYLE SHEET

EXTERNAL STYLE SHEETS

An *external style sheet* is sometimes referred to as a linked style sheet. External
style sheets are stored separately from the XHTML document but contain the
same rules that were used with the embedded style. Since the file is saved
separately, it can be used to apply the same style to every page in a Website.
These files are text files that have a .css extension. The browser recognizes the
extension and interprets the file as a style sheet.

APPLYING EXTERNAL STYLE SHEETS, THE <LINK> ELEMENT

The link element is used to apply an external style sheet to an XHTML document. The href attribute is used to provide the name and location of the style sheet. The value of the href attribute can also be a uniform resource locator (URL) or the file name located in the same directory.

The rel attribute is used to specify the relationship of the page containing the link to the other document. The rel attribute is set to "stylesheet," which specifies that an external style sheet is being used. The type attribute is used to tell the browser what type of file it is reading. The basic syntax for using the link element is:

> tip: Since <link> is an empty element and does not have a closing tag, it must be terminated properly by adding a space and a slash, such as <link />.

```
<link rel="stylesheet" href="exstyle1.css" type="text/css"/>
```

USING EXTERNAL STYLE SHEETS

We will use the link element introduced above to create a basic page that uses an external style sheet.

1. Type the following using your choice of editor and save it as externalstyle1.html.

```
<?xml version="1.0" encoding="UTF-8"?>
<!DOCTYPE html PUBLIC "-//W3C//DTD/XHTML 1.0 Transitional//EN"
"http://www.w3.org/TR/xhtml1/DTD/xhtml1-transitional.dtd">
<html xmlns="http://www.w3.org/1999/xhtml" xml:lang="en" lang="en">
<head>
<title>  Using External Style Sheet </title>
</head>
<body>
    <h1>Paragraph One</h1>
    <p>
        This is a basic XHTML document that has three paragraphs.
        This is the first paragraph, which has a level one heading
        that is red. The font for every paragraph is: sans-serif.
    </p>
    <h3>Paragraph Two</h3>
    <p>
        This is the second paragraph in our external style sheet
        example.  It has a level three heading that is blue
        and italic.
```

```
    </p>
    <h6>Paragraph Three</h6>
    <p>
        This is the third paragraph in our external style sheet
        example. It has a level six heading that is aqua.
    </p>
</body>
</html>
```

2. Add the <link> element to the head section by placing it after the </title> tag.

```
<link rel="stylesheet" href="exstyle1.css"type="text/css"/>
```

3. Save the file externalstyle1.html and, using the text editor, open a new file and save it as exstyle1.css in the same directory as the previous file.

4. Next, add the style rules for the three different levels of headings and paragraphs to the file exstyle1.css.

```
            h1{
                color: red;
                }
            h3{
                font-style: italic;
                color: blue;
                }
            h6{
                color: aqua;
                }
             p{
                font-family: sans-serif;
                color: black;
                }
```

5. Save the document exstyle1.css.

6. In the browser, select Open from the File menu to open externalstyle1.html. Your screen should resemble Figure 12.7.

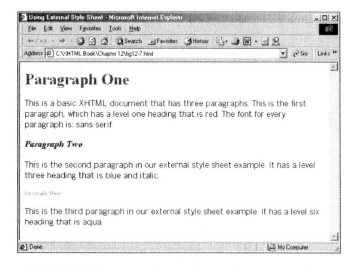

FIGURE 12.7: BASIC XHTML DOCUMENT USING EXTERNAL STYLE SHEET

CREATING A STYLE CLASS

A *style class* allows you to define different styles for the same element or for a group. This allows for different styles to be applied to parts of an XHTML document that are structurally the same. For example, you could define classes to enable the <h1> element to have different appearances instead of just the one defined. Without the use of classes, this would have to be done with inline styles. Style classes are defined within embedded or external style sheets using the following syntax:

```
.class name{
        property:value;
        property:value;
        }
```

The class name is used to identify the class and is preceded by a period. When naming the class, it is a good practice to give it a name that represents function and not style. The following is an example of defining classes in the style element:

```
<style type="text/css">
<!--
  h1.go{
        color: green;
```

```
        }
    h1.caution{
            color: yellow;
            }
    .stop{
        color: red;
        }
    h1{
       font-size:16pt
        }
    p{
      font-style: italic;
      color: black;
      }
-->
</style>
```

In this example, there are two classes targeted specifically at a level-one heading and can be used only with them. These two classes are go and caution. Notice that the class "stop" does not have an XHTML element associated with it. This allows the class to be used with any XHTML element that can display color. Let's apply the classes that we created to the following XHTML document using the class attribute:

```
<?xml version="1.0" encoding="UTF-8"?>
<!DOCTYPE html PUBLIC "-//W3C//DTD/XHTML 1.0 Transitional//EN"
"http://www.w3.org/TR/xhtml1/DTD/xhtml1-transitional.dtd">
<html xmlns="http://www.w3.org/1999/xhtml" xml:lang="en" lang="en">
<head>
<title> Using Classes With Style Sheets </title>
<style type="text/css">
    <!--
        h1.go{
             color: green;
             }
        h1.caution{
               color: yellow;
               }
        .stop{
             color: red;
             }
        h1{
           font-size:16pt
           }
        p{
          font-style: italic;
          color: black;
```

```
            }
      -->
  </style>
  </head>
  <body>
    <h1 class="go">This heading is green because it uses the go
       class.</h1>
    <h1 class="caution">This heading is yellow because it uses the
       caution class.</h1>
    <h1 class="stop">This heading is red because it uses the stop
       class.</h1>
    <p>
       Since the stop class was defined with no associated XHTML
       element, I can use it with the span element to change
       the color of some text to red.  <span class="stop">This text
       is red and italic.</span>
    </p>
  </body>
  </html>
```

The results of the above XHTML are shown in Figure 12.8.

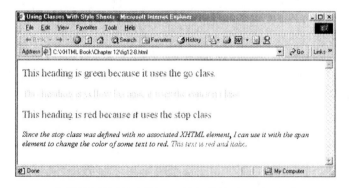

FIGURE 12.8 BASIC XHTML DOCUMENT USING CLASSES

USING STYLE SHEET PROPERTIES

So far in this chapter, we have applied some simple style rules to XHTML documents using style properties that affected color, font size, and font type. There are a great many more properties that could be used, so many that it just would not be practical to cover them in a single chapter. The next part of this chapter will look at the most common style sheet properties and how they can be used.

The properties that are used with style sheets can be divided into two groups: text-level and block-level. Text-level properties would cover color, fonts, space, size, and positioning. Block-level properties deal more with page layout and include borders, margins, text alignment, and indents.

Setting Color

The *color* property has been used in previous examples to change the color of text. The value of this property can be specified using one of 16 color keywords. The 16 standard color names include

aqua	gray	navy	teal
black	green	olive	silver
blue	lime	purple	white
fuchsia	maroon	red	yellow

You are not limited to the 16 standard colors; the hexadecimal color value can also be used to specify colors. When using the hexadecimal value, it is preceded by the # sign. Below are the same 16 standard color names with their hexadecimal values:

aqua	#00FFFF	gray	#808080	navy	#000080	teal	#008080
black	#000000	green	#008000	olive	#808000	silver	#C0C0C0
blue	#0000FF	lime	#00FF00	purple	#800080	white	#FFFFFF
fuchsia	#FF00FF	maroon	#800000	red	#FF0000	yellow	#FFFF00

The following are examples of style rules using the color property to change the color of XHTML elements:

```
h1{color: red;}
h3{color: blue;}
h6{color: aqua;}
 p{color: #0000FF;}
```

Setting Background Color

The *background-color* property is used to set the background color of an element. Although you can define a background color for any element, it is normally used to define a background color for the body element. The color values used with the color property also apply to this property. The following are examples of the style rules using the background-color property with XHTML elements:

```
body{background-color: white;}
h1{background-color:#FF0000;}
```

Figure 12.9 is the result of applying the following style rules to a simple XHTML document:

```
body{background-color:gray;}
h1{color:blue; background-color:white;}
p{color:white; font-family: sans-serif;}
```

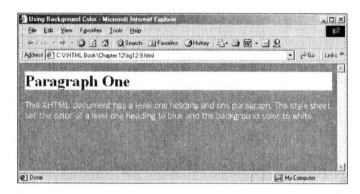

FIGURE 12.9: SIMPLE XHTML DOCUMENT USING BACKGROUND-COLOR PROPERTY

Controlling Font Appearance

Cascading style sheets have a wide range of properties to specify the appearance of a font in an XHTML document. The commonly used cascading style sheet properties used to control fonts are

- font-family
- font-size
- font-style
- line-height
- font-weight

font-family

Cascading style sheets allow for the naming of a specific font to be used for text. The *font-family* property can be assigned a specific font name or generic font family as its value. The only catch is that the specified font must be available on the computer viewing the page. If the specified font is not available, the default font will be used. The following is an example of a CSS rule using the font-family property:

```
p{
    font-family: sans-serif;
}
```

The font-family property can also have multiple family assignments made, which allows for a list of alternatives in case the first choice of font is not available. The list of alternatives is separated by commas and is in order of preference. The browser will start with the first value of the font-family property and work its way to the last. The last value in the list should be a generic font-family. The following is an example of a CSS rule using the font-family property with multiple values:

```
p{
    font-family: helvetica, arial, sans-serif;
}
```

When using a font name that contains multiple words, enclose the name in quotes. For example:

```
p{
    font-family: "century schoolbook", times, serif;
}
```

The following are the five font families recognized by cascading style sheets:
- serif
- sans-serif
- monospace
- script
- fantasy

Figure 12.10 illustrates the different font families.

This is the Sans Serif Font Family

This is the Serif Font Family

This is the Script Font Family

This is the Monospace Font Family

THIS IS THE FANTASY FONT FAMILY

FIGURE 12.10 BASIC FONT FAMILIES

font-size

The *font-size* property can be used to control the size of the font displayed by the browser. The assigned value can be either absolute or relative. The absolute values are based on standard units of measurement such as pixels (px), points (pt), inches (in), centimeters (cm), or picas (pc). A relative value is expressed as a value relative to the size of the parent element. The most common way to express a relative value is by using a percentage. The following are examples of CSS rules using the font-size property:

```
h1{
    font-size:16pt;
  }
p{
    font-size:120%;
  }
```

Figure 12.11 illustrates the effect of the font-size property.

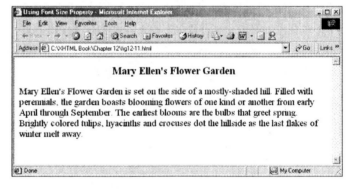

FIGURE 12.11: FONT-SIZE PROPERTY APPLIED

font-style

The *font-style* property defines the appearance of a font in one of three ways: normal, italic, or oblique. The italic and oblique (slanted) are very similar in appearance. The italic style is available in most fonts and should be used over the oblique option. The following is an example of a style sheet declaration using the font-style property:

```
p{
    font-style: italic;
  }
```

font-weight

The *font-weight* property is used to control the line thickness (lighter or bolder) of the text. The weight of a font can be specified by using a number representing how dark it should be or by using a keyword. When using a number to specify the weight, the value is a number ranging from 100, being the lightest, to 900, being the darkest. The number increases in intervals of 100. The weight of 400 for most fonts is normal, while a weight of 700 is considered bold. The keywords bold, bolder, lighter, and normal can also be used to specify the weight of a font. The following are examples of style sheet declarations using the font-weight property:

```
h1{
    font-weight:200;
    }
h3{
    font-weight:bold;
    }
h6{
    font-weight:900;
    }
```

Figure 12.12 illustrates the effect of the font-weight property.

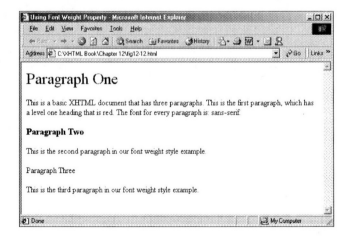

FIGURE 12.12: FONT-WEIGHT PROPERTY APPLIED

line-height

The *line-height* property refers to how much vertical space is displayed between lines of text in a paragraph or other element. The normal vertical space is directly related to the size of the font, but it can be modified by using the line-height property. The value assigned to this property can be expressed in

■ a percentage of font size

■ a specific numeric value specified by a measurement in points, inches, pixels, or centimeters

The following are examples of style sheet declarations using the line-height property:

```
h1{
    line-height:14pt;
    }
p{
    line-height:150%;
    }
```

Figure 12.13 illustrates the effect of the line-height property.

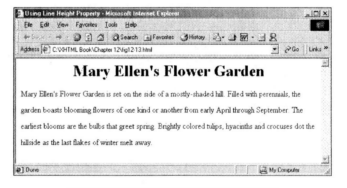

FIGURE 12.13 FONT-HEIGHT PROPERTY APPLIED

Using Block-level Properties to Control Layout

Cascading style sheets have a wide range of properties to improve the layout of an XHTML document. CSS handles block-level properties based on the *box model*, which is shown in Figure 12.14 as a graphical representation. The concept is based on the fact that every block-level element is displayed in a box and could have a box within it. This includes the body element; the browser will create a box for it inside its containing block, which would be the browser window. At the center of every box created by an element is the content; this is what is going to be displayed. The area that surrounds the content is called the *padding,* and if a background color or image were present, it would extend into this area. The border surrounds the padding and is a line around the contents. The *margin* surrounds the border and is the space between any other boxes that may be around it. The margins of a box are always transparent. This allows the background color of the body to be seen.

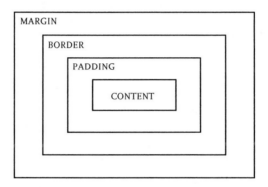

FIGURE 12.14: BOX MODEL

To get a better understanding of the box model, let's look at Figure 12.15, which shows a graphical representation of the following simple XHTML code:

```
<body>
    <p>
        This is a paragraph in an XHTML document.  This is the
        content of the paragraph element.
    </p>
</body>
```

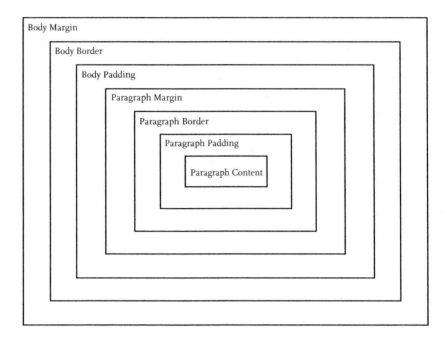

FIGURE 12.15: BOX MODEL USING XHTML EXAMPLE

The commonly used cascading style sheet properties used to improve layout are

- margin-top
- margin-right
- margin-bottom
- margin-left
- padding-top
- padding-right
- padding-bottom
- padding-left
- text-align
- text-indent
- text-transform

Applying Margin Properties

The CSS properties of *margin-top*, *margin-bottom*, *margin-left*, and *margin-right* describe the sides of the margin box. These properties allow for the control of space between the block-level element and the surrounding element. Margin sizes are set using units of lengths expressed as pixels, points, inches, centimeters, or a percentage value. The following is an example of a style sheet with a declaration using the margin properties:

```
body{
    margin-left:10%; margin-right:10%;
}
```

Using the above style sheet declaration, Figures 12.16 and 12.17 illustrate the effect of the margin properties.

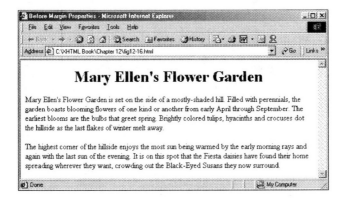

FIGURE 12.16: DOCUMENT BEFORE MARGIN PROPERTIES APPLIED

FIGURE 12.17: DOCUMENT AFTER MARGIN PROPERTIES APPLIED

When a percentage value is used, as in the previous example, the percentage is relative to another length value; in this case, since we are working with the body element, it would be the browser window. The value assigned to the margin size can also be expressed as a negative number. The margin-top and margin-bottom properties can also be used to control the space above and below elements such as headings. The following is an example of a style sheet declaration using the top and bottom margin properties on a level-one heading:

```
h1{
    margin-top:10%; margin-bottom:10%
}
```

Using the above style sheet declaration, compare Figures 12.17 and 12.18, which illustrate the effect of the margin top and bottom properties.

FIGURE 12.18: DOCUMENT AFTER MARGIN TOP AND BOTTOM PROPERTIES APPLIED

Applying Padding Properties

The CSS properties of padding-top, padding-bottom, padding-left, and padding-right describe the sides of the padding box. These properties allow for the control of space

tip: By using a relative value such as a percentage, if the browser window is resized, the margins and padding will adapt to the page's new proportions.

between the border and the content of an element. *Padding* values are set using units of lengths expressed as pixels, points, inches, centimeters, or as a percentage value. The following is an example of a style sheet with a declaration using the padding properties:

```
td{
    padding-left:20pt;
}
```

Padding properties are useful with cells of a table. Figure 12.19 shows an example of a table from an earlier chapter. Notice how each cell has no space between the left border and the contents. Figure 12.20 shows the table after the above style sheet declaration has been added to an embedded style sheet.

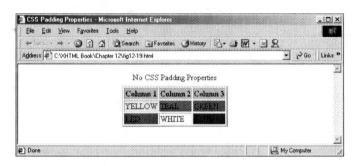

FIGURE 12.19: TABLE BEFORE PADDING PROPERTIES APPLIED

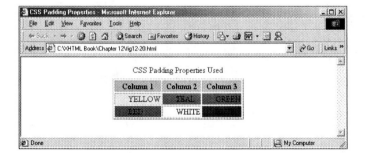

FIGURE 12.20: TABLE AFTER PADDING PROPERTIES APPLIED

Padding can also be added by using the padding property by itself, followed by up to four values, which are used to set padding on each side. For example:

```
td{
    padding:10pt 10pt 10pt 10pt;
  }
```

Figure 12.21 shows the table example after the above style sheet declaration has been applied. Notice the space that has been added around each of the cell contents.

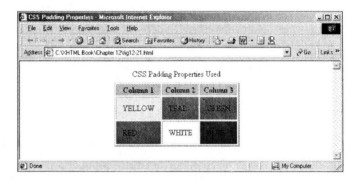

FIGURE 12.21   TABLE AFTER PADDING PROPERTY WITH FOUR VALUES APPLIED

The padding property can take one to four values. The following example is equivalent to the declaration shown above with four values:

```
td{
    padding:10pt;
  }
```

The number of padding property values is interpreted in the following way:

- One value—indicates that the value given will be applied to all sides
- Two values—indicates that the first value will be applied to the top and bottom while the second value will be applied to the left and right
- Three values—indicates that the first value will apply to the top, the second value will apply to the left and right, and the third will be applied to the bottom
- Four values—indicates that the values will be applied to the top, right, bottom, and left, respectively

Applying Text-align Property
The CSS *text-align* property can be applied to block-level elements and allows for the justification of text within the element. The values used to align text within

an element include left, center, and right. The following is an example of a style sheet with a declaration using the text-align property:

```
h1{
    text-align:center;
    }
```

Applying Text-indent Property

The CSS *text-indent* property can be applied to block-level elements and is used to set the amount of indentation of the first line of text within the element. The value used to define the amount of indentation can be expressed as an absolute or relative value. The following is an example of a style sheet with a declaration using the text-align property:

```
p{
    text-indent:5%;
    }
```

Figure 12.22 shows an example of the above style sheet declaration applied to an XHTML document.

FIGURE 12.22: PARAGRAPHS AFTER TEXT-INDENT PROPERTY APPLIED

Applying Text-transform Property

The CSS *text-transform* property can be used to change the case of text. The text is transformed based on the following values:

- capitalize—first character of each word is capitalized
- lowercase—all characters will become small letters
- uppercase—all characters will be capitalized

The following are examples of style sheet declarations applying the text-transform property to the <h1> and <span> elements:

```
h1{
    text-transform:capitalize;
    }
span{
    text-transform:capitalize;
    }
```

Figure 12.23 shows an example of the above style sheet declarations applied to an XHTML document.

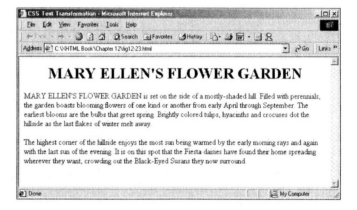

FIGURE 12.23: PARAGRAPHS AFTER TEXT-TRANSFORM PROPERTY APPLIED

CHAPTER SUMMARY

Cascading style sheets allow you to take more control over the presentation of a Web page. This chapter introduced style sheet concepts and how to apply them using inline styles, embedded styles, and external styles. With this language, we can control the text size, color, and font, as well as the background color and white space around a particular element. We learned how to apply CSS properties to block-level elements. Some of the advantages to using style sheets include:

- allows for the styling and layout of multiple pages at the same time
- allows the style of an entire site to be changed easily
- more maintainable because styling is contained in a central location instead of embedded throughout the document

Refer to Appendix B for more on cascading style sheet properties.

KEY TERMS

background-color	margin-bottom
block-level element	margin-left
box model	margin-right
cascading style sheets (CSS)	margin-top
color	padding
embedded style sheet	property
external style sheet	selector
font-family	style
font-size	style class
font-style	text-align
font-weight	text/css
inline style	text-indent
line-height	text-transform
margin	value

REVIEW QUESTIONS

1. What does CSS stand for?
2. What is a style sheet rule?
3. What are the three ways to apply style sheet rules to an XHTML document?
4. What property is used to indent the first line of text within an element?
5. What are the four components of the box model?
6. What type of style sheet is used when the style element is placed within the head element?
7. What type of style sheet would be used to create a style for a Website with multiple pages?

8. What is the difference between inline, embedded, and external style sheets?
9. What is the precedence order for the application of styles?
10. What is a block-level element?

EXERCISES

1. Create an XHTML document that is your résumé. It should include sections for objectives, education, employment, and references. Use the following elements: headings, paragraphs, horizontal rules, lists, images, and links. Use the concepts learned in this chapter to enhance the layout of the page using the properties of text-level and block-level elements. Use the embedded type of style sheet.

2. Using the personal Web page created in Chapter 6, Exercise 3, modify it to use an external style sheet. Using style sheets, make the following changes to each section:

    Family
        Heading—level 2, font style italic, color black, and centered
        Paragraph text—font family sans-serif, color black, and use the span element to change the color of an important sentence to red
    Life before college
        Heading—level 2, font style bold, color blue, and centered
        Paragraph text—font family Times New Roman, color blue, and font size 200%
    Life in college
        Heading—level 2, font style italic, color red, and centered
        Paragraph text—font family arial, color red, and centered

3. Using the text below, create an XHTML document that uses inline styles. The heading should use the font family Times New Roman and have a color of black. Each paragraph should use a different font family and color. Inside each paragraph, use the span element to change the font size of any flower name to 200 percent.

Mary Ellen's Flower Garden

Mary Ellen's Flower Garden is set on the side of a mostly shaded hill. Filled with perennials, the garden boasts blooming flowers of one kind or another from early April through September. The earliest blooms are the bulbs that greet spring. Brightly colored tulips, hyacinths, and crocuses dot the hillside as the last flakes of winter melt away.

The highest corner of the hillside enjoys the most sun, being warmed by the early morning rays and again with the last sun of the evening. It is on this spot that the Fiesta daisies have found their home, spreading wherever they want, crowding out the Black-Eyed Susans they now surround.

The foxgloves grow taller before opening their throaty flowers, which provide a safe haven for fat bumblebees seeking their sweet nectar. And scattered up and down the hill are the carefree daylilies, whose blooms follow the sun as it moves encircling the hill each day.

Sloping down the hill into the shade, the delicate columbine have long since bloomed and turned to seed. Still deeper into the shade are the dark purple irises, with their long, slender green foliage framing their beauty.

PROJECT

As we create our site, we need to account for future changes. One thing we can do now to make future cosmetic changes easy is to implement cascading style sheets for describing how links and text will be rendered by the browser. Do the following:

- Create an external style sheet that gives all of your links and text a uniform and pleasing look.
- Place the necessary links on your pages to reference the style sheet you just created. Make sure to use relative links.

REFERENCES

Cascading Style Sheets, http://www.w3.org/Style/CSS/
CSS Frequently Asked Questions,
   http://www.hwg.org/resources/faqs/cssFAQ.html
WebReview.com's Style Sheet Reference Guide,
   http://www.webreview.com/style/index.shtml

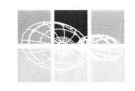

chapter 13
publishing your web page

CHAPTER OVERVIEW

There are many issues to consider in deploying a Website. In this chapter, you will learn how to validate the effectiveness of the content of your Website through the creation of a small usability test. You will also learn how to perform a walk-through of a site in order to identify and fix technical errors. You will learn how to prepare a plan for promoting a Website by considering Website promotion through the lens of traditional marketing. You will explore the issues connected with hiring an external hosting company including server components, hosting platforms, file transfers, and permissions. And finally, you will learn how to transfer files to a Web server using File Transfer Protocol.

CHAPTER OBJECTIVES

- Prepare a small usability test to validate a site
- Perform a site walk-through to identify problems
- Consider Website promotion as a function of traditional marketing
- Select hosting plans
- Use IP numbers or domain names to access Web content
- Transfer files to a Web sever via FTP

WEBSITE PUBLISHING

DEPLOYMENT CHECKLIST

Prior to uploading the site to a Web server, we need to make sure not only that it works from a technical point of view, but also that it addresses the needs of our audience.

Before we make our Website available to the public, we must ensure that it functions properly and that it fills the need for which it was developed. In Chapter 4, we developed a comprehensive vision that identified the goals, content, and organization of our site. Then, in later chapters, we used Web development techniques to create a site that fulfilled that vision. Now it's time to validate our solution by checking if it is technically functional and how it performs when placed in the hands of our target audience.

Throughout the previous chapters, we have addressed the technical details of producing XHTML documents. Before we publish our site, we need to make sure that every feature we implemented works properly by performing a site "walk-through." We should go through our site, using every possible combination. Along the way, we can note any errors and fix them. Some of the specific features that we should check include making sure that

- Graphics are optimized and in the correct format
- All links and images use relative addressing
- All links work
- All images load properly
- Alternate text is used for graphic images
- Common fonts are used (such as Times New Roman, Arial, Helvetica)
- Any meta-tag is fewer than 1,024 characters
- Meta-tags are placed on all key pages
- All tags are balanced

Now we can turn our attention towards checking the effectiveness of the site on our *target audience*. In the site design documentation we completed in Chapter 4, we addressed the goals for our site and the attributes of the target audience for our Website. Some additional issues we considered included the navigation and organization of content, the browsing behavior of our target audience, some possible color schemes, and even some possible fonts. At this stage in our development effort, we need to make sure that our site lives up to the vision we developed in our site design. We also need to ensure that our site is effective at communicating with our audience.

One of the best methods for checking the effectiveness of our site is to conduct a small usability study. We can gauge how well our site works by trying it out on a few users who are representative of the target audience. We ask these users to accomplish a series of tasks and then ask them to give us feedback. For example, if we created a site for our local community to inform people of upcoming events, we could ask the users to look up all of the festivals that occur in November. We would then be able to check if the users could in fact use our site to find that information. We could also time the users to see how long it took them to accomplish the task.

The intricacies of developing usability studies are beyond the scope of this book, but we can still employ the basic tenets of usability tests. We test our site on people who represent the target audience to see if our site works. If something does not work, we fix it. Only after the site works with a small pilot group do we incur the cost of actually deploying it.

WEBSITE PROMOTION

Before uploading our site to a Web server, we need to determine how we plan to promote our site in order to attract visitors. To properly promote a site, we need to do the same analysis and work that a typical marketing firm would go through in promoting a product or a service. While the intricacies of marketing are beyond the scope of this book, we can be guided by the same goals. Ultimately, we want members of our target audience to come to our site.

Before we go out and blindly register our site with every search engine under the sun, join any Web rings, put all types of meta-tags on our pages to attract the search engines, or even try to model the structure of our meta-tags to maximize our ranking with the search engines, we need to identify the following:

- Who is the target audience?
- What's the goal for our site? What do we want people to do when or after they visit our site?
- What can be used to initially attract the target audience to our site?
- What can be used to keep them coming back once we get them there?
- What mode of communication do they use most often?
- What's our budget for promoting the site?

Again, we are not marketing experts, but we can use this information to build a methodical action-plan for *marketing* our site. For example, let's assume that we have built a portal site for the Indianapolis area that will allow people to search for events or "things to do" in the community. Let's ask our questions and see how we could use that information to market our site.

- Who is the target audience?
  - Residents of the Indianapolis area.
- What's the goal for our site? What do we want people to do when or after they visit our site?
  - Increase participation in local community events such as carnivals, fairs, concerts, and so on.
- What can be used to initially attract the target audience to our site?
  - Let them know the site exists, partner with local business to provide free promotional items, do interviews with local celebrities, or add some human interest stories.
- What can be used to keep them coming back once we get them there?
  - Maintain a large database of all local events, have fresh new information on a daily basis, and so on.
- What mode of communication do they use most often?
  - Newspaper, radio, and television.
- What's our budget for promoting the site?
  - $200

Now that we have an idea of whom our Website is trying to impact and have some ideas that specifically address our audience, it is fairly easy to devise a plan of attack for promoting this Website. With only $200 to spend on promoting our site, we can discount using radio or TV advertising. Because we have narrowed the target audience to members of the Indianapolis area, we can concentrate on getting the word out in that arena. A few classified newspaper ads and fliers passed out at strategic places in the community would be much more effective in this case than any Web-based search engine or Web ring. We have also found a link between the goals for our site and how achieving those goals can benefit a third party. Our primary goal is to get people involved in community events. Thus, we can partner with other organizations that would benefit from our success and have them help us promote the site.

The above plan would work only for the situation that we described. This approach would not work if we were trying to promote a site on dog grooming.

But, by addressing the questions we posed earlier, we could devise a plan that would be just as effective for that area. That plan may involve running newspaper ads, partnering with people, registering with search engines, or even joining a Web ring, but the decision to do any of these things should be based on a methodical analysis of the target audience and the goals for the site.

What about Web-based promotion? There are tons of sites with advice on how to promote your site using just the Internet. All or most advise the registration of your site with the major search engines and the use of meta-tags within the pages to alert the search engines of the content of your site. Some even suggest joining Web rings or exchanging banner ads. If you are interested in these techniques, do a search using any of the major search engines for "Website promotion." Tons of sites will appear. There is no shortage of opinions on how to make your site the highest ranking with the search engines.

In the end, though, you will find that Internet-only Web promotion schemes are not effective. It's critical to think of *Website promotion* in the context of traditional marketing.

HOSTING AT A SERVICE PROVIDER

Once we are convinced that our site works, we can turn our attention to actually deploying it to a live Web server. We have two basic options. We can either host the Website ourselves, or we can pay an *Internet service provider* or *hosting provider* to host our site. As always, there are benefits to both of these options.

Hosting the Website can be rewarding because it provides us with an unprecedented amount of freedom in configuring our site, but it comes at the cost of the Web-hosting equipment and the expertise needed to maintain it. In other words, we can set up the Web server any way we want, but we need to be able to afford a machine that can be a Web server and to have the necessary skills to keep the server running. The skills required to set up and maintain a Web server are beyond the scope of this book. Thus, we will concentrate on the issues that accompany hosting a Website at a service provider.

Hosting a Website on a rented Web server is usually easier and more reliable. ISPs take care of configuring the server, registering our domain name, and backing up the data, and often provide faster connectivity.

While all hosting companies are unique and have different procedures for deploying our Website on the Internet, there are numerous issues that we need to consider before selecting a Web-hosting provider. These issues include

- Server type and components
- Bandwidth
- Domain name registration
- Transferring the files

Server Type and Components

Before selecting a hosting plan, we should make sure that our Website will work properly on the service provider's Web servers. There are a variety of different servers on the market, but we will narrow the field by focusing on three basic types of servers. There are (1) Unix servers that can host XHTML content and CGI programs, (2) Microsoft Internet Information Servers (IIS) that can host XHTML content and Active Server Pages (ASP), and (3) Java-based servers that can host XHTML content and JavaServer Pages (JSP). Notice that all three of these choices have the capability to host XHTML content. If our Website contains no server-side scripting, then we can rent space on any server because they can all serve regular Web pages. All of the content we have developed in this book, thus far, will work with any Web server. Later, in Chapter 16, we will develop Active Server Pages, which will require an MS IIS server. As you can see, if we decide to use any type of server-side scripting technology, then we need to rent space on a server that supports it.

Generally, prices for hosting plans partially reflect the type of server that your Web pages require. Microsoft hosting solutions are usually more expensive than Unix hosting solutions. We need to keep in mind that for a Microsoft hosting solution, the hosting provider will need to provide a machine running Microsoft NT Server or Microsoft 2000 Server. For a Unix solution, the ISP can use an open-source version of Linux with Apache; both of these are basically free.

Any specialized *server components* used on the Website will also need to be rented. For example, a popular component for NT-based solutions is called SoftArtisans File-Up. This component allows users to upload files via a Web browser. It is useful for creating auction sites or any site where we would like to provide the user with the capability to send images or other types of files to our Web server. If we use this component, then we must make sure the hosting provider has this component. Just renting a space on an IIS server is not enough.

Bandwidth

Another issue that will affect the price of a hosting plan is the bandwidth required by our site. Typically, hosting providers have extremely fast lines into their facilities. The hosting provider will sell us a portion of the bandwidth available on their leased line. This is usually measured in total bandwidth per month. For example, a typical hosting provider will charge approximately $20 per month for a total of 1.5 gigabytes of traffic per month and a total disk space of 150 megabytes. In other words, for $20 per month, the ISP will provide us with a total of 150 megabytes for our site. Our pictures and Web pages would be stored in this space. The 1.5 gigabytes is the amount of data that we could send in one month. The more users that visit our site, the more bandwidth we would use.

Domain Name Registration

Once we have selected a hosting plan that fits our needs, we need to register a domain name for our site. Each machine on the Internet has a unique number that identifies it, which is called an *IP number*. If we wanted to, we could just use the IP number of the service provider's server as the address to our site. While that would work, it would not be very pretty, and it would be difficult for people to remember our address in IP numbers. We can solve this problem by associating a *domain name* with the IP number of the server that hosts our site. Then we could use the name for constructing our URLs instead of the IP number.

To illustrate this, let's consider the server www.expert.cc.purdue.edu. This Web server has the IP number of 128.210.10.11. Purdue has elected to register the name www.expert.cc.purdue.edu to make it easier for people to remember that Website. If we wanted to access a Web page called index.html from this server, we could use either of these two addresses:

> http://128.210.10.11/index.html
> http://expert.cc.purdue.edu/index.html

As we have just seen, accessing Websites using domain names is much easier than using the IP numbers. You can register a domain name through most service providers or by going directly to one of the domain name authorities such as InterNIC. Regardless of who registers your domain, there will be an extra cost associated with the registration that is not included with your hosting plan. As of this writing, it costs $70 for two years.

Transferring the Files

Once we sign up for a hosting plan and ask the hosting provider to register a domain or transfer a domain name, we need to transfer our Website to the provider's Web server. This is typically done using *File Transfer Protocol (FTP)*. FTP allows computers on the Internet to exchange files. Thus, we can use FTP to copy the files we have developed for our Website from our local machine to the machine that will serve our pages.

FTP is operating-system independent, so it will work with any machine on the Internet, including Macintosh, Windows, and Unix. The way that it is implemented is a little different on each of these machines. If you are running Mac OS 9 or earlier, you will need an FTP client such as Fetch. On Mac OS, Windows, or Unix, you have the option of either using an FTP client or FTPing from the command prompt. Let's first explore how to FTP using a client. Note that you can download shareware FTP clients for any of these operating systems from some of the shareware repositories on the Web such as www.tucows.com, www.shareware.com, or www.cnet.com.

FTPing with a Graphical Client

By far, the easiest way to transfer files via FTP is by using a graphical client. In a nutshell, a graphical FTP program will allow us to graphically drag files from our machine onto a remote machine. In the example below, we will transfer some XHTML files from our machine to the Web server. The exact dialog boxes that you will see with your FTP client will vary, but they all require the same information to work. Namely, all FTP clients will need to know the name or address of the machine that you would like to contact, your user name on that machine, and your password. In Figure 13.1, we are trying to connect to the machine expert.cc.purdue.edu. Our user ID is crmorales, and our password is ******.
box. Again, the boxes might look different depending on the FTP client that we use. Figure 13.2 shows WS_FTP, and Figure 13.3 shows CuteFTP. Note the similarities of the interfaces.

When transferring anything other than XHTML or text files, it is critical to select binary mode for the transfer. In WS_FTP, we can check the Binary radio button. In CuteFTP, we can use the Transfer drop-down menu.

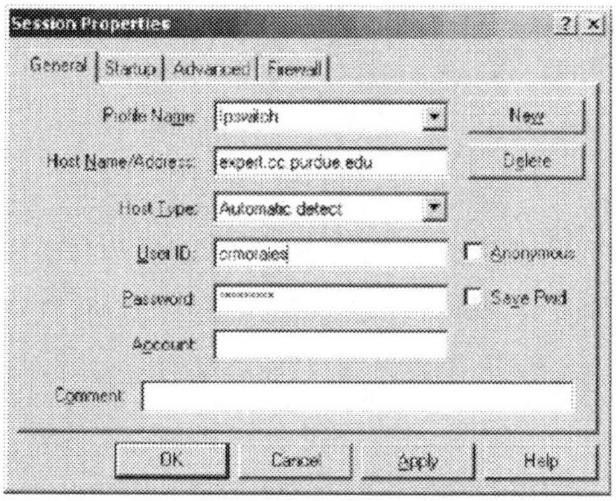

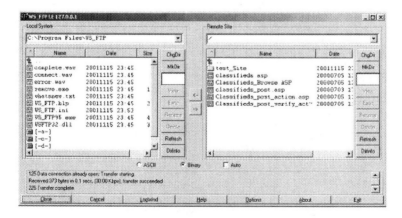

FIGURE 13.1: INITIALIZING AN FTP TRANSFER

When we hit the OK button, our machine will connect to the remote machine. We will see two lists of files. On the left side, we will see the files on our system, and on the right side we will see the files on the server. To send our files to the server, we just drag them from the left box to the right

FIGURE 13.2: WS_FTP FTP CLIENT

Once we drag the files over, the files get transferred and our Web pages are on the Web server.

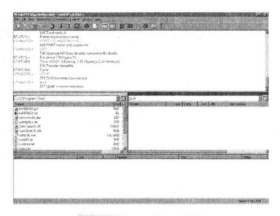

FIGURE 13.3: CUTEFTP CLIENT

FTPing from the command line is also an option for transferring our files. In a nutshell, we open up a command line prompt, change directories to where we have our original files, FTP to the server, and then initiate the transfer. Let's assume that we would like to send a file named myfile.xhtml that resides in c:\data\web_pages\myfile.html. Here is what we would do:

1. Open a command prompt window.
2. Navigate to the file from the current directory. We would type:
   cd data\web_pages\
   This would change our current directory from the root c:\ to where our file resides, c:\data\web_pages\.
3. Now type
   FTP [hostname].
   If we wanted to connect to expert.cc.purdue.edu, we would type ftp expert.cc.purdue.edu.
4. Now we will be asked for our username and password. Type them in.
5. If all is successful, we will be greeted with an ftp> prompt. Here we can type FTP commands to send and receive files.
6. To send a file, we would type
   put *[filename]*
   Thus, to send our myfile.html, we would type put myfile.html. Figure 13.4 shows a typical session.

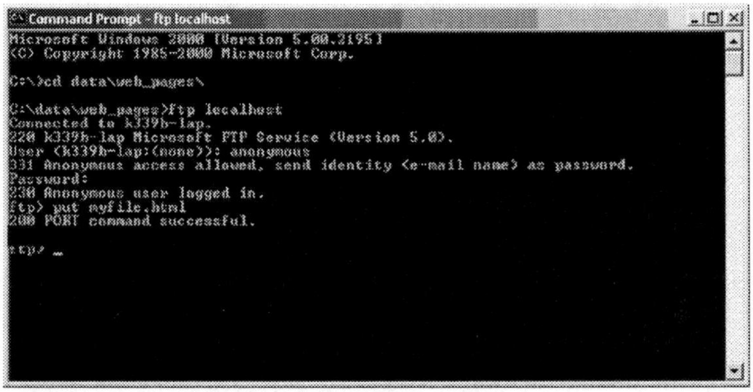

FIGURE 13.4: FTPING FROM THE COMMAND LINE

FTPing from the command line is very similar to using a graphical client but requires that you do everything manually. We still provide the same three basic pieces of information: the host that we would like to contact, our user name, and our password. In situations where no graphical FTP client is available, it is useful to know how to accomplish the transfer in this manner, but in most situations, a graphical client is preferred.

Unix Permissions

Unix shell accounts can be used for much more than just hosting Websites. Many of the accounts that hosting providers rent out are standard Unix accounts that happen to have the ability to serve Web pages. On these accounts, we could run Unix programs, host Web pages, read newsgroup postings, send/receive email, and so on. Because the hosting providers cannot predict the types of activities or the needs for your specific Website, they often leave the task of setting permissions up to the user. For example, we might want to grant read-access to all of our Web pages and also have a folder that users can upload images to. Thus, we would also need to grant that folder write-access. The configuration of the permissions would not only vary per account but also per project. We could host another Website with the same Unix account that requires a different set of permissions.

Most hosting providers will have the permissions for your account set to read-access only for users of your site. If all we are doing is serving standard Web pages, this is enough. In those cases, all we need to do is FTP our files into the server as described above and retrieve our Web pages using the Web address provided by the hosting provider. In some rare circumstances, service providers will provide you with an account with no permissions set for visitors to your site. Again, they assume that you will set these up to meet the needs of your site. In those cases, we would need to telnet into our account and set up our files to be world-readable and world-executable.

1. Open a command prompt window and type

    telnet *[provider's host]*

    If our account were on expert.cc.purdue.edu, we would type telnet expert.cc.purdue.edu. This information will be provided in the information you received when you signed up for the account.

2. We will be asked for a username and password. Again, we would have received these when we signed up for the account.

3. Make our folder world-executable and world-readable by typing

    chmod go+rx ~

The permissions for our account are now properly set for serving Web pages. Again, with most hosting providers, we will not have to set these permissions ourselves.

CHAPTER SUMMARY

In this chapter, we explored the issues that accompany deploying a Website. We validated the content and organization of our solution with a small usability study. We also learned to validate the technical functionality of a site by doing a walk-through. We considered Website promotion from a traditional marketing perspective. We looked at issues connected with hiring an external hosting company including server components, hosting platforms, file transfers, and permissions. Finally, we learned how to transfer files via FTP both from the command line and by using a graphical client.

KEY TERMS

Domain name

File Transfer Protocol (FTP)

hosting provider

Internet service
    provider

IP number

marketing

server component

target audience

Website promotion

REVIEW QUESTIONS

1. What is a domain name?
2. What is File Transfer Protocol?
3. What are some common graphical FTP clients on each of the major platforms: Unix, Macintosh, and Windows?
4. What are three advantages of hosting your own site over hiring a service provider?
5. What are some disadvantages of hosting your own Website?
6. What are three technical issues that should be checked in validating a Website?
7. What are some of the issues we should consider in promoting a Website?

EXERCISES

1. Do a Web search and find three Web-hosting companies that offer NT-hosting plans for sites under 25 megs with less than 1 GB of traffic per month and also offer better than 97 percent up time.
2. Of the three sites, which offers the most technological "extras," such as free components?
3. Which offers the best technical support?
4. Which of the companies will transfer your domain name for free or register your domain for free?
5. Find three Unix-hosting plans that meet the criteria set in Exercise 1.
6. Considering the NT-host and Unix-hosting plans, which one would you select for a personal Website?
7. Do an Internet search for "Website promotion." Write a short proposal for promoting a site based on the information you found in your search.

PROJECT

Now that most of our site has been completed, we need to consider how we can promote it. Let's develop a plan for marketing our site based on the analysis and site design we developed in Chapter 4. Write a two- to five-page proposal for promoting our plan. Be sure to clearly identify the target audience, the goals for our site, how visitors will initially be attracted, and how visitors will be enticed into returning to our site. Make sure to provide specifics. Justify any features you put into the site by addressing how it helps to fulfill the overall goal for the site.

REFERENCES

Baatsee, M., Blair, R., et. al. 2000. *ASP XML*, Birmingham, U.K.:Wrox Press.

Hettihewa, S. 1999. *SAMS Teach Yourself Active Server Pages 2.0 in 21 Days*, Indianapolis: SAMS Publishing.

Weissinger, A. 1999. *ASP in a Nutshell*, Sebastopol, CA: O'Reilly.

Whitehead, P. 2000. *Active Server Pages 3.0*, Mississauga, ON: maranGraphics.

4 Guys From Rolla, www.4GuysFromRolla.com

ASP 101, www.ASP101.com

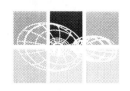

chapter 14

programming with javascript: introduction

CHAPTER OVERVIEW

This chapter is *not* intended to make you a programmer, but we need to have a basic understanding of some programming principles in order to do some basic JavaScript programming. The pages that we have been creating in previous chapters have been static, allowing limited interaction through links. This chapter will introduce JavaScript concepts, which will allow us to build applications that actively process user inputs. This chapter will cover the following topics: capabilities, incorporating JavaScript into XHTML pages, language and syntax, built-in operators, and functions.

CHAPTER OBJECTIVES

- Create simple JavaScript programs
- Understand the basic syntax of the JavaScript language
- Understand how to include JavaScript in an XHTML document
- Understand the relationship of objects, properties, methods, and events
- Understand how to use event handlers
- Create XHTML documents using JavaScript

JAVASCRIPT

JavaScript is an easy-to-use and powerful language that can be embedded into XHTML documents. JavaScript programs are run by the browser and can enhance interactivity with users and the appearance of Web pages. You have probably even used Web pages that contained JavaScript programs without knowing it. These programs are commonly used to perform calculations, display the current date and time, verify information entered on forms, and create special effects on pages.

There are two scripting methodologies in which JavaScript can be used: client-side and server-side scripting. Client-side scripts are embedded into the XHTML document and are interpreted by the browser. They can perform many functions such as data validation and providing interactive feedback to the user. This processing on the client machine has its advantages, such as

- The client has to make fewer trips to the server for information, so potential network bottlenecks are avoided, which can result in an increase in execution speed
- Users are allowed to interact with the Web page, making decisions that may affect how the Web page looks or how information is processed
- Scripts are able to respond to user events such as a mouse click or the resizing of a page

Client-side scripting comes with some disadvantages, such as

- The browser must support the scripting language being used
- Scripts may have different results in different browsers
- The scripts are embedded into the XHTML document, so the source code is easily viewed with the browser, making it difficult to protect your source code

Server-side scripts are not embedded into an XHTML document but are stored and run on a Web server. The server-side script also has its advantages, such as

- The ability to interact with a relational database
- Performing file manipulations on the server
- Generating responses based on users' requests
- No problems with browser support because scripts run on the server
- Only the XHTML is sent to the client, so the source code is not viewable

Server-side scripting also has some disadvantages, such as

- More burden is placed on the Web server to process information and respond to simple user requests
- Increased network traffic
- Possible decrease in execution speed

Given the advantages and disadvantages of client-side and server-side scripting, which one should be used? A lot depends on the situation, but a general rule to follow is to do as much processing on the client as possible, taking advantage of its processing power and flexibility.

JavaScript is often confused with *Java*; they are not the same, even though their names may be similar. JavaScript was originally developed by Netscape as *LiveScript*. Sun Microsystems took an interest in this scripting language and worked together with Netscape to refine it into what is now known as JavaScript. With JavaScript, the script is saved as text as part of the XHTML document. When the XHTML document is read by the browser, the JavaScript is interpreted line by line. It is also important to point out that, as with any other programming language, JavaScript has keywords and syntax, which refers to the structure of statements. As we start to write our JavaScript, we will learn more about the various keywords and syntax rules.

OBJECT-BASED LANGUAGE

JavaScript is an object-based language as opposed to an object-oriented language. JavaScript does not fully comply with the *object-oriented programming (OOP)* philosophy; one such area is in inheritance, which it is not capable of using. Since JavaScript is an object-based language, we should define some of the vocabulary associated with OOP languages, such as objects, properties, methods, and events.

Objects

Objects are real life entities. These entities include things like cars, books, animals, people, browser windows, and page elements.

The XHTML document that we create is an object. Items like buttons, forms, tables, or images that are placed on the XHTML document are also objects. JavaScript has many predefined objects, three of which are used frequently. These three frequently used objects are the window, the navigator, and the document. The following describes some of the JavaScript objects that are available:

Object	Description
window	This object is at the top of the browser object hierarchy and refers to the current browser window.
document	This object represents the body of the current XHTML document, which is displayed within the browser window. The document object is a child of the window object.
history	The history object contains the record of URLs that the browser has visited before the current page. The history object is a child of the window object.
location	The location object contains information about the current document such as the URL, the path, and the domain name. The location object is a child of the window object.
form	This object contains information about forms on the current XHTML document, which can include text fields, buttons, and radio buttons. The form object is a child of the document object.

As you can see from the object descriptions, they provide information about the Web browser environment and have a relationship to each other. This relationship is referred to as the object hierarchy and is depicted in Figure 14.1.

All objects have properties associated with them.

Properties

Properties are characteristics of objects that allow one object to be differentiated from another. These could be things like size, color, or a text value. Properties can also be objects. For example, the window object has the properties of document and navigator, which are also objects. The syntax for changing the value of a property is

```
[object name] . [property name] = new value
```

The following are some JavaScript objects and their properties:

Object	Property	Description
window	status	This property sets the message displayed in the status bar.
	length	This property contains the number of frames in the window.

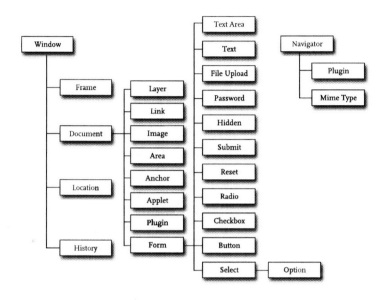

FIGURE 14.1: THE OBJECT HIERARCHY

Object	Property	Description
document	bgColor	This property specifies the background color of the current document.
	fgColor	This property specifies the color of the text on the document.
	lastModified	This property specifies the date when the document was last modified.
	title	This property specifies the title of the document.
	linkColor	This property specifies the color of the links on the document.
history	length	This property contains the number of entries in the history list.
	current	This property specifies the URL of the current history entry.
	next	This property specifies the URL of the next entry in the history list.
	previous	This property specifies the URL of the previous entry in the history list.

Object	Property	Description
location	hostname	This property will specify the host name of the server.
form	name	This property specifies the name of the form.
	method	This property specifies how the input information will be sent to the server.
	action	This property specifies the destination for the data submitted from the form.

Methods

Methods are actions that are performed with or to an object. Methods can be used to

- Open a new browser window
- Write text to the current XHTML document
- Navigate the browser history
- Display a dialog box

The syntax for executing a method in JavaScript is often referred to as the "dot syntax." This syntax is illustrated by the following:

```
[object name] . [method name] (parameters)
```

A period is used to separate the object name from the method name. The following is an example of the write method of the document object:

```
document.write("This will be written on the page")
```

The following are some JavaScript objects and their methods:

Object	Method	Description
window	alert	This method displays an alert dialog box.
	open	This method opens a new browser window.
document	write	This method will write text and XHTML elements to the current document.
	writeln	This method will write text and XHTML elements to the current document. It also adds a line.
history	go	This method will load a URL from the history list.
	back	This method will return to the previous URL in the history list.
	forward	This method will load the next URL in the history list.

Events

Events are actions that can trigger other functions. JavaScript has many *event handlers* that react to specific events. When a particular event is triggered, the code associated with it is executed. Some common examples of JavaScript event handlers are

Event	Description
onclick	Some action will be performed when any mouse button is clicked.
onload	Some action is performed when the document is loaded.
onmouseover	Some action is performed when the mouse is moved over something.
onresize	Some action is performed when a page or element is resized.
onfocus	Some action is performed when a particular element gets focus.
onkeydown	Some action is performed when a key is depressed.
onkeypress	Some action is performed when a key is depressed and the associated code is available.
onkeyup	Some action is performed when a key goes up.
onblur	Some action is performed when a particular element loses focus.

It is important to remember that event support varies by XHTML element.

USING JAVASCRIPT IN AN XHTML DOCUMENT

JavaScript code can be added to an XHTML document in several different ways, such as:
- Embedding the script using a script element
- Using a link to an external file that contains a script
- Using an event handler

EMBEDDING JAVASCRIPT, THE <SCRIPT> ELEMENT

JavaScript code is embedded into an XHTML document using the *script element* and can be placed within the head element or body element. The type and language attributes are used to tell the browser which scripting language is being used. The basic syntax of the script element is

```
<script type="text/javascript" language="javascript">

        (JavaScript code goes here)

</script>
```

Let's add a simple script to an XHTML document and see what happens.

1. Type the following using your choice of editor and save it as jsexample1.html.

```
<?xml version="1.0" encoding="UTF-8"?>
<!DOCTYPE html PUBLIC "-//W3C//DTD/XHTML 1.0 Transitional//EN"
"http://www.w3.org/TR/xhtml1/DTD/xhtml1-transitional.dtd">
<html xmlns="http://www.w3.org/1999/xhtml" xml:lang="en" lang="en">
<head>
<title>  A Simple JavaScript  </title>
</head>
<body>
   <h1>Welcome To The World of JavaScript</h1>
</body>
</html>
```

2. Next, add a script element in the head section after the </title> tag. Enter the following script element:

```
<script type="text/javascript" language="javascript">
  window.alert("Welcome to XHTML using JavaScript")
</script>
```

3. Save the document as jsexample1.html.

4. The completed XHTML document should resemble the following:

```
<?xml version="1.0" encoding="UTF-8"?>
<!DOCTYPE html PUBLIC "-//W3C//DTD/XHTML 1.0 Transitional//EN"
"http://www.w3.org/TR/xhtml1/DTD/xhtml1-transitional.dtd">
<html xmlns="http://www.w3.org/1999/xhtml" xml:lang="en" lang="en">
<head>
<title>  A Simple JavaScript  </title>
<script type="text/javascript" language="javascript">
  window.alert("Welcome to XHTML using JavaScript")
</script>
</head>
<body>
   <h1>Welcome To The World of JavaScript</h1>
</body>
</html>
```

5. In the browser, select Open from the File menu to open jsexample1.html. Your screen should resemble Figure 14.2.

FIGURE 14.2: A SIMPLE XHTML DOCUMENT WITH JAVASCRIPT

This example used the window object's *alert method* to produce a *dialog box*. Notice that the browser stops reading the XHTML once the JavaScript for the alert has been executed. When the user clicks the "OK" button, the browser continues to read the XHTML document and displays it.

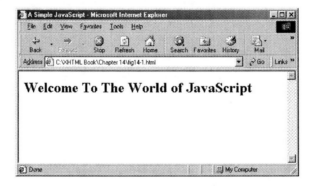

FIGURE 14.3: A SIMPLE XHTML DOCUMENT WITH JAVASCRIPT AFTER OK IS CLICKED

Let's repeat this example using a different object and placing the JavaScript in both the head and body sections.

1. Using your choice of editor, open the file jsexample1.html and save it as jsexample2.html.
2. Modify the script element in the head section as follows:

```
<script type="text/javascript" language="javascript">
  document.writeln("This script is in the head section")
</script>
```

3. In the body, add the following script element after the header:

```
<script type="text/javascript" language="javascript">
  document.writeln("This script is in the body section")
</script>
```

4. Save the document as jsexample2.html.

5. The completed XHTML document should resemble the following:

```
<?xml version="1.0" encoding="UTF-8"?>
<!DOCTYPE html PUBLIC "-//W3C//DTD/XHTML 1.0 Transitional//EN"
"http://www.w3.org/TR/xhtml1/DTD/xhtml1-transitional.dtd">
<html xmlns="http://www.w3.org/1999/xhtml" xml:lang="en" lang="en">
<head>
<title>  A Simple JavaScript  </title>
<script type="text/javascript" language="javascript">
    document.writeln("This script is in the head section")
</script>
</head>
<body>
    <h1>Welcome To The World of JavaScript</h1>
<script type="text/javascript" language="javascript">
    document.writeln("This script is in the body section")
</script>
</body>
</html>
```

6. In the browser, select Open from the File menu to open jsexample2.html.
   Your screen should resemble Figure 14.4.

FIGURE 14.4: AN XHTML DOCUMENT WITH JAVASCRIPT IN HEAD AND BODY SECTIONS

This example used the document object's writeln method to write text to the page. As you can see from the results, the only effect the placement of the JavaScript had was where the line of text was written. We will discuss working with objects and methods a little later in the chapter.

Since an XHTML document can contain several scripts, which one is executed first? The browser executes the <script> elements within the <head> section first and then the <body> section. If the <body> section contains multiple script elements, they are executed in the order that they appear.

EXTERNAL JAVASCRIPT FILES, USING THE SCRIPT ELEMENT

The script element supports the use of the src attribute, which allows JavaScript code that is in a separate file to be included in an XHTML document. To see how this works, create a simple example by doing the following:

1. Type the following using your choice of editor and save it as jsexample3.html.

```
<?xml version="1.0" encoding="UTF-8"?>
<!DOCTYPE html PUBLIC "-//W3C//DTD/XHTML 1.0 Transitional//EN"
"http://www.w3.org/TR/xhtml1/DTD/xhtml1-transitional.dtd">
<html xmlns="http://www.w3.org/1999/xhtml" xml:lang="en" lang="en">
<head>
<title> JavaScript Using An External File </title>
</head>
<body>
    <h1>Welcome To The World of JavaScript</h1>
</body>
</html>
```

2. Next, add a script element in the body section after the heading. Enter the following <script> element:

```
<script type="text/javascript" language="javascript"
   src="extscript.js">
</script>
```

3. Save the file jsexample3.html.
4. Open a new text file and add the following JavaScript code:

```
document.writeln("This was written by an external JavaScript file")
```

5. Save the file as extscript.js.
6. The completed XHTML document should resemble the following:

```
<?xml version="1.0" encoding="UTF-8"?>
<!DOCTYPE html PUBLIC "-//W3C//DTD/XHTML 1.0 Transitional//EN"
"http://www.w3.org/TR/xhtml1/DTD/xhtml1-transitional.dtd">
<html xmlns="http://www.w3.org/1999/xhtml" xml:lang="en" lang="en">
<head>
<title> JavaScript Using An External File </title>
</head>
<body>
   <h1>Welcome To The World of JavaScript</h1>
   <script type="text/javascript" language="javascript"
      src="extscript.js">
   </script>
</body>
</html>
```

7. In the browser, select Open from the File menu to open jsexample3.html.
Your screen should resemble Figure 14.4.

The src attribute functions the same as in a link; it provides the name and
location of the document. You can use any name for the external JavaScript file,
but the standard file extension is .js. The external file in this example contains
only one line of JavaScript.

USING AN EVENT HANDLER SCRIPT

Remember that events are actions that can trigger a response to the user's
actions. To act on these events requires the use of event handlers. Events
are generated every time the user presses a key, clicks the mouse, moves the
mouse, or even when the browser loads the XHTML document. Not every event
is supported by the different browsers. Here is an example of using event
handlers with an XHTML element:

```
<?xml version="1.0" encoding="UTF-8"?>
<!DOCTYPE html PUBLIC "-//W3C//DTD/XHTML 1.0 Transitional//EN"
"http://www.w3.org/TR/xhtml1/DTD/xhtml1-transitional.dtd">
<html xmlns="http://www.w3.org/1999/xhtml" xml:lang="en" lang="en">
<head>
<title>  Using Event Handlers  </title>
</head>
<body>
<h1>Click the button to change background color</h1>
<form>
   <input type="button" value="Change Color"
      onmousedown="document.bgColor='aqua'" />
   <input type="button" value="Reset Color"
      onmousedown="document.bgColor='white'" />
```

```
</form>
</body>
</html>
```

This example creates two buttons using the form input element; one is used for changing the background color, and the other is used to reset the color back to the original value. To change the background color, the <input> element's onmousedown event attribute is used to change the bgcolor property of the document object. Figure 14.5 shows the XHTML document after the Change Color button has been clicked, and Figure 14.6 shows the page after the Reset button has been clicked.

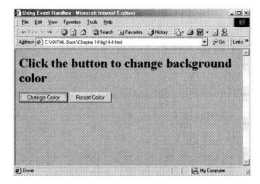

FIGURE 14.5: AN XHTML DOCUMENT AFTER THE CHANGE COLOR BUTTON IS CLICKED

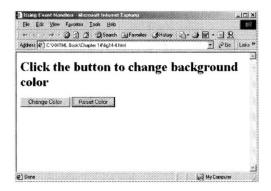

FIGURE 14.6 AN XHTML DOCUMENT AFTER THE RESET BUTTON IS CLICKED

Event handlers are executed when that particular event occurs. We will look at
event handlers more later in the chapter.

JAVASCRIPT ERRORS

Now that we know how to include a script in our XHTML document, what
happens when the browser does not understand the code? In your travels on the
Web, you have probably encountered a JavaScript error message. The following
is an XHTML document with an error in the JavaScript:

```
<?xml version="1.0" encoding="UTF-8"?>
<!DOCTYPE html PUBLIC "-//W3C//DTD/XHTML 1.0 Transitional//EN"
"http://www.w3.org/TR/xhtml1/DTD/xhtml1-transitional.dtd">
<html xmlns="http://www.w3.org/1999/xhtml" xml:lang="en" lang="en">
<head>
<title>  A Simple JavaScript  </title>
<script type="text/javascript" language="javascript">
    document.writeln("This script is in the head section"
</script>
</head>
<body>
    <h1>Welcome To The World of JavaScript</h1>
</body>
</html>
```

Do you see it? The ")" is missing at the end of the JavaScript statement. This
error will produce an error message in Internet Explorer and is shown in
Figure 14.7.

FIGURE 14.7 JAVASCRIPT ERROR MESSAGE

Notice that the browser stops processing the XHTML document. The error message indicates what is wrong and allows you the opportunity to debug. After the No button is clicked on the dialog box, the document finishes loading.

THE JAVASCRIPT LANGUAGE

This chapter is not intended to make you a programmer, but we need to have a basic understanding of some programming principles in order to do some basic JavaScript programming. We will start with some basic information about the language and then discuss the following:

- Comments
- Variables
- Literals
- Functions

JavaScript is no different from any other programming language in that it has keywords and a syntax structure. One of the most important parts of the JavaScript syntax to remember is that it is a case-sensitive language. This means that the correct case must be observed when using keywords, variables, and functions. For example, look at the following JavaScript statements:

number = 3;

Number = 3;

NUMBER = 3;

JavaScript determines that the spellings of the variable names (number) are different; therefore, you must be referring to three different variables. Don't worry if you don't know what a variable is right now; we will discuss variables shortly.

Comments in JavaScript

Comments are a very important feature in any programming language. They allow program developers to place notes within the code either to themselves or to others who might edit the code at a later date. Comments should aid in the understanding of what the purpose of the code is. JavaScript allows for both one-line comments and multiple-line comments. When using a single-line comment, the comment is preceded with //. These characters indicate that what follows is a comment and should be disregarded by the program. A multiple-line comment starts with a /* and also ends with a */. If you are familiar with the Java and C languages, the commenting syntax should look very familiar. Some examples of comments used in JavaScript are

```
//This comment is on a single line
```

```
/* This comment is on multiple lines.  As you can see, I can
   write as much as needed as long as it is terminated properly */
```

Variables

Variables are memory locations that can hold data and be accessed at a later time while the program is running. The term "variable" refers to the fact that the data stored can change or vary during program execution. When naming variables, it is important that a logical name be used, one that reflects what the variable will be used for. Besides giving a variable a logical name, the name must also conform to the following rules:

- Variable names must start with a letter or an underscore (_)
- Variable names can contain alphanumeric characters
- Variable names are case-sensitive
- Spaces and punctuation are not allowed in a variable name
- Variable names cannot be a reserved word

Reserved words or keywords are part of the JavaScript language syntax. The following are some of the keywords:

break	case	continue	default	do
else	for	function	if	new
return	switch	this	var	void
while	with			

All of these words have a specific meaning and function in the JavaScript language. JavaScript variables can store four different types of values:

- Numerical values
- String values
- Boolean or logical values
- Null

Numerical values can be integers, or floating point numbers or can be expressed in scientific notation. Some examples:

7
14.92
3.14159

Strings are values such as "Have a nice day." A string value can be enclosed in either single or double quotes, but not both. For example:

```
"This is a valid string "
'This is a valid string'
'This is not a valid string"
```

Boolean variables hold one of two values, either true or false, and are useful for indicating whether a particular condition is true or false. A variable with a null value has not had a value assigned to it.

Before a variable can be used within a JavaScript program, it must be declared. Unlike many other programming languages, you do not have to specify what type of data a variable will hold when it is declared. A variable can be declared in the following ways:

```
var myVariable;

var myVariable = "We are using JavaScript"

myVariable = "We are using JavaScript"
```

The first declaration creates a variable called myVariable and uses the var keyword, which allows us to declare a variable without assigning a value to it. The second and third declarations declare the variable and assign a value to it. Assigning a value to a variable uses the *assignment operator*, which is the equal sign. The syntax for using the assignment operator is

```
Variable name = value being assigned
```

The assigned value will always be on the right side of the equal sign with the variable on the left. For example:

```
myNumber = 10;
```

This is read from right to left; the value 10 is assigned to the variable myNumber. Using the previous example, any time the variable myNumber is referenced, the value 10 is returned. Remember that the value of a variable can change during program execution. For example, suppose we were to change the value using the following statement:

```
myNumber = 5;
```

Now when we reference the variable myNumber, the value 5 will be returned. Let's look at the following XHTML document, which includes JavaScript that uses variables:

```
<?xml version="1.0" encoding="UTF-8"?>
<!DOCTYPE html PUBLIC "-//W3C//DTD/XHTML 1.0 Transitional//EN"
"http://www.w3.org/TR/xhtml1/DTD/xhtml1-transitional.dtd">
<html xmlns="http://www.w3.org/1999/xhtml" xml:lang="en" lang="en">
<head>
<title>  A Simple JavaScript  </title>
<script type="text/javascript" language="javascript">
    var myVariable;
    var myNumber;
    myVariable = "This is assigned to myVariable in the head
        section and 5 is assigned to myNumber";
    myNumber = 5;
    document.writeln(myVariable);
</script>
</head>
<body>
  <h1>Welcome To The World of JavaScript</h1>
  <script type="text/javascript" language="javascript">
    myVariable = "This is assigned to myVariable in the body
        section. The alert box shows value of myNumber";
    document.writeln(myVariable);
    window.alert(myNumber);
  </script>
</body>
</html>
```

Figure 14.8 shows the results of this XHTML.

FIGURE 14.8 JAVASCRIPT USING VARIABLES

Notice that we were able to use the variables in another part of the XHTML document. The variables are declared in the script element in the head section and then assigned initial values. The value of myVariable is then written to the document using the writeln method of the document object. In the script element in the body section, a new value is assigned to myVariable and again is written to the document. An alert dialog box is then used to display the value of the variable myNumber, which had the value 5 assigned to it in the head section.

When declaring and using variables in JavaScript, you must also understand the concept of variable scope. The term variable scope refers to where in the JavaScript that the variable can be used. Variables have two types of scope:

- **Global**—A variable with global scope is defined outside of a function and is available for use anywhere in the document.
- **Local**—A variable with local scope is defined within a function and can only be used inside of the function where it was declared.

You may not totally understand the concept of scope right now, but keep it in the back of your mind as it may help you solve a problem with one of your scripts where you are not getting the results you expect.

Literals

We have seen the use of literals in many of the previous examples; in JavaScript, literals are used to represent values. They are not variables but are fixed values. In the previous example, we assigned literal values to the variables myVariable and myNumber. The variable myNumber had a string literal value assigned to it, whereas the variable myNumber had a numeric literal assigned. Literals can also be floating-point or Boolean values.

Functions

A function in JavaScript is a set of statements that is treated as a group to perform a specific task. A JavaScript user-defined function consists of the following parts:

- Function keyword
- Function name, which provides a way to identify it
- Parameters, which are values used by the function. Not all functions have parameters.
- Set of statements

The syntax of a JavaScript function is

```
function function_name(parameters)
{
        JavaScript Statements
}
```

The rules for naming a function are the same as those for naming a variable. A function does not have to take any parameters, but when there are multiple parameters, a comma-separated list is used within the parentheses. The JavaScript statements are enclosed within curly braces: {}. The following defines a simple function that has no parameters:

```
function helloalert()
    {
        window.alert("This was created by our function.")
    }
```

The function definition is placed within the script element in the head section. It is not required that you place the function here, but it is the best place. Remember that scripts placed in the head section are executed first, which guarantees that the function is defined before an attempt is made to use it.

The function does not execute until it is called. The calling of the function is usually done in the body of an XHTML document. To call a function, enter a JavaScript statement that contains the name of the function followed by any parameters, also known as arguments, it requires in parentheses. The following would call our helloalert function:

```
        helloalert();
```

The call statement instructs the JavaScript interpreter to transfer control to the function and begin execution with the first statement it contains.

Let's put this function into the following XHTML document and see what happens:

```
<?xml version="1.0" encoding="UTF-8"?>
<!DOCTYPE html PUBLIC "-//W3C//DTD/XHTML 1.0 Transitional//EN"
"http://www.w3.org/TR/xhtml1/DTD/xhtml1-transitional.dtd">
<html xmlns="http://www.w3.org/1999/xhtml" xml:lang="en" lang="en">
<head>
<title>  A Simple JavaScript  </title>
<script type="text/javascript" language="javascript">
    function helloalert()
    {
        window.alert("This was created by our function.")
    }
</script>
</head>
<body>
```

```
    <h1>Welcome To The World of JavaScript</h1>
    <script type="text/javascript" language="javascript">
        helloalert();
    </script>
</body>
</html>
```

Figure 14.9 shows the results of this XHTML.

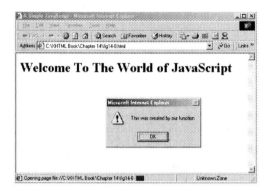

FIGURE 14.9: JAVASCRIPT USING FUNCTION

Once the function has completed its task, control is returned to where it was called. Returning control is accomplished in one of three ways:

- Encountering the right brace, which ends the function
- Executing the return statement and returning no values—return;
- Executing the return statement followed by the value to be returned—return value;

The passing of parameters can add more flexibility to the function. Let's modify the JavaScript in the previous XHTML example to take a parameter. We will modify the XHTML document to create the screen shown in Figure 14.10.

FIGURE 14.10: XHTML DOCUMENT USING FORM FOR INPUT

Create the document as follows:

1. Type the following using your choice of editor and save it as jsexample4.html.

```
<?xml version="1.0" encoding="UTF-8"?>
<!DOCTYPE html PUBLIC "-//W3C//DTD/XHTML 1.0 Transitional//EN"
"http://www.w3.org/TR/xhtml1/DTD/xhtml1-transitional.dtd">
<html xmlns="http://www.w3.org/1999/xhtml" xml:lang="en" lang="en">
<head>
<title>  A Simple JavaScript  </title>
</head>
<body>
  <h1>Welcome To The World of JavaScript</h1>
  <p>
    Please enter your name in the text box and when you have
    finished please click the enter button.
  </p>
</body>
</html>
```

2. Create the JavaScript function in the head section as follows:

```
<script type="text/javascript" language="javascript">
   function helloalert(textinput)
   {
      window.alert("HELLO "+ textinput + " !")
   }
</script>
```

3. Create the XHTML form as follows:

```
<form>
    <input name="nametext"type="text" />
    <input name="enter" type="button"value="Enter"
    onclick="helloalert(form.nametext.value)" />
</form>
```

4. Save the completed XHTML document as jsexample4.html. It should resemble the following:

```
<?xml version="1.0" encoding="UTF-8"?>
<!DOCTYPE html PUBLIC "-//W3C//DTD/XHTML 1.0 Transitional//EN"
"http://www.w3.org/TR/xhtml1/DTD/xhtml1-transitional.dtd">
<html xmlns="http://www.w3.org/1999/xhtml" xml:lang="en" lang="en">
<head>
<title>  A Simple JavaScript  </title>
<script type="text/javascript" language="javascript">
    function helloalert(textinput)
    {
        window.alert("HELLO "+ textinput + " !")
    }
</script>
</head>
<body>
  <h1>Welcome To The World of JavaScript</h1>
  <p>
    Please enter your name in the text box and when you have
    finished please click the enter button.
  </p>
  <form>
    <input name="nametext"type="text" />
    <input name="enter" type="button"value="Enter"
    onclick="helloalert(form.nametext.value)" />
  </form>
</body>
</html>
```

5. In the browser, select Open from the File menu to open jsexample4.html. Your screen should resemble Figure 14.11.

FIGURE 14.11: DIALOG BOX AFTER JAVASCRIPT FUNCTION EXECUTED

This function took what the user entered in the text box and called the function using the text box value as the parameter. In the function, we also introduced a concatenation operator (+), which can be used to combine the values of two strings. For example, if you had variables for first name, last name, and full name, you could take the first and last names, concatenate them together, and assign the result to the full name variable. This is illustrated by the following:

```
firstName = "Joe ";
lastName = "Programmer";
fullName = firstName + lastName
```

The value of the variable fullName would be Joe Programmer.

Functions can also be used to perform a calculation and return the result. These calculations could be as simple as finding the square of a number to calculating the monthly payment on an auto loan. The process of returning a value from a function is accomplished by placing the keyword "return" followed by the value that is to be returned at the end of the function. The following example creates a function to calculate and return the miles per gallon:

```
<?xml version="1.0" encoding="UTF-8"?>
<!DOCTYPE html PUBLIC "-//W3C//DTD/XHTML 1.0 Transitional//EN"
"http://www.w3.org/TR/xhtml1/DTD/xhtml1-transitional.dtd">
<html xmlns="http://www.w3.org/1999/xhtml" xml:lang="en" lang="en">
<head>
<title> JavaScript - Function Returns </title>
<script type="text/javascript" language="javascript">
   var mpg;
```

```
    function mileage(dist, gal)
    {
       var mpg = dist/gal;
       return mpg;
    }
</script>
</head>
<body>
  <script>
     var distance = 500;
     var gallons = 40;
     mpg = mileage(distance, gallons);
     document.writeln("The miles per gallon is: "+ mpg);
  </script>
</body>
</html>
```

Figure 14.12 shows the results of this XHTML.

FIGURE 14.12 JAVASCRIPT RETURNING A VALUE FROM FUNCTION

The JavaScript used to generate Figure 14.12 also illustrates the concepts of variable scope. Remember from earlier in the chapter that a variable could have either local or global scope depending on where it was declared. Local scope variables are declared inside of a function and can be used only within that function. This means that other functions and scripts are not even aware of the variable's existence. Let's take a look at the function from the example:

```
function mileage(dist, gal)
{
   var mpg = dist/gal;
   return mpg;
}
```

This function declares a local variable mpg to store the results of a calculation. The parameters of the function also create variables, which in the above function are dist and gal. These parameters are also considered local.

The JavaScript also creates a global scope variable in the head section of the XHTML document. A global scope variable is one that can be used in any scripts or functions within the document. The following is the variable declaration from the example:

```
var mpg;
```

Notice that the global variable has the same name as a local variable in the function. This is a little bit confusing, but which one gets used? Since the var keyword was used to declare the variable in the function, it creates the local variable and uses it, having no effect on the global variable. In effect, the global variable has been hidden from the function. Although there is nothing wrong with having two variables named the same but with different scope, it should be avoided so problems are not encountered by the two variables being confused.

CHAPTER SUMMARY

This chapter has covered a lot of information about JavaScript, but remember that this material only scratches the surface of this subject. In this chapter, you learned what JavaScript is and how to insert a script into an XHTML document. You have also learned how to create some simple scripts that take little programming to accomplish. You have also learned the basic concepts behind OOP and how they relate to JavaScript. You were introduced to the programming concepts of variables, constants, operators, and functions. The concept of variable scope was also introduced. Chapter 15 will cover some more JavaScript programming concepts.

KEY TERMS

alert method	JavaScript
assignment operator	LiveScript
comment	method
dialog box	object
event	object-oriented programming (OOP)
event handler	property
Java	script element

REVIEW QUESTIONS

1. What are variables used for?
2. What XHTML element is used to enclose a JavaScript script?
3. What is a client-side script?
4. What is a server-side script?
5. What is an object?
6. What is a method?
7. What is an event?
8. Where is the JavaScript code placed within an XHTML document?
9. What document property can be used to change the background color in JavaScript?
10. What are event handlers?

EXERCISES

1. Create an XHTML document that includes eight radio buttons for the following colors:

Aqua	Fuchsia	Red	Yellow
Blue	White	Green	Silver

When one of these radio buttons is clicked, it should change the background color of the document. Use event handlers to determine when a particular button has been clicked and to change the background color to the one requested by the user. The XHTML document should look similar to the following:

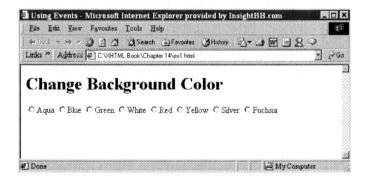

2. Modify the XHTML document used to create Figure 14.12 so that it uses only the global variable for miles per gallon.

3. Create an XHTML document that contains two text boxes and two buttons. When the swap button is clicked, whatever text is in the input text box will be placed in the output text box. When the alert button is clicked, whatever text is in the input text box will be displayed in an alert dialog box. A heading should also be included on the page.

4. Create an XHTML document that contains two text boxes and one button. When the swap button is clicked, call a function swap passing the contents of the two text boxes. The function should swap the contents of each box. A heading should also be included on the page.

5. Modify the XHTML document used to create Figure 14.12 so that it takes input from the user for distance and gallons. It should include two text boxes and a button to initiate the calculation. The results should be displayed below the input boxes and buttons in the current format.

6. Create an XHTML document that will calculate the Celsius temperature for a given Fahrenheit temperature. This document should contain a heading, two text boxes, and one button. The button should be labeled "calculate." When the calculate button is clicked, call a function to convert the given temperature to Celsius. This function should be passed to the input temperature and return the converted value to be displayed in the second text box.

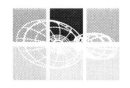

chapter 15

programming with javascript: intermediate

CHAPTER OVERVIEW

This chapter will introduce more JavaScript concepts, which will allow us to build applications that actively process user inputs, and will cover operators, conditional statements, loops, and incorporating dates into XHTML pages. It will show how to validate user input before the data is submitted to the server for processing.

CHAPTER OBJECTIVES

- Understand how to declare and use variables
- Understand the use of JavaScript assignment operators
- Understand the use of JavaScript logical operators
- Understand how to use the IF and IF/ELSE selection structure to select actions
- Understand how to use repetition structures in the JavaScript language
- Understand how to validate data using JavaScript
- Create simple JavaScript programs incorporating dates

JAVASCRIPT

In the previous chapter, we only scratched the surface of what JavaScript is capable of doing. This chapter is also not intended to make you a programmer, but we need to have a basic understanding of some programming principles in order to do some basic JavaScript programming. Remember that JavaScript is no different from any other programming language in that it has keywords and a syntax structure. One of the most important parts of the JavaScript syntax to remember is that it is a case-sensitive language. This means that the correct case must be observed when using keywords, variables, and functions.

The JavaScript that we have created so far has used variables to hold information, functions to perform calculations, and alert boxes to communicate information to the user. The real power of programming comes from being able to perform logical comparisons, to make decisions as to what processing is to be performed, and to repeatedly execute a series of statements. Let's start learning how we can use the following basic programming principles to enhance the JavaScript we create:

- Expression and operators
- Conditional statements
- Loops

EXPRESSIONS AND OPERATORS

JavaScript uses various types of operators to perform operations on *objects* and variables within a script. Most operators require two operands to perform the operation, but there are some that use only one. An expression is formed when an operator connects two operands. An expression will evaluate to a single value. You have seen the assignment operator used in previous examples to assign a literal value to a variable. So the expression myNumber = 5 will evaluate to a single value of 5, and the expression 7 - 2 will also evaluate to a single value of 5. These two examples illustrate how expressions using different operators evaluate to a single value. JavaScript operators include assignment, arithmetic, unary, comparison, and logical.

ASSIGNMENT OPERATORS

The *assignment operator* is used to assign the value of its right operand to its left operand. This is accomplished by using the assignment operator the equal sign (=). The value to the right of the assignment operator can be a literal value, an expression, or an expression that contains other variables. The following are examples of using the assignment operator:

```
myNumber = 5;

myNumber = 3 + 2;

area = height * width;
```

Remember that the equal sign used in the above expression refers to assignment, not to equality as when used in mathematics. JavaScript also supports compound assignment operators, which combine arithmetic operators with the assignment operator. The compound assignment operators are described below:

Operator	Function	Expression	Equivalent To
+=	Addition/Assignment	x += y	x = x + y
-=	Subtraction/Assignment	x -= y	x = x - y
*=	Multiplication/Assignment	x *= y	x = x * y
/=	Division/Assignment	x /= y	x = x / y

As you can see, this is a shorthand method to perform an arithmetic operation and assignment. Some people find the use of the compound assignment operators to be confusing. Let's look at an example of (x += y), which means that the new value of x would be the sum of the previous value of x plus the value of y. So if the following values are assigned:

$$x = 2 \quad y = 5$$

the new value of x would be 7.

ARITHMETIC OPERATORS

Arithmetic operators are used to perform mathematical calculations on two operands. The following are the basic JavaScript arithmetic operators:

Operator	Function	Expression
+	Addition	x = x + y
–	Subtraction	x = x – y
*	Multiplication	x = x * y
/	Division	x = x / y

UNARY OPERATORS

Unary operators perform their operation on one operand. JavaScript provides two, the increment and decrement operators. The increment operator (++) is used to add one to an operand, whereas the decrement operator (--) is used to subtract one from an operand. These operators are useful when using a variable for counting up or down. For example, if we were using a variable called "count" to keep track of how many times an operation was performed, we could use the following examples:

count = count + 1

or

count++

Both examples accomplish the same task of adding one to the variable count. The increment and decrement operators can either be placed before the operand, which is referred to as prefixed, or after the operand, which is referred to as postfixed. This placement can have an effect on how the variable is interpreted. Consider the following examples (independent of each other), assuming that the variable count has the value of 10:

result = ++count

result = count++

In the first example, the operator is prefixed to the variable count; this will increment the value of count by one before the assignment is made to the variable result. The variable result will now have the value of 11. In the second example, the operator is postfixed to the variable count; this causes the assignment of the value of count to be made, and then the variable count will be incremented. The variable result will now have the value of 10, and the variable count will have the value of 11. The placement of this operator can cause problems in the results of your programs, so keep the differences in mind.

COMPARISON OPERATORS

The *comparison operators* allow for two operands to be compared as a relational expression, returning a logical value of true or false based on the results of the comparison. The relational expressions enable our programs to check results of calculations against known values or to validate user input. These operators can be used with numerical or string values. The comparison operators are described in the following:

Operator	Example	Function
==	x == y	Equality, will evaluate to true if the operands are equal
!=	x != y	Not equal, will evaluate to true if the operands are not equal
>	x > y	Greater than, will evaluate to true if the left operand (x) is greater than the right operand (y)
<	x < y	Less than, will evaluate to true if the left operand (x) is less than the right operand (y)
>=	x >= y	Greater than or equal to, will evaluate to true if the left operand (x) is greater than or equal to the right operand (y)
<=	x <= y	Less than or equal to, will evaluate to true if the left operand (x) is less than or equal to the right operand (x)

LOGICAL OPERATORS

The *logical operators* are used to create compound conditions. These operators take logical values as operands and return a logical value based on the evaluation of the operands and the logical operator used. The following are the logical operators:

Operator	Function
&&	AND
||	OR
!	NOT

The logical AND (&&) operator requires both conditions to be true. If one condition is false, it will return a false value. Consider the following example, given x = 5 and y = 9:

$$((x + y) ==15) \ \&\& \ (((x + y)/2) ==7)$$

This would return false because the first expression is false and the last is true. The results of the AND (&&) operator can be illustrated in a truth table shown below.

Expression 1	Expression 2	Returns
T	T	T
T	F	F
F	T	F
F	F	F

The logical OR (||) operator requires that one of the two conditions be true for the entire expression to be true. Consider the following example, given x = 5 and y = 9:

$$((x + y) ==15) \ || \ (((x + y)/2) ==7)$$

This would return true even though the first condition is false because the second condition is true. The results of the OR (||) operator can be illustrated in a truth table shown below.

Expression 1	Expression 2	Returns
T	T	T
T	F	T
F	T	T
F	F	F

The NOT (!) operator is used to reverse the logical value of an expression to which it is applied. Consider the following example, given x = 5 and y = 9:

$$! \ (((x + y)/2) ==7)$$

This would return false. The comparison is true, and the NOT (!) operator reverses the result.

CONDITIONAL STATEMENTS

JavaScript uses *conditional statements* to control the flow of a program. Conditional statements allow for one course of action to be taken if the condition is true or another if it is false. The main conditional statement in JavaScript is the if statement. The if statement consists of two parts: a condition and statements to execute if the condition is true. The syntax for the simplest form of the if statement is:

```
if (condition) {
    statements to execute if the condition is true
}
```

The condition is enclosed in parentheses and is any JavaScript expression that evaluates to true or false. The statements are enclosed in curly braces ({}) and can be single or multiple statements but could also be nested if statements or loops. The flowchart in Figure 15.1 illustrates the simple if statement.

This form of the if statement allows you to execute a set of statements only if a given condition is true. What if you wanted to execute a different set if the condition is false? JavaScript also has an if-else statement. It functions the same as the

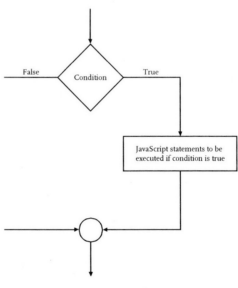

FIGURE 15.1: FLOWCHART FOR SIMPLE IF STATEMENT

simple if statement but offers an alternative course of action if the condition tested is false. The syntax for the if-else statement is:

```
if (condition) {
    statements to execute if the condition is true
}
else
{
    statements to execute if the condition is false
    }
```

The flowchart in Figure 15.2 illustrates the if-else statement.

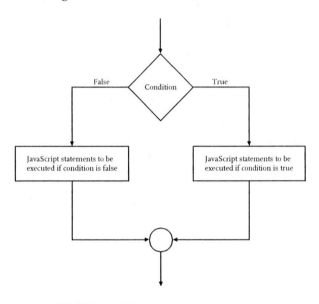

FIGURE 15.2: FLOWCHART FOR IF-ELSE STATEMENT

The if-else statement can contain single or multiple statements. It can also contain other if-else statements; this is referred to as "nesting." These nested if-else statements can be nested in either part of the if-else statement. The following example illustrates nesting:

```
if (condition 1) {
    if (condition 2) {
        statements to execute if condition 1 and
        condition 2 are true
    }
    else
    {
        statements to execute if condition 1 is true and
        condition 2 is false
    }
}
else
{
    statements to execute if condition 1 is false
```

```
if (condition 3) {
    statements to execute if condition 1 is false and
    condition 3 is true
}
}
```

The flowchart in Figure 15.3 illustrates the nested if-else statements.

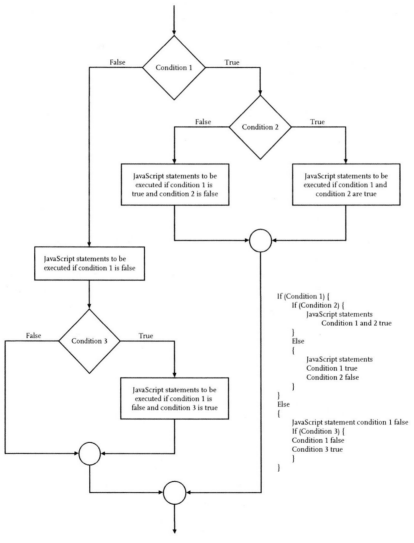

As you may have noticed, nested if-else statements can become somewhat confusing. Since they can be hard to follow, you should try to avoid nesting if-else statements more than three deep (within other if statements).

Let's add a conditional if-else statement to an XHTML document and see what happens. We will create a program to enter two values and then determine which one is larger.

Create the document as follows:

1. Type the following using your choice of editor and save it as jsexample6.html.

```
<?xml version="1.0" encoding="UTF-8"?>
<!DOCTYPE html PUBLIC "-//W3C//DTD/XHTML 1.0 Transitional//EN"
"http://www.w3.org/TR/xhtml1/DTD/xhtml1-transitional.dtd">
<html xmlns="http://www.w3.org/1999/xhtml" xml:lang="en" lang="en">
<head>
<title>  A Simple JavaScript With Conditional Statements  </title>
</head>
<body>
  <h1>Welcome To The World of JavaScript</h1>
  <p>
    Please enter a number in each of the text boxes and when you
    have finished please click the enter button.
  </p>
  <form name = "chk">
    <p>
      <b>Number 1:</b>
      <input type="text" length="6" name="num1" />
    </p>
    <p>
      <b>Number 2:</b>
      <input type="text" length="6" name="num2" />
    </p>
    <p>
      <input name="enter" type="button" value="Enter"
      onclick="check()" />
    </p>
</form>
</body>
</html>
```

2. Next, add a script element in the head section after the </title> tag. Enter the following script element, which creates a function called check:

```
<script type="text/javascript" language="javascript">
 function check() {
      if (document.chk.num1.value == document.chk.num2.value){
```

```
      alert("Number 1 is equal to Number 2.");
      return false;
    }
    else
    {
      if (document.chk.num1.value > document.chk.num2.value){
        alert("Number 1 is greater than Number 2.");
        return false;
      }
      else
      {
        alert("Number 2 is greater than Number 1.");
        return false;
      }
    }
  }
</script>
```

3. Save the completed XHTML document as jsexample6.html. It should resemble the following:

```
<?xml version="1.0" encoding="UTF-8"?>
<!DOCTYPE html PUBLIC "-//W3C//DTD/XHTML 1.0 Transitional//EN"
"http://www.w3.org/TR/xhtml1/DTD/xhtml1-transitional.dtd">
<html xmlns="http://www.w3.org/1999/xhtml" xml:lang="en" lang="en">
<head>
<title> A Simple JavaScript With Conditional Statements  </title>
<script type="text/javascript" language="javascript">
  function check() {
      if (document.chk.num1.value == document.chk.num2.value){
        alert("Number 1 is equal to Number 2.");
        return false;
      }
      else
      {
        if (document.chk.num1.value > document.chk.num2.value){
          alert("Number 1 is greater than Number 2.");
          return false;
        }
        else
        {
          alert("Number 2 is greater than Number 1.");
          return false;
        }
      }
  }
</script>
</head>
```

```
<body>
  <h1>Welcome To The World of JavaScript</h1>
  <p>
    Please enter a number in each of the text boxes and when you
    have finished please click the enter button.
  </p>
  <form name = "chk">
  <p>
    <b>Number 1:</b>
    <input type="text" length="6" name="num1" />
  </p>
  <p>
    <b>Number 2:</b>
    <input type="text" length="6" name="num2" />
  </p>
  <p>
    <input name="enter" type="button" value="Enter"
    onclick="check()" />
  </p>
  </form>

</body>
</html>
```

4. In the browser, select Open from the File menu to open jsexample6.html. Your screen should resemble Figure 15.4.
5. Enter 9 in the text box for Number 1 and 6 in the text box for Number 2, then click the Enter button.   Your screen should resemble Figure 15.5.

FIGURE 15.4: XHTML DOCUMENT USING NESTED IF-ELSE

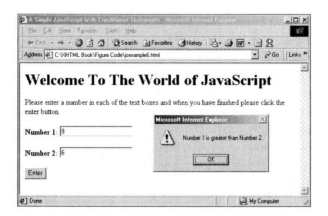

FIGURE 15.5: XHTML DOCUMENT USING NESTED IF-ELSE AFTER COMPARISON

In programming, it is sometimes necessary to use multiple if statements to evaluate a single value using different conditions. For example, if we need to determine the day of the week when given a number, we might use a series of if statements:

```
if (day == 1) {
    document.write("Today is Monday <br />");
}


        if (day == 2) {
    document.write("Today is Tuesday <br />");
}
if (day == 3) {
    document.write("Today is Wednesday <br />");
}
```

Or we could use if-else statements:

```
if (day == 1) {
    document.write("Today is Monday <br />");
        }
else
{
    if (day == 2) {
        document.write("Today is Tuesday <br />");
    }
    else
    {
    if (day == 3) {
     document.write("Today is Wednesday <br />");
```

```
    }
    else
    {
        document.write("I am not sure what day you want <br />");
    }
}
    }
```

JavaScript provides an alternative to using multiple conditions to evaluate an expression; the switch statement can be used to accomplish the task. The switch statement has the following syntax:

```
switch (expression) {
    case value :
            statements;
            break;
    case value :
            statements;
            break;
    default :
            statements;
```

Let's deconstruct the switch statement to see what the different components are:

■ The statement starts with the keyword "switch" and is followed by an expression in parentheses. This expression is what will be evaluated using the different cases. The cases are evaluated sequentially.

■ Just as with the if statement, the braces { and } are used to enclose the switch.

■ Next are the case statements, followed by a value. Each value has a colon after it. These values will be compared to the expression in the switch statement. When the values match, the statements after the case statement are executed.

■ The break statement is used to signal the end of each case and terminates the switch statement. This is a very important statement. When the break statement is omitted from a case, the next statement in the switch statement is executed.

■ The optional default statement is executed when no matching cases are found. If the default statement is omitted and there are no matching cases, the switch statement just ends.

Now let's see what the multiple if statement examples above would look like when they are converted to a switch statement:

```
switch (day) {
    case 1 :
            document.write("Today is Monday <br />");
            break;
    case 2 :
            document.write("Today is Tuesday <br />");
            break;
    case 3 :
            document.write("Today is Wednesday <br />");
            break;
    default :
        document.write("I am not sure what day you want <br />");
}
```

As you can see, the switch statement simplifies the process of testing a single value for multiple conditions.

LOOPS

Loops are a very important and powerful programming tool in any language. Loops allow for actions to be repeated several times while a specified condition is met. JavaScript currently supports three common types of loops; for, while, and do while. All loops have two basic components:

- **Loop control**—This will specify what condition is necessary for the continued execution of the loop.
- **Loop body**—These are the statements that will be repeatedly executed as long as the loop control condition is satisfied.

FOR LOOPS

The *for loop* is useful when you know how many times the action is to be repeated. The for loop consists of three expressions separated by semicolons, which are enclosed in parentheses. The for loop syntax is

```
for (initializing expression; test condition; incrementing
    expression) {
        JavaScript statements comprising loop body
}
```

The following sequence of events occur when a for loop executes:
1. The loop control value is initialized.
2. The test condition is evaluated. If the condition is true, the statements in the loop body execute. If the condition is false, the loop is terminated.

3. The incrementing expression is executed to increment the loop control variable.
4. The loop control returns to step 2.

The flowchart in Figure 15.6 illustrates the for loop.

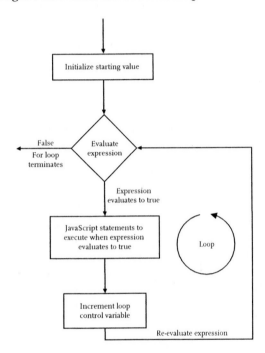

FIGURE 15.6: FLOWCHART ILLUSTRATING FOR LOOP SYNTAX

The following is an example of a for loop:

```
for (count = 1; count <= 10; count++) {
    document.write(This is loop pass:   " , count, "<br />");
}
```

The first expression (count) is a variable used to keep track of the number of times the loop has been executed and is initialized with a starting value. The second expression (count <=10) is the condition that is evaluated on each pass of the loop. If the condition evaluates to true, the statements within the loop are executed. When the condition is false, the loop terminates. The third expression (count++) is executed with each pass of the loop after the statements have been performed. It is used to increment the variable that is used to control the number of times the loop is executed. The body of the loop, which contains the statements, is enclosed within curly braces ({}). The flowchart in Figure 15.7 illustrates this example.

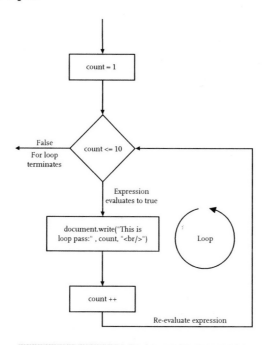

FIGURE 15.7: FLOWCHART ILLUSTRATING A FOR LOOP

Let's add this loop to an XHTML document and see what happens.

Create the document as follows:

1. Type the following using your choice of editor and save it as jsexample7.html.

```
<?xml version="1.0" encoding="UTF-8"?>
<!DOCTYPE html PUBLIC "-//W3C//DTD/XHTML 1.0 Transitional//EN"
"http://www.w3.org/TR/xhtml1/DTD/xhtml1-transitional.dtd">
<html xmlns="http://www.w3.org/1999/xhtml" xml:lang="en" lang="en">
<head>
<title>  A Simple JavaScript With Loop  </title>
</head>
<body>
  <h1>Welcome To The World of JavaScript</h1>
</body>
</html>
```

2. Create the JavaScript function in the body section as follows:

```
<script type="text/javascript" language="javascript">
  for (count = 1; count <= 10; count++) {
     document.write("This is loop pass:  " , count, "<br />");
  }
</script>
```

3. Save the completed XHTML document as jsexample7.html. It should resemble the following:

```
<?xml version="1.0" encoding="UTF-8"?>
<!DOCTYPE html PUBLIC "-//W3C//DTD/XHTML 1.0 Transitional//EN"
"http://www.w3.org/TR/xhtml1/DTD/xhtml1-transitional.dtd">
<html xmlns="http://www.w3.org/1999/xhtml" xml:lang="en" lang="en">
<head>
<title>  A Simple JavaScript With Loop  </title>
</head>
<body>
  <h1>Welcome To The World of JavaScript</h1>
  <script type="text/javascript" language="javascript">
     for (count = 1; count <= 10; count++) {
       document.write("This is loop pass:  " , count, "<br />");
     }
  </script>
</body>
</html>
```

4. In the browser, select Open from the File menu to open jsexample7.html. Your screen should resemble Figure 15.8.

FIGURE 15.8: JAVASCRIPT USING A FOR LOOP

WHILE LOOPS

While loops are usually used when the number of times a loop will be executed is not known. It is similar to the for loop in that it executes a series of statements until a certain condition is met, but it does not include a built-in counter. The syntax for the while loop is

```
while (condition) {
      JavaScript statements comprising loop body
}
```

The following sequence of events occur when a while loop executes:
1. The condition is evaluated.
2. If the condition is true, the statements in the loop body execute. If the condition is false, the loop is terminated.
3. The loop control returns to step 1.

The flowchart in Figure 15.9 illustrates the while loop.

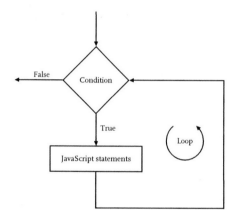

FIGURE 15.9 FLOWCHART ILLUSTRATING WHILE LOOP SYNTAX

The following is an example of a while loop:

```
while (count <= 10) {
    document.write("This is a while loop pass:  " , count, "<br />");
}
```

Notice in the condition that the variable count, which we are using to control the number of loop iterations, is not assigned a starting value or incremented. An infinite loop would result by not incrementing the loop control variable. An infinite loop is one that never ends. In a while loop, the initialization of the loop control variable and its increment is the responsibility of the programmer to include. The following would be the correct use of this while loop:

```
var count = 1;
while (count <= 10) {
   document.write("This is while loop pass:   " , count, "<br />");
   count++;
}
```

The flowchart in Figure 15.10 illustrates the while loop.

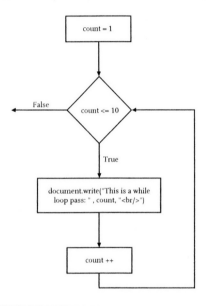

FIGURE 15.10: FLOWCHART ILLUSTRATING A WHILE LOOP

Let's add this while loop to the previous XHTML document and see what happens. The changed XHTML document would resemble the following:

```
<?xml version="1.0" encoding="UTF-8"?>
<!DOCTYPE html PUBLIC "-//W3C//DTD/XHTML 1.0 Transitional//EN"
"http://www.w3.org/TR/xhtml1/DTD/xhtml1-transitional.dtd">
<html xmlns="http://www.w3.org/1999/xhtml" xml:lang="en" lang="en">
<head>
<title>  A Simple JavaScript With Loop  </title>
</head>
<body>
  <h1>Welcome To The World of JavaScript</h1>
```

```
<script type="text/javascript" language="javascript">
  var count = 1;
  while (count <= 10) {
   document.write("This is a while loop pass:  " , count,
    "<br />");
   count++;
   }
  </script>
</body>
</html>
```

Figure 15.11 shows the results of this XHTML. Were the results the same as the for loop?

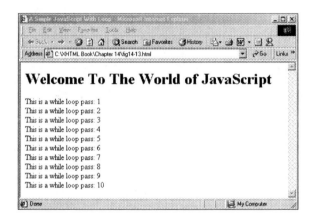

FIGURE 15.11: JAVASCRIPT USING A WHILE LOOP

DO WHILE LOOPS

A *do while loop* is similar to a while loop with one very important difference: the loop body executes before the loop control condition is evaluated. The syntax for the do while loop is

```
do{
      JavaScript statements comprising loop body
  }  while (condition);
```

The following sequence of events occurs when a do while loop executes:

1. The loop body is executed.
2. The condition is evaluated.

3. If the condition is true, the statements in the loop body execute. If the condition is false, the loop is terminated.
4. The loop control returns to step 1.

The flowchart in Figure 15.12 illustrates the do while loop.

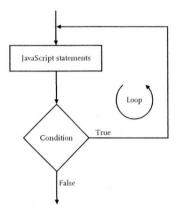

FIGURE 15.12: FLOWCHART ILLUSTRATING DO WHILE LOOP SYNTAX

The following is an example of a do while loop:

```
var count = 1;
do{
    document.write("This is a do while loop pass:  " , count, "<br />");
    count++;
  }  while (count <= 10);
```

Notice that the loop body will be executed at least one time, regardless of how the loop control condition evaluates.

The flowchart in Figure 15.13 illustrates the do while loop.

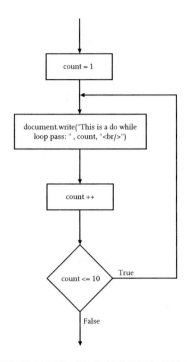

FIGURE 15.13: FLOWCHART ILLUSTRATING A DO WHILE LOOP

Let's add this do while loop to the previous XHTML document and see what happens. The changed XHTML document would resemble the following:

```
<?xml version="1.0" encoding="UTF-8"?>
<!DOCTYPE html PUBLIC "-//W3C//DTD/XHTML 1.0 Transitional//EN"
"http://www.w3.org/TR/xhtml1/DTD/xhtml1-transitional.dtd">
<html xmlns="http://www.w3.org/1999/xhtml" xml:lang="en" lang="en">
<head>
<title>  A Simple JavaScript With Do While Loop  </title>
</head>
<body>
  <h1>Welcome To The World of JavaScript</h1>
  <script type="text/javascript" language="javascript">
    var count = 1;
    do {
     document.write("This is a do while loop pass:  " , count,
      "<br />");
     count++;
    } while (count <= 10);
  </script>
</body>
</html>
```

Figure 15.14 shows the results of this XHTML. Were the results the same as the while loop?

FIGURE 15.14: JAVASCRIPT USING A DO WHILE LOOP

CONTINUE STATEMENT

The *continue statement* can be used to bypass part of a loop body and continue execution with the next loop iteration. The following is an example of using the continue statement in a while loop:

```
x = 0;
y= 0;

while (x < 4) {
    x ++;
    if (x == 3){
        continue;
    }
    y = y + 1
}
```

warning: No matter which loop you choose to use, it is very important to ensure that the loop control condition will eventually become false. If the loop control condition never becomes false, an infinite loop will occur.

In this example, the only time that the continue statement executes is when the value of x is equal to three. When the continue statement does execute, the variable y will not be incremented because the expression is bypassed. The ending value of x is 4 and y is 3.

BREAK STATEMENT

The *break statement* provides an easy way to terminate a loop. When the break statement is executed, the rest of the loop will be skipped, and execution will continue with the first statement following the loop's ending brace. The following is an example of using the break statement in a while loop:

```
x = 0;
y = 0;

while (x < 4) {
  x ++;
  if (x == 3) {
      break;
  }
  y = y + 1
}
```

In this example, the break statement executes when the value of x is equal to three. When the break statement executes, the rest of the loop is bypassed and control is passed to the end of the loop. The ending value of x is 3 and y is 2.

WRITING XHTML WITH JAVASCRIPT

Since the document.write method performs its task by displaying whatever text is enclosed in parentheses, the text could also include XHTML elements. When the text includes XHTML elements, the browser will interpret them appropriately and render them in the browser window. Let's give this a try to see how this works.

Let's add a simple script to an XHTML document and see what happens.

1. Type the following using your choice of editor and save it as jsexample8.html.

```
<?xml version="1.0" encoding="UTF-8"?>
<!DOCTYPE html PUBLIC "-//W3C//DTD/XHTML 1.0 Transitional//EN"
"http://www.w3.org/TR/xhtml1/DTD/xhtml1-transitional.dtd">
<html xmlns="http://www.w3.org/1999/xhtml" xml:lang="en" lang="en">
<head>
<title>  A Simple JavaScript  </title>
</head>
<body>
</body>
</html>
```

2. Next, add a script element in the body section after the <body> tag. Enter the following script element:

```
<script type="text/javascript" language="javascript">
  document.write("<h1>Welcome To The World of JavaScript</h1>");
  document.write("<p>This is an example of using the document write
                  method to include XHTML elements controlling
                  how the browser will render the text.</p>");
</script>
```

3. Save the document as jsexample8.html.

4. The completed XHTML document should resemble the following:

```
<?xml version="1.0" encoding="UTF-8"?>
<!DOCTYPE html PUBLIC "-//W3C//DTD/XHTML 1.0 Transitional//EN"
"http://www.w3.org/TR/xhtml1/DTD/xhtml1-transitional.dtd">
<html xmlns="http://www.w3.org/1999/xhtml" xml:lang="en" lang="en">
<head>
<title>  A Simple JavaScript  </title>
</head>
<body>
  <script type="text/javascript" language="javascript">
  document.write("<h1>Welcome To The World of JavaScript</h1>");
  document.write("<p>This is an example of using the document write
                  method to include XHTML elements controlling
                  how the browser will render the text.</p>");
  </script>
</body>
</html>
```

5. In the browser, select Open from the File menu to open jsexample8.html. Your screen should resemble Figure 15.15.

FIGURE 15.15: USING DOCUMENT.WRITE METHOD WITH XHTML ELEMENTS

This example used the document object's write method to include XHTML elements to control how the browser would render the text. Notice that the body section did not contain any headings or text, but the page was rendered with a heading and text. This technique enables you to dynamically change the content of your page.

PUTTING JAVASCRIPT TO WORK—SIMPLE DATA VALIDATION

One of the most common uses of JavaScript is to validate the information that a user has entered on a form before it is submitted to the server for processing. A common way to validate data is to include checking to see if data has been entered in a particular field or if it is in the correct format. Validation is usually performed by a function that includes the validations for all of the fields on a form. The function must return a "true" or "false" value. Let's add data validation to the following XHTML document, which includes a form:

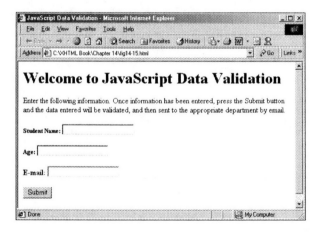

FIGURE 15.16: XHTML DOCUMENT WITH A FORM

1. Create the document by typing the following using your choice of editor and save it as jsexample9.html.

```
<?xml version="1.0" encoding="UTF-8"?>
<!DOCTYPE html PUBLIC "-//W3C//DTD/XHTML 1.0 Transitional//EN"
"http://www.w3.org/TR/xhtml1/DTD/xhtml1-transitional.dtd">
<html xmlns="http://www.w3.org/1999/xhtml" xml:lang="en" lang="en">
<head>
<title>  JavaScript Data Validation  </title>
</head>
```

```
<body>
  <h1>Welcome to JavaScript Data Validation</h1>
  <p>Enter the following information.  Once information has been
     entered, press the Submit button and the data entered will be
     validated, and then sent to the appropriate department
     by email.
  </p>
  <form name="info" action="mailto:user@company.com"
       enctype="text/plain" onSubmit="return validate();">
  <p>
    <b>Student Name:</b>
    <input type="text" length="25" name="studentname" />
  </p>
  <p>
    <b>Age:</b>
    <input type="text" length="3" name="age" />
  </p>
  <p>
    <b>E-mail:</b>
    <input type="text" length="15" name="email" />
  </p>
  <p>
    <input type="SUBMIT" value="Submit" />
  </p>
  </form>
</body>
</html>
```

2. Next, add a script element in the head section after the </title> tag. Enter
the following script element, which creates a function called validate:

```
<script type="text/javascript" language="javascript">
 function validate() {
  if (document.info.studentname.value.length < 1){
    alert("Student name is required, please enter your name.");
    return false;
  }
  if (document.info.age.value < 17){
    alert("Student age cannot be less than 17, please enter your
          correct age.");
    return false;
  }
  if (document.info.email.value < 7){
    alert("E-mail address is required, please enter your email
          address.");
    return false;
  }
  return true;
```

```
    }
</script>
```

3. Save the document as jsexample9.html.

4. The completed XHTML document should resemble the following:

```
<?xml version="1.0" encoding="UTF-8"?>
<!DOCTYPE html PUBLIC "-//W3C//DTD/XHTML 1.0 Transitional//EN"
"http://www.w3.org/TR/xhtml1/DTD/xhtml1-transitional.dtd">
<html xmlns="http://www.w3.org/1999/xhtml" xml:lang="en" lang="en">
<head>
<title> JavaScript Data Validation </title>
<script type="text/javascript" language="javascript">
 function validate() {
  if (document.info.studentname.value.length < 1){
    alert("Student name is required, please enter your name.");
    return false;
  }
  if (document.info.age.value < 17){
    alert("Student age cannot be less than 17, please enter
          your correct age.");
    return false;
  }
  if (document.info.email.value < 7){
    alert("E-mail address is required, please enter your email
          address.");
    return false;
  }
  return true;
 }
</script>
</head>
<body>
  <h1>Welcome to JavaScript Data Validation</h1>
  <p>Enter the following information.  Once information has been
    entered, press the Submit button and the data entered will be
    validated, and then sent to the appropriate department by
    email.
  </p>
  <form name="info" action="mailto:user@company.com"
      enctype="text/plain" onSubmit="return validate();">
  <p>
    <b>Student Name:</b>
    <input type="text" length="25" name="studentname" />
  </p>
  <p>
    <b>Age:</b>
    <input type="text" length="3" name="age" />
```

```
    </p>
    <p>
      <b>E-mail:</b>
      <input type="text" length="15" name="email" />
    </p>
    <p>
      <input type="SUBMIT" value="Submit" />
    </p>
    </form>
</body>
</html>
```

5. In the browser, select Open from the File menu to open jsexample9.html.
   Your screen should resemble Figure 15.17.
6. Click the Submit button with no data entered in the fields. Your screen
   should resemble Figure 15.18.

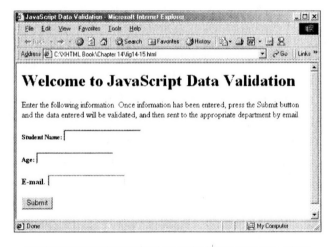

FIGURE 15.17: XHTML DOCUMENT FORM WITH NO DATA ENTERED

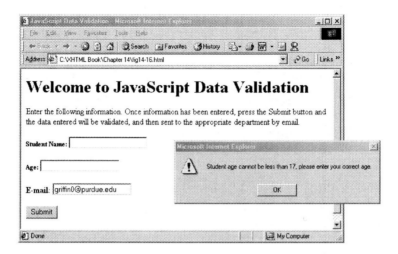

FIGURE 15.18: XHTML DOCUMENT FORM WITH VALIDATION ERROR

The form used the validate function to verify that the user had entered data into each of the three fields. It also checked to verify that the age was not below a given value. If the data entered passes the three validations, the function returns true and your email program is started to email the information to its destination.

WORKING WITH DATES

This section introduces you to the very powerful JavaScript built-in *date object*, which can be used to manipulate the current system date and time. Since JavaScript does not include a date data type, a new object instance must be created before you can manipulate the date. Once the new date object has been created, the information stored in the object can be changed and manipulated in the desired format. The syntax for creating a new date object is

```
var currentdate = new Date()
```

The new object in the above syntax is currentdate. The keyword new is used to create the new object instance. The Date() object with empty parentheses indicates that the current system date and time will be passed on to the new object. The Date() object can also be passed optional parameters to define a specific date. In the above example, what does the new date object contain?

If you said the current system date, you are correct, and it is in the following format:

Sun Aug 26 16:31:36 EST 2001

This format may not be what we wanted to use in our application, but it can be changed by using one of many date object methods. JavaScript has eight methods that can be used to extract specific date and time information from the new date object that was created. These extraction methods include:

Method	Description
getSeconds()	Returns seconds
getMinutes()	Returns minutes of hour
getHours()	Returns the hour (24) of day
getDate()	Returns day of the month
getDay()	Returns day of the week (Sun = 0, Mon = 1, ...)
getMonth	Returns the month of the year (Jan = 0, Feb = 1, Mar = 2, ...)
getFullYear	Returns the full year
getTime	Returns the time in milliseconds since 1/1/1970

The following XHTML shows the use of the date object methods:

```
<?xml version="1.0" encoding="UTF-8"?>
<!DOCTYPE html PUBLIC "-//W3C//DTD/XHTML 1.0 Transitional//EN"
"http://www.w3.org/TR/xhtml1/DTD/xhtml1-transitional.dtd">
<html xmlns="http://www.w3.org/1999/xhtml" xml:lang="en" lang="en">
<head>
<title>  JavaScript Date Object </title>
<script type="text/javascript" language="javascript">
var currentdate = new Date()
var seconds = currentdate.getSeconds();
var minutes = currentdate.getMinutes();
var hours = currentdate.getHours();
var day = currentdate.getDay();
var date = currentdate.getDate();
var month = currentdate.getMonth() + 1;
var year = currentdate.getFullYear();
var time = currentdate.getTime();
document.write("<h1>Results of Date Object Methods</h1>");
document.write("Current date: " + currentdate + "<br />");
document.write("Seconds: " + seconds + "<br />");
```

```
document.write("Minutes: " + minutes + "<br />");
document.write("Hours: " + hours + "<br />");
document.write("Day: " + day + "<br />");
document.write("Day of Month: " + date + "<br />");
document.write("Month: " + month + "<br />");
document.write("Year: " + year + "<br />");
document.write("Time: " + time + "<br />");

document.write("<h1>Creating Usable Date Format</h1>");
document.write("<b>Today is </b>" + month + "/" + date + "/" +
year );
</script>
</head>
<body>
</body>
</html>
```

Figure 15.19 shows the results of the above XHTML document.

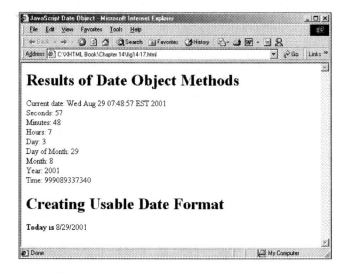

FIGURE 15.19: USING JAVASCRIPT DATE OBJECT METHODS

Notice that the syntax for using the date object methods is

```
variable = name of object.method()
```

We can also create a clock for our page by using these same methods. Let's take a look at how that could be done. The following XHTML illustrates how to create an on-screen clock:

```
<?xml version="1.0" encoding="UTF-8"?>
<!DOCTYPE html PUBLIC "-//W3C//DTD/XHTML 1.0 Transitional//EN"
"http://www.w3.org/TR/xhtml1/DTD/xhtml1-transitional.dtd">
<html xmlns="http://www.w3.org/1999/xhtml" xml:lang="en" lang="en">
<head>
<title>  JavaScript Date Object </title>
<script type="text/javascript" language="javascript">
  document.write("<h1>Current Time</h1>");

  function time(){
      var currentdate = new Date()
      var seconds = currentdate.getSeconds();
      var minutes = currentdate.getMinutes();
      var hours = currentdate.getHours()


      if (hours < 10) {
        hours = "  " + hours
      }

      if (minutes < 10) {
        minutes = "0" + minutes
      }

      if (seconds < 10) {
        seconds = "0" + seconds
      }

      document.time.numbers.value = hours + ":" + minutes
      + ":" + seconds
      setTimeout("time()", 1000)
    }
</script>

</head>
<body onLoad = "time()">
<form name="time">
<input type="text" name="numbers" />
</form>
</body>
</html>
```

Figure 15.20 shows the results of the above XHTML document.

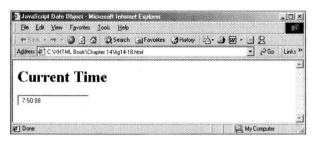

FIGURE 15.20: USING JAVASCRIPT DATE OBJECT METHODS TO CREATE A CLOCK

CHAPTER SUMMARY

This chapter has covered a lot of information about JavaScript, but remember that this material only scratches the surface of this subject. You have learned how to create some simple scripts that take little programming to accomplish. You were introduced to the programming concepts of operators, expressions, loops, and functions. This chapter demonstrated how dates and times could be manipulated into different date formats for use in your XHTML documents. You also learned how JavaScript could be used to validate user input before the data is submitted to the server for processing.

KEY TERMS

arithmetic operators	date object
assignment operators	do while loop
break statement	for loop
comparison operators	logical operators
continue statement	object
conditional	unary operators
statements	while loop

REVIEW QUESTIONS

1. What are variables used for?
2. What is the difference between constants and variables?
3. What three types of loops can be used in JavaScript?
4. What is an assignment operator used for?
5. Write the equivalent compound assignment statement for x = x + 1.
6. What are unary operators and how are they used?
7. What is the purpose of the switch statement?
8. What are comparison operators?
9. What does the expression $(((5 + 9)/2) == 7)$ evaluate to—true or false?
10. The following is a truth table for which logical operator?

Expression 1	Expression 2	Returns
T	T	T
T	F	T
F	T	T
F	F	F

EXERCISES

1. Write a script and place it in an XHTML document that uses a while loop to count from 0 to 100 by increments of three. Display the count on the page.
2. Modify the XHTML document used to create Figure 15.17 so that it includes the date and time.

3. Write a script and place it in an XHTML document that will display the current date in the following format: July 4, 2001. Incorporate the use of a switch that determines the month into the script.

4. Write a function that accepts parameters for a student's name and numeric grade. The script in the function should determine the student's letter grade based on the numeric grade using the following criteria:

A	Greater than 90
B	Greater than 80 but less than 90
C	Greater than 70 but less than 80
D	Greater than 60 but less than 70
F	Less than 60

After the grade has been determined, display the student's name in an alert box with the letter grade. Also provide one of the following messages based on if the student passed or failed:

Congratulations, you have passed!
Sorry, you failed the test!

The function should be called from the body of the XHTML document.

5. Modify the XHTML document created in the previous exercise to include a form for the user to enter the student's name and score. The form should be validated for correct information before calling the grade function. Validate that the user has entered something in the name text box and score text box. The score should also be validated to ensure that it is not less than 0 and not greater than 100.

PROJECT

We will now focus on using JavaScript to add client-side functionality to our site. Do the following:

- Add validation to the forms you created in Chapter 11 for entering events and items. Do not allow any of the fields to be left blank.
- Add JavaScript to the home page that will display the current date.

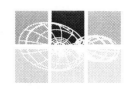

chapter 16
active server pages

CHAPTER OVERVIEW

Active Server Pages (ASP) allow us to create dynamic Web content by providing us with the ability to alter Web pages moments before the user receives them. This allows us to personalize content based on the user, automate content updating, and perform any other task that would benefit from having the latest information. This chapter will introduce you to creating ASP pages. You will learn the structure of ASP and how to integrate it with XHTML. You will see how to use the ASP built-in objects to conditionally send content to the user and to use pre-built components to create complex interactions with very little code.

CHAPTER OBJECTIVES

- Create an ASP document by encapsulating XHTML within ASP
- Use ASP expressions to insert ASP into XHTML
- Use if statements to change Web content based on a set of criteria
- Use the response object to construct XHTML
- Use built-in components to integrate a page counter, random text content, and random banner ads into a Web page
- Set up a free ASP-hosting account

ACTIVE SERVER PAGES

Today's Web surfers expect content to be up to date and many times even personalized to them. In order to accomplish this economically, we need a technology that allows us to dynamically build Web content. By waiting until the user requests a Web page to construct it, we gain the ability to use the latest information within the page. Each time the user returns, he or she sees something new.

Microsoft's Active Server Pages is a server-side technology that allows us to create pages or change Web pages on the server and then send them to the user. Some uses for ASP include processing forms, performing calculations, placing banner ads, and retrieving information from a database. This technology offers the benefit of allowing developers to set a single template page that will yield different results to users depending on their particular situation. For example, we can set up a single product information page that will display information for products in an online catalog. If cosmetic changes are needed, we need to change only the one page. The net result is a highly efficient and economical technology. The possibilities are endless.

REQUIREMENTS AND SETUP

Active Server Pages is a Microsoft technology and therefore runs only on Microsoft's Web servers. The code in this chapter will require access to such a server. If you do not currently have access to one, don't despair. Microsoft gives its server out for free to anyone who owns Windows 95, Windows 98, Windows 2000, Windows NT, or Windows XP.

If your school does not provide access to an ASP-capable server, sign up for a free ASP-hosting account. While we do not endorse any specific free hosting companies, these are some possibilities: www.brinkster.com , www.webhostme.com, and www.aspfree.com.

If you have Windows 95, Windows 98, or Windows NT 4.0, you will need to install Personal Web Server 4.0. Personal Web Server (PWS) is a scaled-down version of Microsoft's enterprise-level Web server called *Internet Information Server (IIS)*. There are two main limitations with PWS. First, it can only support a maximum of 10 concurrent hits. Second, it does not include some of the components included with IIS.

You may download a copy of PWS from www.microsoft.com. If you have Windows 98, do not use the copy that came with your Windows 98 CD-ROM. The version on that CD-ROM is Personal Web Server 3.0.

If you have any version of Windows 2000 or Windows XP, your installation CD-ROM contains a version of Internet Information Server 5.0. It is not installed by default. To install it, go to Start → Settings → Control Panel → Add/Remove Programs. This will bring up a dialog box with all of the programs installed on your computer. Now, select the third button in the left column titled "Add/Remove Windows Components." Another dialog box will open. Put a check mark in front of "Internet Information Services" and click on "Next." This will install the IIS Web server and an FTP server on your computer.

Regardless of which operating system you use, IIS creates a folder named /InetPub/wwwroot on your boot drive. Our boot drive is the D drive. On the D drive, there is a folder named InetPub, and inside of that folder is another one called wwwroot. If your boot drive is your C drive, then the folders will be located there. Check to see if this folder exists before continuing on to the next section.

ASP STRUCTURE

At its most basic level, ASP is nothing more than XHTML with special tags that run on the server. The server executes the ASP code and sends the resulting XHTML to the user. Let's try an example to get the general structure of an ASP document.

Type the following using your choice of editor and save it as hello.asp in your C:\InetPut\wwwroot\XHTML directory.

1. We need to let the server know that we are creating an ASP document. We are using the extension .asp on our files. We must inform the server of the language that we are using for our documents. In this case, we are using Visual Basic Script or *VBScript*. This line must appear at the start of all ASP documents and is called the *language declaration*. Notice the inclusion of the @ sign. All ASP sections of code must appear between <% %>, but only the language declaration is allowed to use the @ sign after the opening <% delimiter.

   ```
   <%@ Language="VBScript" %>
   ```

2. Now we add some HTML headers.

   ```
   <html><head></head><body>
   ```

3. Here we output some regular XHTML. We print *"Hello there, the date is:"* in bold.

```
<b>Hello there, the date is: </b>
```

4. Now we let the server know that the lines that follow are written in ASP.

```
<%
```

5. This line causes the server to retrieve the current date and send it to the user. If we look at the resulting rendered document in Figure 16.2 and the resulting XHTML code in Figure 16.3, we will notice that this line has been replaced with 5/7/2001. The code is fully executed, and only its results are sent to the user. In this case, the result is 5/7/2001. Looking at this line more closely, we notice that there are two statements. The Response.Write statement causes the server to print whatever happens to be in parentheses. If we were to write "Response.Write ("Today is a great day.")," the server would print "Today is a great day." The second statement on this line is date(). This is a function that causes VBScript to retrieve today's date. Thus, by putting the date() function inside of the Response.Write statement, we can cause ASP to retrieve today's date and send it to the user.

```
Response.Write ( date() )
```

6. Here we cause the Response.Write statement to send a breakline (
) and "I guess that's ok" to the user. Notice that there are double quotes around the text we are sending to the user. This is because we would like to send the user a string. In this case, the string is "I guess that's ok". All strings in ASP must be surrounded by double quotes.

```
Response.Write ("<br/>I guess that's ok")
```

7. Now we let the server know that we are done with ASP.

```
%>
```

8. Finally, we close the page and the document.

```
</body></html>
```

Your final code should look like Figure 16.1.

```
<%@ Language="VBScript" %>
<html><head></head><body>
<b>Hello There, the date is: </b>
<%
   Response.Write ( date() )
   Response.Write ("<br/>I guess that's ok")
%>
</body></html>
```

FIGURE 16.1: ASP CODE EXAMPLE 1

Open your Web browser and type the following address in your address line: http://localhost/XHTML/hello.asp. You should get a document similar to Figure 16.2. If you get a dialog box asking you to save the document, you have forgotten to include the http:// in your address. This is critical because this will cause your Web server to process the document.

FIGURE 16.2 EXAMPLE 1 RENDERING

```
<html><head></head><body>
<b>Hello There, the date is: </b>
5/7/2001<br/>I guess that's ok
</body>
</html>
```

FIGURE 16.3 XHTML CODE FOR EXAMPLE 1

INTEGRATING ASP AND XHTML

XHTML and ASP can appear on the same page, but XHTML cannot appear inside of the *ASP delimiters*, <% %>. This limitation leaves us with two ways for intermixing XHTML and ASP code. We can encapsulate all XHTML tags inside of Response.Write statements or we can place ASP expressions within our XHTML. Both methods have advantages and disadvantages. Let's create the same output both ways as we contrast the strengths and weaknesses of each method.

ENCAPSULATING XHTML INSIDE ASP

With this method, we will encapsulate the XHTML tags inside of the Response.Write statements. An advantage to this method is cleaner code. A disadvantage is that this method often leads to complex string constructions, as we will see below when we consider the construction of line 6.

Create a folder inside of your XHTML folder and call it "images". On the CD-ROM, you will find a file called asp_header.gif. Copy it to c:\InetPub\wwwroot\XHTML\images. Type the following using your choice of editor and save it as fonts_encap.asp in your C:\InetPut\wwwroot\XHTML directory.

1. Here we place our language declaration. It is identical to the declaration we used in the last document because we are still using VBScript for our ASP pages.

   ```
   <%@ Language="VBScript" %>
   ```

2. Now we let the server know we are going to use ASP code.

   ```
   <%
   ```

3. Now we use the Response.Write statement to print strings to the user. Note that all of the XHTML tags appear inside of the string.

```
Response.Write ("<html>")
Response.Write ("<head><title>Font Sizes </title></head>")
Response.Write ("<body>")
```

Now we place an image by using the image tag. We need to pay particular attention to this line because it appears to have extra quotes. As we discussed earlier, the Response.Write statement requires strings to appear in double quotes. Thus, the double quotes are used as delimiters inside of the Response.Write statement to indicate the start and end of a string. In line 6, we are attempting to create an XHTML <img> tag for the purpose of including an image on our page. As you recall, the <img> tag follows the following general form:

```
<img src="imageName.jpg">
```

This requires us to be able to print double quotes. We can instruct the Response.Write statement to include a single set of double quotes by including consecutive double quotes in our string. Thus,

```
Response.Write ("<img src=""images/asp_header.gif"">")
```

produces

```
<img src="images/asp_header.gif">
```

4. Now we print a line break and "Look at the fonts" formatted as a second-level header.

```
Response.Write ("<br/>")
Response.Write ("<h2>Look at the fonts</h2>")
```

5. Now we use a loop to print the same statement in multiple font sizes.

```
for s=1 to 3
  Response.Write ("<font size=" &s& ">ASP is fun</font>")
  Response.Write ("<br/>")
next
```

We define a loop with s as a counter that will go from one to three. This will cause anything between the for statement and the next statement to be executed three times. Each time through the loop, the variable s will be increased by one. The first time through s will have a value of 1, then 2, and finally 3.

If we turn our attention to the first Response.Write statement within the loop, we notice that we are constructing a string that says "<font size=" followed by an ampersand (&), the letter s, another ampersand (&), and finally another string that says ">ASP is fun</font>". This will create one large string that will say:

```
<font size=1>ASP is fun</font>
<font size=2>ASP is fun</font>
<font size=3>ASP is fun</font>
```
the first time through the loop, then
the second time through the loop, then
the third time through the loop

The value of the variable s is inserted into the string by using the ampersand character. The net result is that we get the words "ASP is fun" in increasing font sizes.

What would we need to change if we wanted our ASP page to output the words "ASP is fun" 100 times at a font size of two? Because our for statement dictates how many times we go through the loop, we would want the for statement to read

```
for s=1 to 100
```

Finally, we would need to change the first Response.Write statement to not use the variable s as a basis for font size. It would read:

```
Response.Write ("<font size=2>ASP is fun</font>")
```

6. Now we print "This is not too bad."

```
Response.Write ("This is not too bad <br/>")
```

7. Then we close the document and the page.

```
Response.Write ("</body></html>")
%>
```

Your finished code should look similar to Figure 16.4.

```
<%@ Language="vbscript" %>
<%
Response.Write ("<html>")
Response.Write ("<head><title>Font Sizes </title></head>")
Response.Write ("<body>")
Response.Write ("<img src=""images/asp_header.gif"">")
Response.Write ("<br/>")
Response.Write ("<h2>look at the fonts</h2>")
for s=1 to 3
  Response.Write ("<font size=" &s& ">Asp is fun</font>")
  Response.Write ("<br/>")
next
```

```
Response.Write ("This is not too bad <br/>")
Response.Write ("</body></html>")
%>
```

FIGURE 16.4 SOURCE FOR FONTS_ENCAP.ASP

To see our page, open http://localhost/xhtml/fonts_encap.asp with your Web browser. It should look similar to Figure 16.5.

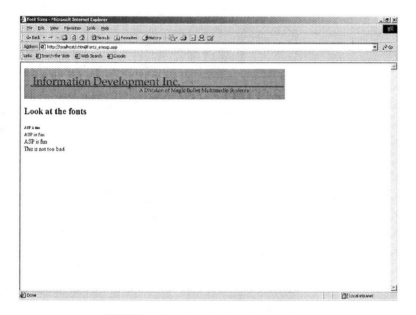

FIGURE 16.5: RENDERING OF FONTS_ENCAP.ASP

THE ASP EXPRESSION FORMAT

Now, let's create an identical document but use the expression form of the Response.Write statement. We use a special delimiter called the ASP expression format that stands for Response.Write to insert ASP results into our document. This is useful when you have an XHTML document into which you want to place a limited amount of text or images coming from an ASP source. Let's examine how this is done.

Type the following using your choice of editor and save it as fonts_exprs.asp in your C:\InetPut\wwwroot\XHTML directory.

1. Declare the language for our ASP page.

```
<%@ Language="VBScript" %>
```

2. Print some normal XHTML. Notice that these XHTML tags are placed outside of the ASP delimiters.

```
<html>
<head>
<title>Font Sizes</title>
</head>
<body>
<img src="images/asp_header.gif">
<br><h2>Look at the fonts</h2>
```

3. Here we include the <% delimiter, signaling that ASP code will follow and define our for statement. Notice that the for statement has the ASP delimiters on both sides of it.

```
<% for s=1 to 3 %>
```

ASP does not require its loops or if statements to occur within one contiguous code block. This makes it possible to have a loop that starts in an isolated ASP code segment and terminates with an isolated next statement. The lines between the two do not need to be ASP code.

4. Next, we have the line that will print "ASP is fun" in increasing font sizes.

```
<font size= <%=s%> >ASP is fun </font> <br>
```

As before, we are attempting to create a loop that will increment the size of the font by one each time this loop is executed by using the value of the variable s as the value for our font size. Thus, we are trying to construct the following statements:

```
<font size=1>ASP is fun</font>    where 1 is coming from variable s
<font size=2>ASP is fun</font>    where 2 is coming from variable s
<font size=3>ASP is fun</font>    where 3 is coming from variable s
```

To accomplish this, we need to print the value of the variable s within our font xhtml statement. The following would accomplish this:

```
<font size= <%Response.Write (s)%> >ASP is fun</Font>
```

If we turn our attention back to our line, we notice that it looks different from the line above. That is because <%= %> is equivalent to <% Response.Write %>. This is called the *expression format* because it allows us to insert results from ASP code directly into the middle of our XHTML. To illustrate this further, let's create an XHTML table with some ASP expressions within the cells of our table.

5. Now we close our for loop by inserting the next statement. Note that it is surrounded by the ASP delimiters.

```
<%next %>
```

6. Finally, we output some regular XHTML and close the page.

```
<br>This is not too bad <br>
</body>
<html>
```

Your finished code should look similar to Figure 16.6.

```
<%@ Language="VBScript" %>
<html>
<head>
<title>Font Sizes</title>
</head>
<body>
<img src="images/asp_header.gif">
<br><h2>Look at the fonts</h2>
<% for s=1 to 3 %>
      <font size= <%=s%> >ASP is fun </font> <br>
<%next %>
<br>This is not too bad <br>
</body>
<html>
```

FIGURE 16.6: SOURCE FOR FONTS_EXPRS.ASP

We can see our document by opening http://localhost/xhtml/ fonts_exprs.asp with any Web browser. It should look similar to Figure 16.7. While our ASP code was different, the resulting page is the same.

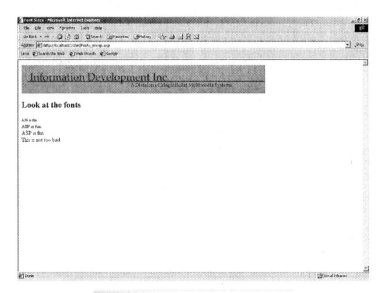

FIGURE 16.7 RENDERING OF FONTS_EXPRS.ASP

To further explore the power of using expressions, let's create another document. We will use expressions within the cells of a table to output the date and the value of a variable. Type the following using your choice of editor and save it as exprs_example.asp in your C:\InetPut\wwwroot\XHTML directory.

1. We start by declaring the language for our ASP language as VBScript.

```
<%@ Language="VBScript" %>
```

2. Here we declare a variable called vname and initialize it with the value of Joe Smith. Notice the ASP delimiters around the entire line.

```
<% vname="Joe Smith" %>
```

3. Now we output some regular XHTML.

```
<html>
<head>
  <title>Expressions</title>
</head>
<body>
<table border="1">
<tr>
```

4. On these lines, we use the expression delimiter to insert the result of the ASP expressions into our table cells. With the first line, we insert the

result of the date function. This is how we get 7/23/2001 into the first cell. On the line after, we insert the string "The date is:" followed by the results of the date function in long format. This is how we get "The date is: Tuesday, May 08, 2001" into the second cell. On the final line, we insert "Your name is:" followed by the value inside of vname. This is how we get "Your name is: Joe Smith" into the last cell of our table. In all cases, we have used the <%= %> delimiters to surround the ASP expression that we want to appear inside of our XHTML code.

```
<td> <%= date() %> </td>
<td> <%="The date is: "& formatdatetime (date, vblongdate))  %>
</td>
<td> <%= "Your name is: "& vname %> </td>
```

5. Next, we close the table and the page.

```
</tr>
  </table>
</body>
<html>
```

The final code should look similar to Figure 16.8.

```
<%@ Language="VBScript" %>
<% vname="Joe Smith" %>
<html>
<head>
  <title>Expressions</title>
</head>
<body>
  <table border="1">
        <tr>
            <td> <%= date() %> </td>
            <td> <%="The date is: "& formatdatetime (date,
            vblongdate))  %> </td>
            <td> <%= "Your name is: "& vname %> </td>
        </tr>
  </table>
</body>
<html>
```

FIGURE 16.8: SOURCE FOR EXPRS_EXAMPLE.ASP

Open the page in your Web browser by opening http://localhost/xhtml/ exprs_example.asp. The document results should look like Figure 16.9.

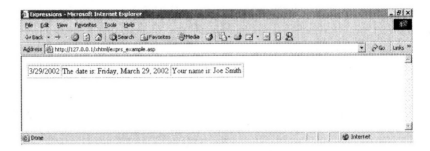

FIGURE 16.9: RENDERING OF EXPRS_EXAMPLE.ASP

CONDITIONAL CONTENT

We have examined the general structure of ASP and learned how to dynamically alter the appearance of a Web document through the use of Response.Write statements. While this is powerful, we have not considered how to change our Web content based on a condition on the server or on the user's previous actions. In this section, we will create an ASP document that will send the user a different banner image based on the time of the day.

Type the following using your choice of editor and save it as TimeOfDay.asp in your C:\InetPut\wwwroot\XHTML directory. Copy the following files to your c:\InetPub\wwwroot\XHTML\images directory: asp_good_m.gif, asp_good_a.gif, and asp_good_e.gif. You will find the originals on the CD-ROM.

1. Declare the language.

```
<%@ Language="VBScript" %>
```

2. Write out the HTML heads and a heading using regular XHTML.

```
<html>
<head>
<title>Time of Day</title>
</head>
<body>
<h2> I wonder what time of the day it is: </h2>
```

3. Declare the next lines as ASP with the <% delimiter.

```
<%
```

4. Now we use an extended if statement to check if the time of the server falls within the specified ranges. First, we check if the time is between 0100 hours and 1200 hours. If it is, we Response.Write an image tag that puts the "Good Morning" on the screen. We also Response.Write the phrase "It is morning!!" We then repeat this for each frame of time that we are searching.

```
if (hour(time) > 1) and (hour(time) < 12) then
  response.write ("<img src=""images/asp_good_m.gif"">")
  response.write ("<br/>It is morning!!")
elseif (hour(time) > 13) and (hour(time) < 18) then
  response.write ("<img src=""images/asp_good_a.gif"">")
  response.write ("<br/>It is sometime in the afternoon")
elseif (hour(time) > 18) and (hour(time) < 23) then
  response.write ("<img src=""images/asp_good_e.gif"">")
  response.write ("<br/>It is sometime in the afternoon")
end if
```

5. Finally, we close the page.

```
%>
</body>
<html>
```

The final code should look similar to Figure 16.10.

```
<%@ language="vbscript" %>
<html>
<head>
<title>Time of day</title>
</head>
<body>
<h2> I wonder what time of the day it is: </h2>
<%
```

```
if (hour(time) > 1) and (hour(time) < 12) then
  response.write ("<img src=""images/asp_good_m.gif"">")
  response.write ("<br/>It is morning!!")
elseif (hour(time) > 13) and (hour(time) < 18) then
  response.write ("<img src=""images/asp_good_a.gif"">")
  response.write ("<br/>It is sometime in the afternoon")
elseif (hour(time) > 18) and (hour(time) < 23) then
  response.write ("<img src=""images/asp_good_e.gif"">")
  response.write ("<br/>It is sometime in the afternoon")
end if
%>
</body>
<html>
```

FIGURE 16.10: SOURCE FOR TIMEOFDAY.ASP

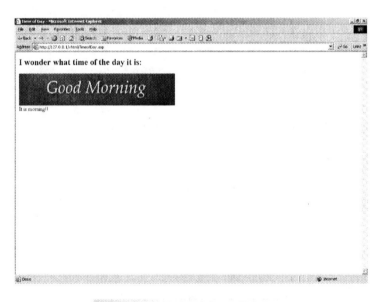

FIGURE 16.11: RENDERING OF TIMEOFDAY.ASP

ASP OBJECTS AND COMPONENTS

ASP includes a series of objects and components that provide us with a tremendous amount of functionality. By using these objects, we can create very complex Web documents with very little coding. For example, using the Ad Rotator component, we can add rotating banners to a Web page with two lines of code, or by using the Page Counter component, we can add a page counter to any page with one line of code. In this section, we are going to look at all of the objects of ASP and the most common components.

THE SIX OBJECTS OF ASP

All Active Server Pages are built around six objects. Each object is responsible for major aspects of our Website and provides us with functions, called methods, that we can call upon to perform a specific action. For example, the Response object is responsible for sending information from the server to the user. It has a method called Write that specifically handles strings. Therefore, when we need to send a string, such as an XHTML line of code, from the server to the user, we call the Write method of the Response object. It looks like Response.Write. The general format is always NameOfObject.MethodName.

In the next chapter, we will be building an online classified site in which we will use most of the objects and components of ASP. For right now, let's do a quick run-through of these objects and components.

Response Object

The *response object* carries information from the server to the client. We can think of it as the server *responding* to the user. It can be used to send body text, HTTP header information, and even binary information. The most useful methods are the Write, ContentType, and Cookies methods. As we discovered earlier, Response.Write sends a string to the user.

Response.ContentType is used to change the content type reported by the HTTP header in the document sent to the user. For example, under normal conditions, when we send XHTML content to a user, the browser automatically renders the XHTML into a Web document. But what if we wanted to have the browser show the actual XHTML tags instead of rendering the document? We can accomplish this by changing the ContentType header in our file to "text/plain". If this is not included, the server automatically adds a ContentType header into all files of the type "text/plain". This is how the user's browser knows that it is receiving XHTML instead of plain text, a movie file, or some other type of file.

Response.Cookies allows us to write a cookie into users' systems. This is useful for personalizing content for users. For example, we could place a cookie on the users' systems with their first name. Then when they visited at a later date, we could retrieve the cookie off their system and greet them by using their first name.

Request Object

The *request object* is used when we want the server to retrieve information from the user. We can think of it as the server requesting information from the user. This is useful for retrieving information from forms the user has filled out, for determining the browser being used, or for retrieving cookies that we have deposited onto the client's machine.

Session Object

The *session object* allows us to store information about the user for a temporary period of time. Under normal conditions, the user's browser and the server forget all of the information about each other between consequent page accesses. This is because HTTP, the protocol used for the Web, is a stateless protocol. Session objects are a special type of variable that allow our Web pages to remember information we have put in them beyond the page we created the variable in. By default, these variables are destroyed after 20 minutes of no user activity.

Application Object

The *application object* serves a similar function as the session object. It allows us to define variables that everyone who is accessing our Website can access. This is useful for situations where we want users to exchange information with one another, such as in a live chatting scenario. Session variables can be accessed on any page an individual user goes to, while any user on any page of the site can access application variables.

Server Object

The *server object* does not provide us with any visible functionality like the other objects we have looked at thus far. This object allows us to create and destroy objects on the server. For example, ASP lacks the capabilities to allow the user to upload files to the server via a Web page. But a company called SoftwareArtisans sells a component that provides this functionality. The server object allows us to create an instance of the SoftwareArtisans FileUpload object. If it sounds a bit confusing, don't worry. We will see all of these objects in operation in the next chapter.

ObjectContext Object

The *ObjectContext object* is very powerful but extremely narrow in the functionality that it provides. It provides ASP with the ability to manage transactions using Microsoft Transaction Server. Most sites can be completed without using this component.

ASP COMPONENTS

The Microsoft Internet Information Server provides a series of components that allow us to perform relatively complex tasks with a few lines of code. These tasks range from displaying banner ads to accessing databases.

To use any component, we must create an instance of the component by assigning it to a variable. This is done using the *Server.CreateObject*. The general format is always

```
Set variableName = Server.CreateObject("ObjectName")
```

Let's create an ASP document with some of these components to see them in operation.

Ad Rotator Component

The Microsoft *Ad Rotator component* can be used to place a banner ad on a page. The component takes care of selecting the appropriate image and randomly placing it on our page.

Type the following using your choice of editor and save it as adsComponent.asp in your C:\InetPut\wwwroot\XHTML directory. Copy the following files to your C:\InetPub\wwwroot\XHTML\images directory: Banner01.gif, Banner02.gif, and Banner03.gif. You will find the originals on the CD.

1. Declare the language we are going to use.

```
<%@ Language="VBScript" %>
```

2. Create the page headers.

```
<html><head><Title>My Portal</title></head>
```

3. Create an instance of the Microsoft Web component Ad Rotator and assign it to the variable AdObj. This is the object that is responsible for randomly selecting images and sending them to the user.

```
<%
set AdObj = Server.CreateObject("MSWC.AdRotator")
```

4. Use the GetAdvertisement method of the object we created on line 4 (AdObj) to assign an image to the ad variable. At this point, the component will place a string of the form <img src=...> into the variable.

```
ad = AdObj.GetAdvertisement("/XHTML/banners/AdSchedule.txt")
```

5. We then use the Response.Write statement to send the user the <img src> source, which causes the user's browser to load the appropriate image.

```
Response.Write ad
```

6. We then destroy our object.

```
set aAdvObject = nothing
```

7. We then close the ASP delimiter and output some regular XHTML.

```
%>
<body>
<h1><font color=sienna>Welcome to my portal site</font></h1>
</body></html>
```

Figure 16.12 depicts the finished source code.

```
<%@ Language="VBScript" %>
<html><head><TITLE>My Portal</title></head>
<%
set AdObj = Server.CreateObject("MSWC.AdRotator")
ad = AdObj.GetAdvertisement("/XHTML/banners/AdSchedule.txt")
Response.Write ad

set aAdvObject = nothing
%>
<body>
<h1><font color=sienna>Welcome to my portal site</font></h1>
</body></html>
```

FIGURE 16.12: SOURCE FOR ADSCOMPONENT.ASP

If we try to view our page at this point, we will generate an error because we have not created a schedule file for our document. If we look at the code we just created, we passed the GetAdvertisement method a parameter that says "/XHTML/banners/AdSchedule.txt." This is a specially formatted text file that contains information about the images we want to show. Create a text file with the name of AdSchedule.txt and save it in C:\InetPub\wwwroot\XHTML\ banners.

Type the following into the file and save it.

```
REDIRECT http://localhost/XHTML/goToSponsor.asp
WIDTH 371
HEIGHT 53
BORDER 0
*
/XHTML/banners/Banner01.gif
http://www.apple.com
Please click on me.
3
/XHTML/banners/Banner02.gif
http://www.intel.com
Let go to visit Intel
1
/XHTML/banners/Banner03.gif
http://www.microsoft.com
Click on me
1
```

FIGURE 16.13 ADSCHEDULE FILE

Line 1 of the file tells the component that we would like to use a redirector file. This is useful for recording which banners the user has clicked on. In other words, this is a file on our server that records what banner was just clicked on and then sends the user to the final destination. This line is optional. Lines 2 through 4 declare the size of our banners and the size of the border we would like. Notice that this is a global declaration for all of the banners, and therefore all of the banners we want to use must be of the same size. Lines 5 through 9 represent a single entry in our banner schedule and can repeat indefinitely. The first line in each entry must be an asterisk. The second line points to the location of the image we would like to use for a banner. This must be a GIF, JPG, or PNG image. The next line represents what the alternate tag for the image will hold. This would be the texts users would see if they browsed the site with a non-graphical browser. Finally, the last line is a weight. It tells the component how often to show an image. In this schedule file, the first banner would be shown three times more than either of the other two entries.

Content Rotator Component

The *Content Rotator component* is similar to the Ad Rotator component, but instead of displaying random images, it displays random lines of text. It is useful for implementing features such as "saying of the day" or "get your daily fortune." This component does not come with IIS 4.0 or PWS. Therefore, it will not work with Windows 98 or Windows NT 4.0 unless the Microsoft IIS Resource Pack is also installed. It will work flawlessly with any version of Windows 2000 or Windows XP. The listing below shows this component in operation.

```
1:   <%@ Language="VBScript" %>
2:   <html><head><title>My Portal</title></head>
3:   <%
4:   set rndSaying = Server.CreateObject("MSWC.ContentRotator")
5:   Response.Write rndSaying.choosecontent("sayings.txt")
6:
7:   set rndSaying = nothing
8:   %>
9:   <Body>
10:  <h1><font color=sienna>Welcome to my portal site</font></h1>
11:  </gody></html>
```

Line 4 creates an instance of the Microsoft Web component Content Rotator and assigns it to the variable rndSaying. Then line 5 retrieves a random chunk of text from the file sayings.txt and uses the Response.Write statement to send it to the user. Notice that we are taking the output of the choosecontent method or the rndSaying object and feeding its results to the Write method of the response object. Using objects in this manner allows us to get a lot of functionality with very little code. In this case, two lines of code is all that is needed.

```
1:   <%@ Language="VBScript" %>
2:   <html><head><title>My Portal</title></head>
3:   <%
4:   set rndSaying = Server.CreateObject("MSWC.ContentRotator")
5:   Response.Write rndSaying.choosecontent("sayings.txt")
6:
7:   set rndSaying = nothing
8:   %>
9:   <body>
```

```
10:    <h1><font color=sienna>Welcome to my portal site</font></h1>
11:    </body></html>
```

We should also look at the structure of the sayings.txt file we used as an argument on line 5. The file can contain an unlimited number of stories. Each one is delimited by a double percent sign followed by a space, a pound sign, and the weight the story should be given. A double set of slashes is optional and can be used to denote a comment. On line 1 below, we find the delimiter for the first story. It has been given a weight of 2; therefore, it will be displayed twice for each time the other stories are shown. It also contains a comment, "ASP Code is Fun." This will not be shown to the user. On line 5, we find the delimiter for the second story. This one has a weight of 1 and no comment.

```
1:     %% #2 // ASP Code is Fun
2:     The Surgeon General of the United States has determined that
3:     coding ASP on a daily basis reduces the chances of
4:     heart disease
5:     %% #1
6:     Is your marriage on the rocks?  Don't despair! ASP coding
7:     can help.  A romantic night of ASP coding can bring the
8:     romance back into your life.
9:     %% #1 // Man found saved by ASP
10:    A man who had been missing since 1940 was found in excellent
11:    health after being stranded on an island for over 60 years.
12:    When asked, "How did you do it?" the man replied, "A strong
13:    regiment of daily ASP was all I required."
```

Remember that ASP code can be intermixed within XHTML. This gives us the capabilities of changing the appearance of the text delivered by the component. If we wanted to assign the text a heading of 2, we would change line 5 to

```
Response.Write ("<h2>"&rndSaying.choosecontent("sayings.txt")&"</h2>")
```

Page Counter Component

The *Page Counter component* allows us to insert a page counter into our ASP documents. Like the Content Rotator component, it does not come with the basic version of IIS 4. It will work with Windows 2000 and Windows XP, both of which come with IIS 5. Let's add a page counter to the document we constructed for the content rotator. Delete line 11 and enter the code below.

```
11:  <br/>
12:  <% set pc=server.CreateObject("MSWC.PageCounter") %>
13:  You have been here <b> <%= pc.pageHit %> </b> times
14:  </body></html>
```

You should see a page similar to the one shown in Figure 16.14 when you execute the code.

FIGURE 16.14: CONTENT ROTATOR AND PAGE COUNTER

On line 12, we enter an ASP code segment and instantiate a version of the Microsoft Web component Page Counter by assigning it to the variable pc. On line 13, we use the expression format to insert the results of the pageHit method inside of the bold tags. It is this line that actually prints the number of hits on the Web page.

CHAPTER SUMMARY

In this chapter, we learned how to build dynamic Web content through the integration of ASP and XHTML. We saw that ASP is a type of markup language that gets executed on the server before pages are sent to the user. We learned how to integrate ASP and XHTML using both the encapsulation and expression techniques. We learned how to use if statements to conditionally execute ASP code. We encountered the six ASP objects. Finally, we learned how to use components to rotate banner ads, show random text, and insert page counters into our documents.

KEY TERMS

Ad Rotator component
application object
ASP delimiter
ASP expression format
Content Rotator component
Internet Information Server (IIS)
language declaration
ObjectContext object

Page Counter component
request object
response object
Response.Write
Server.CreateObject
server object
session object
VBScript

REVIEW QUESTIONS

1. List two ways that ASP and XHTML can be integrated.
2. What must surround all ASP code segments?
3. What would be the result of the following?
   Response.Write ("<h2>"&date()&"</h2>")
4. What function does the scheduling file serve for the Content Rotator component?
5. What is the relationship between the response and the Request objects?
6. How many ASP objects are there and what function do they serve?
7. What are some of the advantages of using components?
8. How does the server know what language the ASP code segments will be written in?

EXERCISES

1. Create a personal Web page by using nothing but ASP. All of your XHTML code should be encapsulated inside of Response.Write statements.
2. Now create a Web page for your family in XHTML. Then go back and insert ASP statements to show today's date using the expression format.
3. Go back to the page you created for Exercise 1 and add the Content Rotator component to randomly show some of your hobbies.
4. Now add the Ad Rotator and have the page show random images of yourself, your friends, your family, and so on.

5. Now change the page to show a different set of images during the night than those shown during the day.

6. Why would the following code not work?

```
<%@ Language="VBScript" %>
<html><head></head><body>
<%
    <b>Hello There, the date is: </b>
    Response.Write ( date() )
    Response.Write ("<br/>I guess that's ok")
%>
</body></html>
```

PROJECT

Now that we know how to use server-side scripting, we can focus on adding even more functionality to our site. Do the following:

▪ Change your home page to display the date on the server instead of the date on the client's machine. This will ensure that the date will display properly even if the users do not have their machines set up properly. Because our site targets a single geographical community, we do not have to account for the current date across international lines.

▪ Add a dynamic banner to your site.

▪ Add a page counter.

▪ Add a random saying of the day.

REFERENCES

Baatsee, M., Blair, R., et. al. 2000. *ASP XML*, Birmingham, U.K.:Wrox Press.

Hettihewa, S. 1999. *SAMS Teach Yourself Active Server Pages 2.0 in 21 Days*, Indianapolis: SAMS Publishing.

Weissinger, A. 1999. *ASP in a Nutshell*, Sabasotopol, CA: O'Reilly.

Whitehead, P. 2000. *Active Server Pages 3.0*, Mississauga, ON: maranGraphics.

4 Guys From Rolla, www.4GuysFromRolla.com

ASP 101, www.ASP101.com

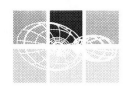

chapter 17
extensible markup language

CHAPTER OVERVIEW

The Extensible Markup Language (XML) enables us to
create highly flexible documents by separating the content
of a document from its appearance. By using XML to store
information and then using other technologies such as
XSL, XML enables us to efficiently disseminate our data
in multiple forms. This chapter covers how to create XML
documents to maintain data, how to use document type
definitions to validate data, and how to use namespaces for
extending XML documents.

CHAPTER OBJECTIVES

- Create well-formed XML documents
- Create valid documents by using a DTD to validate the
  XML content
- Use namespaces to expand an XML document
- Create a DTD
- Create element definitions
- Use occurrence indicators and connectors in declaring ele-
  ment definitions

EXTENSIBLE MARKUP LANGUAGE

At its most basic level, the *Extensible Markup Language (XML)* is a text-based language used for describing data and its structure. In isolation, XML does nothing other than hold data, much as a database or a file stores information. But, when combined with other technologies such as Extensible Stylesheet Language or document type definitions, XML provides an extremely robust toolset.

It can be used to separate data from how our Web applications present information. One advantage of this approach is that we can use the data supplied by a single XML document to create various forms to output documents. For example, if we maintained an XML file of menu items for a restaurant, we could construct an XHTML version and a printed text-based version of the menu from the same XML file. Any changes made to the data stored in the XML document would immediately be reflected on our Web page and on any new menus printed out. As you can see, XML can be used to create files for HTML, XHTML, and many other languages. As a result, we call XML a meta-language. Another use for XML is for facilitating the exchange of information among disparate systems. By providing an industry standard for encoding data, XML makes it easy to share information.

In more specific terms, XML is a text-based markup language similar in structure to HTML. Because it is intended to be extensible, the tags are not predefined. We invent tags that best describe the information we need to maintain. In contrast, HTML has predetermined tags that describe how the browsers should display the data. For example, <h1> hello there </h1> informs the browser that it should render the data "hello there" as a level-one header.

XML STRUCTURE

XML provides us with a tremendous amount of flexibility in modeling information at the expense of an extremely rigid syntax. In order for the language to allow extensibility, it cannot make any assumptions about our tags. As a result, there are a number of rules that we need to follow in order to create XML documents. Let's create our first XML document while we examine its syntax.

Type the following using your choice of editor and save it as memo.xml.

1. The first thing we need to do when we create an XML document is to explicitly declare it as XML using a *processing instruction*.

```
<?xml version="1.0" encoding="ISO-8859-1"?>
```

Processing instructions are reserved keywords that communicate with the XML parser. This particular one declares our document as being an XML version 1.0 document that has been encoded using Latin 1/Western European characters (ISO-8859-1). Each XML document must contain this processing instruction on line 1.

2. Now we will create an element called memo.

```
<memo>
```

This is the root element of our document. Elements can be nested, but each XML document can contain one and only one root element, also called a root node. In our document, the root element is memo. Its children are the elements to, cc, from, time, subject, and message. Notice that the element from also has children of its own—it has the elements first and last.

3. Now we add child elements to the memo element.

```
<to>Dr. Bertoline</to>
<cc/>
<from>
<first>Carlos</first>
<last>Morales</last>
</from>
```

An XML document is composed of *markup tags* and *character data*. In our document, we find Dr. Bertoline as our character data and the tag <to> as our markup tag. Combined, the character data and the markup tag make up an *element*. The name of the tag is the name of the element. Notice that the element from is a child of the element memo, but it has the child elements first and last.

The naming requirements for the elements are also strict. Tags are case-sensitive. So the elements <to>, <To>, and <TO> are not the same. Elements' names must start with a letter or an underscore. We must also not include any spaces in our elements' names. And finally, we must never start an element name with the letters xml. This is because processing instructions begin with the letters xml.

Another structural requirement for our XML document is that each element must have an opening and a closing tag. This is different from HTML, where it is typical to not close paragraph tags or break-line tags. If there is no data for a particular tag, then we can use the self-closing format. If we look at the cc element that we just added, we can see a self-closing empty element. We could have written <cc></cc> to indicate that it is empty or written <cc/>. Both are equivalent and indicate no data for the element.

4. Now we add an element called time with the attribute clock, which has been set to military time.

```
<time clock="military">13:43</time>
```

Attributes can be thought of as being parameters of the element that they belong to and always follow the general format <element attribute="value">. The value part of the attribute must always appear in double quotes. On this line, we notice that the element time has an attribute called clock that has been set to the value of military. The intended purpose of this attribute, in this case, is to inform the application reading this document that the time element is military time format.

If we look back at our first line, we will notice that the name of the element is xml with the attributes version and encoding, which have been set to "1" and "ISO-8859-1" respectively.

5. We continue adding elements.

```
<subject>Resources</subject>
<message>Resources are adequate</message>
```

6. Now we close our document.

```
</memo>
```

The completed document should look similar to Figure 17.1

```
<?xml version="1.0" encoding="ISO-8859-1"?>
   <memo>
      <to>Dr. Bertoline</to>
      <cc/>
      <from>
           <first>Carlos</first>
           <last>Morales</last>
      </from>
      <time clock="military">13:43</time>
      <subject>Resources</subject>
      <message>Resources are adequate</message>
   </memo>
```

FIGURE 17.1 MEMO.XML

Now open Internet Explorer 5.0 or higher or Netscape 6.0. View the
XML document you just created. It should look similar to the document in
Figure 17.2.

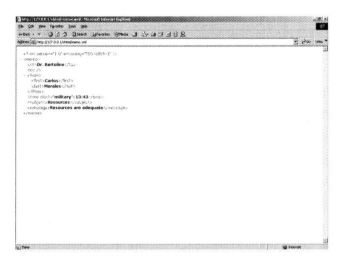

FIGURE 17.2 XML RESULTS

Characters that are normally used as delimiters within the XML document
cannot appear directly within the character data of an element. To use these,
you must utilize their escape-character equivalents. Table 17.1 below portrays
these characters.

Character	Escape-Character Equivalent
<	&lt
&	&amp
>	&gt
'	&apo
"	&quot

TABLE 17.1: XML ESCAPE CHARACTERS

All elements have two special attributes that are automatically included.
The first of these is the xml:lang attribute, which can be used to indicate the
language in which the character data of a particular element is written. The

second is the xml:space attribute that can be used to indicate if we want to preserve white spaces. Both of these attributes are optional. The example below shows a heading written in English from the United States that preserves white space.

```
<h2 xml:lang="en-US"> Hello There.    How are you? </h2>
```

NAMESPACES

Namespaces are mechanisms for documenting and determining the origin and the meaning of the elements we use in XML. Two central benefits of XML that make it an ideal format for data exchange are that it is extensible and that it is self-describing. We should be able to send an XML document to people in another company and have them be able to not only read our document but also add their own elements to it. In other words, the recipient has the option of extending our document by adding his or her own tags.

Sounds great, but what happens if someone tries to extend our document by using the same element names we have but in another manner? For example, in the XML document above, we use the element <to> to designate the full name of the recipient—in our case, Dr. Bertoline. What if someone extended our document by adding a second <to> element, but instead it indicated the user name of the recipient, such as gbertoline? Both of these entries would refer to the same person, but the data would be in different forms. This would confuse future people or applications trying to read our document.

Namespaces allow us to indicate the party that is responsible for a particular set of elements. Let's create a document that has two namespaces and then examine it:

1. Type the following using your choice of editor and save it as namespaces.xml. Do not type in the numbers in the left-hand column. These will be used for us to discuss the code.

```
1:   <?xml version="1.0" encoding="ISO-8859-1"?>
2:    <memo xmlns="http://www.loke.com/ref/4"
3:          xmlns:cm="http://www.purdue.edu/1.0"
4:          xmlns:lb="http://www.lb.com/lb/2.3">
5:       <cm:to>Dr. Bertoline</cm:to>
6:       <lb:to>gbertoline</lb:to>
7:       <cc/>
8:       <from>
9:            <first>Carlos</first>
```

```
10:                <last>Morales</last>
11:           </from>
12:           <time clock="military">13:43</time>
13:           <subject>Resources</subject>
14:           <lb:dept>Web Development</lb:dept>
15:           <message>Resources are adequate</message>
16:      </memo>
```

Namespaces are declared as attributes of the root element using the xmlns attribute. If we examine lines 2 through 4, we will find three namespaces being declared for this XML document. The address within the quotes is called a *Universal Resource Identifier (URI)*. It uniquely identifies the author of a set of XML elements or tags. Note that it does not point to an actual Web document. Instead, it points at a unique location on the server of the element author. In other words, line 3 defines a namespace, but if we used our Web browser to go to ="http://www.purdue.edu/1.0", we would not find a Web page or XML document there.

Line 2 declares the default namespace for this document. Notice that it does not have a colon on the xmlns declaration. Line 3 declares a namespace that will be referred to within this XML document as cm. Any tags that have been added or altered by the owner of this namespace will take the form <namespace:tag>, such as <cm:to> shown on line 5. Notice that both lines 5 and 6 have data that belongs to the element <to>, but the data on line 5 is in a format specified by the namespace declared on line 3. On line 14, there is an element that only exists for the lb namespace. Tags that do not have a colon were declared by the original author and therefore belong to the namespace declared on line 2.

DOCUMENT TYPE DEFINITION

Namespaces provide us with a way to identify the parties responsible for defining the tags of an XML document but not with a way to determine if we have a good document. We need to consider two issues when determining the status of our XML document. If our XML document adheres to all of the syntactical rules that we examined in the last section, then we say the document is *well-formed*. If the document is well-formed and it also makes sense, then we say the document is *valid*.

To determine the validity of an XML document, we need a second type of document called a *document type definition (DTD)*, which describes the type of data and the order that our XML data can use. This is particularly important

because the combination of a DTD and XML provide us with a way to share data among independent applications. If we have access to a document that describes the structure of XML documents coming from a particular source, then we can adapt our Web applications to best be able to exchange data with that source. In short, DTDs are what allow us to use XML for universal data exchange while maintaining the flexibility that comes with extensibility.

Let's create a DTD for the XML document we created in the last section. Type the following using your choice of editor and save it in the same directory you saved the namespaces.xml file. Name this one memo.dtd.

1. We'll start by inserting a processing instruction that identifies our DTD as adhering to XML 1.0 rules.

   ```
   <?xml version="1.0"?>
   ```

   While this processing instruction identifies our document as an XML 1.0 document, we need to beware because the DTD does not follow the format of an XML file exactly. Each line contains an *element name* and a *content model*. If we look at line 5, the element name is from and the content model is (first, last). Each line of the form <!ELEMENT element-name content-model> declares an element and the possible contents for that element.

2. Now we define the rules for the element memo.

   ```
   <!ELEMENT memo (to, cc?, from, time, subject,
   (dept|deptID)?, message)>
   ```

   This line states that there will be an element called memo that will have children elements by the name of to, cc, from, time, subject, dept, and message. We can then find the possible content of any of the children of memo by looking at their content model.

3. Now we define the rules for the element to.

   ```
   <!ELEMENT to (#PCDATA)>
   ```

   This element can have only one child of the type #PCDATA. PCDATA stands for parsed character data, which is just plain text.

4. We now add the content model for the element cc.

   ```
   <!ELEMENT cc (#PCDATA)>
   ```

5. Now we add the content model for the element from, which we define as having two child elements.

```
<!ELEMENT from (first, last)>
```

We could then track down the content models for those two children by continuing to scan our DTD for the definition for those elements.

6. We continue by adding rules for the rest of the elements.

```
<!ELEMENT first (#PCDATA)>
<!ELEMENT last (#PCDATA)>
<!ELEMENT time (#PCDATA)>
<!ATTLIST time clock CDATA #REQUIRED>
<!ELEMENT subject (#PCDATA)>
<!ELEMENT message (#PCDATA)>
```

Notice that the element time has both an element and an attribute definition. We define the element time as being composed of parsed character data. Then we define an attribute, using the <!ATTLIST> tag, for the element time that can hold character data and is required.

Your final document should look like Figure 17.3.

```
<?xml version="1.0"?>
<!ELEMENT memo (to, cc?, from, time, subject, (dept|deptID)?,
message)>
<!ELEMENT to (#PCDATA)>
<!ELEMENT cc (#PCDATA)>
<!ELEMENT from (first, last)>
<!ELEMENT first (#PCDATA)>
<!ELEMENT last (#PCDATA)>
<!ELEMENT time (#PCDATA)>
<!ATTLIST time clock CDATA #REQUIRED>
<!ELEMENT subject (#PCDATA)>
<!ELEMENT message (#PCDATA)>
```

FIGURE 17.3: DOCUMENT TYPE DEFINITION FOR MEMO.DTD

Now, let's edit the namespaces.xml document you created in the last section to use your newly created DTD. Change the document to read as follows:

```
1:    <?xml version="1.0" encoding="ISO-8859-1"?>
2:    <!DOCTYPE memo SYSTEM "memo.dtd">
3:      <memo xmlns="http://www.loke.com/ref/4"
4:            xmlns:cm="http://www.purdue.edu/1.0"
5:            xmlns:lb="http://www.lb.com/lb/2.3">
```

```
6:          <cm:to>Dr. Bertoline</cm:to>
7:          <lb:to>gbertoline</lb:to>
8:          <cc/>
9:          <from>
10:             <first>Carlos</first>
11:             <last>Morales</last>
12:         </from>
13:         <time clock="military">13:43</time>
14:         <subject>Resources</subject>
15:         <lb:dept>Web</lb:dept>
16:         <message>Resources are adequate</message>
17:      </memo>
```

When the XML parser reaches line 2 of the document above, it will load the memo.dtd file and attempt to validate the rest of the XML document against the rules we defined in memo.dtd. If any of the data in the rest of our XML document does not adhere to our DTD, an error will be generated and the XML page will fail to load. The goal of our DTD file is to describe the type of data and the order of XML elements.

Occurrence Indicators and Connectors
If our XML document is to truly be flexible, then our DTD must provide a way for us to indicate optional attributes. We can specify the order and frequency of the XML elements using the *occurrence indicators* reflected in Table 17.2 and the *connectors* reflected in Table 17.3.

Indicator	Meaning
+	Element may appear one or more times
*	Element may appear zero or more times
?	Element may appear zero or one time
No indicator	Element must appear once and only once

TABLE 17.2: DTD OCCURRENCE INDICATORS

Connector	Meaning
,	Element must appear in the order shown
|	One and only one of the elements must appear

TABLE 17.3: DTD CONNECTORS

Let's dissect the content model for the element memo to see these modifiers in action.

```
<!ELEMENT memo (to, cc?, from, time, subject, (dept|deptID)?,
message)>
```

Reading from left to right, we see that memo must have one and only one child element named to. This is because the to element does not have an occurrence indicator. No indicator means that it must appear once and only once. The next element, cc?, must appear once or not at all. Therefore, this element is optional. The next three elements (from, time, and subject) have no occurrence indicators and have commas separating them. The lack of indicator, again, means that they are mandatory, and the comma means that these elements must appear in the order they are listed.

For the next element, we have a nested term. Inside of the parentheses, we see that we can have either an element called dept or an element called deptID but not both. This is indicated by the vertical bar. Outside of the parentheses, we see a question mark, which means that this element may or may not occur. In other words, listing a department element is optional, but if one is listed, it must either be the elements dept or deptID but not both. The final element, message, is also mandatory, as we have it listed in our DTD.

Attributes

Our DTD must indicate not only the order and frequency of our XML elements but also the contents of any attributes that our elements may contain. On line 10, we see a declaration for the attribute clock for the element time. Attributes are declared using the general format: <!ATTLIST element-name attribute-name attribute-type default-value>. Our declaration states that time has an attribute called clock that can contain character data and that it is required.

CHAPTER SUMMARY

In this chapter, we learned how to create XML documents and their accompanying DTDs. We learned the syntactical requirements for constructing well-formed documents. We discussed how to create elements and attributes and how to process instructions. We also examined namespaces and their impact on expandability. We learned how to create document type definitions for validat-

ing documents. Specifically, we looked at the declaration of element definitions and their content models as well as the occurrence indicators and connectors.

KEY TERMS

attributes	markup tags
character data	namespaces
connectors	occurrence indicators
content model	processing instruction
document type definition (DTD)	Universal Resource
element	Identifier (URI)
element name	valid
Extensible Markup Language (XML)	well-formed

REVIEW QUESTIONS

1. List and explain the two parts of all XML elements.
2. What is the function of a namespace?
3. What are the major differences between a well-formed and a valid XML document?
4. Name at least three syntactical requirements that must be followed in order to have a well-formed XML document.
5. What is the function of a DTD?
6. How many root nodes can an XML document contain?
7. How can you denote that an element is empty by self-closing its markup tag?
8. How do a URL and a URI differ?
9. List the occurrence indicators and their impact.
10. What are two portions of an element declaration in a DTD?

EXERCISES

1. Assume you have a drawer with the following items inside of it: a book (which costs $5), a yellow pen (50¢), a red pen (20¢), and a stapler ($7). Create a well-formed XML document to track the name, the cost, and the color of each item in the drawer.
2. Now create a DTD to validate the document you created in Exercise 1.
3. Create a personal Web page in which all of the XHTML tags conform to the XML standard.
4. Rewrite the document portrayed in Figure 17.1 to include an optional attribute for the element <to>, which could be used to indicate if the recipient is male or female.
5. Create a DTD to reflect the change in the document you created for Exercise 4.

PROJECT

While the client never asked for the site to list local sporting events, we feel that this would help the cause of facilitating collaboration in the community. We will accomplish this by creating an additional page that shows this information using XML and XSL. Because the dates of sporting events are known well in advance and often do not change, we will not pull these values from a database. In this chapter, we will create the XML and in the next chapter the XSL necessary to display the information as XHTML. Do the following:

- Create a structure for an XML document that lists local sporting events. Track the two teams playing, the location, the time, and the type of sport.
- Create a sample XML document with this structure you created. Make sure to include at least five records in your XML document.
- Create a DTD that will be used to validate your document.

REFERENCES

Baatsee, M., Blair, R., et. al. 2000. *ASP XML*, Birmingham, U.K: Wrox Press.

Liberty, J., Kraley, M. 2000. *XML Web Document from Scratch*, Indianapolis: Que Publishing.

Marchal, B. 2000. *XML by Example*, Indianapolis: Que Publishing.

4 Guys From Rolla.com, www.4GuysFromRolla.com

ASP 101, www.ASP101.com

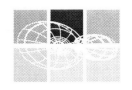

chapter 18
extensible stylesheet language

CHAPTER OVERVIEW

The Extensible Stylesheet Language (XSL) allows us to transform XML data into just about any number of forms including HTML, XHTML, and plain text. By utilizing different XSL documents to access the same XML data, it is possible to more efficiently create documents that rely on the same underlying data. This chapter covers the structure of XSL and how to integrate it with XML on both the client and the server. Emphasis is placed on the role of XSLT.

CHAPTER OBJECTIVES

- Create XSL documents
- Create XHTML output by combining XML using client-side technology
- Use server-side technology to integrate XML and XSL
- Use JavaScript to integrate XML and XSL
- Use match parameters to navigate the XML element tree structure
- Use content-selecting XSL functions

EXTENSIBLE STYLESHEET LANGUAGE

If we think of XML as a language to describe data, then we can think of *Extensible Stylesheet Language (XSL)* as the language that describes how to display that data. By manipulating XML data into any number of outputs, XSL can present the same information in various ways.

XSL is composed of two main technologies. The first, *XSLT (XSL Transformations)*, allows us to take the data contained inside of an XML document and change it into another form. This capability allows us to transform an XML document into HTML, XHTML, plain text, or even another XML document.

Many people indicate that it is possible to recreate HTML with XML. This is true, but the real power of XML becomes apparent when we need to show the same data in multiple ways. For example, if we have a list of real-estate properties in an XML document, we could use XSL to transform this data into an XHTML Web document, a Microsoft Word document, and a simple text document. As new houses are added to our XML document, all of the documents are automatically updated to reflect these changes. It is this advantage that favors XML/XSL over XHTML when multiple forms of output are needed from the same data.

XSL/FO (XSL Formatting Objects), the second technology that comprises XSL, allows us to describe how XML should be displayed. We can think of it as cascading style sheets for XML. In reality, XSL/FO is seldom used for displaying XML data for two main reasons. First, most vendors have not integrated support for XSL in their software. Neither Microsoft Internet Explorer 5.5 nor Netscape 6.0 fully implements XSLFO.

Before we look at XSL in action, let's briefly touch on the tools that we are going to need and the overall process. Before we can start, we will need access to an *XSL processor*. This software is responsible for integrating the results of XML and XSL. Some of the available XSL processors include Microsoft Internet Explorer 5.5, Netscape 6.0, and Lotus AlphaWorks. We will use the XSL processor included with Internet Explorer 5.5 for the examples in this chapter, due to its widespread market penetration.

At its most basic level, an XSL processor works by reading an XSL document and an XML document, integrating the two based on the instructions in the XSL document, and outputting the results. Figure 18.1 illustrates this process.

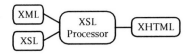

FIGURE 18.1: XML/XSL RELATIONSHIP WITH XSL PROCESSOR

In a more complex scenario, we have a single XML document that needs to be displayed in a multitude of forms (see Figure 18.2). In this case, our XML document contains a list of properties for sale by Ballinger Realty. We would like to create a text document and a Web page from the same data. As a result, we create two different stylesheets. One stylesheet will transform the XML into plain text and the other into XHTML. Notice that both access the same XML document and that the same XSL processor processes both sets of documents.

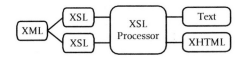

FIGURE 18.2: MULTIPLE STYLESHEETS FOR ONE XML DATA SOURCE

XSL STRUCTURE

Before we can delve into the world of XSL, we must have some XML document or data that our XSL can act upon. We will take the memo XML document we created in the last chapter and modify it for this purpose.

Open the memo.xml document from the last chapter and modify it to reflect Figure 18.3. We have made three main changes. First, we have changed the name of the root element from memo to memos. This was necessary because an XML document can have only one root element. We wanted to have multiple memo elements in our document. Thus, we had to place a node above all of the memo nodes in our tree. It did not have to be called memos; it just seemed logical to call it memos.

The second change occurs on line 2, where we explicitly set this document to use the document memo.xsl as its stylesheet. The third change was the addition of a second memo. Save the document as memo.xml when you make these changes.

```
<?xml version="1.0" encoding="ISO-8859-1"?>
<?xml-stylesheet type="text/xsl" href="memo.xsl"?>
<memos>
    <memo>
        <to>Dr. Bertoline</to>
        <cc />
        <from>
            <first>Carlos</first>
        <last>Morales</last>
        </from>
        <time clock="military">13:43</time>
        <subject>Resources</subject>
        <message>Resources are adequate</message>
    </memo>
    <memo>
        <to>Dr. Ballinger</to>
        <cc />
        <from>
            <first>Loke</first>
            <last>Dog</last>
        </from>
        <time clock="military">13:43</time>
        <subject>Need resources</subject>
        <message>We need more stuff</message>
    </memo>
</memos>
```

FIGURE 18.3: MEMO.XML

Now we can move on to creating an XSL document that will format our memo.xml document into an XHTML document. Type the following using your choice of editor and save it as memo.xsl.

1. We start by letting the XSL processor know that we will be using elements as described by the W3C XSL namespace.

```
<xsl:stylesheet xmlns:xsl="http://www.w3.org/TR/WD-xsl">
```

2. Now we select the root node of our XML document.

```
<xsl:template match="/">
```

3. Now we output regular XHTML.

```
<html>
    <head />
    <body>
```

```
<table border="2" bgcolor="green">
   <tr>
      <th>From</th>

      <th>Subject</th>

      <th>Message</th>
   </tr>
```

Note, the content does not need to be XHTML or HTML. It can be text if we wanted to produce a text document. But in this case, we want to create a Web page. So after we select the root node (line 2), we proceed to write out the HTML we want to output prior to outputting content from the XML elements.

4. Now begin to output content from the XML document into the XHTML document that we are creating.

```
<xsl:for-each select="memos/memo">
     <tr>
       <td bgcolor="yellow">
           <xsl:value-of select="from/first"/>
       </td>
       <td>
           <xsl:value-of select="subject"/>
       </td>
       <td>
<xsl:value-of select="message"/>
                 </td>
             </tr>
         </xsl:for-each>
```

We are telling the processor that we would like to repeat all of the lines in between these two for each instance of a memo inside of the element <memos>. The syntax for this is <xsl:for-each select="memos/memo">. Notice that because we had the root node selected, we had to go down two levels in our XML tree. First we went down to the element memos and then to the element memo. It is useful to think of the XML tree as an MS-DOS or Unix directory structure.

We then output table rows and cells. We then fill in the last table cell we created with the first name of the person who sent this memo. Recall that our memo.xml document has the first and last names of the sender as two elements, <first> and <last>, which are children of the element <from>. This is why we select this data by using <xsl:value-of select="from/first"/>. This statement says to select the contents of the ele-

ments held in from/first based on our current position in the document tree. We then repeat this procedure to select the contents of the elements <subject> and <message>. When the XSL processor hits the <xsl:value-of> tag, it reads values from the XML document and outputs them.

5. Finally, we close our table, the HTML document we are creating, our template, and the stylesheet.

```
            </table>
          </body>
        </html>
      </xsl:template>
    </xsl:stylesheet>
```

The final XSL document should look similar to Figure 18.4.

```
<xsl:stylesheet xmlns:xsl="http://www.w3.org/TR/WD-xsl">
    <xsl:template match="/">
        <html>
            <head />
            <body>
                <table border="2" bgcolor="green">
                    <tr>
                        <th>From</th>

                        <th>Subject</th>

                        <th>Message</th>
                    </tr>
                    <xsl:for-each select="memos/memo">
                        <tr>
                            <td bgcolor="yellow">
                              <xsl:value-of select="from/first"/>
                            </td>
                            <td>
                              <xsl:value-of select="subject"/>
                            </td>
                            <td>
                              <xsl:value-of select="message"/>
                            </td>
                        </tr>
                    </xsl:for-each>
                </table>
            </body>
        </html>
    </xsl:template>
</xsl:stylesheet>
```

FIGURE 18.4: MEMO.XSL

Open the memo.xml file you created with Microsoft Internet Explorer 5.0 or above. Make sure the memo.xsl document is in the same directory. It should look similar to Figure 18.5.

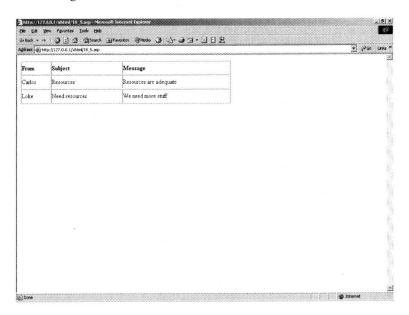

FIGURE 18.5   XML/XSL RESULTANT PAGE

Let's quickly recap how we arrived at the document depicted in Figure 18.5. We started by modifying the memo.xml document from the last chapter to allow us to include multiple memo elements. We did this to satisfy the requirement of having only one root node per XML document. We then set the stylesheet for our XML document to memo.xsl. When we ask Internet Explorer 5.5 to display memo.xml, it encounters the directive to use the memo.xsl stylesheet. This is why MS IE 5.5 showed us a table instead of the tree structure that we saw with our XML documents in the last chapter. If you have MS IE 5.5 show you the source code, you will notice that it is XML and not XHTML or HTML.

The second document we typed, memo.xsl, contained the instructions for what data out of the XML document should be displayed and how it should be displayed. Notice that while our memo.xml document contained all types of information about the memos, we decided to show only the first name, subject, and actual message for each memo. Let's step through our XSL and see how it functions.

XSL SYNTAX

Now that we have seen how XML and XSL are integrated, let's take a more formal look at the syntax of XSL. We should notice that XSL documents are themselves XML documents and follow the rules for well-formed XML documents. Each stylesheet is composed of *template tags*, which in turn are composed of match parameters and content. The *match parameter* indicates the path to the element in the XML tree. The content indicates what content should be output. On line 20 of our XSL document, we have

```
<xsl:value-of select="subject"/>
```

The content of this template is value-of, which outputs the actual content held by the selected element. The match parameter of this template is "subject". The match parameter is always preceded by select=.

As we have indicated the XML document creates a tree structure, with the root element of the XML document serving as the trunk. We can move through the tree much as we would in an MS-DOS or Unix directory.

XML/XSL INTEGRATION OPTIONS

Thus far, we have used the XSL processor in MS IE 5.5 to integrate our XML and XSL on the client side. We have also hard-coded our XML document to use a specific stylesheet by putting the stylesheet declaration inside of our XML document. Look at line 2 of the memo.xml document. There you will find <?xml-stylesheet type="text/xsl" href="memo.xsl"?> . This tells the parser to always use the file memo.xsl as a stylesheet.

Neither of these choices is very sound. First, we are requiring users to not only have Microsoft Internet Explorer 5.5 on their machine but also use it to access our site. There are many users who do not have MS IE 5.5 on their computer, or they may have it loaded but prefer to use Netscape. Second, we have tied our XML data source to one specific form of output. The parser would never allow you to output a Web page and a simple text document out of our memo.xml document because the document explicitly states to use the stylesheet memo.xsl. The output will look as prescribed in that memo.xsl file.

The solution to both of these issues lies in understanding how and where the XML and XSL documents are being integrated. In our previous example, we asked Internet Explorer to read both the XML and XSL documents. Both documents were sent to the user's browser where the MS IE XSL processor then integrated both of these and showed them to the user. The advantage of this method is that it is easy to implement for the Web developer. But, as we have seen, it has the disadvantage of dictating to users the software they will use.

JAVASCRIPT XML/XSL INTEGRATION

We can also integrate the XML and XSL on the client side using the Microsoft IE XMLDOM object. In other words, we can use the same engine that MS IE 5.5 uses to integrate our document. The advantage is that we no longer have to tie our XML document to one specific stylesheet and that we can use this method with Netscape. We are still using the IE 5.5 engine. So the user must have MS IE 5.5 loaded on their machine, but they do not have to use it.

Let's see this at work. Change the memo.xml file you typed earlier to read as shown below. We have deleted the second line, <?xml-stylesheet type="text/xsl" href="memo.xsl"?>, which tied our XML document to a specific XSL document. Now we can use this XML document with any stylesheet.

```
<?xml version="1.0" encoding="ISO-8859-1"?>
<memos>
        <memo>
                <to>Dr. Bertoline</to>
                <cc />
                <from>
                        <first>Carlos</first>
                        <last>Morales</last>
                </from>
                <time clock="military">13:43</time>
                <subject>Resources</subject>
                <message>Resources are adequate</message>
        </memo>
        <memo>
                <to>Dr. Ballinger</to>
                <cc />
                <from>
                        <first>Loke</first>
                        <last>Dog</last>
                </from>
```

```
                    <time clock="military">13:43</time>
                    <subject>Need resources</subject>
                    <message>We need more stuff</message>
          </memo>
</memos>
```

FIGURE 18.6: MODIFIED MEMO.XML DOCUMENT

Now create a file named memo.html and type the code shown below. We are going to use the *MS XMLDOM object* using JavaScript to merge our XML and XSL documents.

1. Create an HTML document with proper headers.

```
<html>
<head/>
<body>
```

2. Set our scripting language to JavaScript.

```
<script language="javascript">
```

3. Instantiate a copy of the MS XMLDOM object.

```
var xml = new ActiveXObject("Microsoft.XMLDOM")
xml.async = false
```

We create an instance of the Microsoft XMLDOM object and assign it to a variable called xml. The XMLDOM object is supplied by MS IE 5.5 and can be used by any program on the machine to process XML and XSL. Then we set the async property of the object we created to false. This lets the object know that this is not an asynchronous load and therefore it should wait until the entire document is loaded into memory before it proceeds.

4. Load the memo.xml document.

```
xml.load("memo.xml")
```

We instruct the object to load our XML document into memory. Had we set the async property to true, the object would perform the next instruction even if our file had been fully loaded into memory.

5. Instantiate another copy of the MS XMLDOM object.

```
var xsl = new ActiveXObject("Microsoft.XMLDOM")
xsl.async = false
```

We then repeat this same thing for our XSL document. Remember that an XSL document is formatted just like an XML document. That is why loading it into memory is done the same way that we used to load the memo.xml document. Notice that the name of the variable we used to hold the XSL document is xsl.

6. Load the memo.xsl document.

```
xsl.load("memo.xsl")
```

7. Integrate the two documents.

```
document.write(xml.transformNode(xsl))
```

This line actually combines the XML and XSL to create the XHTML. We use the transformNode method of the object holding the document and pass it the variable holding the XSL document. In other words, this command is all that it takes for the processor to create the output.

8. Close the document.

```
</script>
</body>
</html>
```

Using JavaScript to integrate our XML with XSL on the client side frees up the hard link between the XML and XSL. By constructing multiple stylesheets and then changing which one we load, the JavaScript method allows us to show the same XML document in multiple ways. Figure 18.7 shows the final code.

```
<html>
<head/>
<body>
<script language="javascript">

var xml = new ActiveXObject("Microsoft.XMLDOM")
xml.async = false
xml.load("memo.xml")

var xsl = new ActiveXObject("Microsoft.XMLDOM")
xsl.async = false
xsl.load("memo.xsl")

document.write(xml.transformNode(xsl))
</script>
```

```
</body>
</html>
```

FIGURE 18.7: JAVASCRIPT XML/XSL INTEGRATION

Open the memo.html file with either Netscape or Internet Explorer. The resulting page will still look similar to the one depicted in Figure 18.8. Note that this will not work on a Macintosh because ActiveX technology is not available on that platform.

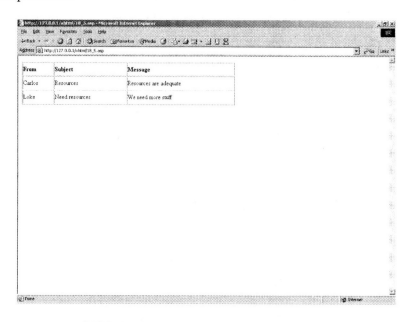

FIGURE 18.8: JAVASCRIPT XML/XSL INTEGRATION RESULTS

ASP SERVER-SIDE XML/XSL INTEGRATION

Using JavaScript on the server still requires users to have a copy of Microsoft Internet Explorer 5.5 on their computer and only works on PCs. A better method would be to combine the XML and XSL on the server and then send the resulting XHTML to the user's browser. We can do this by using ASP and MS IE 5.5 on the server. Any program on the same machine can use the XMLDOM object that comes with MS IE 5.5. We can capitalize on this by loading MS IE 5.5 on the same machine as our Web server and then processing our XML/XSL there.

As we saw during our earlier encounter with ASP code, you will need access to a machine running Microsoft Internet Information Server for this code to work.

Create a directory inside of the IIS wwwroot folder called XMLExample. Copy the memo.xml and memo.xsl files into this directory. Now create a file named memo.asp and type the code shown below.

1. Declare the language for our ASP document as VBScript.

```
<%@ Language="VBScript" %>
```

2. Instantiate a copy of the MS XMLDOM object.

```
set xml = Server.CreateObject("Microsoft.XMLDOM")
xml.async = false
```

This is the same object that we used on the client's machine with Java-Script to integrate our XML and XSL.

3. Load the memo.xml document.

```
xml.load(Server.MapPath("memo.xml"))
```

4. Instantiate another copy of the MS XMLDOM object.

```
set xsl = Server.CreateObject("Microsoft.XMLDOM")
xsl.async = false
```

We then repeat this same thing for our XSL document. Remember that an XSL document is formatted just like an XML document. That is why loading it into memory is done the same way that we used to load the memo.xml document. Notice that the name of the variable we used to hold the XSL document is xsl.

5. Load the memo.xsl document.

```
xsl.load(Server.MapPath("memo.xsl"))
```

6. Integrate the two documents.

```
document.write(xml.transformNode(xsl))
```

While the object that redirects the output to the screen has changed for our JavaScript example, the object that actually integrates the XML and XSL has remained the same.

7. Destroy the objects.

```
Set xml=nothing
Set xsl=nothing
%>
```

The final code is shown in Figure 18.9.

```
<%@ Language="VBScript" %>
<%

set xml = Server.CreateObject("Microsoft.XMLDOM")
xml.async = false
xml.load(Server.MapPath("memo.xml"))

set xsl = Server.CreateObject("Microsoft.XMLDOM")
xsl.async = false
xsl.load(Server.MapPath("memo.xsl"))

theHTML= xml.transformNode(xsl)
Response.Write(theHTML)

Set xml=nothing
Set xsl=nothing
%>
```

FIGURE 18.9: ASP CODE OF XML/XSL INTEGRATION

CHAPTER SUMMARY

In this chapter, we learned how to integrate XML and XSL using a variety of different techniques including browser-based client-side technology; JavaScript-based, client-side scripting; and ASP-based, server-side scripting. We created XSL documents that navigated and selected content from an XML document. We also learned the syntax of XSL and the relationship of XSL to XSLT and XSL/FO.

KEY TERMS

Extensible Stylesheet Language
  (XSL)
match parameter
MS XMLDOM object

template tag
XSL Transformations (XSLT)
XSL Formatting Objects (XSL/FO)
XSL processor

REVIEW QUESTIONS

1. What are the two components of XSL?
2. Of the methods presented for integrating XML and XSL, which one would work across all browsers and why?
3. What statement is used by XSL to select the root node of an XML document?
4. What statement is used by XSL to select the contents of an XML element?
5. What are two advantages of using JavaScript on the client side to integrate XSL and XML over using a server-side approach?
6. Why can XSLT be used to accomplish much of what XSL/FO is meant to do?

EXERCISES

1. Create an XML document with contact information for your friends. Include their first name, last name, street, city, and phone number. Call it friends.xml.
2. Now create an XSL document that formats friends.xml into XHTML using Internet Explorer 5.5. Only display the first name and phone number of each person. Call this XSL document friends1.xsl.
3. Now create a second XSL document that also uses friends.xml as a data source, but this time your output should display last names and streets. Call this XSL document friends2.xsl.
4. Now create an HTML document that uses JavaScript to integrate the XML and the XSL. Include a link at the bottom of the document to allow the user to select between friends1.xsl and friends2.xsl.
5. Now create an ASP page that displays friends.xml using friends.xsl. Make sure to transform the XML into XHTML on the server.

PROJECT

Next, we need to take the XML document we developed in Chapter 17 and display it to the user through the use of XSL. We want to reach the widest possible audience. As a result, we should do XML/XSL transformation on the server and send just XHTML to the client. Do the following:

- Create an XSL document to transform your XML document into XHTML. Make sure the resulting XHTML fits into the look you have developed for your site.

REFERENCES

Baatsee, M., Blair, R., et. al. 2000. *ASP XML*, Birmingham, U.K.: Wrox Press.

Liberty, J., Kraley, M. 2000. *XML Web Document from Scratch*, Indianapolis: Que Publishing.

Marchal, B. 2000. *XML by Example*, Indianapolis: Que Publishing.

4 Guy From Rolla.com, www.4GuysFromRolla.com

ASP 101, www.ASP101.com

XHTML elements

<!-- ... -->

Definition:	Comments can be used to help organize or clarify parts of an XHTML document. Comments are not displayed and have no impact on the functioning of the document.
Syntax:	<!-- content -->
Attributes:	None.
Events:	None.
Example:	

```
<!-- Author: Joe Designer -->
<!-- Purpose: Demonstrate Basic XHTML Document  -->
<!-- Last Update: May 1, 2002  -->
```

<!DOCTYPE>

Definition:	The <!DOCTYPE> element indicates what DTD the document is validated against. This element appears at the top of the XHTML document.
Syntax:	<!DOCTYPE top element name of DTD URL to DTD>
Attributes:	None.
Events:	None.
Example:	

```
<!DOCTYPE html PUBLIC "-//W3C//DTD/XHTML 1.0 Transitional//EN"
"http://www.w3.org/TR/xhtml1/DTD/xhtml1-transitional.dtd">
```

This <!DOCTYPE> element contains the following parts:

- html—indicates that <html> is the root element and will contain all other elements within the document.
- PUBLIC—identifies the name of the DTD, in this case it is "-//W3C//DTD/XHTML 1.0 Transitional//EN". The EN at the end of the name indicates that the DTD is written in English.
- The URL—indicates where the browser can locate the DTD by providing a URL.

<a>...</a>

Definition:	The anchor element allows an XHTML document to attach or anchor itself to another document in the various locations. The text that is between the opening <a> tag and the closing </a> tag is the link that will be highlighted and underlined for the user to click.
Syntax:	<a attributes> content </a>
Attributes:	**charset** ="character set". Used to specify character encoding of the linked page.
	href ="location of linked document". Used to specify the location of the document to be linked. This location is usually an URL.
	name ="text". Used to specify certain points within the document that are available as targets of links.
	rel ="link type". Used to define the link relationship between the current document and the destination document.
	target ="_blank	_self	_ parent	_ top". Used to identify where the linked document is to be opened.

_blank	This attribute opens the selected file in a new browser window.
_self	This attribute instructs the browser to open the file in the current frame.
_parent	This attribute instructs the browser to replace the current document (frameset) with the new file.
_top	This attribute instructs the browser to clear all current frames and load the new page into the main browser window.

Standard Attributes: id, class, title, style, dir, lang

Events: onblur, onclick, ondblclick, onfocus, onkeydown, onkeypress, onkeyup, onmousedown, onmouseup, onmouseover, onmousemove, onmouseout

Example:
```
<a href = "http://www.fbeedle.com">Click for the FBA home
page.</a>
```

<abbr>...</abbr>

Definition: A descriptive element that indicates the abbreviation of a word. The text used with this element is usually rendered as italics or plain text.

Syntax: <abbr attributes> content </abbr>

Attributes: title ="expansion of abbreviation". Used to show the expanded form of the expression when the mouse is held over the abbreviation.

Standard Attributes: id, class, title, style, dir, lang

Events: onclick, ondblclick, onkeydown, onkeypress, onkeyup, onmousedown, onmouseup, onmouseover, onmousemove, onmouseout

Example:
```
<abbr title = "Indiana">IN</abbr>
```

<acronym>...</acronym>

Definition: A descriptive element that indicates a word that is formed by using the initial letters of several words. The text used with this element is usually rendered as italics or plain text.

Syntax: <acronym attributes> content </acronym>

Attributes: title ="expansion of acronym". Used to show the expanded form of the acronym when the mouse is held over the acronym.

Standard Attributes: id, class, title, style, dir, lang

Events: onclick, ondblclick, onkeydown, onkeypress, onkeyup, onmousedown, onmouseup, onmouseover, onmousemove, onmouseout

Example:
```
<acronym title = "Program Development Life Cycle">PDLC</acronym>
```

<address>...</address>

Definition: This element provides a special format for defining addresses, signatures, or authors of documents.

Syntax: <address attributes> content </address>

Standard Attributes: id, class, title, style, dir, lang

Events: onclick, ondblclick, onkeydown, onkeypress, onkeyup, onmousedown, onmouseup, onmouseover, onmousemove, onmouseout

Example:
```
<address>Joe Programmer, 2300 South Washington Street, Kokomo,
IN, 46902. Email: Joe Programmer@anywhere.net</address>
```

\<area>...\</area>

Definition: The \<area> element is an empty element used to specify the hotspot of a client-side image map. Since \<area> is an empty element and does not have a closing tag, it must be terminated properly in XHTML by adding a space and a slash before the closing angle bracket.

Syntax: \<area shape="shape name" coords="coordinate values" href="link" alt="description of hotspot" />

Attributes: **coords** ="coordinate values". Used to specify coordinates of the hotspot. The values of this attribute depend on the value used for the shape attribute. Coordinates are expressed in pixels and are listed separated by commas.

href ="location of linked document". Used to specify the location of the document that is to be linked to for display. This location is usually a URL.

shape ="shape name". Used to specify the shape of the mapped area. If no shape attribute is given, the default value is rect. The possible values of the shape attribute are rect, circle, poly, and default. The default is any area not covered by another \<area> element. When an area is set up using the default shape, the user clicking outside of one of the hotspots will activate the URL setup for the default.

alt ="alternate text". The value of this attribute is a text description of the defined hotspot. This text is displayed when an image is encountered by a non-graphical browser or a browser that has graphics disabled.

target ="_blank | _self | _parent | _top". Used to identify where the linked document is to be opened.

    _blank   This attribute opens the selected file in a new browser window.

    _self   This attribute instructs the browser to open the file in the current frame.

    _parent This attribute instructs the browser to replace the current document (frameset) with the new file.

    _top   This attribute instructs the browser to clear all current frames and load the new page into the main browser window.

Standard Attributes: id, class, title, style, dir, lang

Events: onblur, onclick, ondblclick, onfocus, onkeydown, onkeypress, onkeyup, onmousedown, onmouseup, onmouseover, onmousemove, onmouseout

Example:
```
<map id="shapes"name="shapes">
            <area shape="rect" coords="52,54,196,1126"
      href="rectangle.html" alt="rectangle hotspot" />
            <area shape="poly"
coords="326,52,326,182,404,222,450,147,393,129,389,55"
href="polygon.html" alt="polygon hotspot" />
<area shape="circle" coords="217,238,x" href="circle.html"
alt="circle hotspot" />
</map>
```

\<b>...\</b>

Definition: This is a physical element used to render text in a boldface font style.

Syntax: \<b attributes> content \</b>

Attributes: None.

Standard Attributes: id, class, title, style, dir, lang

Events: onclick, ondblclick, onkeydown, onkeypress, onkeyup, onmousedown, onmouseup, onmouseover, onmousemove, onmouseout

Example: `<div>This is the <b>bold</b> style.</div>`

\<base /\>

Definition:	This element is used to specify a base URL for all hyperlinks used in the document. This element does not have a closing tag, so should be closed by using a forward slash before the closing angle bracket. When the base is not specified, the browser uses the current document URL. The base element must be in the head element and be before any references to external resources.
Attributes:	**href** ="location of linked document". Used to specify the base location for relative linked documents. This location is usually a URL.
	target ="_blank | _self | _parent | _top". Used to identify where the linked document is to be opened.

	_blank	This attribute opens the selected file in a new browser window.
	_self	This attribute instructs the browser to open the file in the current frame.
	_parent	This attribute instructs the browser to replace the current document (frameset) with the new file.
	_top	This attribute instructs the browser to clear all current frames and load the new page into the main browser window.

Standard Attributes:	none.
Events:	none.
Example:	`<head>`
	`  <base href ="http://www.fbeedle.com"/>`
	`</head>`

\<big\>...\</big\>

Definition:	This is a physical element used to render text in a larger font size.
Syntax:	<big attributes> content </big>
Attributes:	None.
Standard Attributes:	id, class, title, style, dir, lang
Events:	onclick, ondblclick, onkeydown, onkeypress, onkeyup, onmousedown, onmouseup, onmouseover, onmousemove, onmouseout
Example:	`<div>This is the <big>big</big> style.</div>`

\<blockquote\>...\</blockqoute\>

Definition:	This element is a container element that will enclose a block of text that is to be treated as a quote. White space is created on both sides of the text and is usually indented.
Syntax:	<blockquote attributes> content </blockquote>
Attributes:	**cite** ="location of linked document". Used to specify the URL source of the quote.
Standard Attributes:	id, class, title, style, dir, lang
Events:	onclick, ondblclick, onkeydown, onkeypress, onkeyup, onmousedown, onmouseup, onmouseover, onmousemove, onmouseout
Example:	`<blockquote>`
	`"The Surgeon General of the United States has determined that the consumption of alcoholic beverages impairs your ability to drive a car or operate machinery, and may cause health problems"`
	`</blockquote>`

<body>...</body>

Definition: The body element is a container element that will contain several other elements that are used to describe the content of the Web page. It contains the largest part of the document.

Syntax: <body attributes> content </body>

Attributes: **background** ="URL". Specifies the location of a background image to be displayed.

bgcolor ="color". Sets the background color of the document. The color value can be expressed by using the RGB hexadecimal format (rrggbb = hexadecimal color value) or by using a predefined color name.

text ="color". Sets the text color of the document. The color value can be expressed by using the RGB hexadecimal format (rrggbb = hexadecimal color value) or by using a predefined color name.

link ="color". Used to set the link color in the document. The color value can be expressed by using the RGB hexadecimal format (rrggbb = hexadecimal color value) or by using a predefined color name.

vlink ="color". Used to set the visited link color in the document. The color value can be expressed by using the RGB hexadecimal format (rrggbb = hexadecimal color value) or by using a predefined color name.

alink ="color". Used to set the active link color in the document. The color value can be expressed by using the RGB hexadecimal format (rrggbb = hexadecimal color value) or by using a predefined color name.

Note: The above presentation attributes have been depreciated in favor of style sheets.

Standard Attributes: id, class, title, style, dir, lang

Events: onload, onunload, onclick, ondblclick, onkeydown, onkeypress, onkeyup, onmousedown, onmouseup, onmouseover, onmousemove, onmouseout

Example:
```
<head>
<title>  Using Paragraphs </title>
</head>
<body>
    <p>
This is a basic XHTML document that has two paragraphs. They
may be simple, but I think they will get the point across. This
is the first paragraph.
    </p>
    <p>
This is the second paragraph of our document. It has one blank
line before it starts. I also included carriage returns, blank
lines, and indentations.
    </p>
</body>
```


Definition: Used to insert a single line break. This element is an empty element used to end a line of text and start the next line at the left margin. The <br /> element will not include an extra space before or after the new line. It can be placed at any point within a line of text and the break occurs when the tag is encountered.

Syntax: <br attributes />

Standard Attributes: id, class, title, style

Example:
```
<p>
This is a basic XHTML document that has two paragraphs.<br
/> They may be simple, but I think they will get the point
across.<br /> This is the first paragraph.
</p>
```

<button>...</button>

Definition:	Used to define a push button on a web page.
Syntax:	<button attributes> content </button>
Attributes:	**disabled** = "disabled". Used to identify that the button is unavailable.
	name = "button name". Used to provide a name for the button allowing it to be used in a form or script.
	type = "button	submit	reset". Used to specify the type of button to be created.

    button   This value is used to create a push button.

    submit   This value is used to create a submit button.

    reset   This value is used to create a reset button.

    value = "data value". Used to assign an initial value.

Standard Attributes: id, class, title, style, dir, lang

<caption>...</caption>

Definition:	The table caption element specifies a title for the table and that it is centered either above or below the table, depending upon the align attribute.
Syntax:	<caption attributes> content </caption>
Attributes:	**align** ="top"	"bottom"	"left"	"right". Used to align the table caption relative to the table.
Standard Attributes:	id, class, title, style, dir, lang
Events:	onclick, ondblclick, onkeydown, onkeypress, onkeyup, onmousedown, onmouseup, onmouseover, onmousemove, onmouseout

Example:
```
<table>
<caption>Favorite Fruits</caption>
<tr>
   <td>Apples</td>
   <td>Oranges</td>
   <td>Bananas</td>
</tr>
</table>
```

<cite>...</cite>

Definition:	This element is used to indicate a quotation or citation. The text used with this element is usually rendered as italics.
Syntax:	<cite attributes> content </cite>
Attributes:	None.
Standard Attributes:	id, class, title, style, dir, lang
Events:	onclick, ondblclick, onkeydown, onkeypress, onkeyup, onmousedown, onmouseup, onmouseover, onmousemove, onmouseout

Example:
```
<cite>Jeff Griffin</cite> was one of the authors who wrote the
second edition of the Web Page Workbook.
```

\<code>...\</code>

Definition:	The code element is a descriptive element that is used to indicate programming code. The text content used with this element is usually rendered as a monospaced font. When multiple lines of code need to be displayed, it should be formatted as `pre`.
Syntax:	\<code attributes> text content \</code>
Attributes:	None.
Standard Attributes:	id, class, title, style, dir, lang
Events:	onclick, ondblclick, onkeydown, onkeypress, onkeyup, onmousedown, onmouseup, onmouseover, onmousemove, onmouseout
Example:	`<code>If ( a == b)</code>`

\<col>...\</col>

Definition:	This element is an empty element that allows for a structure to be defined within a \<colgroup> element. This will allow us to format individual columns of a group. When this element is not used, columns inherit all their attribute values from the column group. This element is not used to provide a structural grouping, but groups columns to share attribute values.
Syntax:	\<col attributes />
Attributes:	**align** ="center" | "justify" | "left" | "right". Used to horizontally align the contents of cells.
	width ="pixels" | "percent". It is used to specify the width (in pixels or percentage) of each column, which is spanned by the col element. This attribute will override any width set in the colgroup element.
	valign ="top" | "middle" | "bottom" | "baseline". Vertically aligns text at the top or the bottom of the cell.
	span ="number of columns". Used to set the number of columns that the col element spans. The spanned columns will inherit the attributes from the col element.
Standard Attributes:	id, class, title, style, dir, lang
Events:	onclick, ondblclick, onkeydown, onkeypress, onkeyup, onmousedown, onmouseup, onmouseover, onmousemove, onmouseout
Example:	

```
<table>
<colgroup width="10%"></colgroup>
<colgroup span="3">
   <col align="left" width="20%"/>
   <col align="center" width="30%"/>
   <col align="right" width="40%"/>
</colgroup>
<tr>
   <td>1</td>
   <td>2</td>
   <td>3</td>
   <td>4</td>
</tr>
</table>
```

\<colgroup>...\</colgroup>

Definition:	An empty element that creates column groups, which allows for formatting of grouped columns.

Syntax:	<colgroup attributes > content </colgroup> or <colgroup attributes /> content
Attributes:	**align** ="center" | "justify" | "left" | "right". Used to horizontally align the contents of cells in the colgroup. **width** ="pixels" | "percent". Used to specify the width (in pixels or percentage) of the colgroup. **valign** ="top" | "middle" | "bottom" | "baseline". Vertically aligns contents of the cells in the colgroup. **span** ="number of columns". Used to set the number of columns that the colgroup should span.
Standard Attributes:	id, class, title, style, dir, lang
Events:	onclick, ondblclick, onkeydown, onkeypress, onkeyup, onmousedown, onmouseup, onmouseover, onmousemove, onmouseout
Example:	

```
<table>
<colgroup width="10%"></colgroup>
<colgroup span="3">
   <col align="left" width="20%"/>
   <col align="center" width="30%"/>
   <col align="right" width="40%"/>
</colgroup>
<tr>
   <td>1</td>
   <td>2</td>
   <td>3</td>
   <td>4</td>
</tr>
</table>
```

<dd>...</dd>

Definition:	This element is a container element that will enclose text that is to be treated as the definition of the term. It is part of a definition list.
Syntax:	<dd attributes > content </dd>
Attributes:	None.
Standard Attributes:	id, class, title, style, dir, lang
Events:	onclick, ondblclick, onkeydown, onkeypress, onkeyup, onmousedown, onmouseup, onmouseover, onmousemove, onmouseout
Example:	

```
<body>
<p>Here is a definition list</p>
  <dl>
     <dt>Orange</dt>
        <dd>Juicy citrus fruit with reddish yellow rind</dd>
     <dt>Apple</dt>
        <dd>A rounded fruit with firm white flesh</dd>
     <dt>Banana</dt>
        <dd>A yellow or reddish finger-shaped fruit</dd>
  </dl>
</body>
```

\<div>...\</div>

Definition:	This element is used to divide an XHTML document into sections and allows information within that section to be aligned. The \<div> element is very useful when using style sheets, but also is an effective way to handle a block of text when not using style sheets. The \<div> element allows for aligning entire sections of text as well as adding style to the same.
Syntax:	\<div attributes > content \</div>
Attributes:	**align** ="center" | "justify" | "left" | "right". Used to horizontally align the text content.
Standard Attributes:	id, class, title, style, dir, lang
Events:	onclick, ondblclick, onkeydown, onkeypress, onkeyup, onmousedown, onmouseup, onmouseover, onmousemove, onmouseout
Example:	

```
<div align = "center">
 This book is a practical approach to web design and coding
</div>
<div>
 This is the second division.
</div>
```

\<dl>...\</dl>

Definition:	This element is a container element that will enclose a block of text that is formatted with the \<dt> and \<dd> elements.
Syntax:	\<dl attributes > content \</dl>
Attributes:	None.
Standard Attributes:	id, class, title, style, dir, lang
Events:	onclick, ondblclick, onkeydown, onkeypress, onkeyup, onmousedown, onmouseup, onmouseover, onmousemove, onmouseout
Example:	

```
<dl>
<dt>Orange</dt>
  <dd>Juicy citrus fruit with reddish yellow rind</dd>
<dt>Apple</dt>
  <dd>A rounded fruit with firm white flesh</dd>
<dt>Banana</dt>
  <dd>A yellow or reddish finger-shaped fruit</dd>
  </dl>
```

\<dt>...\</dt>

Definition:	This element is a container element that will enclose text that is to be treated as the term to be defined.
Syntax:	\<dt attributes > content \</dt>
Attributes:	None.
Standard Attributes:	id, class, title, style, dir, lang
Events:	onclick, ondblclick, onkeydown, onkeypress, onkeyup, onmousedown, onmouseup, onmouseover, onmousemove, onmouseout

Example: `<dl>`
`<dt>Orange</dt>`
`  <dd>Juicy citrus fruit with reddish yellow rind</dd>`
`<dt>Apple</dt>`
`  <dd>A rounded fruit with firm white flesh</dd>`
`<dt>Banana</dt>`
`  <dd>A yellow or reddish finger-shaped fruit</dd>`
`</dl>`

`<em>`...`</em>`

Definition:	This element is used to indicate some text is to be emphasized. The text used with this element is usually rendered as italics.
Syntax:	`<em attributes > content </em>`
Attributes:	None.
Standard Attributes:	id, class, title, style, dir, lang
Events:	onclick, ondblclick, onkeydown, onkeypress, onkeyup, onmousedown, onmouseup, onmouseover, onmousemove, onmouseout
Example:	`<div>This is the <em>emphasis</em> style.</div>`

`<font>`...`</font>`

Definition:	This element is used to specify a font size, color, or typeface. Although this element is still widely used, it has been depreciated in favor of style sheets.
Syntax:	`<font attributes> content </font>`
Attributes:	**color** ="#rrggbb" | "colorname". The color value can be expressed by using the RGB hexadecimal format (rrggbb = hexadecimal color value) or by using a predefined color name.
	size ="n" | "+n" | "-n". Used to set the font size where "n" is a size between 1 (smallest) and 7 (largest). To increase or decrease the font size relative to the base font, a plus or minus is placed in front of the number.
	face ="name of font, name of font..". Used to specify one or more typefaces.
Standard Attributes:	id, class, title, style, dir, lang
Example:	`<font size ="3">Go Boilers</font>`

`<form>`...`</form>`

Definition:	This element is used to specify the layout of a form and contains the controls used for user input. It also will determine how the submitted form will be handled.
Syntax:	`<form attributes > content </form>`
Attributes:	**action** ="URL". Mandatory. It determines where form content is sent when the submit button is selected.
	method ="get" | "post". This attribute indicates how to send the information to the server. When get is specified, the form's data will be appended to the form's URL separated by a question mark (url?form_data). When the form's input is greater than 100 characters or it contains non-ASCII characters the post method must be used. The post allows more information to be transferred by sending a message block.
	enctype ="mime type". Used to specify the format for encoding the submitted data.
	accept ="mime type list". Used to specify a comma-separated list of the mime types accepted by the server.
	target ="_blank | _self | _ parent | _ top". Used to identify where the linked document is to be opened.

_blank   This attribute opens the selected file in a new browser window.

_self   This attribute instructs the browser to open the link in the current frame.

_parent This attribute instructs the browser to replace the current document (frameset) with the new file.

_top   This attribute instructs the browser to clear all current frames and load the new page into the main browser window.

Standard Attributes: id, class, title, style, dir, lang

Events: onsubmit, onreset, onclick, ondblclick, onkeydown, onkeypress, onkeyup, onmousedown, onmouseup, onmouseover, onmousemove, onmouseout

Example:
```
<form name="info" action="mailto:user@company.com" enctype="text/
plain"    onSubmit="return validate();">
  <p>
    <b>Student Name:</b>
    <input type="text" length="25" name="studentname" />
  </p>
  <p>
    <b>Age:</b>
    <input type="text" length="3" name="age" />
  </p>
  <p>
    <b>E-mail:</b>
    <input type="text" length="15" name="email" />
  </p>
  <p>
    <input type="SUBMIT" value="Submit" />
  </p>
</form>
```

<frame />

Definition: Defines a single frame within the frameset and identifies the content to be placed within that frame.

Syntax: <frame attributes />

Attributes: **src** ="source". Specifies the source URL of the document that will become the content of the frame.

name ="frame name". Used to define a name for an individual frame. This name can be used as a target of hyperlinks in the <a>, <form>, <area>, and <base> elements.

scrolling ="yes | no | auto". By default scrollbars are displayed for frames when their content exceeds the allotted space. The frame scrolling attribute will give you control over the appearance of scrollbars for each frame.

noresize ="noresize". When using the noresize attribute, the user will not be allowed to alter the frame size. This attribute takes its own name as a value.

marginheight ="pixels". Used to specify the amount of separation (in pixels) between the border of a frame and the frame's content. When marginheight is used the white space around any content will be at the top and the bottom.

marginwidth ="pixels". Used to specify the amount of separation (in pixels) between the border of a frame and the frames content. When marginwidth is used the white space around the content will be on the sides.

longdesc ="url". Provides a link to a long description of the frame.

frameborder ="0 | 1 ". Determines if borders are drawn around the frame.

Standard Attributes: id, class, title, style
Example:

```
<frameset cols="33%,33%,34%">
  <frame src="frame1.html" noresize="noresize"/>
  <frame src="frame2.html"/>
  <frame src="frame3.html"/>
</frameset>
```

\<frameset>...\</frameset>

Definition:	Determines the frame structure, and the number and size of frames that will be displayed within a document.
Syntax:	\<frameset attributes > content \</ frameset>
Attributes:	**cols** ="pixels | % | * ". Used to define the size of each column.
	rows =" pixels | % | * ". This list defines the size of each row.
Standard Attributes:	id, class, title, style
Events:	onload, onunload

Example:

```
<frameset cols="33%,33%,34%">
  <frame src="frame1.html"/>
  <frame src="frame2.html"/>
  <frame src="frame3.html"/>
</frameset>
```

\<h1>...\</h1> through \<h6>...\</h6>

Definition:	The heading element is a container element that will enclose text used for document headings. XHTML allows six levels of headings numbered 1 through 6.
Syntax:	\<hn attributes > content \</ hn>
Attributes:	**align** ="center" | "justify" | "left" | "right". Used to horizontally align the text content.
Standard Attributes:	id, class, title, style, dir, lang
Events:	onclick, ondblclick, onkeydown, onkeypress, onkeyup, onmousedown, onmouseup, onmouseover, onmousemove, onmouseout

Example:

```
<h1>Level 1 headings are the Largest</h1>
<h2>Level 2 heading</h2>
<h3>Level 3 heading</h3>
<h4>Level 4 heading</h4>
<h5>Level 5 heading</h5>
<h6>Level 6 headings are the Smallest</h6>
```

\<head>...\</head>

Definition:	The head element is a container element that can contain several other elements that are used to describe a Web page. The information contained within the \<head> element is usually not displayed as Web page content.
Syntax:	\<head attributes > content \</ head>
Attributes:	**profile** ="url". Used to specify a location that contains meta-data information about the page.
Standard Attributes:	dir, lang

Example:

```
<html xmlns="http://www.w3.org/1999/xhtml" xml:lang="en"
lang="en">
<head>
```

```
<title>Basic XHTML Document Structure</title>
</head>
<body>
</body>
</html>
```

\<hr />

Definition:	This element is an empty element used to draw horizontal lines to vertically separate sections of the document. The rule's size, width, and alignment can also be control using different attributes.
Syntax:	\<hr attributes />
Attributes:	**align** ="center" | "justify" | "left" | "right". Used to horizontally align the rule. **width** ="height". Used to set line width. **size** ="length". Used to set line length.
Standard Attributes:	id, class, title, style, dir, lang
Example:	

```
<h3 align ="center">Changing Size</hr>
<hr align="center" size="1" width="10%">
<hr align="center" size="5" width="25%">
<hr align="center" size="10" width="50%">
<hr align="center" size="15" width="100%">
```

\<html>...\</html>

Definition:	Used to indicate the XHTML document content is written using the HTML language. The \<html> element will be the container for the entire XHTML document.
Syntax:	\<html attributes > content \</html>
Standard Attributes:	dir, lang
Example:	

```
<html xmlns="http://www.w3.org/1999/xhtml" xml:lang="en"
lang="en">
<head>
<title>Basic XHTML Document Structure</title>
</head>
<body>
</body>
</html>
```

\<i>...\</i>

Definition:	Used to display italicized text.
Syntax:	\<i attributes > content \</i>
Standard Attributes:	id, class, title, style, dir, lang
Events:	onclick, ondblclick, onkeydown, onkeypress, onkeyup, onmousedown, onmouseup, onmouseover, onmousemove, onmouseout
Example:	\<div>This is the \<i>italic\</i> style.\</div>

\<iframe>...\</iframe>

Definition:	The inline or floating frame can appear any place that you want and is displayed as part of the document's text. These inline frames can be added to a regular XHTML document, one without a \<frameset>.

Syntax:	<iframe attributes > content </iframe>
Attributes:	**src** ="source". Specifies the source URL of the document that will become the content of the frame.
	width ="pixels"| "%". Used to set the width of the inline frame.
	height ="pixels"| "%". Used to set the height of the inline frame.
	name ="frame name". Used to define a name for an individual frame. This name can be used as a target of hyperlinks in the <a>, <form>, <area>, and <base> elements.
	scrolling ="yes	no	auto". By default scrollbars are displayed for frames when their content exceeds the allotted space. The frame scrolling attribute will give you control over the appearance of scrollbars for each frame.
	marginheight ="pixels". Used to specify the amount of separation (in pixels) between the border of a frame and the frame's content. When marginheight is used the white space around any content will be at the top and the bottom.
	marginwidth ="pixels" Used to specify the amount of separation (in pixels) between the border of a frame and the frames content. When marginwidth is used the white space around the content will be on the sides.
	longdesc ="url". Provides a link to a long description of the frame.
	frameborder ="0	1 ". Determines if borders are drawn around the frame.
Standard Attributes:	id, class, title, style
Example:	`<h1>Inline Frames</h1>`
	`<p>This is an example of how to use basic inline frames. In the inline frame you will see a chapter overview. </p>`
	`<iframe src="chapter3.html" height="300" width="300">`
	`</iframe>`

<img />

Definition:	This element is an empty element used to specify the image that is to be inserted into the Web page. Since <img> is an empty element and does not have a closing tag, it must be terminated properly in XHTML by adding a space and a slash before the closing angle bracket. The <img> element has two required attributes, src and alt.
Syntax:	<img attributes />
Attributes:	**src** ="url of image". Attribute used to include an image in a document. Src stands for "source" and directs the browser to get the file at the specified location.
	alt ="alternative text". The alt attribute stands for "alternate." The value of this attribute is a text description of the image. This text is displayed when an image is encountered by a non-graphical browser or a browser that has graphics disabled.
	width ="pixels"| "%". Used to set the width of an image.
	height ="pixels"| "%". Used to set the height of the image.
	align ="top"	"middle"	"bottom"	"left"| "right". Used to align an image with the text baseline.
	border ="pixels". Used to set the border width around the image.
	vspace ="pixels". Used to create white space at the top and bottom of the image.
	hspace ="pixels". Used to create white space on the left and right sides of the image.
	ismap = "url". Used to set the image as a server-side image map.
	usemap = "url". Used to set the image as a client-side image map.
	longdesc ="url". Provides a link to a long description of the image.
Standard Attributes:	id, class, title, style, dir, lang
Events:	onclick, ondblclick, onkeydown, onkeypress, onkeyup, onmousedown, onmouseup, onmouseover, onmousemove, onmouseout

Example:
```
<img src="FlagsEagle.jpg" alt="American Flags and Eagle"
align="bottom" />
```

\<input />

Definition: This element is an empty element used to define controls used in forms, which can be used to enter data. Since \<input> is an empty element and does not have a closing tag, it must be terminated properly in XHTML by adding a space and a slash before the closing angle bracket.

Syntax: \<input attributes />

Attributes: **type** ="text" | "password" | "checkbox" | "hidden" | "radio" | "submit" | "reset". Used to set the type of input element.

name =" name". Used to assign the name of the input element.

src ="url"=. Specifies the url of an image. This is used with type="image".

accept ="mime type list". Used to specify a comma-separated list of the MIME types accepted by the server.

value ="value". Used with type ="radio" | "checkbox" to specify the initial value of the control.

size ="number". Used to specify the initial size of the control. When used with type ="text" | "password", it specifies the width of the input field.

maxlength ="number". Used to specify the maximum number of characters that can be entered into the control.

align ="top" | "middle" | "bottom" | "left" | "right". Used to align the object with the text baseline.

checked = "checked". Boolean value used to specify if the control is checked when the form loads. This attribute is used with type ="checkbox" | "radio".

Standard Attributes: id, class, title, style, dir, lang

Example:
```
First name: <input type="text" name="first">
<br/>
Last name: <input type="text" name="last">
<br/>
```

\<ins>...\</ins>

Definition: Identifies inserted text.

Syntax: \<ins attributes > content \</ins>

Attributes: **cite** ="url". Used to specify a URL of a document that provides the reason for the change.

datetime ="yyyymmdd". Used to set the date and time the change was made.

Standard Attributes: id, class, title, style, dir, lang

Events: onclick, ondblclick, onkeydown, onkeypress, onkeyup, onmousedown, onmouseup, onmouseover, onmousemove, onmouseout

Example:
```
This text was <ins>inserted</ins> here.
```

\<kbd>...\</kbd>

Definition: This element is used to indicate some text is to be defined as keyboard text. The text used with this element is usually rendered as a monospaced font.

Syntax: \<kbd attributes > content \</kbd>

Standard Attributes: id, class, title, style, dir, lang

Events: onclick, ondblclick, onkeydown, onkeypress, onkeyup, onmousedown, onmouseup, onmouseover, onmousemove, onmouseout

Example:
```
<p>Press the <kbd>ENTER</kbd> key to continue
```

<li>...</li>

Definition:	This element is a container element that will enclose text that is to be treated as a list item in either an ordered or an unordered list.
Syntax:	<li attributes > content </li>
Standard Attributes:	id, class, title, style, dir, lang
Events:	onclick, ondblclick, onkeydown, onkeypress, onkeyup, onmousedown, onmouseup, onmouseover, onmousemove, onmouseout
Example:	

```
<ol>
<li>Analyze the problem</li>
<li>Design the logic</li>
<li>Code the program</li>
<li>Test and Debug program</li>
<li>Create program documentation</li>
        </ol>
```

<link />

Definition:	This element is used to describe the relationship between two linked documents. Since <link > is an empty element and does not have a closing tag, it must be terminated properly by adding a space and a slash.
Syntax:	<link attributes />
Attributes:	**charset** ="character set". Used to specify character encoding of the linked page.
	href ="location of linked document". Used to specify the location of the document to be linked. This location is usually a URL.
	rel ="link type". Used to define the link relationship between the current document and the destination document.
	target ="_blank	_self	_ parent	_ top". Used to identify where the linked document is to be opened.

	_blank	This attribute opens the selected file in a new browser window.
	_self	This attribute instructs the browser to open the file in the current frame.
	_parent	This attribute instructs the browser to replace the current document (frameset) with the new file.
	_top	This attribute instructs the browser to clear all current frames and loads the new page into the main browser window.

	type ="type". Used to tell the browser what type of file it is reading.
Standard Attributes:	id, class, title, style, dir, lang
Events:	onblur, onclick, ondblclick, onfocus, onkeydown, onkeypress, onkeyup, onmousedown, onmouseup, onmouseover, onmousemove, onmouseout
Example:	

```
<head>
<title>  Using External Style Sheet </title>
<link rel="stylesheet" href="exstyle1.css"type="text/css"/>
</head>
```

<map>...</map>

Definition:	Specifies a client-side image map. This element is used to create the map specification and will enclose the <area> elements. It also defines the map name, which is used by the <img> element.

Syntax:	<map attributes> content </map>
Attributes:	**name** ="map name". Used to define a name for an image map.
	id ="map name". Used to define a name for an image map.
	Note:In XHTML, the name attribute has been deprecated and will be removed in later versions, but some browsers do not support the id attribute, so we need to use both for now.
Standard Attributes:	id, class, title, style, dir, lang
Events:	onblur, onclick, ondblclick, onfocus, onkeydown, onkeypress, onkeyup, onmousedown, onmouseup, onmouseover, onmousemove, onmouseout, tabindex, accesskey, onfocus, onblur

Example:

```
<map id="shapes"name="shapes">
    <area shape="rect" coords="52,54,196,1126"
href="rectangle.html" alt="rectangle hotspot" />
    <area shape="poly"
coords="326,52,326,182,404,222,450,147,393,129,389,55"
href="polygon.html" alt="polygon hotspot" />
    <area shape="circle" coords="217,238,x" href="circle.html"
alt="circle hotspot" />
    </map>
```

<meta />

Definition:	This element provides information about the content of a document, which can be used by Internet search engines to index the Web pages.
Syntax:	<meta attributes />
Attributes:	content ="text". Used to set meta-information that is associated with the name.
	name ="text". Used to identify a name with the meta-object. This attribute has some pre-defined values, such as:

- Author
- Keywords
- Description
- Generator
- Formatter
- Copyright

	http-equiv ="name". Used to identify a name with meta-information.
Standard Attributes:	dir, lang

Example:

```
<meta name="keywords" content="Antique Cars, Ford, Model T,
Model A, Chalmers" />
<meta name="description" content="Using XHTML to design and
create Web pages. Visual Design techniques are discussed." />
<meta name="generator" content="Microsoft FrontPage 4.0" />
<meta name="author" content="Jeff Griffin" />
<meta name="copyright" content"&copy; 2001 Jeff Griffin" />
```

<noframes>...</noframes>

Definition:	Displays text for browsers that do not support the use of frames and is used inside the frameset element.
Syntax:	<noframes attributes> content </noframes>
Standard Attributes:	id, class, title, style, dir, lang
Events:	onclick, ondblclick, onkeydown, onkeypress, onkeyup, onmousedown, onmouseup, onmouseover, onmousemove, onmouseout

Example:
```
<noframes>
Your current browser does not handle frames. Please upgrade
your browser to view this page.
</noframes>
```

<noscript>...</noscript>

Definition:	This element is used to define alternate text to be displayed if the browser does not recognize the script element.
Syntax:	<noscript attributes> content </noscript>
Standard Attributes:	id, class, title, style, dir, lang
Events:	onclick, ondblclick, onkeydown, onkeypress, onkeyup, onmousedown, onmouseup, onmouseover, onmousemove, onmouseout

Example:
```
<script type="text/javascript">
<!--
document.write("Hello World!")
//-->
</script>
<noscript>Your current browser does not support JavaScript!
Please upgrade your browser to view this page
</noscript>
```

<object>...</object>

Definition:	This element is used to include an external object in the XHTML document.
Syntax:	<object attributes> content </object>
Attributes:	**codetype** ="mime type". Used to set the Internet media type.
	data = "url". Used to identify the location of the object's data.
	name = "text". Used to set the name of the object.
	width ="pixels"| "%". Used to set the width of the object.
	height ="pixels"| "%". Used to set the height of the object.
	align ="top"	"middle"	"bottom"	"left"	"right". Used to align the object with the text baseline.
	vspace ="pixels". Used to create white space at the top and bottom of the element.
	hspace ="pixels". Used to create white space on the left and right sides of the element.
	usemap = "url". Used to set the image as a client-side image map.
Standard Attributes:	id, class, title, style, dir, lang
Events:	onclick, ondblclick, onkeydown, onkeypress, onkeyup, onmousedown, onmouseup, onmouseover, onmousemove, onmouseout, tabindex

<ol>...</ol>

Definition:	This element is a container element that will enclose a block of text that is to be treated as a list. Ordered lists are sometimes referred to as numbered lists.
Syntax:	<ol attributes> content </ol>
Attributes:	**type** = "1	a	A	I	i". Used to define what type of numbering to use on an ordered list.
	start = "number". Used to set the starting number of an ordered list.
	compact. Used to instruct the browser to display the list in a compact form.
Standard Attributes:	id, class, title, style, dir, lang
Events:	onclick, ondblclick, onkeydown, onkeypress, onkeyup, onmousedown, onmouseup, onmouseover, onmousemove, onmouseout

Example:
```
<ol>
    <li>Analyze the problem</li>
    <li>Design the logic</li>
    <li>Code the program</li>
    <li>Test and Debug program</li>
    <li>Create program documentation</li>
</ol>
```

\<optgroup\>...\</optgroup\>

Definition:	This element is used to define an option group, which allows the grouping of option elements within select statements.
Syntax:	\<optgroup attributes\> content \</optgroup\>
Attributes:	**label** ="text". Used to label the option group.
	disabled ="disabled". Used to disable the option group.
Standard Attributes:	id, class, title, style, dir, lang
Events:	onclick, ondblclick, onkeydown, onkeypress, onkeyup, onmousedown, onmouseup, onmouseover, onmousemove, onmouseout, tabindex

---

\<option\>...\</option\>

Definition:	The element specifies the options available inside a select element.
Syntax:	\<option attributes\> content \</option\>
Attributes:	**value** ="text". Used to specify the initial value of the control.
	selected. Boolean value used to specify that an option is preselected.
	disabled. Used to disable the control for user input.
Standard Attributes:	id, class, title, style, dir, lang
Events:	onclick, ondblclick, onkeydown, onkeypress, onkeyup, onmousedown, onmouseup, onmouseover, onmousemove, onmouseout

---

\<p\>...\</p\>

Definition:	The paragraph element is a container element that will enclose a block of text that is to be treated as a paragraph.
Syntax:	\<p attributes\> content \</p\>
Attributes:	**align** ="center" | "left" | "right". Used to horizontally align the paragraph.
Standard Attributes:	id, class, title, style, dir, lang
Events:	onclick, ondblclick, onkeydown, onkeypress, onkeyup, onmousedown, onmouseup, onmouseover, onmousemove, onmouseout

Example:
```
<p>
    This is a basic XHTML document that has two paragraphs.
    They may be simple, but I think they will get the point
    across. This is the first paragraph.
</p>
<p>
    This is the second paragraph of our document. It has one blank
    line before it starts. It also included carriage returns, blank
    lines, and indentations.
</p>
```

<param />

Definition:	This element allows settings to be specified at runtime for objects.
Syntax:	<param attributes />
Attributes:	**name** = "text". Used to define the name of a parameter required by the object.
	value = "data". Sets the value of the identified parameter.
	type ="content type". Used to specify the content or media type of the object.
	valuetype ="data" | "ref" | "object". Used to identify the type of the parameter in the value attribute.
Standard Attributes:	id

<pre>...</pre>

Definition:	This element is a container element that will enclose a block of text that is preformatted. The <pre> tag identifies the text as preformatted and instructs the browser that it should be displayed as entered and preserves spacing.
Syntax:	<pre attributes> content </pre>
Attributes:	width ="number". Used to specify the width of the content block.
Standard Attributes:	id, class, title, style, dir, lang
Events:	onclick, ondblclick, onkeydown, onkeypress, onkeyup, onmousedown, onmouseup, onmouseover, onmousemove, onmouseout
Example:	

```
<pre>
              M E M O R A N D U M

     Date      January 9, 2001
     To        CPT 250 Class
     From      Jeff Griffin, Computer Technology Department
     Subject   Activities for Lab 1 on Thursday January 11, 2001

</pre>
```

<q>...</q>

Definition:	This element is a container element that will identify a short quotation.
Syntax:	<q attributes> content </q>
Attributes:	**cite** ="location of linked document". Used to specify the URL source of the quote.
Standard Attributes:	id, class, title, style, dir, lang
Events:	onclick, ondblclick, onkeydown, onkeypress, onkeyup, onmousedown, onmouseup, onmouseover, onmousemove, onmouseout
Example:	`This an example of a short quotation: <q>XHTML is fun.</q>`

<samp>...</samp>

Definition:	This element is used to indicate sample text. The text used with this element is usually rendered as a monospaced font.
Syntax:	<samp attributes> content </samp>
Standard Attributes:	id, class, title, style, dir, lang
Events:	onclick, ondblclick, onkeydown, onkeypress, onkeyup, onmousedown, onmouseup, onmouseover, onmousemove, onmouseout
Example:	`<div>This is the <samp>sample</samp> style.</div>`

\<script\>...\</script\>

Definition:	This element is used to embed a script into an XHTML document. This element can be placed within the \<head\> element or the \<body\> element.
Syntax:	\<script attributes\> content \</script\>
Attributes:	**type** ="content type". Used to specify type of script.
	src ="url of script". Attribute used to include a script in a document. Src stands for "source" and directs the browser to get the file at the specified location.
	langauge ="content type". Used to specify type of script.
Example:	

```
<script type="text/javascript" language="javascript">
window.alert("Welecome to XHTML using JavaScript")
</script>
```

\<select\>...\</select\>

Definition:	The select element creates a pop-up menu or scrolled list box to list choices.
Attributes:	**multiple** ="true | false". Boolean value used to indicate if multiple selections are allowed.
	name ="text". Used to set the name associated with the select element.
	size ="number". Used to set the number of displayed rows in a scroll box.
Standard Attributes:	id, class, title, style, dir, lang
Events:	onclick, ondblclick, onkeydown, onkeypress, onkeyup, onmousedown, onmouseup, onmouseover, onmousemove, onmouseout, tabindex
Example:	

```
<select name ="State">
      <option value = "IN">Indiana</option>
      <option value = "IL">Illinios</option>
      <option value = "OH">Ohio</option>
</select>
```

\<small\>...\</small\>

Definition:	This is a physical element used to render text smaller.
Syntax:	\<small attributes\> content \</small\>
Standard Attributes:	id, class, title, style, dir, lang
Events:	onclick, ondblclick, onkeydown, onkeypress, onkeyup, onmousedown, onmouseup, onmouseover, onmousemove, onmouseout
Example:	\<div\>This is the \<small\>small\</small\> style.\</div\>

\<span\>...\</span\>

Definition:	The \<span\> is an inline element, which is used to select a portion of inline text and apply a style to that part. The style will override the default settings.
Syntax:	\<span attributes\> content \</span\>
Standard Attributes:	id, class, title, style, dir, lang
Events:	onclick, ondblclick, onkeydown, onkeypress, onkeyup, onmousedown, onmouseup, onmouseover, onmousemove, onmouseout
Example:	

```
<p>
This is a basic XHTML document that uses the span element to
change the font size of the second sentence. <span style=
"font-size:200%;">It may be simple, but I think you will get
the idea.</span> The font size is now back to normal for the
remainder of the paragraph.
</p>
```

\...\

Definition:	This element is used to indicate some text is to be emphasized more than \. The text used with this element is usually rendered as bold.
Syntax:	\<strong attributes> content \
Standard Attributes:	id, class, title, style, dir, lang
Events:	onclick, ondblclick, onkeydown, onkeypress, onkeyup, onmousedown, onmouseup, onmouseover, onmousemove, onmouseout
Example:	```<p>Let's emphasize <em>XHTML</em>a little and <strong>XML</strong> even more.</p>```

\<style>...\</style>

Definition:	This element is used to create styles within a single document. It contains the rules that the browser will use to render the document.
Syntax:	\<style attributes> content \</style>
Attributes:	**media** ="type". Used to specify the destination medium of the style information.
	type ="content type". Used to specify the content type of the style language.
Standard Attributes:	title, dir, lang
Events:	onclick, ondblclick, onkeydown, onkeypress, onkeyup, onmousedown, onmouseup, onmouseover, onmousemove, onmouseout
Example:	```<style type="text/css">```

```
<style type="text/css">
<!--
  h1{
     color: red;
     }
-->
</style>
```

_{...\}

Definition:	This is a physical element used to render text lower than surrounding text.
Syntax:	_{content \}
Standard Attributes:	id, class, title, style, dir, lang
Events:	onclick, ondblclick, onkeydown, onkeypress, onkeyup, onmousedown, onmouseup, onmouseover, onmousemove, onmouseout
Example:	```<div>This is the _{subscript} style.</div>```

\^{...\}

Definition:	This is a physical element used to render text higher than surrounding text.
Syntax:	\^{content \}
Standard Attributes:	id, class, title, style, dir, lang
Events:	onclick, ondblclick, onkeydown, onkeypress, onkeyup, onmousedown, onmouseup, onmouseover, onmousemove, onmouseout
Example:	```<div>This is the ^{superscript} style.</div>```

<table>...</table>

Definition:	This element is used to define a table.
Syntax:	<table attributes> content </table>
Attributes:	**border** ="pixels". Used to set the border width around the table.
	cellspacing ="pixels". Used to specify the amount of separation (in pixels) between the border of one cell and the border of the adjacent cells.
	cellpadding ="pixels". Used to control the amount of space (in pixels) between the border of each table cell and the contents of that cell.
	width ="pixels"| "%". Used to control the width of a table.
	align = "center"	"left"	"right". Used to align a table with respect to the page.
	bgcolor ="color". Sets the background color for the cells of a table. The color value can be expressed by using the RGB hexadecimal format (rrggbb = hexadecimal color value) or by using a predefined color name.
	rules ="none"	"groups"	"rows"	"cols"	"all". Used to specify if interior lines of a table are visible.
Standard Attributes:	id, class, title, style, dir, lang
Events:	onclick, ondblclick, onkeydown, onkeypress, onkeyup, onmousedown, onmouseup, onmouseover, onmousemove, onmouseout
Example:	

```
<table>
    <tr>
        <td>Mercury</td>
        <td>Venus</td>
        <td>Earth</td>
        <td>Mars</td>
    </tr>
</table>
```

<tbody>...</tbody>

Definition:	This element is used to create a table body. The <tbody> elements define the row groups and a table can have any number of these elements.
Syntax:	<table attributes> content </table>
Attributes:	**align** = "center"	"left"	"right"	"justify". Used to align text within table cells.
	valign ="top"	"middle"	"bottom"	"baseline". Used to vertically align text within table cells.
Standard Attributes:	id, class, title, style, dir, lang
Events:	onclick, ondblclick, onkeydown, onkeypress, onkeyup, onmousedown, onmouseup, onmouseover, onmousemove, onmouseout
Example:	

```
<tbody>
    <tr>
        <th> ROW 1 </th>
        <td> ROW 1, COL 1</td>
        <td> ROW 1, COL 2</td>
        <td> ROW 1, COL 3</td>
    </tr>
    <tr>
        <th> ROW 2 </th>
        <td> ROW 2, COL 1</td>
        <td> ROW 2, COL 2</td>
        <td> ROW 2, COL 3</td>
    </tr>
</tbody>
```

<td>...</td>

Definition:	This element defines individual cells that hold the data in the rows of a table.
Syntax:	<td attributes> content </td>
Attributes:	**align** = "center" | "left"| "right" | "justify". Used to horizontally align contents of table cells.
	valign ="top" | "middle"| "bottom" | "baseline". Used to vertically align contents of table cells.
	colspan ="number". Used to set number of columns this cell should span.
	rowspan ="number". Used to set number of rows this cell should span.
Standard Attributes:	id, class, title, style, dir, lang
Events:	onclick, ondblclick, onkeydown, onkeypress, onkeyup, onmousedown, onmouseup, onmouseover, onmousemove, onmouseout
Example:	

```
<table>
   <tr>
    <th> ROW 1 </th>
    <td> ROW 1, COL 1</td>
    <td> ROW 1, COL 2</td>
    <td> ROW 1, COL 3</td>
   </tr>
   <tr>
    <th> ROW 2 </th>
    <td> ROW 2, COL 1</td>
    <td> ROW 2, COL 2</td>
    <td> ROW 2, COL 3</td>
   </tr>
</table>
```

<textarea>...</textarea>

Definition:	This element creates a multi-line input control.
Syntax:	<textarea attributes> content </textarea>
Attributes:	**name** ="name". Used to set the name of the control name.
	cols ="number". Used to specify the width of the text area, in characters.
	rows ="*number*". Used to specify the height of the text area, in rows.
Standard Attributes:	id, class, title, style, dir, lang
Events:	tabindex, onfocus, onblur, onselect, onchange, onclick, ondblclick, onmousedown, onmouseup, onmouseover, onmousemove, onmouseout, onkeypress, onkeydown, onkeyup

<tfoot>...</tfoot>

Definition:	This element is used to create a table footer when rows are being grouped. The table footer will typically contain column totals or provide a description about all the columns.
Syntax:	<tfoot attributes> content </tfoot>
Attributes:	**align** = "center" | "left"| "right" | "justify". Used to horizontally align contents of table cells.
	valign ="top" | "middle"| "bottom" | "baseline". Used to vertically align contents of table cells.
Standard Attributes:	id, class, title, style, dir, lang
Events:	onclick, ondblclick, onkeydown, onkeypress, onkeyup, onmousedown, onmouseup, onmouseover, onmousemove, onmouseout
Example:	

```
<tfoot>
   <tr>
     <td colspan="4" align="center"> THIS IS THE FOOTER </td>
   </tr>
</tfoot>
```

<th>...</th>

Definition:	Defines a header in a table. A table header element is automatically formatted as boldfaced and centered to set it apart from other table cells in that column.
Syntax:	<th attributes> content </th>
Attributes:	**align** = "center" | "left"| "right" | "justify". Used to horizontally align contents of table cells.
	valign ="top" | "middle"| "bottom" | "baseline". Used to vertically align contents of table cells.
	colspan ="number". Used to set number of columns this cell should span.
	rowspan ="number". Used to set number of rows this cell should span.
	bgcolor ="color". Sets the background color for the cells of a table. The color value can be expressed by using the RGB hexadecimal format (rrggbb = hexadecimal color value) or by using a predefined color name.
Standard Attributes:	id, class, title, style, dir, lang
Events:	onclick, ondblclick, onkeydown, onkeypress, onkeyup, onmousedown, onmouseup, onmouseover, onmousemove, onmouseout
Example:	

```
<tr>
    <th>LEFT</th>
    <th>CENTER</th>
    <th>RIGHT</th>
</tr>
<tr>
    <td align = "left">Cell 1</td>
    <td align = "center">Cell 2 </td>
    <td align = "right">Cell 3</td>
</tr>
```

<thead>...</thead>

Definition:	This element is used to create a header for a table. Typically it is the same information that you place in the header cells to describe the columns using the <th> elements.
Syntax:	<thead attributes> content </thead>
Attributes:	**align** = "center" | "left"| "right" | "justify". Used to horizontally align contents of table cells.
	valign ="top" | "middle"| "bottom" | "baseline". Used to vertically align contents of table cells.
Standard Attributes:	id, class, title, style, dir, lang
Events:	onclick, ondblclick, onkeydown, onkeypress, onkeyup, onmousedown, onmouseup, onmouseover, onmousemove, onmouseout
Example:	

```
<thead bgcolor = "blue">
    <tr>
        <th>Row Number</th>
        <th>Column 1</th>
        <th>Column 2</th>
        <th>Column 3</th>
    </tr>
</thead>
```

<title>...</title>

Definition:	This element is used to add a title to your XHTML document. It appears in the title bar of the browser.
Syntax:	<title attributes> content </title>
Standard Attributes:	dir, lang

Example:
```
<head>
  <title>  A Basic XHTML Document  </title>
</head>
```

`<tr>...</tr>`

Definition:	This element creates a new row in the table.
Syntax:	<tr attributes> content </tr>
Attributes:	**align** = "center" | "left"| "right" | "justify". Used to horizontally align contents of table cells.
	valign ="top" | "middle"| "bottom" | "baseline". Used to vertically align contents of table cells.
	bgcolor ="color". Sets the background color for the cells of a table. The color value can be expressed by using the RGB hexadecimal format (rrggbb = hexadecimal color value) or by using a predefined color name.
Standard Attributes:	id, class, title, style, dir, lang
Events:	onclick, ondblclick, onkeydown, onkeypress, onkeyup, onmousedown, onmouseup, onmouseover, onmousemove, onmouseout

Example:
```
<tr>
    <th>LEFT</th>
    <th>CENTER</th>
    <th>RIGHT</th>
</tr>
<tr>
    <td align = "left">Cell 1</td>
    <td align = "center">Cell 2 </td>
    <td align = "right">Cell 3</td>
</tr>
```

`<tt>...</tt>`

Definition:	This is a physical element used to render text as teletype or monospaced.
Syntax:	<tt attributes> content </tt>
Standard Attributes:	id, class, title, style, dir, lang
Events:	onclick, ondblclick, onkeydown, onkeypress, onkeyup, onmousedown, onmouseup, onmouseover, onmousemove, onmouseout
Example:	<div>This is the <tt>true type</tt> style.</div>

`<ul>...</ul>`

Definition:	This element is a container element that will enclose a block of text that is to be treated as an unordered list. Unordered lists are sometimes referred to as bulleted lists.
Syntax:	<ul attributes> content </ul>
Attributes:	**type** = "disc | square | circle". Used to define what style of bullets is used with the unordered list.
	compact. Used to instruct the browser to display the list in a compact form.
Standard Attributes:	id, class, title, style, dir, lang
Events:	onclick, ondblclick, onkeydown, onkeypress, onkeyup, onmousedown, onmouseup, onmouseover, onmousemove, onmouseout

Example:	`<p>Unordered List Using Square</p>`
	`<ul type = "square">`
	`<li>Oranges</li>`
	`<li>Apples</li>`
	`<li>Banana</li>`
	`<li>Strawberry</li>`
	`</ul>`

`<var>...</var>`

Definition:	This element is used to highlight a variable to be supplied by the user. It is usually rendered in italic.
Syntax:	`<var attributes> content </var>`
Standard Attributes:	id, class, title, style, dir, lang
Events:	onclick, ondblclick, onkeydown, onkeypress, onkeyup, onmousedown, onmouseup, onmouseover, onmousemove, onmouseout
Example:	`<div>This is the <var>variable</var> style.</div>`

STANDARD ATTRIBUTES

Attribute	Description
id = 'identifier'	An alphanumeric identifier used to identify an object.
style = 'styles'	Used to include inline styles, indicating how the element will be rendered.
class = 'class rule' | 'style rule'	Used to indicate the class of the element.
title = 'text'	Contains additional information for an element, which could be displayed in the tool tip.
dir = 'ltr' | 'rtl'	Used to indicate the text direction of an element. The value ltr indicates left-to-right and rtl indicates right-to-left.
lang = 'language code'	Used to indicate the base language of the element's content or attributes.

FORM EVENTS

Event	Description
onfocus	Some action is performed when a particular element gets focus.
onblur	Some action is performed when a particular element loses focus.
onchange	Some action is performed when data in a control changes.
onsubmit	Some action is performed when the user clicks the submit button.
onreset	Some action is performed when the user clicks the reset button.
onselect	Some action is performed when a selection occurs.

KEYBOARD EVENTS

Event	Description
onkeydown	Some action is performed when a key is depressed.
onkeypress	Some action is performed when a key is depressed and the associated code is available.
onkeyup	Some action is performed when a key goes up.

MOUSE EVENTS

Event	Description
onclick	Some action is performed when any mouse button is clicked.
ondbclick	Some action is performed when an element is double-clicked.
onmouseover	Some action is performed when the mouse is moved over something.
onmousedown	Some action is performed when a mouse button goes down.
onmousemove	Some action is performed when the mouse moves.
onmouseout	Some action is performed when a mouse leaves an element.
onmouseup	Some action is performed when a mouse button goes up.

WINDOW EVENTS

Event	Description
onload	Some action is performed when the document is loaded.
onunload	Some action is performed when the document is unloaded.

cascading style sheet (css2) reference

This appendix contains CSS2 properties that are grouped by their function. Before using this appendix it is important that you understand style sheet concepts such as selectors, rules, properties, and box model. These topics are presented in Chapter 12. The following CSS2 property groups are included:

- Backgrounds and Colors
- Fonts
- Text
- Box Model
- Tables
- Visual Formatting and Positioning
- Generated Content and Lists
- Paged Media

The CSS2 property group Aural Style is not included in this appendix. This style group is used to create Web pages for visually impaired individuals, or to provide audio information. A complete listing of the CSS2 specifications can be found at http://www.w3.org/TR/REC-CSS2/.

BACKGROUND AND COLOR PROPERTIES

color

Purpose:	Specifies color of an element.
Values:	<color>	inherit
Inherited:	Yes
Used in:	All elements
Example:	{color: aqua;}
	or
	{color: #0000FF;}

background-color

Purpose:	Specifies background color of an element.
Values:	<color>	transparent	inherit
Inherited:	No
Used in:	All elements
Example:	{background-color: white;}
	or
	{background-color:#FF0000;}

background-image

Purpose:	Inserts background image of element.
Values:	<url>	none	inherit
Inherited:	No
Used in:	All elements

background-repeat

Purpose:	Specifies how a background image of an element is repeated.
Values:	repeat | repeat-x | repeat-y | no-repeat | inherit
	repeat—repeats image both horizontally and vertically
	repeat-x—repeats image only horizontally
	repeat-y—repeats image only vertically
	no-repeat—image does not repeat
Inherited:	No
Used in:	All elements

background-attachment

Purpose:	Determines if the background image scrolls or remains fixed.
Values:	scroll | fixed | inherit
Inherited:	No
Used in:	All elements

background-position

Purpose:	Specifies how a background image is positioned within the element.
Values:	[<percentage> | <length>] {1, 2} | top | center | bottom || left | center | right | inherit
Inherited:	No
Used in:	Block-level and replaced elements

background

Purpose:	A shorthand method used to group background properties.
Values:	[<background-color> || <background-image> || <background-repeat> || <background-attacment> || <background-position>] | inherit
Inherited:	No
Used in:	All elements

FONT PROPERTIES

font-family

Purpose:	Defines a font and alternatives to use for an element's text.
Values:	[[<family-name> | [serif | sans-serif | cursive | fantasy | monospace]] | inherit
Inherited:	Yes
Used in:	All elements
Example:	{font-family: sans-serif;}

font-style

Purpose:	Defines a font style for text.
Values:	normal | italic | oblique | inherit
Inherited:	Yes
Used in:	All elements
Example:	{font-style: italic;}

font-variant

Purpose:	Enables a font to be rendered as small caps.
Values:	normal	small-caps	inherit
Inherited:	Yes
Used in:	All elements

font-weight

Purpose:	Determines the thickness (boldness) of the text.
Values:	normal	bold	bolder	lighter	100–900	inherit
	A number from 100 to 900 is used to indicate the thickness of the font with 100 being the lightest to 900 being the boldest.
Inherited:	Yes
Used in:	All elements
Example:	`{font-weight:  200;}`
	`{font-weight:bold;}`
	`{font-weight:900;}`

font-stretch

Purpose:	Defines the width of the font.
Values:	normal	wider	narrower	ultra-condensed	extra-condensed	condensed	semi-condensed	semi-expanded	expanded	extra-expanded	ultra-expanded	inherit
Inherited:	Yes
Used in:	All elements

font-size

Purpose:	Used to control the size of the font displayed by the browser.
Values:	<absolute-size>	<relative-size>	<length>	<percentage>	inherit
Inherited:	Yes
Used in:	All elements
Example:	`{font-size:16pt;}`
	`{font-size:120%;}`

font-size-adjust

Purpose:	Defines an aspect ratio to be maintained when resizing the height of a font.
Values:	<number>	none	inherit
Inherited:	Yes
Used in:	All elements

font

Purpose:	A shorthand method used to define all font properties at one time.
Values:	[[<font-style> || <font-variant> || <font-weight>] ? <font-size> [/ <line-height>] ? <font-family>]	caption	icon	menu	message-box	small-caption	status-bar	inherit
Inherited:	Yes
Used in:	All elements

TEXT PROPERTIES

text-indent

Purpose:	Used to set the amount of indentation of the first line of text within the element.
Values:	<length>	<percentage>	inherit
Inherited:	Yes
Used in:	Block-level elements
Example:	{text-indent:5%;}

text-align

Purpose:	Allows for the justification of text within the element.
Values:	left	right	center	justify	<string>	inherit
Inherited:	Yes
Used in:	Block-level elements
Example:	{text-align: right;}

text-transform

Purpose:	Used to change the case of text.
Values:	capitalize	uppercase	lowercase	none	inherit
Inherited:	Yes
Used in:	All elements
Example:	{text-transform:capitalize;}

text-decoration

Purpose:	Used to add decoration to the text of an element.
Values:	underline	overline	line-through	blink	none	inherit
Inherited:	No
Used in:	All elements

text-shadow

Purpose:	Used to create a text shadow effect.
Values:	none	[<color> || <length> <length> <length>? ,]* [<color> || <length> <length> <length>?]	inherit
	First length—defines horizontal distance to the right of the text
	Second length—positive number defines vertical distance below the text and a negative number defines distance above the text
	Third length—defines the text shadow blur radius
Inherited:	No
Used in:	All elements

white-space

Purpose:	Used to control how white space is handled with an element.
Values:	normal	pre	nowrap	inherit
Inherited:	Yes
Used in:	Block elements

letter-spacing

Purpose:	Defines the space between text characters and can be used to increase the default spacing.
Values:	normal	<length>	inherit
Inherited:	Yes
Used in:	All elements

word-spacing

Purpose:	Defines the space between words and can be used to increase the default spacing.
Values:	normal	<length>	inherit
Inherited:	Yes
Used in:	All elements

BOX MODEL PROPERTIES

border-color

Purpose:	Shorthand property used to specify color settings for all sides of an element at one time.
Values:	<color>{1,4}	transparent	inherit
Inherited:	No
Used in:	All elements

border-bottom-color

Purpose:	Used to specify the color setting for the bottom side of the box.
Values:	<color>	inherit
Inherited:	No
Used in:	All elements

border-top-color

Purpose:	Used to specify the color setting for the top side of the box.
Values:	<color>	inherit
Inherited:	No
Used in:	All elements

border-left-color

Purpose:	Used to specify the color setting for the left side of the box.
Values:	<color>	inherit
Inherited:	No
Used in:	All elements

border-right-color

Purpose:	Used to specify the color setting for the right side of the box.
Values:	<color>	inherit
Inherited:	No
Used in:	All elements

border-width

Purpose:	Shorthand property used to specify width settings for all borders of an element at one time.
Values:	[thin | medium | thick | <length>]{1,4} | inherit
Inherited:	No
Used in:	All elements

border-bottom-width

Purpose:	Used to specify the border width for the bottom side of the box.
Values:	[thin | medium | thick | <length>] | inherit
Inherited:	No
Used in:	All elements

border-left-width

Purpose:	Used to specify the border width for the left side of the box.
Values:	[thin | medium | thick | <length>] | inherit
Inherited:	No
Used in:	All elements

border-right-width

Purpose:	Used to specify the border width for the right side of the box.
Values:	[thin | medium | thick | <length>] | inherit
Inherited:	No
Used in:	All elements

border-top-width

Purpose:	Used to specify the border width for the top side of the box.
Values:	[thin | medium | thick | <length>] | inherit
Inherited:	No
Used in:	All elements

border-style

Purpose:	Shorthand property used to specify style for all borders of an element at one time.
Values:	[none | hidden | dotted | dashed | solid | double | groove | ridge | inset | outset]{1,4} | inherit
Inherited:	No
Used in:	All elements

border-bottom-style

Purpose:	Used to specify the border style for the bottom side of the box.
Values:	[none | hidden | dotted | dashed | solid | double | groove | ridge | inset | outset] | inherit
Inherited:	No
Used in:	All elements

border-top-style

Purpose:	Used to specify the border style for the top side of the box.
Values:	[none | hidden | dotted | dashed | solid | double | groove | ridge | inset | outset] | inherit
Inherited:	No
Used in:	All elements

border-right-style

Purpose:	Used to specify the border style for the right side of the box.
Values:	[none | hidden | dotted | dashed | solid | double | groove | ridge | inset | outset] | inherit
Inherited:	No
Used in:	All elements

border-left-style

Purpose:	Used to specify the border style for the left side of the box.
Values:	[none | hidden | dotted | dashed | solid | double | groove | ridge | inset | outset] | inherit
Inherited:	No
Used in:	All elements

margin

Purpose:	Shorthand property used to specify margins for all sides of an element at one time.
Values:	[<length> | <percentage> | auto]{1,4} | inherit
Inherited:	No
Used in:	All elements

margin-bottom

Purpose:	Used to specify the width for the bottom margin.
Values:	<length> | <percentage> | auto | inherit
Inherited:	No
Used in:	All elements
Example:	{margin-bottom:10%;}

margin-top

Purpose:	Used to specify the width for the top margin.
Values:	<length> | <percentage> | auto | inherit
Inherited:	No
Used in:	All elements
Example:	{margin-top:10%;}

margin-left

Purpose:	Used to specify the width for the left margin.
Values:	<length> | <percentage> | auto | inherit
Inherited:	No
Used in:	All elements
Example:	{margin-left:10%;}

margin-right

Purpose:	Used to specify the width for the right margin.
Values:	<length>	<percentage>	auto	inherit
Inherited:	No
Used in:	All elements
Example:	{margin-right:10%;}

padding

Purpose:	Shorthand property used to specify padding widths for all sides of an element at one time. The padding property can take one to four values.
Values:	[<length>	<percentage>]{1,4}	inherit
Inherited:	No
Used in:	All elements
Example:	{padding:10pt 10pt 10pt 10pt;}

padding-bottom

Purpose:	Used to specify the padding width for the bottom.
Values:	<length>	<percentage>	inherit
Inherited:	No
Used in:	All elements
Example:	{ padding-bottom:20pt;}

padding-top

Purpose:	Used to specify the padding width for the top.
Values:	<length>	<percentage>	inherit
Inherited:	No
Used in:	All elements
Example:	{ padding-top:20pt;}

padding-right

Purpose:	Used to specify the padding width for the right side.
Values:	<length>	<percentage>	inherit
Inherited:	No
Used in:	All elements
Example:	{ padding-right:20pt;}

padding-left

Purpose:	Used to specify the padding width for the left side.
Values:	<length>	<percentage>	inherit
Inherited:	No
Used in:	All elements
Example:	{ padding-left:20pt;}

TABLE PROPERTIES

caption-side

Purpose:	Used to specify the position of a table caption in relation to the table.
Values:	top | bottom | left | right | inherit
Inherited:	Yes
Used in:	Table caption elements

table-layout

Purpose:	Specifies how the table is laid out.
Values:	auto | fixed | inherit
Inherited:	No
Used in:	Table and inline-table elements

border-collapse

Purpose:	Specifies how the table borders are displayed.
Values:	collapse | separate | inherit
Inherited:	Yes
Used in:	Table and inline-table elements

border-spacing

Purpose:	Specifies the spacing between table borders.
Values:	<length> <length> ? | inherit
Inherited:	Yes
Used in:	Table and inline-table elements

empty-cells

Purpose:	Specifies how the border of empty cells will be rendered.
Values:	show | hide | inherit
Inherited:	Yes
Used in:	Table cell elements

VISUAL FORMATTING PROPERTIES

display

Purpose:	Used to specify the type of display box the element will create.
Values:	block | list-item | inline | run-in | compact | marker | table | inline-table | table-row-group | table-header-group | table-footer-group | table-row | table-column-group | table-column | table-cell | table-caption | none | inherit
Inherited:	No
Used in:	All elements

position

Purpose:	Specifies the positioning method used.
Values:	static | relative | absolute | fixed | inherit
Inherited:	No
Used in:	All elements except generated content

top

Purpose:	Specifies the offset width from the top edge.
Values:	<length> | <percentage> | auto | inherit
Inherited:	No
Used in:	Positioned elements

right

Purpose:	Specifies the offset width from the right edge.
Values:	<length> | <percentage> | auto | inherit
Inherited:	No
Used in:	Positioned elements

left

Purpose:	Specifies the offset width from the left edge.
Values:	<length> | <percentage> | auto | inherit
Inherited:	No
Used in:	Positioned elements

bottom

Purpose:	Specifies the offset width from the bottom edge.
Values:	<length> | <percentage> | auto | inherit
Inherited:	No
Used in:	Positioned elements

float

Purpose:	Used to specify if the display box will float to the left or right.
Values:	left | right | none | inherit
Inherited:	No
Used in:	All but positioned elements and generated content

clear

Purpose:	Determines if text appears next to the side of a float box.
Values:	none | right | left | both | inherit
Inherited:	No
Used in:	Block-level elements

width

Purpose:	Used to specify the width of the display box.
Values:	<length>	<percentage>	auto	inherit
Inherited:	No
Used in:	All elements but non-replaced inline elements, table rows, and row groups

min-width

Purpose:	Used to specify the minimum width of the display box.
Values:	<length>	<percentage>	auto	inherit
Inherited:	No
Used in:	All elements but non-replaced inline elements and table elements

max-width

Purpose:	Used to specify the maximum width of the display box.
Values:	<length>	<percentage>	auto	inherit
Inherited:	No
Used in:	All elements but non-replaced inline elements and table elements

height

Purpose:	Used to specify the height of the display box.
Values:	<length>	<percentage>	auto	inherit
Inherited:	No
Used in:	All elements but non-replaced inline elements, table columns, and column groups

min-height

Purpose:	Used to specify the minimum height of the display box.
Values:	<length>	<percentage>	auto	inherit
Inherited:	No
Used in:	All elements but non-replaced inline elements and table elements

max-height

Purpose:	Used to specify the maximum height of the display box.
Values:	<length>	<percentage>	auto	inherit
Inherited:	No
Used in:	All elements but non-replaced inline elements and table elements

line-height

Purpose:	Used to specify line spacing for an element box.
Values:	normal	<number>	<length>	<percentage>	inherit
Inherited:	Yes
Used in:	All elements

vertical-align

Purpose:	Used to specify vertical positioning inside a line box.
Values:	baseline | sub | super | top | text-top | middle | bottom | text-bottom | \<percentage\> | \<length\> | inherit
Inherited:	No
Used in:	Inline and table cell elements

visibility

Purpose:	Specifies if an element is visible.
Values:	visible | hidden | collapse | inherit
Inherited:	No
Used in:	All elements

clip

Purpose:	Used to define the clipping area for overflowed sections.
Values:	\<shape\> | auto | inherit
Inherited:	No
Used in:	Block-level and replaced elements

GENERATED CONTENT, NUMBERING, AND LIST PROPERTIES

list-style-type

Purpose:	Specifies the list style to be applied to the bullets or numbers.
Values:	disc | circle | square | decimal | decimal-leading-zero | lower-roman | lower-greek | lower-alpha | lower-latin | upper-alpha | upper-latin | hebrew | armenian | georgian | cjk-ideographic | hiragana | katakana | hiragana-iroha | katakana-iroha | none | inherit
Inherited:	Yes
Used in:	Elements with display list item

list-style-image

Purpose:	Specifies graphic to be used in place of a bullet.
Values:	\<url\> | none | inherit
Inherited:	Yes
Used in:	Elements with display list item

list-style-position

Purpose:	Defines how the list item marker is positioned relative to the list content.
Values:	inside | outside | inherit
Inherited:	Yes
Used in:	Elements with display list item

marker-offset

Purpose:	Specifies the distance between a list marker and text.
Values:	<length> | auto | inherit
Inherited:	Yes
Used in:	Elements with display marker.

counter-increment

Purpose:	Used to increment the value of a specified counter.
Values:	[<identifier> <integer>?] + | none | inherit
Inherited:	No
Used in:	All elements

counter-reset

Purpose:	Used to reset the value of a specified counter.
Values:	[<identifier> <integer>?] + | none | inherit
Inherited:	No
Used in:	All elements

quotes

Purpose:	Used to define pairs of quotation marks.
Values:	[<string> <string>] + | none | inherit
Inherited:	Yes
Used in:	All elements

PAGED MEDIA PROPERTIES

size

Purpose:	Used to specify the size and orientation of a page.
Values:	<length> {1,2} | auto | portrait | landscape | inherit
Inherited:	N/A
Used in:	Page context

marks

Purpose:	Used to specify what marks are rendered outside the page box.
Values:	[crop || cross] | none | inherit
Inherited:	N/A
Used in:	Page context

page-break-before

Purpose:	Used to specify how the page breaks before an element.
Values:	auto | always | avoid | left | right | inherit
Inherited:	No
Used in:	Block-level elements

page-break-after

Purpose:	Used to specify how the page breaks after an element.
Values:	auto	always	avoid	left	right	inherit
Inherited:	No
Used in:	Block-level elements

page-break-inside

Purpose:	Used to specify how the page breaks inside an element.
Values:	avoid	auto	inherit
Inherited:	Yes
Used in:	Block-level elements

page

Purpose:	Used to specify page type when displaying an element.
Values:	<identifier>	auto	inherit
Inherited:	Yes
Used in:	Block-level elements

orphans

Purpose:	Used to specify the minimum number of content lines that must be left at the bottom of a displayed page.
Values:	<integer>	inherit
Inherited:	Yes
Used in:	Block-level elements

widows

Purpose:	Used to specify the minimum number of content lines that must be left at the top of a displayed page.
Values:	<integer>	inherit
Inherited:	Yes
Used in:	Block-level elements

selected color resources on the internet

The URLs in this appendix are available on the accompanying CD in electronic format for ease of access to the links.

http://www.colormatters.com/entercolormatters.html
Color Matters—a site about color and the world around us

http://www.color.org/
International Color Consortium site

http://www.pantone.com
Pantone's color site. Pantone matching system is a standard in print color.

http://www.webreference.com/authoring/graphics/color
Web reference articles

http://www.colormarketing.org
The Color Marketing Group

http://www.lynda.com
Lynda Weinman's site—lots of Web design and color information here

http://www.lynda.com/hex.html
http://www.lynda.com/hexh.html
Color chart by hue

http://www.visibone.com/colorlab/
Visibone color chart

http://www.inforamp.net/~poynton/Poynton-colour.html
http://www.inforamp.net/~poynton/GammaFAQ.html
http://www.inforamp.net/~poynton/ColorFAQ.html
Charles Poynton's articles on gamma and color

http://www.colorschemer.com/online/
Create online color schemes!

http://www.sanford-artedventures.com/study/study.html
A variety of subjects

http://www.zspc.com/color/index-e.html
This page allows you to select text color and background color and see how they go together

http://eies.njit.edu/~kevin/rgb.txt.html
All colors, not just Web colors

http://www.bagism.com/colormaker/
Choose text, links, and background colors

http://hotwired.lycos.com/webmonkey/reference/color_codes/
Visual chart and hexadecimal code of web colors

http://library.thinkquest.org/50065/
Educational site on color, color psychology, and color theory

http://plato.stanford.edu/entries/color/
Lengthy treatise on color

http://www.w3.org/Graphics/Color/sRGB.html
A Standard Default Color Space for the Internet—sRGB

http://www.hypersolutions.org/rgb.html
RGB to hexadecimal charts and more

http://www.webtemplates.com/colors/
WebTemplates site—Web color picker, Design 101, and more

http://www.cis.rit.edu/mcsl/
Munsell Color Science Laboratory at Rochester Institute of Technology

http://www.physics.sfasu.edu/astro/color.html
Color science site

http://www.webreference.com/dev/graphics/palette.html
Article on optimizing for different platforms including Unix, Mac, and Windows

http://www.immigration-usa.com/html_colors.html
Another Web color chart

http://www.adobe.com/support/techguides/color/main.html
Adobe's site on color

http://tigger.uic.edu/~hilbert/Glossary.html
A glossary of color science terms

http://www.shibuya.com/garden/colorpsycho.html
Color psychology site

appendix d
XHTML special character entities

Sometimes it is necessary to include special characters like ©, ®, or < in an XHTML document. The special character you want to use is not always available on your keyboard. These special characters can be included in an XHTML document by using codes referred to as character entities, which when inserted into the document allow the browser to render the corresponding characters. Character entities are often used to display an XHTML element in a document. For example, if you were explaining how to use the <a> element and wanted to display the element in the paragraph explaining it, you could not just enter the following:

```
<p>
     This is how the <a> element is used.
</p>
```

The <a> element in the paragraph would be interpreted as an XHTML element by the browser and would not be rendered. The element could be displayed by using character entities as follows:

```
<p>
     This is how the &lt;a&gt; element is used.
</p>
```

Adding the character entities for the less than and greater than symbols allows <a> to be treated as characters and rendered as such in the XHTML document.

Special character entities can be included in your document by referring to their entity name or decimal number. Both entity formats begin with an ampersand (&) and end with a semicolon (;). The syntax for the use of the named entity and number would be as follows:

```
&name;
&#number;
```

One of the most common special characters seen in a Web page is the copyright symbol. For example, to add the following line to a web page:

Copyright © 2002 Franklin, Beedle & Associates

could be accomplished by using the named entity or the numeric entity value. Let's look at how to code this using both formats.

Using the named entity would look like the following:

```
Copyright &copy; 2002 Franklin, Beedle &amp; Associates
```

Using the numeric entity value would look like the following:

```
Copyright &#169; 2002 Franklin, Beedle &#38; Associates
```

The following table represents the most common character symbols. It is only a subset of the symbols that are available for use.

Character	Description	Entity Code	Mnemonic
"	Double quotation mark	&#34;	&quot;
&	Ampersand	&#38;	&amp;
<	Less-than sign	&#60;	&lt;
>	Greater-than sign	&#62;	&gt;
™	Trademark sign	&#8482	&8482;
	Non-breaking space		
¡	Inverted exclamation point	&#161;	&iexcel;
¢	Cent sign	&#162;	&cent;
£	Pound sterling sign	&#163;	&pound;
◊	General currency sign	&#164;	&curren;
¥	Yen sign	&#165;	&yen;
¦	Broken vertical bar	&#166;	&brvbar;
§	Section sign	&#167;	&sect;
¨	Dieresis	&#168;	&uml;
©	Copyright sign	&#169;	&copy;
ª	Feminine ordinal indicator	&#170;	&ordf;
«	Small left-angle mark	&#171;	&laquo;
¬	Not sign	&#172;	&not;
-	Soft hyphen	&#173;	&shy;
®	Registered trademark sign	&#174;	&reg;
¯	Macron accent	&#175;	&macr;
°	Degree sign	&#176;	&deg;
±	Plus-or-minus sign	&#177;	&plusmn;
²	Superscript two	&#178;	&sup2;
³	Superscript three	&#179;	&sup3;
´	Acute accent	&#180;	&acute;
µ	Micro sign	&#181;	&micro;
¶	Paragraph sign	&#182;	&para;
·	Middle dot	&#183;	&middot;
¸	Cedilla	&#184;	&cedil;
¹	Superscript one	&#185;	&sup1;
º	Masculine ordinal	&#186;	&ordm;
»	Small right-angle mark	&#187;	&raquo
¼	Fraction one-fourth	&#188;	&frac14;
½	Fraction one-half	&#189;	&frac12;
¾	Fraction three-fourths	&#190;	&frac34;
¿	Inverted question mark	&#191;	&iquest;
À	Capital A, grave accent	&#192;	&Agrave
Á	Capital A, acute accent	&#193;	&Aacute;
Â	Capital A, circumflex accent	&#194;	&Acirc;
Ã	Capital A, tilde	&#195;	&Atilde;
Ä	Capital A, dieresis or umlaut	&#196;	&Auml;
Å	Capital A, ring	&#197;	&Aring;
Æ	Capital AE diphthong (ligature)	&#198;	&AElig;
Ç	Capital C, cedilla	&#199;	&Ccedil;
È	Capital E, grave accent	&#200;	&Egrave;
É	Capital E, acute accent	&#201;	&Eacute;
Ê	Capital E, circumflex accent	&#202;	&Ecirc;

Character	Description	Entity Code	Mnemonic
Ë	Capital E, dieresis or umlaut	&#203;	&Euml;
Ì	Capital I, grave accent	&#204;	&Igrave;
Í	Capital I, acute accent	&#205;	&Iacute;
Î	Capital I, circumflex accent	&#206;	&Icirc;
Ï	Capital I, dieresis or umlaut	&#207;	&Iuml;
Ð	Capital Eth, Icelandic	&#208;	&ETH;
Ñ	Capital N, tilde	&#209;	&Ntilde;
Ò	Capital O, grave accent	&#210;	&Ograve;
Ó	Capital O, acute accent	&#211;	&Oacute;
Ô	Capital O, circumflex accent	&#212;	&Ocirc;
Õ	Capital O, tilde	&#213;	&Otilde;
Ö	Capital O, dieresis or umlaut	&#214;	&Ouml;
×	Multiplication sign	&#215;	&times;
Ø	Capital O, slash	&#216;	&Oslash;
Ù	Capital U, grave accent	&#217;	&Ugrave;
Ú	Capital U, acute accent	&#218;	&Uacute;
Û	Capital U, circumflex accent	&#219;	&Ucirc;
Ü	Capital U, dieresis or umlaut	&#220;	&Uuml;
Ý	Capital Y, acute accent	&#221;	&Yacute;
Þ	Capital THORN, Icelandic	&#222;	&THORN;
ß	Small sharp s, German (sz ligature)	&#223;	&szlig;
à	Small a, grave accent	&#224;	&agrave;
á	Small a, acute accent	&#225;	&aacute;
â	Small a, circumflex accent	&#226;	&acirc;
ã	Small a, tilde	&#227;	&atilde;
ä	Small a, dieresis or umlaut	&#228;	&auml;
å	Small a, ring	&#229;	&aring;
æ	Small ae dipthong (ligature)	&#230;	&aelig;
ç	Small c, cedilla	&#231;	&ccedil;
è	Small e, grave accent	&#232;	&egrave;
é	Small e, acute accent	&#233;	&eacute;
ê	Small e, circumflex accent	&#234;	&ecirc;
ë	Small e, dieresis or umlaut	&#235;	&euml;
ì	Small i, grave accent	&#236;	&igrave;
í	Small i, acute accent	&#237;	&iacute;
î	Small i, circumflex accent	&#238;	&icirc;
ï	Small i, dieresis or umlaut	&#239;	&iuml;
ð	Small eth, Icelandic	&#240;	&eth;
ñ	Small n, tilde	&#241;	&ntilde;
ò	Small o, grave accent	&#242;	&ograve;
ó	Small o, acute accent	&#243;	&oacute;
ô	Small o, circumflex accent	&#244;	&ocirc;
õ	Small o, tilde	&#245;	&otilde;
ö	Small o, dieresis or umlaut	&#246;	&ouml;
÷	Division sign	&#247;	&divide;
ø	Small o, slash	&#248;	&oslash;
ù	Small u, grave accent	&#249;	&ugrave;
ú	Small u, acute accent	&#250;	&uacute;
û	Small u, circumflex accent	&#251;	&ucirc;

Character	Description	Entity Code	Mnemonic
ü	Small u, dieresis or umlaut	ü	ü
ý	Small y, acute accent	ý	ý
þ	Small thorn, Icelandic	þ	þ
ÿ	Small y, dieresis or umlaut	ÿ	ÿ

glossary

640x480 pixels

The minimum resolution to which Web pages currently are designed so as not to exclude potential users who don't have more sophisticated equipment.

8-bit color

The equivalent of 256 colors.

abbreviation element

A descriptive element that indicates when a word is abbreviated.

absolute frame measurement

A measurement that fixes the frame sizes. They don't change if the browser window is resized.

absolute link

A link used to load and display a page located on a server other than the one on which the linking text or element is located. It requires the full URL.

accessibility

An issue related to usability, but also concerned with the ability of disabled users to access a Website. An audio description for the blind would be an accessibility issue.

acronym element

A descriptive element identifying a word made up from the initial letters of multiple words.

Ad Rotator component

The Microsoft Ad Rotator component can be used to place a banner ad on a page.

ADA

The Americans with Disabilities Act, the legislation that governs accessibility issues.

ADO

ActiveX Data Objects.

alert method

An object associated with the window that calls up an alert dialog box.

align attribute

Sets either vertical or horizontal alignment of the contents of a cell or group of cells.

alt attribute

An alternate text description of an image. It is required for ADA compliance.

analogous colors

Any four consecutive colors on the color wheel.

anchor

The part of a hypertext link that is the destination text or location for the link.

anchor element

The element that contains the anchor and the href.

Apache

Free Web server software.

application object

The application object serves a similar function as the session object. It allows us to define variables that everyone who is accessing our Website can access.

arithmetic operators

Relating to JavaScript, the multiplication (*), division (/), sum (+), and difference (-) signs are arithmetic operators.

ARPANET

The Internet began as a simple network of only four computers. The project, named the Advanced Research Projects Agency Network (ARPANET), was funded by the Department of Defense (DOD).

ASP delimiter <% %>

The coding that defines where the ASP code goes. No XHTML can go inside the ASP delimiters.

ASP expression format <%= %>

Allows for ASP to go inside XHTML.

assignment operator

Relating to JavaScript, the equal sign (=) is an assignment operator.

attribute

A parameter of an element.

attribute minimization

A stand-alone attribute not supported by XHTML. HTML has a number of attributes that don't require a value.

background color

The color of the background. It can be defined for any element, not just the body element.

backslash (\)

A symbol used in directory addresses.

balance

The visual equilibrium achieved or manipulated through the placement of elements in a design. Balance can be achieved through symmetry or asymmetry.

base element

The element used to specify a base URL for all hypertext links in a document.

base line

An imaginary line on which the base of a line of type (excluding descenders) rests.

block-level element

An element that can contain other XHTML elements.

blockquote element

The element that contains a block of text to be treated as a quotation.

body element

A container element that will contain other elements.

border attribute

Determines whether an image is surrounded by a border.

box model

How CSS handles block-level properties.

brainstorming

Engaging in thoughtful word and idea play in order to explore the full range of ideas that might touch a particular project.

branding

Creating an identity that becomes synonymous with either a product or a company. This is then used on all communications that relate to the company. Often a client already has a branded identity and it is up to the Web team to match the Website with that brand identity.

break element

An empty element that indicates the end of a line.

browser

A program that sends a message to a server requesting information. The browser then displays this information in either text or graphical format

business rules

The rules that dictate how a site will interact with the user.

cascading style sheets (CSS)

Contain rules that define the appearance of elements within an XHTML document.

cell

The part of a table where data can be entered.

centered

Aligned down the center.

CERN

European Particle Physics Laboratory.

CGI

Common Gateway Interface. CGI scripts are used to process form information once it is submitted with POST or GET.

character data

The information between markup tags that is displayed on a Web page.

check box

A clickable icon on a form that indicates multiple choices to be made.

citation element

The element indicating a quotation or citation.

class attribute

Used to apply the classes that are defined.

client

The person or company that you work for.

code element

A descriptive element that indicates programming code.

color

A property used to change the color of text. Also, the result in the brain of light wave stimulation of the retina in the eye.

colspan attribute

The attribute that allows table cells to span more than one column at a time.

column

A vertical array of cells. Also, a design aid used in layout that usually contains text and graphics.

comments

Used to clarify parts of an XHTML document.

comparison operators

The comparison operators allow for two operands to be compared as a relational expression returning a logical value of true or false based on the results of the comparison.

complementary color

The color directly opposite another color on the color wheel. Red and green are complementary colors.

concept

An overarching and unifying idea that is applied to a project.

condensed type

A typeface with an elongated or narrow appearance.

consistency

Describes the use in a similar fashion visual and interactive elements so that there are no surprises for the user.

contact information

Information on the home page that allows users to know how to get in touch with the Webmaster, the one in charge of maintaining the site.

content

The meat of a site. It is usually provided by the client or taken from printed collateral pieces the client may already be using.

Content Rotator component

Similar to the Ad Rotator component, but instead of displaying random images it displays random lines of text.

contrast

Differ in some way, as in black and white, hard and soft, and large and small.

cool colors

The colors containing greens, blues, and purples.

decorative

A typeface category that consists of primarily fanciful type that is used for headlines or as line art.

definition description element

A container element that indicates a term's definition.

definition list element

A container element indicating that what follows is a list of terms and their definitions.

definition term element

A container element that indicates a term.

depth clues

Ideas in viewer's minds such as the idea that objects closer to the viewer overlap other objects in the visual field and the idea that elements that are higher in the visual field are farther away. Perspective skewing is the idea that as a element goes from being viewed flat on by the viewer to edge on, the back edge shrinks and the sides converge to a central vanishing point. See also *perspective*.

dialog box

A window that pops up to alert users to a condition that needs their input.

division element

A block element that is used to divide an XHTML page into sections.

document header

A portion of a document that contains information about the page that is used by browsers and Web servers.

document information

The document information consists of a version declaration and document type definition. The version declaration indicates what version of the XML standard is being used. This XML declaration is not required to be included in an XHTML document, but is highly recommended by the XHTML 1.0 standard.

DOD

The U.S. Department of Defense.

domain name

The text version of a numeric IP address.

domain name resolution

The association of a text domain name with a numeric IP address.

domain name system

Software that translates a text domain name into a numeric IP address.

DTD

Document type definition, a collection of XML declarations that, as a collection, defines the legal structure, elements, and attributes that are available for use in a document that complies to the DTD. Simply put, it defines how the contents of an XHTML document are going to be displayed by a browser.

element

XHTML tags and their content are referred to as elements.

email

Electronic mail.

embedded style sheets

Part of an XHTML document. They contain the style rules. They are used to apply styles to the entire document.

emphasis element

The element used to indicate text to be emphasized.

empty elements

HTML elements that don't have a close (/) tag associated with them. They are tolerated by HTML and not by XHTML.

event

Relating to JavaScript, events are actions that can trigger other functions.

event handler

Relating to JavaScript, event handlers are predefined actions that respond to specific actions.

expanded/extended type

A wider version of a typeface's standard design.

extensibility

Related to the idea that XHTML as a subset of XML

can be extended beyond its predefined elements.

external style sheets
External style sheets are stored separately from the XHTML document, but contain the same rules that were used with the embedded style.

figure/ground
Figures tend to have positive space in a visual field. The ground is the context on which a figure is recognized. The ground is sometimes the negative space. See also *positive and negative space*.

fill
The interior of a shape, which generally contains the attribute of color or texture.

flow chart
An organizational sketch that details the relationship of pages within a site and shows how users might get from one place to another. See also *schematic*.

font
All the characters, including numbers and punctuation marks, of a particular typeface.

font-family
Allows the naming of a specific font to be used for text.

font-size
The property that can be used to control the size of a font displayed by the browser.

font-style
The property that defines the appearance of a font in one of three ways: normal, italic, or oblique. The italic and oblique (slanted) are similar in appearance.

form
A Web page formatted to include fields for gathering input from users.

forward slash (/)
A symbol used in directory addresses and URLs.

frame
The visual organizational tool our brains use to give a context to our visual experiences. This is sometimes referred to as the "frame of reference."

frame element
The element that establishes the source, or location, of a frame's contents.

frame id attribute
The attribute used to define a name for an individual frame.

frame marginheight attribute
The attribute used to specify the amount of separation (in pixels) between the border of a frame and the frame's content.

frame marginwidth attribute
The attribute used to specify the amount of separation (in pixels) between the border of a frame and the frame's content

frame name attribute
See *frame id attribute*.

frame noresize attribute
The attribute that specifies that users cannot alter a frame's size.

frame scrolling attribute
The attribute that gives the designer control over the appearance of scrollbars for each frame.

frame src attribute
The attribute that specifies the source URL of the document that will become the content of a frame.

frameset column attribute
The <frameset> element requires a rows or cols attribute, which is used to determine the number and size of the size of the vertical and/or horizontal frames.

frameset DTD
This DTD is used when presentational markup needs to be embedded in the document.

frameset element
The element that defines whether a page is a framed page or not. These elements will replace the <body> </body> elements of a non-framed page.

frameset row attribute
The <frameset> element requires a rows or cols attribute, which is used to determine the number and size of the size of the vertical and/or horizontal frames.

FTP
File Transfer Protocol.

gamma
Related to the brightness and contrast of computer monitor displays.

Gestalt
The school of psychology concerned with the human perception of information. The Gestalt psychologists believe that the human response to a stimulus is an unanalyzable whole and not a sum of each response to each element in a given situation.

GET
One of two methods available for transferring form data to the server.

GIF
Graphics Interchange Format, the file format that allows noncontinuous tone artwork to be displayed

in a Web browser.

goals and objectives

The specific, identifiable results you wish to achieve on a given project.

graphic designer

The team member that is responsible for the creation of the visual elements of a Website. The graphic designer may also be responsible for the visual concept as well in lieu of a creative lead.

grid

An aid in design used to achieve unity. It is helpful in figuring out the alignment of elements in a design.

grouping principles

The Gestalt organization principles known as proximity, similarity, continuation, and closure.

GUI

Graphical user interface. The buttons, icons, and links on which users click in order to use a Website or computer application.

halign attribute

Controls the horizontal alignment of the contents of a cell. Left, middle, and right are the possible choices. See also *align attribute* and *valign attribute*.

hash mark

#.

HCI

Human/computer interface. The field of study that investigates how humans and computers interact.

head element

See *document header*.

height attribute

The attribute used to specify the height (in pixels) of a cell, excluding any cell padding. It is also the attribute used to specify the height of an image.

hexadecimal

The base 16 numbering system. Web color is notated in hexadecimal.

hidden text field

A placeholder text field to save information that needs to be passed to another page along the way.

hierarchical

Describes a multilevel Website. It describes a pyramid-like structure.

home.html

The initial or first page of a Website, the base from which a user explores a site. It is sometimes called index.html.

horizontal

Describes the direction left and right in the visual field.

horizontal frame

A frame that stretches from left to right across a page.

horizontal rule element

An empty element that defines a horizontal rule's size, width, and alignment in a document.

hosting provider

The company that hosts a Website once it is created.

href attribute

Stands for hypertext reference. The attribute that specifies the location of the document that is to be linked to for display.

hspace attribute

The attribute used to add horizontal space between images.

HTML

Hypertext Markup Language.

HTTP

Hypertext Transfer Protocol, the protocol used to send information across the World Wide Web.

hub

A Website structure that resembles a wheel with a central hub and pages that radiate from that hub.

hue

The name of a color, such as blue.

hypertext

Text that is designated as a link to some other part of the document, to some other part of the site, or to another site.

id attribute

The attribute used in XHTML to create a named anchor point for a link.

if-then statement

A programming logic statement meaning "if this, then that."

iframe element

The element used to add an inline or floating frame to a non-frames XHTML document.

img element

An empty element used to specify the image that is to be inserted into the Web page.

index.html

The initial or first page of a Website. See also *home.html*.

inline style

A style that overrides any other style. This style affect only the particular element that it has been added to.

interactive

Describes when a communication piece for a company insists that customers or users provide input or make an effort to utilize and find the information they are seeking.

Internet
A global collection of computer networks.

Internet Information Server
Microsoft's Web server software.

Internet service provider
A company that provides access to the Internet through a modem or other connection.

intersected
Describes the operation of shapes that leaves only the part shared by both shapes to remain. This is sometimes called "difference."

intra-page linking
Linking within an XHTML document.

IP address
The unique numerical address of a machine on the World Wide Web.

IP number
See *IP address.*

ismap attribute
The image tag attribute used for server-side image maps.

Java
A programming language separate from JavaScript.

JavaScript
A scripting language used to enhance and extend HTML and XHTML.

JPEG
Joint Photographic Experts Group. The file format that allows continuous tone photos to display properly in a Web browser.

kerning
Adjusting the space between letters.

language declaration
Indicates which language is being used to write ASP.

left justified
Describes text and graphics that align to the left.

line
Made up of an infinite number of points. It is also the path a point would make if a point moved through space. It forms the edge of a plane.

linear
A flat Website structure where the progression is logical from page one to page two. This is similar to the way a book is laid out.

link
A hypertext interactive element that initiates a change in the current state of a Web page.

list
Ordered, unordered, and definition lists are the three types of lists defined in XHTML.

Livescript
The original name for JavaScript as developed by Netscape.

logical operators
Logical operators are used to create compound conditions.

logical styles
Logical style elements are used to describe how text is used, not how it will be displayed. These elements allow the browser to determine the appearance of the text.

lossless compression
Allows an image file to be compressed and when it is later decompressed, there is no loss of data. This means that the decompressed file is identical to the original.

lossy compression
Eliminates information that is unimportant when the file is compressed. This means that the decompressed file will not be identical to the original. This is accomplished in such a way that the loss of data will not be noticed.

margin
Surrounds the border and is the space between any other boxes that may be around it.

margin-bottom
Describes the sides of a margin box. These properties allow for the control of space between the block-level element and the surrounding element.

margin-left
Describes the sides of a margin box. These properties allow for the control of space between the block-level element and the surrounding element.

margin-right
Describes the sides of a margin box. These properties allow for the control of space between the block-level element and the surrounding element.

margin-top
Describes the sides of a margin box. These properties allow for the control of space between the block-level element and the surrounding element.

markup tags
Part of the HTML/DHTML/XHTML element. <td> is a markup tag.

meta attribute
An element that provides information about the content of a document, which can be used by Internet search engines to index the Web pages.

metaphor
A figure of speech that contains within it a comparison of one thing to another.

method
Relating to JavaScript, methods are actions that are performed with or to an object.

Microsoft Access
Microsoft's database program.

modern
A typeface category that refers to serif type that has a cold and machined appearance. There is little or no transition from the main stroke of a letterform to the serif. The vertical stress of round letters is vertical at 12:00 and 6:00.

monospace
A type category that contains typefaces in which each letter occupies exactly the same space. Most type on the computer is proportionally spaced to enhance readability and the aesthetic look.

MOS
Mission objective statement. The mission statement identifies the goals and objectives of a particular project.

name attribute
The attribute used to identify certain points within a document that are available to be used as targets of links.

namespaces
Mechanisms for documenting and determining the origin and the meaning of the elements used in XML.

navigation
The elements on a Web page that allow you to move from page to page or site to site.

nested frame
A frame within a frame.

nested list
An inner list. A list within a list.

nested table
A table within a table.

nesting
Making sure that elements are properly contained within other elements. Order is important.

noframe element
Provides an alternative for browsers that are not capable of displaying frames.

nowrap attribute
The attribute used to disable automatic word wrapping within the contents of a cell.

object
Relating to JavaScript, objects are real-life entities. These entities include things like cars, books, animals, people, browser windows, and page elements.

Object Context object
Provides ASP with the ability to manage transactions using Microsoft Transaction Server.

occurrence indicator
Specify the order and frequency of the XML elements.

oldstyle
A typeface category referring to serif type that has a graceful and elegant appearance. It primarily refers to the gentle transition from the main stroke of a letterform to the serif of the letterform. It also identifies the visual stress of letters such as "o" and "e" as being off center at about 10:00 and 4:00.

OOP
Relating to JavaScript, object-oriented programming.

ordered list element
A container element that encloses a block of text that is to be treated as a list.

padding
Relating to CSS, the area that surrounds the content.

Page Counter component
This component allows us to insert a page counter into our ASP documents.

paragraph align attribute
The attribute that allows us to define where a paragraph aligns other than left alignment, which is the default.

paragraph element
A container element that encloses a block of text that is to be treated as a paragraph.

parent directory (..)
Symbology used in directory addresses to indicate the directory above the current directory.

password field
A field that accepts a password.

pattern
A sustained rhythm over a defined visual area.

personality
The unique identity of something, the thing that makes it different from others of its kind.

perspective

A visual system that mimics reality. It consists of the idea of a horizon line and edges that recede from the viewer. Perspective also includes the idea that as things are farther from the viewer, they are less distinct and that they move toward a medium value. This category of ideas is called "depth clues."

physical styles

Physical style elements are used to specify exactly how the browser displays text.

pica

A standard unit of measurement in layout and design. Related to typography in that 1 pica equals 12 points and that 6 picas equals an inch. Using the pica/point measuring system for layout allows a designer to make visual decisions based on the size of the type in a paragraph or heading. This assists in the unification of a design.

pixel

The smallest display unit of a computer monitor. It is short for "picture element."

plane

A plane is made up on an infinite number of lines. It is also the area a line would scribe if it traveled through space.

PNG format

Portable Network Graphics. It uses a lossless compression technique.

point

A conceptual visual element, a single identifiable coordinate in x, y space. Also, a standard unit of measure in typography. Seventy-two points is equal to one inch. Twelve points equals one pica.

portability

The idea that Web documents are going to be viewed on smaller and more portable devices such as PDAs (personal digital assistants), cell phones, and on screen in automobiles.

positive and negative space

The idea relating to the fact that we perceive form and volume to occupy space (positive space) and that we perceive there to be space around the form (negative space).

POST

One of two methods available for transferring form data to the server.

preformatted text element

A container element that encloses a block of text that is preformatted and preserves the spacing.

primary colors (light/computer color)

Red, green, and blue.

primary colors (pigment)

Red, yellow, and blue.

print collateral material

Marketing materials, annual reports, and advertising materials that might assist in creating the Web presence for a client.

properties

Relating to JavaScript, properties are characteristics of objects that allow one object to be differentiated from another. These could be things like size, color, or a text value.

property

Relating to CSS, the property indicates the style that is to be applied to the XHTML element identified by the selector. A style sheet can contain many properties to define a particular selector. Properties include attributes such as color, margins, or fonts.

punched

The operation of shapes that allows one to be cut from another. This is sometimes referred to as subtraction.

radio button

A clickable icon on a form that indicates a single choice picked from many choices.

relative frame measurement

A measurement that keeps proportional frame sizes even if the browser window is resized.

relative link

A link used when we want to load a document that is located on the same server as the current page that is displayed in the browser window.

repetition

The repeating of visual elements in a design. It is most powerful when the similarity of the visual elements is strong.

Request object

The Request object is used when we want the server to retrieve information from the user.

resolution

The size (width and height) in pixels of a graphic image.

Response object

Responsible for sending information from the server to the user.

RGB

The primary colors of light used by computer monitor displays.

rhythm

Sustained repetition used to assist in the organizational flow of a visual design.

right justified

Describes text and graphics that align to the right.

row

A horizontal array of table cells.

rowspan attribute

An attribute that allows a table cell to span more than one row at a time.

sample element

The element used to indicate sample text.

sans serif

A typeface category that refers to type without serifs. "Sans" means "without" in French and Latin.

schematic

An organizational sketch that visualizes a site's architecture.

script

A typeface category that refers to type that emulates cursive handwriting.

script attribute

The element used to embed scripts written in JavaScript or VBScript into an XHTML document.

script element

The XHTML element that defines where a script goes.

search engine

A card catalog of the Internet. It allows a user to search the vast array of information on the Internet.

second-level domain

The part of the URL after the www. In the URL www.purdue.edu, purdue is the second-level domain.

secondary colors (light)

Cyan, magenta, and amber (yellow).

secondary colors (pigment)

Green, purple, and orange.

selection box

A drop-down selection menu on a form that has choices for the user to make.

selector

Relating to CSS, selectors identify an XHTML element that is to be linked to the style being defined, such as a header or paragraph. The selector could also identify a class to which the rule is to apply.

serif

The "hands and feet" of serif type.

server components

Special hardware and software that facilitate dynamic server-side technology used in Web design.

Server object

This object allows us to create and destroy objects on the server.

Session object

The Session object allows us to store information about the user for a temporary amount of time.

SGML

Standard Generalized Markup Language. Developed in the 1980s, SGML is a very complex markup language.

shade

Add black to a color to achieve related, darker values of a single hue.

shape

The organization of points and lines to form recognizable, named, regular or irregular images in the field of perception. Some shapes are predefined, as in geometric shapes.

site architecture

The physical layout of a Website.

size

The attribute assigned to an element in a design that is either physically measurable or visually noted in relation to other elements in the design. Larger than, smaller than, or equal to are expressions of relative size.

slab serif

A typeface category that refers to letterforms that have very large, blocky serifs.

splash page

The temporary first page of a Website. It often contains animated graphics. The finished state of a splash page is the home page.

split complement color scheme

A color scheme that uses a hue and the color to the left or right of its direct complement.

SQL INSERT statement

The SQL command asking the database to insert information into a table or other object.

SQL SELECT statement

The SQL command asking the database to retrieve some information.

SQL

Structured Query Language, a language that most databases understand.

src attribute
An attribute that directs the browser to get the image file at the specified location.

stakeholder
The person in the client company who has the authority to make or break the project.

stateless protocol
A protocol that forgets the information you have typed into a form once you leave a page.

stored query
A query placed inside of a database. This is done to circumvent the current limitation in the current MS Access ADO drivers.

storyboard
An organizational tool that helps in the visualization stage of design. See also *schematic* and *flow chart*.

strict DTD
The DTD that is used for a document adhering to the XHTML 1.0 standard.

stroke
The main line of a character. Also, the expression and realization of the line that surrounds a shape. It is separate from a shape's fill.

strong element
The element used to indicate that some text is to be emphasized more than the emphasis element.

style
A tag relating to CSS. It is used to create styles within a single document. Also, the unifying application of a metaphor, concept, or personality.

style class
A class that allows you to define different styles for the same element or for a group. Style classes are defined within embedded or external style sheets.

style element
The element used to create styles for an entire Web page.

table
A horizontal and vertical array of cells that can contain information.

table align attribute
The attribute that allows you to align table data other than left aligned.

table border attribute
The attribute that defines whether a table has a border and how wide it is.

table caption tag
The attribute that defines the caption associated with a given table.

table cellpadding attribute
The attribute that controls the amount of space (in pixels) between the border of each table cell and the contents of that cell.

table cellspacing attribute
The attribute used to specify the amount of separation (in pixels) between the border of one cell and the border of the adjacent cells.

table data tag
The tag that allows data to be entered into an individual cell.

table header tag
Similar in function and placement to the table data tag, but the table header tag is automatically formatted as boldfaced and centered to set it apart from other table cells in that column.

table row tag
The tag that defines a new row of cells in a table.

table tag
The tag that defines the beginning and end of a table. All other table-related tags are contained within these tags.

table width attribute
The tag used to control the absolute width of a table. If left undefined, the contents of the cells define the width.

tag editor
A tool used to create HTML/XHTML pages.

target audience
The client's customers to whom you are marketing and to whom you will be designing your communication piece.

TCP/IP
Transmission Control Protocol/Internet Protocol.

technical writer
A writer who can take technical concepts and extract their essence and make them understandable to the target audience.

telnet
A protocol allows users to log onto Unix servers mostly at universities and libraries. Users can access directories and search for files. You can often search databases of information remotely.

template tag
XSL stylesheets are composed of template tags, which in turn are composed of match parameters and content.

tertiary colors (pigment)
Red-orange, orange-yellow, yellow-green, green-blue, blue-purple, and red-purple.

text editor
A tool used to create HTML/XHTML pages.

text field
A field on a page that accepts text.

text wrap
The ability in word processors and other text creation software to automatically return text to the left margin without a carriage return.

text/css
The <style> element's type attribute specifies the media type, which is text/css when using cascading style sheets.

text-align
Applied to block-level elements, it allows for the justification of text within the element.

text-indent
Applied to block-level elements, it is used to set the amount of indentation of the first line of text within the element.

text-transform
Used to change the case of text.

texture
A tactile pattern. A use of a pattern that elicits more than just a visual response. A pattern that appears to be able to be felt.

thick/thin
The contrast in the thickness of the curved strokes.

Tim Burners-Lee
The man who came up with the idea of the World Wide Web and codified the HTML language.

tint
Add white to a color to achieve related, lighter values of a single hue.

title attribute
The element used to add a title to an XHTML document.

top-level domain
The part of the URL that indicates which category a Website falls into, such as .edu, .gov, or .com. In the URL www.purdue.edu, .edu is the top-level domain.

tracking
Increasing or decreasing the amount of space between all the letters in a block of text.

transitional
A typeface category that falls between oldstyle and modern. The transition from stroke to serif is not as severe as modern, but may not be as gentle as oldstyle. The vertical stress of round letters is approaching vertical, but remains more at 11:00 and 5:00.

transitional DTD
The DTD is used on a document that needs to use frames.

type attribute
The attribute that allows you to change the type of numbering in an ordered list from Arabic to Roman.

type family
The range of typefaces that are all variations of a single design. Helvetica, Helvetica Narrow, and Helvetica Heavy are all the same type family.

typography
The art of specifying and using type.

unary operator
Unary operators perform their operation on one operand. JavaScript provides two, the increment and decrement operators.

union
The coming together of two shapes to form a new shape.

Universal Resource Identifier
URI. It uniquely identifies the author of a set of XML elements or tags. Note that it does not point to an actual Web document. Instead it points at a unique location on the server of an element's author.

unordered list element
A container element that encloses a block of text that is to be treated as an unordered list.

URL
Uniform Resource Locator. The address of the information or page being requested.

usability
The ease of use with which visitors to a Website can find what they came looking for.

usemap attribute
The attribute used to connect an image with map information.

Usenet
The electronic news network of the Internet. It is comprised of newsgroups that are accessed with news readers.

valid XML
If a document is well-formed and makes sense, it is described as "valid."

valign attribute
The attribute that controls the vertical alignment of the contents of a cell. Top, middle, or bottom are the possible choices. See also *align attribute*.

value

Relating to CSS, the value describes how a property is to be displayed. Also, the lightness or darkness of an element in a design.

variable element

The element that is used to indicate a variable name that is to be replaced with some value.

VBScript

Visual Basic Script. A script written in the Visual Basic programming language and syntax.

vertical

The direction up and down in the visual field.

vertical frame

A frame that goes from top to bottom on a page.

VGA colors

The 16 colors that most PCs recognize and that can be specified on a Web page by name. Not all 16 are technically Web safe.

vspace attribute

The attribute used to add vertical space between images.

W3C

The World Wide Web Consortium, the governing body for the World Wide Web.

warm colors

The colors containing reds, oranges, and yellows.

Web-safe color

One of a predetermined 216 color set that is acceptable to most browsers.

well-formed XML

If an XML document adheres to syntactical rules, then we say the document is "well-formed."

white space

In page layout, the negative space around text or graphic images that help to focus the user's attention on the image or text. It allows a design to feel open and not cramped.

width attribute

The attribute used to specify the width (in pixels) of a cell, excluding any cell padding. Also, the attribute used to specify the width of an image.

WYSIWYG

What You See Is What You Get.

x-height

Creates the impression of the font's size.

XHTML

Extensible Hypertext Markup Language.

XHTML element

An element having three parts: opening tags, content, and closing tags.

XML

Extensible Markup Language. Based on SGML, it is an easier language to learn and use. It allows anyone to create and define tags.

XML namespace

A collection of names, identified by a URL reference, that is used in XML documents as element types and attribute names.

XSL

Extensible Stylesheet Language.

XSL FO (XSL Formatting Objects)

The second technology that comprises XSL, it allows us to describe how XML should be displayed. We can think of it as cascading style sheets for XML.

XSL processor

Software that is responsible for integrating the results of XML and XSL.

XSLT (XSL Transformations)

Allows us to take the data contained inside of an XML document and change it into another form. This capability allows us to transform an XML document into HTML, XHTML, plain text, or even another XML document.

index